D1520782

THE
COLLEGE
PRESS
NIV
COMMENTARY

JUDGES-RUTH

THE COLLEGE PRESS NIV COMMENTARY

JOSHUA

ROB FLEENOR

MARK S. ZIESE

Old Testament Series Co-Editors:

Terry Briley, Ph.D.
Lipscomb University

Paul Kissling, Ph.D.
Great Lakes Christian College

 COLLEGE PRESS
PUBLISHING COMPANY
Joplin, Missouri

International Standard Book Number 978-0-89900-934-6

A WORD
FROM THE PUBLISHER

Years ago a movement was begun with the dream of uniting all Christians on the basis of a common purpose (world evangelism) under a common authority (the Word of God). The College Press NIV Commentary Series is a serious effort to join the scholarship of two branches of this unity movement so as to speak with one voice concerning the Word of God. Our desire is to provide a resource for your study of the Old Testament that will benefit you whether you are preparing a Bible School lesson, a sermon, a college course, or your own personal devotions. Today as we survey the wreckage of a broken world, we must turn again to the Lord and his Word, unite under his banner and communicate the life-giving message to those who are in desperate need. This is our purpose.

ABBREVIATIONS

AB . . . . *Anchor Bible*
AnBib . . . . *Analecta biblica*
ASOR . . . . *American Schools of Oriental Research*
BA . . . . *Biblical Archaeologist*
BAR . . . . . *Biblical Archaeological Review*
BASOR . . . *Bulletin of the American Schools of Oriental Research*
BCBC . . . . *Believers Church Bible Commentary*
BDB . . . . . *The New Brown, Driver, and Briggs Hebrew and English Lexicon of the Old Testament*
BHS . . . . . *Biblica Hebraica Stuttgartensia*
BI . . . . *Biblical Interpretation*
BJRL . . . . . *Bulletin of the John Rylands University Library of Manchester*
BR . . . . *Bible Review*
BSac . . . . . *Bibliotheca Sacra*
BT . . . . *Bible Translator*
BTB . . . . . *Biblical Theology Bulletin*
CBQ . . . . . *The Catholic Biblical Quarterly*
Did . . . . . . *Didaskalia*
EncJud . . . . *Encyclopedia Judaica*
GKC . . . . . *Gesenius' Hebrew Grammar*
HALOT . . . *Hebrew and Aramaic Lexicon of the Old Testament*
HAR . . . . . *Hebrew Annual Review*
HBT . . . . . *Horizons in Biblical Theology*
HTR . . . . . *Harvard Theological Review*
HUCA . . . . *Hebrew Union College Annual*
IEJ . . . . *Israel Exploration Journal*
JAAR . . . . . *Journal of the American Academy of Religion*
JAOS . . . . . *Journal of the American Oriental Society*
JBL . . . . . . *Journal of Biblical Literature*

JBQ . . . . . . *Jewish Biblical Quarterly*
JETS . . . . . *Journal of the Evangelical Theological Society*
JNES . . . . . *Journal of Near Eastern Studies*
JSOT . . . . . *Journal for the Study of the Old Testament*
JSOTSup . . *Journal for the Study of the Old Testament Supplement*
LXX . . . . . *Septuagint*
MT . . . . . . *Masoretic Text*
NASB . . . . *New American Standard Bible, 1995*
NAC . . . . . *New American Commentary*
NCB . . . . . *New Century Bible*
NEA . . . . . *Near Eastern Archaeology*
NICOT . . . *The New International Commentary on the Old Testament*
NIDOTTE . *New International Dictionary of Old Testament Theology & Exegesis*
NIV . . . . . . *New International Version*
OEANE . . . *The Oxford Encyclopedia of Archaeology in the Near East*
OLA . . . . . *Orientalia Lovaniensia Periodica*
OTL . . . . . *Old Testament Library*
Proof . . . . . *Prooftexts: A Journal of Jewish Literary History*
RQ . . . . . . *Restoration Quarterly*
SBJT . . . . . *Southern Baptist Journal of Theology*
SBL . . . . . . *Society of Biblical Literature*
SJOT . . . . . *Scandinavian Journal of the Old Testament*
SJT . . . . . . *Scottish Journal of Theology*
TBT . . . . . *The Bible Today*
TDOT . . . . *Theological Dictionary of the Old Testament*
TOTC . . . *Tyndale Old Testament Commentaries*
TWOT . . . *Theological Wordbook of the Old Testament*
TynBul . . . *Tyndale Bulletin*
VT . . . . *Vetus Testamentum*
WBC . . . . . *Word Biblical Commentary*
WTJ . . . . . *Westminster Theological Journal*
ZAW . . . . . *Zeitschrift für die Alttestamentliche Wissenschaft*

Simplified Guide to Hebrew Writing

Heb. letter	Translit.	Pronunciation guide
א	'	Has no sound of its own; like smooth breathing mark in Greek
ב	b	Pronounced like English B *or* V
ג	g	Pronounced like English G
ד	d	Pronounced like English D
ה	h	Pronounced like English H, silent at the end of words in the combination āh
ו	w	As a consonant, pronounced like English V or German W
וּ	û	Represents a vowel sound, pronounced like English long OO
ו	ô	Represents a vowel sound, pronounced like English long O
ז	z	Pronounced like English Z
ח	ḥ	Pronounced like German and Scottish CH and Greek χ (chi)
ט	ṭ	Pronounced like English T
י	y	Pronounced like English Y
כ/ך	k	Pronounced like English K
ל	l	Pronounced like English L
מ/ם	m	Pronounced like English M
נ/ן	n	Pronounced like English N
ס	s	Pronounced like English S
ע	'	Stop in breath deep in throat before pronouncing the vowel
פ/ף	p/ph	Pronounced like English P *or* F
צ/ץ	ṣ	Pronounced like English TS/TZ
ק	q	Pronounced very much like כ (k)
ר	r	Pronounced like English R
שׂ	ś	Pronounced like English S, much the same as ס
שׁ	š	Pronounced like English SH
ת	t/th	Pronounced like English T *or* TH

Note that different forms of some letters appear at the end of the word (written right to left), as in כָּפַף (*kāphaph*, "bend") and מֶלֶךְ (*melek*, "king").

Vowels in Hebrew (except where the ו is used to represent a vowel sound), are represented by "vowel points" added to the consonant. For example: הַ (*ha*, "the"). The letter *yod* (י, *y*) also becomes a *part of* certain vowel sounds, as in the conjunction כִּי (*kî*, "that"). Originally, Hebrew was written as "unpointed" text, with just the consonants. For convenience, the different vowel points are shown below on the letter Aleph (א).

אָ	ā	Pronounced not like long A in English, but like the broad A or AH sound
אַ	a	The Hebrew short A sound, but more closely resembles the broad A (pronounced for a shorter period of time) than the English short A
אֶ	e	Pronounced like English short E

אֵ	ē	Pronounced like English long A, or Greek η (eta)
אִ	i	Pronounced like English short I
אִ	î	The same vowel point is sometimes pronounced like 'אִ (see below)
אָ	o	This vowel point sometimes represents the short O sound
אֹ	ō	Pronounced like English long O
אֻ	u	The vowel point ֻ sometimes represents a shorter U sound and
אוּ	ū	is sometimes pronounced like the וּ (û, see above)
'אֵ	ê	Pronounced much the same as אֵ
'אֶ	ê	Pronounced much the same as אֶ
'אִ	î	Pronounced like long I in many languages, or English long E
אְ	ə	An unstressed vowel sound, like the first E in the word "severe"
אֳ, אֲ, אֱ	ŏ, ă, ĕ	Shortened, unstressed forms of the vowels אָ, אַ, and אֶ, pronounced very similarly to אְ

THE BOOK OF
JUDGES

PREFACE AND ACKNOWLEDGMENTS

Like many people, I recall childhood Sunday school lessons from the book of Judges: the strong hero Samson saves Israel from the Philistines; through the underdog Gideon and a few troops, God defeats a vast army; the left-handed assassin Ehud kills the evil Eglon. Also like many, exploring Judges has become an integral part of my own spiritual journey. At its very core, Judges expresses the profound grace of God. The God of Israel responds to human suffering, even when that suffering is rooted in rebellion against him. The heroes in the stories are often spiritually frail — foolish, immoral, doubting — and yet God patiently and powerfully uses them. Judges is about God's power thriving in the midst of human limitations.

There is a certain sense of excitement in writing now about the stories that so intrigued me when I was a child. Yet writing a book on Judges is a daunting task. Entire books have been written on single chapters of Judges. Multiple methods have been applied to the text, examining form, structure, language, story, chronology, gender, or history — each approach giving rise to multiple volumes on every topic. The cacophony of noise surrounding the book can be deafening. But the vast amount of material written about Judges reveals that it is an important book. It is part of the overarching story of Scripture regarding how God brings salvation to humanity. In the immediate context of the Old Testament, Judges forms a link between the exodus of the Hebrews from Egypt and the rise of the Jewish monarchy. The period reflected in Judges is crucial to the development of the Israelite psyche as God begins the lesson that the exiles to Assyria and Babylon later finish: blessing is connected to fidelity to God; suffering is the natural consequence of disobedience.

The stories in Judges have no less relevance for our day. One need look no further than a nightly newscast in order to sense Judges' subtle wisdom beckoning to a society seemingly gone mad. As society abandons its spiritual roots, our hearts cry out for leaders with real integrity; we thirst for an end to violence; we long for freedom from the evil spiritual forces that saturate our culture; we yearn for peace.

In this volume I have approached Judges as a history that the biblical author writes in a creative and entertaining way. I have therefore focused on many of the literary aspects related to the text as well as on the historical and theological elements. The Bible is not a stale record of information God wants us to know; it is an inspired, powerful, and living story that at a very basic level is enjoyable to read. Any story God tells, after all, is a good story.

Along the way I have tried to wrestle with Hebrews 11:32 — the reference in the "Great Chapter of Faith" to four judges: Gideon, Barak, Samson, and Jephthah. These examples of faith have often been puzzling to me. How do disobedience, doubt, immorality, and murder coexist — easily, apparently — with a faith that pleases God? The reality of God using deeply flawed people to accomplish his purposes provides hope to all of us constantly coming to grips with our own imperfections.

To my father, Don Fleenor, and to my friend Fritz Koopmann, I affectionately dedicate this work. One an engineer, one a farmer — both humble models of a love of learning and truth. My wife, Shawnee, has been a constant support, continually providing insight, proofreading, and encouragement. This book would not be possible without her. I pray that God will use this work to enrich his kingdom and increase his glory.

JUDGES
INTRODUCTION

The book of Judges continues the history of Israel after their entry into the Promised Land. Their conquest was not fully completed, and their continued interaction with the remaining Canaanite inhabitants created political and religious friction. The stories are exciting, well-told tales of intrigue, suspense, seduction, violence, revenge, and triumph. Through them all, the hand of the God of Israel moves — sometimes obviously and sometimes furtively — to teach his people their need for him.

TITLE

The title for Judges is taken from the Hebrew word שָׁפַט (*šāphaṭ*)[1], the term for a ruler incorporating all the functions of government — executive as well as judicial. These rulers not only made decisions regarding law, but also enforced those decisions. The judges themselves seem to serve a dual role within the book: military leaders (Gideon, Jephthah, Samson) and civil administrators responsible for maintaining justice (Deborah, Tolah, Jair). The NIV often translates the verbal form of the word as "led," a word that comprehensively summarizes their function. Their authority was limited regionally, and their leadership often relied on the good will of Israelite tribes to cooperate.

AUTHOR AND COMPOSITION

The Book of Judges nowhere mentions its author. In the late nineteenth century, Wellhausen's theory of various sources com-

---

[1]The cognates of the term held similar meaning throughout the ancient Near East. *Encyclopedia Judaica* notes that *šāphaṭ* is an Akkadian cognate of *šapiṭu*, indicating a "district governor" or "high administrative official."

prising the Pentateuch was also extended to Judges, understanding the text as an intermingled product of different writers.[2] This idea later gave way to Martin Noth's theory that Joshua through Second Kings was composed during the time of Israel's exile using earlier sources.[3] This position considers Judges to be part of the Deuteronomistic History, the history of Joshua through 2 Kings written during the age of exile in the 6th century B.C. The "Deuteronomist" is not considered to be a single person but a Deuteronomistic school, a sophisticated group of scribes writing over decades or centuries.[4]

More recent studies argue that Judges represents the highly unified product of a single mind.[5] While the author of Judges no doubt makes use of various sources from which to construct an account, the intricacy with which the book is constructed suggests a single guiding hand responsible for producing the material. Both oral traditions and written texts were passed down through the generations until the author collected, compiled, and presented them in written form.[6] Ancient rabbis held that Judges was written by Samuel,[7] a position still defended by many today.[8] Other suggestions for a specific author have not achieved consensus.[9]

---

[2]C.F. Burney (*The Book of Judges, with Introduction and Notes, and Notes on the Hebrew Text of the Books of Kings, with an Introduction and Appendix* [New York: KTAV Pub. House, 1970], pp. xli-l), attributes Judges to the Elohist writer.

[3]Mark A. O'Brien, "Judges and the Deuteronomistic History," in *The History of Israel's Traditions: The Heritage of Martin Noth*, ed. by Steven L. McKenzie and Matt Patrick Graham (Sheffield: Sheffield Academic, 1994), p. 239.

[4]O'Brien, "Judges and the Deuteronomistic History," p. 257.

[5]See Gregory T.K. Wong, *Compositional Strategy of the Book of Judges: An Inductive, Rhetorical Study* (Leiden: Brill, 2006). Wong examines the interconnectedness of multiple elements within the text, suggesting a much more unified text in composition than previously allowed by scholars.

[6]The Bible itself refers to sources used that are no longer available (Num 21:14; Josh 10:13; 2 Sam 1:18). The author's use of sources does not undermine the idea of inspiration. Individual sources are merely one of many components utilized by the Holy Spirit to produce the text.

[7]*Bava Batra, Babylonian Talmud* (London: Soncino Press, 1938), 14b.

[8]See C.J. Goslinga's *Joshua, Judges, Ruth* (Grand Rapids: Zondervan, 1986), pp. 198-223, for a discussion on the unity and authorship of Joshua, Judges, and Ruth. Goslinga rightly notes that the discussion of authorship is relevant only if the book is part of a unity, i.e., written by a single author.

[9]Adrien J. Bledstein's "Is Judges a Woman's Satire on Men Who Play

DATE AND CHRONOLOGY

INTERNAL EVIDENCE

The date of Judges' composition, like the authorship, is uncertain. The text, however, contains numerous useful internal clues related to the date of its composition. These chronological markers prove more useful to a position maintaining that the book was composed by a single author at a given point in time. If the text is considered to be merely a collection of individual sources, a marker may be helpful for dating a particular source, but is of little use in dating the entire book.

The first chronological marker is the phrase, "to this day." The phrase occurs seven times in the Hebrew text of Judges (1:21,26; 6:24; 10:4; 15:19; 18:12; 19:30),[10] and assists in narrowing down the latter limit of the date range for the composition of the text. "To this day" is used to describe a past event with effects still lingering at the time of writing. Judges 1:21, for instance, mentions that because the tribe of Benjamin failed to drive the Jebusites from the city of Jerusalem, the two groups coexisted in Jerusalem "until this day." Jerusalem will later be conquered by David (2 Sam 5:6-9),[11] which places the date of the Judges prior to the second king of Israel.

God?" in *The Feminist Companion to Judges*, ed. by Athalya Brenner (Sheffield: Sheffield Academic, 1999), for instance, suggests Judges is written by a woman satirist with the intention of condemning violent men. Bledstein goes further in suggesting the Deuteronomist was Huldah from 2 Kings 22, who redacted Judges and is also responsible for the portrayals of Naomi, Ruth, and Hannah. Unfortunately, Bledstein incorrectly imposes modern feminist motivations on the ancient writer. If gender is a concern to the author of Judges at all, it is secondary to the author's intended theological purpose.

[10]The Jebusites cohabitated with the Benjamites in Jerusalem (1:21); the traitor of Bethel built a city he named Luz in the land of the Hittites (1:26); Gideon's altar still stood in Ophrah (6:24); the regional villages controlled by Jair's sons were still named Havvoth Jair (10:4); the spring from which Samson drank was still present at Lehi (15:19); the area west of Kiriath Jearim where the Danite army camped was still designated as such (18:12); and Danite idolatry continued "all the time the house of God was in Shiloh" (18:31). All of these instances likely describe premonarchal events, and are seemingly fresh in the memory of the author.

[11]Jebusites are still present in Jerusalem after the conquest of the city. David purchases the threshing floor of Araunah the Jebusite in order to

A second chronological marker is the phrase, "In those days." The saying occurs seven times (17:6; 18:1(2×); 19:1; 20:27,28; 21:25) and helps pinpoint the early limits of the composition date. "In those days" is used to describe a past condition that no longer applies at the time of writing. Four of the uses of "in those days" are linked to a time before Israel had a king. Judges then was written after the beginning of the monarchy, no earlier than the reign of Saul. Israel's lack of a king is also connected to anarchy and chaos in the land, suggesting that Judges was written during a time of comparative stability before the division of the kingdom.[12] The early reigns of Saul and David — as well as the reign of Solomon — provided such seasons of stability. "In those days" is also used to indicate a previous time when the Ark of the Covenant was located in Bethel and the grandson of the High Priest Aaron was priest (20:27-28). These markers indicate an initial composition date for Judges as early as David's early reign from Hebron (2 Sam 2:11).[13]

A third enigmatic marker is the reference in Judges 18:30 to "the time of captivity in the land." While the majority of chronological markers suggest a date for Judges during the early united kingdom, this phrase is often understood to refer to the Assyrian exile in the eighth century B.C. That identification is used as one basis for assuming Judges (or at least chapters 17–21) has a later composition date. There is, however, no reason to assume that the "captivity" referred to does not represent a historical context known to the original audience but lost to modern readers. The Ark of the Covenant, for instance, was captured in 1 Samuel 4, and could also fit the context of a "time of captivity." Judges 18:31 refers to a parallel marker — a time when "the house of God was in Shiloh." This second reference predates Solomon's temple, probably referring to the early Israelite cultic center established around the Tabernacle at Shiloh. Unless the phrase "time of captivity in the land" is an editorial addi-

---

offer a sacrifice in 2 Sam 24:18-25. After David's victory and occupation of the city, however, the Jebusites became subservient to the Hebrews as David's power and influence increased. Had the writer of Judges known about David's conquest of Jerusalem, it surely would have been the chronological marker used.

[12]Goslinga, *Joshua, Judges, Ruth*, p. 219.

[13]Robert H. O'Connell, *The Rhetoric of the Book of Judges* (Leiden: E.J. Brill, 1996), pp. 332-338.

tion added by a later scribe for clarification, the phrase does not refer to the Assyrian exile. Ultimately, the reference is unspecific enough to warrant interpretation based on the other multiple chronological markers present throughout the text.[14]

EXTERNAL EVIDENCE

Adding up the years of the various oppressions and times of peace recorded throughout the book returns a span of more than 400 years. Based on 1 Kings 6:1, there were 480 years between the Exodus and Solomon's fourth year. Attempts have been made to reconcile the chronology of the Judges accounts, but these are misguided. Treating Judges as a straightforward chronology creates difficulties, not the least of which is limiting the events of Joshua, Samuel and Saul to only sixty years.[15] A better solution is to consider the individual accounts of judges as occurring independently of the others. The judges were regional leaders, and many of their experiences likely overlapped, occurring at the same time.[16] Second, many numbers in Judges likely represent rounded and symbolic numbers. The use of forty years (3:11; 5:31; 8:28; 13:1), for instance, probably represents a full generation rather than a specific duration.[17]

TEXT

The text of Judges is well preserved, with few corruptions in the Hebrew Masoretic Text. The two main traditions of the Septuagint (LXX), however, are in less agreement regarding the text and contain many points of divergence.[18] Though Judges is not directly quoted in the New Testament, Hebrews 11:32 lists Gideon, Barak, Samson, and Jephthah as examples of faith. Paul also refers to the judges in

[14]Ibid., p. 336.

[15]A. Cohen, *Joshua and Judges: Hebrew Text & English Translation with an Introduction and Commentary* (London: Soncino Press, 1970), p. 153.

[16]Goslinga, *Joshua, Judges, Ruth*, pp. 223-234.

[17]Burney, *Judges*, p. liv.

[18]See Walter Ray Bodine, *The Greek Text of Judges: Recensional Developments* (Chico, CA: Scholars Press, 1980).

a sermon at Pisidian Antioch (Acts 13:19-20). Other less certain parallels between Judges and the New Testament have also been suggested, such as Thomas Brodie's suggestion that Luke's Gospel makes heavy use of patterns and themes from Judges.[19]

CANONICITY

In the Hebrew Bible, Judges is grouped with the Former Prophets along with Joshua and Samuel–Kings. The book fills in the gap between the Conquest and the monarchy. While the presence of violence and the inability of God's people to succeed have historically unnerved interpreters, the book's strong theology and crucial role in the history of Israel have ensured its place in the canon.

HISTORICAL BACKGROUND

THE ISRAELITE CONTEXT

By the beginning of Judges, the Hebrew culture has been heavily influenced by three events. First, the identity of Israel was shaped by the Exodus from Egypt. The Exodus positioned Yahweh as the sole deity of the Hebrews. In Egypt, the people had been subjected to Egyptian control. In the ancient world, the nation with the most power was understood to have the most powerful deities. If Egypt controlled the Hebrews, then there was no question that the Egyptian deities were more powerful than the god of the Hebrews. But God is not limited by human perceptions or theology. Through the ten plagues and the ministry of Moses, God makes it clear to both Egyptians and Hebrews that he is the most powerful by systematically dismantling Egyptian theology. Egyptian deities were shown to have not *lesser* power than Yahweh, but *no* power. Establishing the power of their deity was crucial for developing the identity of the Hebrews.

Beyond God's expression of his power through the Exodus, the

---

[19]Thomas L. Brodie, *The Birthing of the New Testament: The Intertextual Development of the New Testament Writings* (Sheffield: Phoenix Press, 2004), pp. 86-92, 447-519.

Israelite identity was shaped by the Sinai covenant. God's demonstration of his power verified his right to author the covenant he gave to the Israelites. The covenant created a new religious identity for Israel. Much of the Law created a distinction between Israel and her neighbors, and that distinction would be crucial for maintaining an independent identity while surrounded by polytheistic nations.

The third factor shaping the identity of early Israel is the incomplete nature of the Conquest. As the reader of Joshua knows, the people failed to conquer fully the land God promised to them. The reality of possessing only a partially captured land creates two difficulties for the Israelite identity. The first is syncretism — the blending of the different religious cultures that plagued Israel until the Assyrian and Babylonian Exiles. "Whenever two groups of peoples come into contact there is an inevitable tendency to syncretism, the gods become identified, or, in the case of a conquered country, their gods find an inferior place in the pantheon of their conquerors. This process is not conscious or deliberate, but it is nevertheless real."[20] The Israelite identity was contaminated by exposure to the various available religious alternatives. The resulting syncretized culture effectively diluted Yahweh to a powerful god among many, which in turn diluted Israel's uniqueness among the surrounding cultures. Further, from the Israelite perspective, Yahweh had not fully delivered a conquered land, so it was natural for the Israelites to diversify their theological portfolio and look to many of the other available deities for favor. Judges 10:10-16 reveals the syncretism from Yahweh's perspective. When the Ammonites oppress the people, they complain to God. God's response in verse 14 abandons the people to their own paradigm. God has no desire to be the most powerful god among many; he wants to be the Only God.

Judges corrects the misconception that Yahweh has not conquered the land. God is not the one at fault for the continued presence of the various groups in Canaan; the text of Judges places the responsibility squarely on the shoulders of the people: five times in the first chapter the failure to drive out the occupants of the land is attributed to a particular tribe's inability to rout the occupants because of an enemy's technological abilities (1:19) or a nation's tenacity (1:27). The failure to

---

[20]Arthur Ernest Cundall, *Judges: An Introduction and Commentary* (Downers Grove, IL: InterVarsity, 1968), p. 40.

take over the land completely is rooted in human causes. Even in 2:20-21 the people's disobedience, not God's lack of power, is the cause of failure. The blame for any failures during the conquest is laid at the feet of the Israelites, not at the feet of Yahweh.

The second problem created by a partial conquest is the external pressure created by the remaining people groups. Because the possession of land was crucial to survival in the ancient world, it was vigorously defended. No one was too interested in sharing territory. The Israelites are the new kids on the block, and these interlopers are not viewed favorably by the surrounding nations. The result is the constant military pressure applied against Israel seen in the book of Judges.

THE BROADER CONTEXT OF CANAAN
AND THE ANCIENT NEAR EAST

Little extrabiblical data from the time of Judges exists. This period coincided with the collapse of power centers during the late Bronze Age and the inability on the part of any regional entity to control Canaan. The Egyptians no longer maintained control over the area, the Hittites had been defeated by an obscure people group known as the Mushkaya, and Babylon and Assyria were too disorganized to exert power over Canaan. "We have arrived at an age in which no external great power was strong enough or free enough to interfere in the affairs of Cana'an."[21]

The situation in Canaan reflected this reality. Only tiny local powers controlled any significant area, and it is these groups that will cause problems for the nation of Israel. Groups such as the Midianites and Ammonites were nomadic peoples and periodically applied pressure to Israel. The Philistines, on the other hand, were better organized, more deeply rooted, and better established than the groups surrounding them. They had the additional advantage of possessing a technological monopoly over all types of metalworking, including valuable iron.[22] Mathews compares the social context to twelfth-century England. The climate was political anarchy, and the

---

[21]Burney, *Judges*, p. xcvii.
[22]Victor Harold Matthews, *Judges and Ruth* (Cambridge: Cambridge University Press, 2004), p. 17.

majority of population centers were villages sized from 75-100, limited by the amount of resources in the area.[23] Such conditions allowed for the frequent rise of small rulers who organized groups around the acquisition and defense of available resources.

HISTORICITY

Much of the debate of the historicity of Judges relates not to the method of composition, but to the date. An earlier dating of the book (ca. 10th century B.C.) commonly accompanies a belief in its historical validity. Those preferring a later date of composition tend to assume a lower level of historical accuracy, instead opting for a perspective that considers the text to be heavily redacted over time.[24] Generally, the later the assumed date of composition, the more the text is assumed to have been edited. Further, those preferring later dates also assume the changes made to the text are connected to particular theological or political agendas that further obscure the view of whatever history might be underlying the text. Philippe Guillaume concludes, "The period of the Judges is therefore a literary construct that should not be used as evidence for the reconstitution of the factual history of Israel before statehood. The term should be definitively banned from serious Histories of Israel."[25]

As with all of Scripture, one's fundamental assumptions determine beliefs about historicity. The stories of Samson's phenomenal strength or Gideon's defeating an army of 120,000 with a paltry squad of 300 are considered simply unbelievable by some. But to those allowing for a God who interacts in human events, the events described in Judges present no historical difficulties.

PURPOSE

Many different purposes have been suggested as the reason for writing Judges. The most common position is that Judges was writ-

[23]Ibid., pp. 12-13.
[24]Barnabas Lindars, *Judges 1–5: A New Translation and Commentary* (Edinburgh: T & T Clark, 1995) performs just such a meticulous analysis of the text, determining the presence of omissions, glosses, and redactions in the text.
[25]Philippe Guillaume, *Waiting for Josiah: The Judges* (London: T & T Clark, 2004), p. 252.

ten as propaganda in support of the monarchy. The identity of the king depends on the date of the book. If Judges was written early in the monarchy, its elevation of the tribe of Judah and the undermining of Benjamin would suggest that the book was compiled in support of the early Davidic monarchy.[26] Others suggest the book was composed during Josiah's reign and therefore functioned as a polemic for Josiah's rule.[27]

Judges' purpose, however, is first and foremost theological in nature. The book of Judges intends to do more than merely support David or Josiah as the legitimate monarch of the Hebrews; it promotes Israel as a people struggling in faithfulness to their God. The leadership vacuum that Judges observes is secondary to the negative commentary provided on Israel's abandonment of commitment to Yahweh. "The theocratic rule of YHWH is [the author's] uppermost concern, rather than providing an apologia for any earthly monarch, however apparently beneficial or successful."[28] This perspective better fits the literary composition techniques used by Judges' author. Many commentators point out Judges' author's use of the cyclical pattern of sin, oppression, repentance, and deliverance as a literary device within the book.[29] This repeated pattern of decline effectively maps the degeneration of a society that abandons Yahweh.[30]

---

[26]Mark Zvi Brettler's *The Book of Judges* is typical in asserting that Judges represents a political polemic supporting the Davidic kingship (United Kingdom: Routledge, 2003). See also J. Clinton McCann's *Judges* (Louisville, KY: John Knox Press, 2002) and Robert H. O'Connell's *The Rhetoric of the Book of Judges*.

[27]E. John Hamlin, *At Risk in the Promised Land: A Commentary on the Book of Judges* (Grand Rapids: Eerdmans, 1990), p. 4.

[28]David Jackman, *Judges, Ruth* (Dallas: Word, 1991), p. 24. Daniel Block presents a similar perspective in *Judges, Ruth* (Nashville: Broadman & Holman, 1999), pp. 57-59.

[29]David Jobling, "Structuralist Criticism: The Text's World of Meaning," in *Judges and Method: New Approaches in Biblical Studies*, ed. by Gale Yee (Minneapolis: Fortress Press, 1995), p. 96. See also Lillian Klein's *The Triumph of Irony in the Book of Judges* (Sheffield: Almond Press, 1989). For those taking a structural approach to Judges, the Othniel narrative functions as the paradigm for the cycles within the book. Some works, such as Tammi Schneider's *Judges* (Collegeville, MN: Liturgical Press, 1999), modify the approach and present the cycles as progressively degenerative.

[30]Wong (*Compositional Strategy of the Book of Judges*) argues that the key to the purpose of Judges is reflected best in the prologue and epilogue. He

Judges reminds readers that Yahweh is merciful and faithful to his covenant in spite of disobedience.

LITERARY STYLE AND CHARACTER

Judges is a carefully written book and has many features that surely would have delighted ancient readers. At its most basic, Judges is simply a collection of engaging stories. But looking just beneath the surface of the text reveals a treasure of storytelling features. By capturing the attention and imagination of the reader, Judges powerfully provides an encounter with the God of Israel. The book of Judges is best read as a story with God at the center. Judges is not merely a skillfully told story. The author constructs the narrative skillfully in order to motivate the reader to interact with the God of Israel.

GEOGRAPHY

Geography plays a central role in Judges. The movements of the tribes, the locations of the inhabitants of the area, rivers, battlefields, and the terrain all factor into the author's construction of this era of Israel's history. Geography determines the area that may be controlled by iron chariots, hampers the escape of retreating troops, and indirectly leads to the idolatry of a wandering tribe. The events recorded in Judges occur in real locations, and the author repeatedly provides places not only as frames of reference for the reader, but as factors in shaping the outcome of events.

THE HERO THEME

Everyone loves a good underdog-becomes-the-hero story, and Judges delivers. The individual judges stand against big odds and still succeed. The Old Testament is full of the motif of hero — Joshua, Samson, David and his mighty men, and Elijah all come through for God in the nick of time. The structure of the hero stories in the book of Judges parallels that of hero stories told in simi-

argues that the purpose is to catalogue Israel's "progressive deterioration" during this period of history. The solution to the Israelite's problem, then, becomes spiritual in nature.

lar cultures for millennia. Yet behind Old Testament hero stories lurks God's powerful hand. Yahweh is the ultimate hero of Judges.

THE TRICKSTER THEME

Judges is filled with characters who deceive in order to achieve the desired results. Rather than being considered dishonest, such characters should be understood to use trickery to gain leverage from a weaker position. Ehud, Jael, Samson, and Delilah all employ trickery to gain an advantage. Trickery in a narrative allows the reader knowledge that the characters lack until the deceit comes to fruition.

THE RETRIBUTION THEME

The powerful theological theme of retribution threads its way through Judges. The book fuels the Hebrew paradigm that retribution for evil must be meted out to the guilty. Abimelech, the tribe of Benjamin, Adoni-Bezek, and Sisera are all divinely repaid for their evil. Judges reminds the reader that the God of Israel has constructed a universe where injustice does not go unanswered.

WORDPLAY

The Hebrew of Judges makes heavy use of wordplay and puns. The names of characters, bitter remarks, repeated phrases, crass humor, and subtle allusions all contribute to the humor and demonstrate the skill of the author. Such elements make the stories all the more engaging to the reader.

ECHO NARRATIVE

Another literary aspect of Judges is its repeated reference to previous events in Israel's history, particularly events occurring in Genesis. Daniel Block uses the term "echo narrative" to describe how a passage connects to a previous event.[31] Jephthah's daughter and the

---

[31]Daniel Block, "Echo Narrative Technique in Hebrew Literature: A Study in Judges 19," *WTJ* 52 (1990): 325-341. The more common and current aca-

Levite's concubine elicit echoes of Abraham's sacrifice of Isaac. The Levite's arrival in Gibeah and the intervention of the host bring to mind Lot's predicament with the angels in Sodom in Genesis 19. The prediction of Samson's birth brings to mind the promised birth of Isaac.[32] Judges' author relies on the broader history of Israel to provide a sense of continuity and scope to the book's readers.

AMBIGUITY

Judges' author is a master of ambiguity. While many commentators wrestle over the absence of detail in the text, it is more likely that the author deliberately intends to be vague and playful. Jael and Sisera are seen in a tent. Did they or didn't they? A concubine is murdered, but is it by a mob or by a Levite with a knife? Micah steals silver from his mother, oddly the same amount paid by one of the Philistine lords to Delilah. The author repeatedly leaves a haze over the details that forces the reader to second guess what has just been read. Millennia later, the literary product still forces the reader to wrestle with both meaning and imagination.

INVERSION

A favorite literary tool of Judges' author is the use of inversion. The reader continually encounters the unexpected as the author changes the outcome to the opposite of what the reader naturally expects.[33] These inversions may be as simple as repeated small twists encountered along the way. In keeping with the Hebrew mind-set of trust expressed in Psalm 44:6-7, even the weapons used in Judges represent a surprise for the reader. God delivers through an ox goad, a tent peg, a jawbone, pitchers and torches, and even bare hands.

Often, the inversions are more significant. Moral inversion powerfully overturns the reader's expectation of finding righteousness and faith in the lives of Israelite readers. A Levite, expected to lead

demic term is "intertextuality," relating to one text's reference to another for an author's literary agenda.

[32]These examples will be explored more fully in the commentary section.

[33]Klein's *The Triumph of Irony in the Book of Judges*, for instance, explores a complex structure in Judges that highlights the irony of the text.

in the pure worship of Yahweh, contracts out his religious services to the highest bidder. Samson, who should be the holiest man in the book, denigrates every aspect of his Nazirite covenant. The supposedly safe Jewish city of Gibeah becomes a nightmare for a band of travelers. Just as Joshua inverts moral expectations and toys with the definitions of "Israelite" and "Canaanite,"[34] Judges upends the moral expectations of the reader.

The most significant kind of inversion used by Judges' author is gender inversion.[35] The narrative repeatedly inverts the expected gender roles of both sexes, in effect inverting the patriarchal paradigm the reader expects to encounter. Powerful male warriors (Sisera, Abimelech, Samson) are conquered by seemingly helpless women. Men are sidelined as women are elevated (Deborah, Manoah's wife). The typical roles expected for both sexes are constantly overturned in the text. Where the readers expect the man to be victorious, they see the woman standing and the man vanquished at her feet. Where a man is humiliated, a woman is honored. Women succeed physically, socially, financially, and spiritually in connection with men who fail. When a woman suffers in the book of Judges, she always does so at the hands of a man. Men, however, suffer at the hands of both men and women. The author is not exhibiting a sexist attitude. Rather, the author has a clear understanding of the gender models of the era in which he writes and deliberately inverts those models for literary effect.

---

[34]Rahab may be considered an immoral prostitute from a pagan people who becomes a faithful follower of Yahweh, while the Hebrew warrior Achan rebels and is killed for his rejection of Yahweh, becoming, in effect, Canaanite. See Mark Ziese, *Joshua* (Joplin, MO: College Press, 2008).

[35]Several biblical commentators have noted literary inversion specifically linked to gender. Mary Shields suggests that the Shunammite woman in 2 Kings 4 is exalted at Elisha's expense ("Subverting a Man of God, Elevating a Woman: Role and Power Reversals in 2 Kings 4," *JSOT* 58 [June 1993]: 59-69). Robert Alter also points out that the Song of Deborah "plays almost teasingly with the expected roles of man and woman" (*The Art of Biblical Poetry* [London: T & T Clark, 1985], p. 46). See also Robert B. Chisholm Jr., "The Role of Women in the Rhetorical Strategy of the Book of Judges," in *Integrity of Heart, Skillfulness of Hands* (Grand Rapids: Baker, 1994).

A WORD ON GENDER

Judges, with its portrayal of both positive and negative images of women, provides fruitful soil for Bible study focused on gender. Achsah, Deborah, Jael, Manoah's wife, and Delilah are all women who succeed powerfully in Judges, often at the expense of men. But Judges is also replete with victimized women: Jephthah's daughter, Samson's wife, the Levite's concubine, and the daughters of Shiloh. While Judges reflects a patriarchal society, contrary to the opinion of much of feminist scholarship, patriarchy is not in and of itself abusive. At the same time, because Judges observes horrible wounds delivered by people in positions of power, it still has implications for both women and men in the modern audience. A victim of sexual assault hears the text of Judges in ways others cannot imagine, so it is imperative that those who handle the book interpret it not only accurately, but also sensitively.

STRUCTURE AND OUTLINE

Judges may be divided into four main sections. The book is composed of two prologues (1:1–2:5 and 2:6–3:6), a central section telling the story of the judges (3:7–16:31), and a concluding section comprised of two separate narratives (17–18 and 19–21). Many modern commentators follow Lillian Klein's understanding of the structure of the central section of Judges as reflecting the "Othniel paradigm": that the first judge is the standard to which all other judges are compared.[36]

---

[36]*The Triumph of Irony in the Book of Judges.*

JUDGES
OUTLINE

JUDGES
BIBLIOGRAPHY

Ackerman J.S. "Prophecy and Warfare in Early Israel: A Study of the Deborah-Barak Story." *BASOR* 220 (1976): 5-13.

Ackerman, Susan. *Warrior, Dancer, Seductress, Queen: Women in Judges and Biblical Israel*. New York: Doubleday, 1998.

Alter, Robert. *The Art of Biblical Narrative*. New York: Basic Books, 1981.

—————. *The Art of Biblical Poetry*. London: T & T Clark, 1985.

Amit, Y. *The Book of Judges: The Art of Editing*. Translated by J. Chipman. Biblical Interpretation Series 38. Leiden: Brill, 1999.

—————. "Hidden Polemic in the Conquest of Dan: Judges 17–18." *VT* 40 (1990): 4-20.

Armerding, C.E. *Judges: A Bible Commentary for Today*. London: Pickering and Inglis, 1979.

Assis, Eliyahu. *Self-interest or Communal Interest: An Ideology of Leadership in the Gideon, Abimelech, and Jephthah Narratives (Judg. 6–12)*. VTSupp. Leiden: Brill, 2005.

Atkinson, Clarissa W., Constance H. Buchanan, and Margaret R. Miles. *Immaculate and Powerful: The Female in Sacred Image and Social Reality*. Boston: Beacon Press, 1985.

Auld, A. Graeme. "Gideon: Hacking at the Heart of the Old Testament." *VT* 39 (1989): 257-267.

The Babylonian Talmud. London: Soncino Press, 1935.

Bach, A. "Rereading the Body Politic: Women and Violence in Judges 21." In *A Feminist Companion to Reading the Bible*, pp. 143-159. Edited by Athalya Brenner and C. Fontaine. Sheffield: Sheffield Academic Press, 1997.

Bahrani, Zainab. "Sex as Symbolic Form: Erotism and the Body in Mesopotamian Art." In *Sex and Gender in the Ancient Near East, Proceedings of the 47th Rencontre Assyriologique Internationale, Helsinki, July 2-6, 2001*, pp. 53-58 (Helsinki: Neo-Assyrian Text Corpus Project, 2002).

Bal, Mieke, ed. *Anti-covenant: Counter-Reading Women's Lives in the Hebrew Bible.* Sheffield: Almond Press, 1989.

Bal, Mieke. "Dealing with Women: Daughters in the Book of Judges." In *Book and the Text: The Bible and Literary Theory*, pp. 16-39. Ed. by Regina Schwartz. Oxford: Basil Blackwell, 1990.

_____ . *Death and Dissymmetry: The Politics of Coherence in the Book of Judges.* Chicago: University of Chicago, 1988.

_____ . *Murder and Difference: Gender, Genre, and Scholarship on Sisera's Death.* Bloomington, IN: Indiana University Press, 1988.

Bledstein, Adrien J. "Is Judges a Woman's Satire on Men Who Play God?" In *A Feminist Companion to Judges*, pp. 34-54. Edited by Athalya Brenner. Sheffield: Sheffield Academic Press, 1993.

Blenkinsopp, J. "Structure and Style in Judges 13–16." *JBL* 82 (1963): 65-76.

Block, Daniel Isaac. "Echo Narrative Technique in Hebrew Literature: A Study in Judges 1." *WTJ* 52 (1990): 325-341.

_____ . "Empowered by the Spirit of God: The Holy Spirit in the Historiographic Writings of the Old Testament." *SBJT* 1 (1997): 42-61.

_____ . *Judges, Ruth.* The New American Commentary. Nashville: Broadman & Holman, 1999.

_____ . "The Period of the Judges: Religious Disintegration under Tribal Rule." In *Israel's Apostasy and Restoration*, pp. 39-57. Edited by A. Gileadi. Grand Rapids: Baker, 1988.

_____ . "Unspeakable Crimes: The Abuse of Women in the Book of Judges." *SBJT* 2 (Fall 1998): 46-55.

_____ . "Will the Real Gideon Please Stand Up? Narrative Style and Intention in Judges 6–9." *JETS* 40 (1997): 353-366.

Bluedorn, Wolfgang. *Yahweh versus Baalism: A Theological Reading of the Gideon-Abimelech Narrative.* JSOTSupp 329. Sheffield: Sheffield Academic Press, 2002.

Bodine, Walter Ray. *The Greek Text of Judges: Recensional Developments*. Chico, CA: Scholars Press, 1980.

Boling, Robert G. *Judges, Introduction, Translation, and Commentary*. Garden City, NY: Doubleday, 1975.

Boogaart, T.A. "Stone for Stone: Retribution in the Story of Abimelech and Shechem." *JSOT* 32 (1985): 45-56.

Borowski, O. *Agriculture in Iron Age Israel*. Winona Lake, IN: Eisenbrauns, 1988.

Botterweck, G. Johannes, and Helmer Ringgren, eds. *Theological Dictionary of the Old Testament*. Grand Rapids: Eerdmans, 1977.

Bray, Jason S. *Sacred Dan: Religious Tradition and Cultic Practice in Judges 17–18*. Library of Hebrew Bible/Old Testament Studies. New York: T & T Clark, 2006.

Brenner, Athalya, ed. *A Feminist Companion to Judges*. Sheffield: Sheffield Academic Press, 1993.

Brenner, Athalya, and C. Fontaine, eds. *A Feminist Companion to Reading the Bible: Methods and Strategies*. Sheffield: Sheffield Academic Press, 1997.

Brensinger, Terry L. *Judges*. Believers Church Bible Commentary. Scottdale, PA: Herald Press, 1999.

Brettler, Marc Zvi. *The Book of Judges*. New York: Routledge, 2001.

_____ . *The Creation of History in Ancient Israel*. London: Routledge, 1995.

Brodie, Thomas L. *The Birthing of the New Testament: The Intertextual Development of the New Testament Writings*. Sheffield: Phoenix Press, 2004.

Brown, Francis, et al., eds. *The New Brown, Driver, and Briggs Hebrew and English Lexicon of the Old Testament, Based on the Lexicon of William Gesenius as Translated by Edward Robinson*. Lafayette, IN: Associated Publishers and Authors, 1981.

Burney, C.F. *The Book of Judges*. New York: KTAV Pub. House, 1970.

Bush, George. *Notes, Critical and Practical on the Book of Judges: Designed as a General Help to Biblical Reading and Instruction*. New York: Saxton, Pierce, 1844.

Cassel, Paulus. *The Book of Judges: Commentary on the Holy Scriptures, Critical, Doctrinal, and Homiletical*. Edited by J.P. Lange. New York: Scribner, 1890.

Chisholm, Robert B. Jr. "The Role of Women in the Rhetorical Strategy of the Book of Judges." In *Integrity of Heart, Skillfulness of Hands: Biblical and Leadership Studies in Honor of Donald K. Campbell*, pp. 34-49. Edited by Roy B. Zuck. Grand Rapids: Baker, 1994.

Christianson, Eric S. "A Fistful of Shekels: Scrutinizing Ehud's Entertaining Violence (Judges 3:12-30)." *BI* 11 (2003): 53-78.

Claassens, L.J.M. "The Character of God in Judges 6–8: The Gideon Narrative as Theological and Moral Response." *HBT* 23 (2001): 51-71.

Cohen, A., ed. *Joshua and Judges: Hebrew Text and English Translation*. London: Soncino Press, 1961.

Coogan, Michael David, ed. *Stories from Ancient Canaan*. Philadelphia: Westminster Press, 1978.

Craigie, Peter C. "Parallel Word Pairs in the Song of Deborah (Judges 5)." *JETS* 20 (March 1977): 15-22.

_____ . "Reconsideration of Shamgar Ben Anath (Judg 3:31 and 5:6)." *JBL* 91 (1972): 239-240.

_____ . "Song of Deborah and the Epic of Tukulti-Ninurta." *JBL* 88 (1969): 253-265.

_____ . "Three Ugaritic Notes on the Song of Deborah." *JSOT* (April 1977): 33-49.

Crenshaw, J.L. "Samson Saga: Filial Devotion or Erotic Attachment?" *ZAW* 86 (1974): 470-504.

Cundall, Arthur Ernest. *Judges: An Introduction and Commentary*. Downers Grove, IL: InterVarsity, 1968.

Davis, Ralph Dale. *Such a Great Salvation: Exposition of the Book of Judges*. Grand Rapids: Baker, 1990.

de Moor, Johannes Cornelis. "The Twelve Tribes in the Song of Deborah." *VT* 43 (October 1993): 483-494.

Dothan, Trude. "Aspects of Egyptian and Philistine Presence in Canaan during the Late Bronze-Early Iron Ages." *OLA* 19 (1985): 55-75.

Drews, Robert. "The 'Chariots of Iron' of Joshua and Judges." *JSOT* 45 (October 1989): 15-23.

Echols, C.L. "The Eclipse of God in the Song of Deborah (Judges 5): The Role of Yhwh in the Light of Heroic Poetry." *TynBul* 56 (2005): 149-152.

Enns, Paul P. *Judges*. Bible Study Commentary Series. Grand Rapids: Zondervan, 1982.

Exum, J. Cheryl. Feminist Criticism: Whose Interests Are Being Served?" In *Judges and Method: New Approaches in Biblical Studies*, pp. 65-90. Ed. by Gale A. Yee. Minneapolis: Fortress Press, 1995.

_____. *Fragmented Women: Feminist (Sub)versions of Biblical Narratives*. Valley Forge, PA: Trinity, 1993.

Faiman, David. "Chronology in the Book of Judges." *JBQ* 21 (Jan 1993): 31-40.

Fewell, Danna Nolan, and David M. Gunn. "Controlling Perspectives: Women, Men, and the Authority of Violence in Judges 4 and 5." *JAAR* 58 (1990): 389-411.

Fleenor, Rob. *The Inversion of Patriarchy in the Book of Judges: Androcentricity as a Literary Mechanism of Male Self-Retribution*. MA thesis, Cincinnati Christian University, 2007.

Fuchs, Esther. "The Literary Characterization of Mothers and Sexual Politics in the Hebrew Bible." *Semeia* 46 (1989): 151-166.

Garstang, John. *Joshua, Judges*. Grand Rapids: Kregel, 1978.

Goslinga, C.J. *Joshua, Judges, Ruth*. Grand Rapids: Zondervan, 1987.

Gottlieb, Freema. "Three Mothers." *Judaism* 30 (1981): 194-203.

Gray, John. *Joshua, Judges, Ruth*. Grand Rapids. Eerdmans, 1986.

Green, Jay, ed. *The Book of Judges*. Wilmington, DE: Associated Publishers and Authors, 1976.

Guillaume, Philippe. *Waiting for Josiah: The Judges*. London: T & T Clark International, 2004.

Gunn, D.M. *Judges*. Malden, MA: Blackwell, 2005.

Gur-Klein, Thalia. "Sexual Hospitality in the Hebrew Bible?" *Lectio Difficilior – European Electronic Journal for Feminist Exegesis* (February 2003): http://www.lectio.unibe.ch/03_2/gur.htm.

Halpern, Baruch. "The Assassination of Eglon: The First Locked-room Murder Mystery." *BR* 4 (December 1988): 33-41.

_____ . "The Resourceful Israelite Historian: The Song of Deborah and Israelite Historiography." *HTR* 76 (October 1983): 379-401.

Hamlin, E. John. *At Risk in the Promised Land: A Commentary on the Book of Judges*. International Theological Commentary. Grand Rapids: W.B. Eerdmans, 1990.

Hammond, Gerald. "The Bible and Literary Criticism — Part II." *Critical Quarterly* 25 (Autumn 1983): 5-20.

Harris, R. Laird, et al., eds. *Theological Wordbook of the Old Testament*. Chicago: Moody Press, 1980.

Hauser, Alan J. "Judges 5: Parataxis in Hebrew Poetry." *JBL* 99 (March 1980): 23-41.

_____ . "Minor Judges: A Re-evaluation." *JBL* 94 (June 1975): 190-200.

_____ . "Unity and Diversity in Early Israel before Samuel." *JETS* 22 (December 1979): 289-303.

Heath, Elaine A. "The Levite's Concubine: Domestic Violence and the People of God." *Priscilla Papers* 13 (Winter 1999): 10-20.

Helyer, Larry R. "Hero and Heroine Narratives in the Old Testament." *SBJT* 2 (1998): 34-45.

Hervey, A.C. *Judges*. London: Funk & Wagnalls, 1913.

Hudson, Don Michael. "Living in a Land of Epithets: Anonymity in Judges 19–21." *JSOT* 62 (June 1994): 49-66.

Jackman, David. *Judges, Ruth*. The Communicator's Commentary Series. Dallas: Word Books, 1991.

Janzen, J.G. "A Certain Woman in the Rhetoric of Judges 9." *JSOT* 39 (1987): 33-37.

Jastrow, Marcus. *A Dictionary of the Targumim, the Talmud Babli and Yerushalmi, and the Midrashic Literature*. Peabody, MA: Hendrickson, 2005.

Jobling, David. "Structuralist Criticism: The Text's World of Meaning." In *Gender and Law in the Hebrew Bible and the Ancient Near East*, pp. 91-118. Ed. by Victor H. Matthews, Bernard M. Levinson, and Tikva Frymer-Kensky. Sheffield: Sheffield Academic Press, 1998.

Keefe, Alice A. "Rapes of Women/Wars of Men." *Semeia* 61 (1993): 79-97.

Keil, C.F., and F. Delitzsch. *Joshua, Judges, Ruth*. Translated by James Martin. Commentary on the Old Testament. 10 Vols. Reprint ed. Grand Rapids: Eerdmans, 1982.

Klein, Lillian R. "The Book of Judges: Paradigm and Derivation in Images of Women." In *A Feminist Companion to Judges*, pp. 55-71. Ed. by Athalya Brenner. Sheffield: Sheffield Academic Press, 1993.

——————. *The Triumph of Irony in the Book of Judges*. Sheffield: Almond Press, 1988.

Kline, Meredith G. *Treaty of the Great King: The Covenant Structure of Deuteronomy*. Grand Rapids: Eerdmans, 1963.

Knowles, Gordon James. "Male Prison Rape: A Search for Causation and Prevention." *Howard Journal of Criminal Justice* 38 (1999): 267-282.

Lasine, S. "Guest and Host in Judges 19: Lot's Hospitality in an Inverted World." *JSOT* 29 (1984): 37-59.

Levine, Mordecai. "A Polemic: In the Days of Jael: Reclaiming the History of Women in Ancient Israel." In *Immaculate and Powerful: The Female Sacred Image and Social Reality*, pp. 15-38. Edited by C.W. Atkinson, C.H. Buchanan, and M.R. Miles. Boston: Beacon, 1985.

Lewis, Arthur H. *Judges/Ruth*. Chicago: Moody Press, 1979.

Lindars, Barnabas. "Deborah's Song: Women in the Old Testament." *Bulletin of the John Rylands University Library of Manchester* 65 (Spring 1983): 158-175.

——————. "Jotham's Fable: A New Form-Critical Analysis." *JETS* 24 (October 1973): 355-366.

——————. *Judges 1–5: A New Translation and Commentary*. Edinburgh: T & T Clark, 1995.

Linton, Anna. "Sacrificed or Spared? The Fate of Jephthah's Daughter in Early Modern Theological and Literary Texts." *German Life and Letters* 57 (July 2004): 237-255.

Marcus, David. *Jephthah and His Vow*. Lubbock, TX: Texas Tech Press, 1986.

Margalith, Othniel. "Samson's Riddle and Samson's Magic Locks." *VT* 36 (1986): 225-234.

Martin, James D. *The Book of Judges*. Cambridge: Cambridge University Press, 1975.

Matthews, Victor H. "Female Voices: Upholding the Honor of the Household." *BTB* 24 (Spring 1994): 8-15.

_____. *Judges and Ruth*. New Cambridge Bible Commentary. Cambridge: Cambridge University Press, 2004.

Matthews, Victor H., and Don C. Benjamin. "Jael: Host or Judge?" *TBT* (September 1992): 291-296.

Mayes, A.D.H. *Judges*. Sheffield: Sheffield Academic Press, 1995.

Mazar, Amihai. "Philistine Temple at Tell Qasile." *BA* 36 (May 1973): 42-48.

Mazar, Benjamin, ed. *The World History of the Jewish People: Judges, Volume III*. Israel: Rutgers University Press, 1971.

McCann, J. Clinton. *Judges*. 1st ed. Louisville, KY: John Knox Press, 2002.

McDaniel, Karl. "Samson's Riddle." *Did* 12 (Spring 2001): 47-57.

McKenzie, Steven L., and Matt Patrick Graham, eds. *The History of Israel's Traditions: The Heritage of Martin Noth*. Sheffield: Sheffield Academic Press, 1994.

McMillion, P.E. "Worship in Judges 17–18." In *Worship in the Hebrew Bible*, pp. 225-243. Edited by M.P. Graham et al. JSOTSupp 284. Sheffield: Sheffield Academic Press, 1999.

Merideth, Betsy. "Desire and Danger: The Drama of Betrayal." In *Anti-covenant: Counter-Reading Women's Lives in the Hebrew Bible*, pp. 63-78. Ed. by Mieke Bal. Sheffield: Almond Press, 1989.

Miller, G. "Verbal Feud in the Hebrew Bible: Judg 3:12-30 and 19–21." *JNES* 55 (1996): 114-115.

Miller, Geoffrey P. "A Riposte Form in the Song of Deborah." In *Gender and Law in the Hebrew Bible and the Ancient Near East*, pp. 113-127. Edited by Victor H. Matthews, Bernard M. Levinson, and Tikva Frymer-Kensky. Sheffield: Sheffield Academic Press, 1998.

Miller, Paul. "Moral Formation and the Book of Judges." *EQ* 75 (2003): 99-115.

Moore, G.F. *The Book of Judges: A New English Translation Printed in Colors Exhibiting the Composite Structure of the Book: With Explanatory Notes and Pictorial Illustrations*. New York: Dodd, Mead, and Company, 1898.

Mullen, E Theodore. "The 'Minor Judges': Some Literary and Historical Considerations." *CBQ* 44 (April 1982): 185-201.

Nelson, Richard D. "Ideology, Geography, and the List of Minor Judges." *JSOT* 31 (March 2007): 347-364.

Niditch, Susan. "Eroticism and Death in the Tale of Jael." In *Gender and Difference in Ancient Israel*, pp. 43-57. Edited by Peggy Day. Minneapolis: Fortress Press, 1989.

_____. *Judges: A Commentary*. Westminster John Knox Press, 2008.

_____. "Samson as Culture Hero, Trickster, and Bandit: The Empowerment of the Weak." *CBQ* 52 (1990): 608-624.

Noth, Martin. *The Deuteronomistic History*. Translated by D. Orton. JSOTSupp 15. Sheffield: JSOT Press, 1981.

O'Brien, Mark. "Judges and the Deuteronomistic History." In *History of Israel's Traditions*, pp. 235-259. Sheffield: Sheffield Academic Press, 1994.

O'Connell, Robert H. *The Rhetoric of the Book of Judges*. VTSupp. Leiden: E.J. Brill, 1996.

Olson, Dennis T. "Dialogues of Life and Death." In *Postmodern Interpretations of the Bible*, pp. 43-54. Edited by A.K.M. Adam. St. Louis: Chalice Press, 2001.

Olson, Dennis. *Judges: The New Interpreter's Bible*. Nashville: Abingdon Press, 2005.

Ovid, *Fasti*, Book IV, 701-712 (Cambridge, Harvard University Press, 1996).

Patton, Corrine L. "From Heroic Individual to Nameless Victim: Women in the Social World of the Judges." In *Biblical and Humane: A Festschrift for John F. Priest*, pp. 33-46. Ed. by Linda Bennett Elder, David L. Barr, and Elizabeth Struthers Malbon. Atlanta: Scholars Press, 1996.

Reich, R. "Anonymity as a Literary Device in Judges 19–21." *Beit Mikra* 158 (1999): 256-260.

Reinhartz, Adele. "Samson's Mother: An Unnamed Protagonist." *JSOT* 55 (1992): 25-37.

Reis, Pamela Tamarkin. "Spoiled Child: A Fresh Look at Jephthah's Daughter." *Proof* (Spring 1997): 279-298.

Reviv, Hanoch. "The Government of Shechem in the El-Amarna Period and in the Days of Abimelech." *IEJ* 16 (1966): 252-257.

Richter, W. *Die Bearbeitungen des "Retterbuches" in der Deuteronomischen Epoche.* Bonn: Bonner Biblische Beiträge, 1964.

Ridout, Samuel. *Judges and Ruth.* Neptune, NJ: Loizeaux Brothers, 1981.

Rogers, Richard. *A Commentary on Judges.* Edinburgh: Banner of Truth, 1983.

Romer, Thomas C. "Why Would the Deuteronomists Tell about the Sacrifice of Jephthah's Daughter?" *JSOT* 77 (March 1998): 27-38.

Schipper, Jeremy. "Narrative Obscurity of Samson's *Hydh* in Judges 14.14 and 18." *JSOT* 27 (2003): 339-353.

Schneider, Tammi. *Judges.* Berit Olam. Collegeville, MN: Liturgical Press, 1999.

Schwartz, Regina, ed. *Book and the Text: The Bible and Literary Theory.* Oxford: Basil Blackwell, 1990.

Segert S. "Paronomasia in the Samson Narrative in Judges 13–16." *VT* 34 (1986): 454-461.

Shields, Mary E. "Subverting a Man of God, Elevating a Woman: Role and Power Reversals in 2 Kings 4." *JSOT* 58 (June 1993): 59-69.

Simons, Louise. "An Immortality Rather Than a Life: Milton and the Concubine of Judges 19–21." In *Old Testament Women in Western Literature*, pp. 144-173. Edited by R. Frontain and J. Wojcik. Conway, AR: UCA Press, 1991.

Simpson, C.A. *The Composition of the Book of Judges.* Oxford: Basil Blackwell, 1957.

Smelik, Willem F. *The Targum of Judges.* Oudtestamentische Studien. Leiden: E.J. Brill, 1995.

Smith, Mark S. "Remembering God: Collective Memory in Israelite Religion." *CBQ* 64 (2002): 631-651.

Soggin, J. Alberto. *Judges, a Commentary*. Philadelphia: Westminster Press, 1981.

Sternberg, Meir. *Expositional Modes and Temporal Ordering in Fiction*. Baltimore: Johns Hopkins, 1978.

Stone, L.G. *From Tribal Confederation to Monarchic State: The Editorial Perspective of the Book of Judges*, unpublished Ph.D. dissertation, Yale, 1988.

Sweeney, A. "Davidic Polemic in the Book of Judges." *VT* 47 (1997): 517-529.

Tanner, J. Paul. "The Gideon Narrative as the Focal Point of Judges." *BSac* 149 (Apr–Jun 1992): 146-161.

Taylor, J. Glen. "The Song of Deborah and Two Canaanite Goddesses." *JSOT* 23 (July 1982): 99-108.

Trible, Phyllis. *Texts of Terror*. Philadelphia: Fortress Press, 1984.

van der Toorn, K. "Judges 16:2l in the Light of the Akkadian Sources." *VT* 36 (l986): 248-253.

VanGemeren, Willem A., ed. *New International Dictionary of Old Testament Theology & Exegesis*. Grand Rapids: Zondervan, 1997.

Vincent, Mark A. "The Song of Deborah: A Structural and Literary Consideration." *JSOT* 91 (2000): 61-82.

Watson, Robert Alexander. *Judges and Ruth*. The Expositor's Bible. New York: A.C. Armstrong, 1893.

Webb, Barry G. *The Book of the Judges: An Integrated Reading*. JSOTSupp 46. Sheffield: JSOT Press, 1987.

Wessels, J.P.H. "'Postmodern' Rhetoric and the Former Prophetic Literature." In *Rhetoric, Scripture and Theology*, pp. 182-194. Ed. by Stanley E. Porter and Thomas H. Olbricht. Sheffield: Sheffield Academic Press, 1996.

Williams, Jay G. "The Structure of Judges 2:6–16:31." *JSOT* 49 (February 1991): 77-86.

Wong, Gregory T.K. *Compositional Strategy of the Book of Judges: An Inductive, Rhetorical Study*. VTSupp. Leiden: Brill, 2006.

_____. "Is There a Direct Pro-Judah Polemic in Judges?" *SJOT* 19 (2005:, 84-110.

Wood, Leon. *Distressing Days of the Judges*. Grand Rapids: Zondervan, 1975.

Yee, Gale A. "Ideological Criticism: Judges 17–21 and the Dismembered Body." In *Judges and Method*, pp. 146-170. Ed. by Gale A. Yee. Minneapolis: Fortress Press, 1995.

Yee, Gale A., ed. *Judges and Method: New Approaches in Biblical Studies*. Minneapolis: Fortress Press, 1995.

Younger, K. Lawson, *The NIV Application Commentary: Judges, Ruth*. Grand Rapids: Zondervan, 2002.

Ziese, Mark. *Joshua*. Joplin, MO: College Press, 2008.

JUDGES 1

I. THE FIRST PROLOGUE (1:1-2:5)

A. MIXED SUCCESS FOR THE TRIBES (1:1-36)

1. Israelites Defeat Adoni-Bezek (1:1-7)

[1]After the death of Joshua, the Israelites asked the LORD, "Who will be the first to go up and fight for us against the Canaanites?"

[2]The LORD answered, "Judah is to go; I have given the land into their hands."

[3]Then the men of Judah said to the Simeonites their brothers, "Come up with us into the territory allotted to us, to fight against the Canaanites. We in turn will go with you into yours." So the Simeonites went with them.

[4]When Judah attacked, the LORD gave the Canaanites and Perizzites into their hands and they struck down ten thousand men at Bezek. [5]It was there that they found Adoni-Bezek and fought against him, putting to rout the Canaanites and Perizzites. [6]Adoni-Bezek fled, but they chased him and caught him, and cut off his thumbs and big toes.

[7]Then Adoni-Bezek said, "Seventy kings with their thumbs and big toes cut off have picked up scraps under my table. Now God has paid me back for what I did to them." They brought him to Jerusalem, and he died there.

1:1 The book opens with a link to Joshua's death in Joshua 24 and the need to complete the conquest. The text will soon reveal the reasons the Israelites failed to capture the land. The immediate focus for now, however, is on the cleanup activities in and around the territory of Judah.

1:2 With Joshua gone from the scene, the Israelites lack leadership. Although it will not last, their first instinct is to seek God's input. Rather than divide the tribes and fight the different people groups in the land concurrently, the Israelites realize that a progressive push against the remaining Canaanite people groups will be the most successful. God's response is to send **Judah** against the Canaanites. Sending Judah makes good sense, since Judah is the largest tribe at this point. The devastation created by Israel's largest tribe would no doubt reinforce the psychological impact on the Canaanites already produced by news of the Exodus.

1:3 Judah makes a generous offer to the smallest tribe of the **Simeonites**: if the Simeonites will fight on behalf of Judah, Judah will fight with Simeon. Judah's offer is clearly advantageous to Simeon. Numbers 26 lists the population of Judah at more than three times the size of Simeon, so when Simeon battles the inhabitants of Zephath in 1:17, the large army of Judah will be present to quickly bring the battle to a close. And because the cities allotted to Simeon were within the territory of Judah, a cooperative effort clearly benefits both tribes.

1:4-5 The first military victory seen in Judges is given **into their hands** by Yahweh. The **Canaanites and Perizzites** were both part of the organized resistance to the Israelite invasion mentioned in Joshua 9:1-2. The Perizzites were first mentioned in Genesis 13:7, and survived at least through the exile (Ezra 9:1). Intermarriage with them will soon be a problem for Israel (Judg 3:6).

1:6-7 After the defeat of 10,000 troops, the Israelites capture the enemy leader, **Adoni-Bezek**.[1] When Adoni-Bezek is captured, the Israelites **cut off** his **thumbs and big toes**. Mutilation was not generally practiced by the Israelites[2], but in this case, both Adoni-Bezek and the Israelites understood this as retributive justice. Mutilating this man was not so much payback as it was delivering to him the same justice he had meted out to others. For the sake of his own

---

[1]His name means "Lord of Bezek." This name may have simply been his personal name, or may have been a royal title.

[2]Israel certainly knew mutilation at the hands of its enemies when they lost conflicts. Saul feared that very thing were he to be captured by the Philistines (1 Sam 31:4), and Samson's and Zedekiah's last visual memory is of a knife being applied to their eyes after being captured (Judg 16:21; 2 Kgs 25:7). Only one of Moses' laws carried physical mutilation as a consequence of violation (Deut 25:11-12).

glory, Adoni-Bezek mutilated the kings of conquered enemies and deliberately treated them like dogs by feeding them with his table scraps. The humiliation he delivered to others was delivered to him. "What goes around, comes around" is a common theme found in Scripture. God himself claims that he will right wrongs in a way that reflects the nature of the wrong done. God's idea of justice address-es the root motivation of the wrong, and he reserves the right to punish the heart sure about its judgments toward others (Matt 7:1-5; 18:21-35).

The Adoni-Bezek story might be intended to foreshadow the Abimelech story. Both men murdered seventy other men who stood in the way of their ambitions,[3] and both received divine retribution from the hand of God. Both Judges and the larger context of Scripture make it clear that no one who practices evil can escape the reach of God's retribution. For Adoni-Bezek, his remaining days were spent marginalized in Jerusalem, his hands and feet a visible reminder of God's judgment on brutality.

2. Othniel Captures Jerusalem (1:8-15)

⁸The men of Judah attacked Jerusalem also and took it. They put the city to the sword and set it on fire.

⁹After that, the men of Judah went down to fight against the Canaanites living in the hill country, the Negev and the western foothills. ¹⁰They advanced against the Canaanites living in Hebron (formerly called Kiriath Arba) and defeated Sheshai, Ahiman and Talmai.

¹¹From there they advanced against the people living in Debir (formerly called Kiriath Sepher). ¹²And Caleb said, "I will give my daughter Acsah in marriage to the man who attacks and captures Kiriath Sepher." ¹³Othniel son of Kenaz, Caleb's younger brother, took it; so Caleb gave his daughter Acsah to him in marriage.

¹⁴One day when she came to Othniel, she urged him[a] to ask her father for a field. When she got off her donkey, Caleb asked her, "What can I do for you?"

¹⁵She replied, "Do me a special favor. Since you have given me

---

[3]Wong, *Compositional Strategy*, pp. 204-205.

**land in the Negev, give me also springs of water." Then Caleb gave
her the upper and lower springs.**

ª*14* Hebrew; Septuagint and Vulgate *Othniel, he urged her*

1:8-9 Judges 1:8-15 is a retelling of Joshua 15:13-19. With only a
few minor alterations, the text is essentially the same.[4] Reading
through Joshua gives the impression that Joshua is still alive at the
time of Othniel's attack on Debir. The events in Judges 1, however,
are clearly described as occurring *after* Joshua's death. The best reconciliation for this apparent contradiction is to consider Joshua
13–21 as a summary of the conquest independent of the time of
Joshua's death. The focus of the book of Joshua is on the successful
conquest of the land that God provides through Joshua's leadership.
Judges, however, instead focuses on the people's failure to capture
the land because of their own disobedience. In evaluating both
books, it is important to understand the authors' viewpoints regarding the conquest. God provides the land for his people in Joshua;
but in Judges, the people suffer for failing to satisfy their responsi-
bilities. The successful conquest portrayed in Joshua is attributed to
skilled leadership and is placed between Joshua's old age (13:1) and
his death (24:29). The aspects of the conquest that failed are blamed
on the people in Judges, and so occur after Joshua's death.

1:10 Sheshai, Ahiman and Talmai are described in verse 20 as
"the three sons of Anak." Numbers 13:33 mentions that the enigmatic Nephilim (Gen 6:4) were the ancestors of Anak. After the initial investigation of the Promised Land, the ten faithless Israelite
spies cited the Nephilim as the reason conquest of the land would
be impossible. The initial readers of Judges certainly understood
that these three sons of Anak were heavyweight rulers, making
Judah's victory at **Hebron** a significant accomplishment.

---

[4]With the exception of the possibly significant נתן/יהב (*yhb/ntn*) difference, the differences in the Judges text are 1) in v. 13, Kenaz is identified as
Caleb's "younger" (הַקָּטֹן מִמֶּן, *haqqāṭōn mimmen*) brother; 2) the definite article ה (*ha*) is added to שָׂדֶה (*śādeh*) in v. 14; 3) the use of Caleb's proper name
in v. 15; 4) a variant spelling for Debir; 5) a feminine singular adjective
rather than a feminine plural of תַּחְתִּי (*taḥtî*), the word for the "lower"
springs. The only significant difference is Acsah's imperative use of יְהַב
(*yāhab*) in the Judges passage instead of the more common נָתַן (*nāthan*). An
argument might be made for a more emphatic understanding *yāhab* as
"give," but support is sparse.

Pre-Davidic Jerusalem was a small city located on the western side of the Kidron Valley along the central ridges and was naturally defended by steep terrain on the south, east, and west. Along with the military advantages that came with occupying Jerusalem, the Canaanites had a propensity to build religious cultic centers in elevated and central locations. Although prior to the temple, the Israelites had not used Jerusalem as a center for religious activity, the military advantage of Jerusalem was obvious. Judah captures the city, and from there moves to the south and west to capture the Negev and the foothills. "Going up" and "going down" should be generally understood in terms of elevation rather than north and south.

Judah's southward expansion brought them against Kiriath-Arba, literally "City of Four," a title reflecting a deity, likely a moon god.[5] Since the Israelites were not likely to refer to a location with a name reflecting a pagan deity, the city later became known as Hebron.

1:11-13 Caleb, along with Joshua, was one of two spies who brought back a positive report to Moses about the possibility of capturing the land (Num 13:6,30). His well-known loyalty to the LORD gives him name recognition here, with no need for an introduction or genealogy. As an incentive to capture the town of **Debir**, Caleb offers his **daughter Acsah** as a war prize to the man who captures the city. A marriage aligning with Caleb's household would be advantageous to the recipient, adding to the honor of Acsah's groom. **Caleb's younger brother**, **Othniel**, takes the challenge. Although his service as a judge will not be addressed until 3:9, Othniel is first addressed here, when he succeeds in capturing Debir, and is given Acsah as his bride.

It is within this story that the reader is introduced to the first of many female characters to make an appearance in Judges.[6] Being

---

[5]Burney, *Judges*, p. 9.

[6]Just as the story of Othniel represents a possible outline for the structure of Judges, Klein suggests that Acsah, too, represents a paradigm: "The first dramatized narrative of the exposition, the story of Acsah and Othniel (1.12-15), offers a feminine model and a model of relations between the sexes; the last, of Othniel (3:2-11), is a complementary masculine model of leadership" (14). Ultimately, "Acsah emerges as an image of ideal Yahwist womanhood" (*Triumph of Irony*, p. 26). For Klein, Othniel and Acsah have the ideal relationship. If Klein is correct, Judges puts a model relationship at the forefront,

given as a war prize would not have offended Acsah the way it does modern sensibilities. Fathers controlled the marriages of their daughters, and Acsah likely would have achieved some status as a result of being betrothed to a war hero. But Acsah apparently carries a broader interest than just marriage. Apparently unsatisfied with the land allotted to her, she negotiates with her father for more.

The temptation for many modern commentators is to read into the text contemporary societal concepts of equality. Through such a lens, Acsah becomes little more than property subject to the whims of her father and uncle. Such interpretations, however, ignore the sociological norms of the day, in which Acsah would not be considered slighted in such an arrangement, but would be honored through marriage to a successful man. As always, beyond his concern with unjust circumstances, God is also concerned with how we conduct ourselves in those circumstances.

While some suggest that the text depicts Othniel and Acsah in a state of marital bliss, uniting to increase the value of their property, the text is better understood as communicating at least slight discord between the newlyweds. Rather than a marriage arranged within family and community, Acsah's marriage is determined by the lottery of Debir's conquest. An arranged marriage typically would have involved family and the daughter's input, whereas a marriage-as-war-prize would not.[7] Although the conqueror of Debir would have been highly esteemed, and being given in marriage to a hero was likely an honorable fate, Acsah does communicate her displeasure with Caleb's stingy wedding gift.[8]

1:14-15 The dowry for Acsah is the city of Debir. Acsah, however, is apparently not satisfied with the amount of wealth belonging

---

suggesting that all other gender interactions in Judges in some way violate that perfect paradigm. Even the narrative of the Levite and his concubine becomes a warped reflection of the interaction between Othniel and Acsah. Victor Matthews echoes Klein, suggesting that Acsah's confrontation of her father is her fulfilling of the expected role of wife, being loyal to her household. "Acsah thereby demonstrates the proper role of the wife, or even the betrothed woman, whose loyalties are immediately transferred to the household of her husband" (Victor H. Matthews, "Female Voices: Upholding the Honor of the Household," *BTB* 24 [Spring 1994]: 9).

[7]Saul twice made his daughters available as war prizes (1 Sam 17:25 and 18:25).

[8]Block, *Judges*, p. 94.

to her new husband. She incites her husband to ask Caleb for land. Much debate revolves around whether Acsah enticed Othniel to ask Caleb for additional property, or whether Othniel directed Acsah to enquire. The MT takes the former position, the LXX and Vulgate, the latter in an attempt to correct what was perceived as gender error in the suffix.[9] The verb סות (sûth) carries "an underlying idea of cunningness in this root."[10] It connotes a persuasion opposite to the intended course of action.[11] In this case, the MT is to be preferred. The Vulgate and LXX portray Othniel as enticing Acsah to ask Caleb for land, but then omit both her actual request and her motive for seeking the additional boon of springs.

So Acsah coerces Othniel to ask Caleb for "a field."[12] Immediately after, Acsah approaches her father to ask for an additional blessing of a desperately needed water supply for the arid property. The reader is left to wonder why Acsah approaches her father to ask for the springs. Caleb may be parsimonious in parting with land, not feeling the need to give Othniel any more than his daughter in marriage. Or, Othniel may have been too diffident before Caleb in making his request. Both scenarios may be true. In any case, the solution of the men is inadequate, and the woman must correct things herself. "Although she remains gracious and respectful, she will not be simply a passive object of men's deals. Instead she seizes the opportunity to achieve something neither her father nor husband contemplated. But she does so without overstepping the bounds of female propriety."[13] Acsah, on her own, concludes that the result of the conversation between Caleb and Othniel was inadequate and decides to take action.

While Acsah clearly takes her fate into her own hands, she hardly does so with the sense of feminine propriety that Daniel Block

---

[9]Schneider, *Judges*, pp. 28-29.

[10]R.D. Patterson, "סות (sût)," *TWOT*, p. 621.

[11]G. Wallis, "סות swt," *TDOT*, 10:207.

[12]Some understand the infinitive construct בְּבוֹאָהּ (bᵊbōʾāh), "when she came," as connoting Acsah's approaching Othniel sexually, in which context she could easily coerce him into asking Caleb for land. It should be noted that while this is a possible and reasonable interpretation, the use of בוא (bwʾ) in the infinitive to render sexual activity is uncommon, and even then, never occurs without a person as the object of the preposition. It is unlikely, then, that the text is suggesting Acsah's use of sex as a tool of coercion.

[13]Block, *Judges*, p. 96.

suggests.[14] Her coercion of her husband is hardly reflective of the decorum appropriate for a new wife in that culture. Asking or pleading with respectful titles such as "my lord" or "my master" would have placed Acsah within the expected female stereotype. As it is, she acts outside both the authority of her new husband and her culture's bounds of feminine propriety.

The narrative sidelines Othniel as Acsah takes center stage. She is dissatisfied with both her father's generosity and her husband's inadequate acquisition of property. Her assertive initiative is a public (and literary) commentary on Othniel's poor performance as a husband. Acsah coerces Othniel to ask Caleb for land and then proceeds to demonstrate by her actions that his asking was not good enough. Acsah herself coaxes her father into giving her **springs** to feed the arid **Negev** land. The narrator presents Acsah as the one who walks away from the negotiations with the most gained.

3. Judah's Territory (1:16-21)

[16]**The descendants of Moses' father-in-law, the Kenite, went up from the City of Palms[a] with the men of Judah to live among the people of the Desert of Judah in the Negev near Arad.**

[17]**Then the men of Judah went with the Simeonites their brothers and attacked the Canaanites living in Zephath, and they totally destroyed[b] the city. Therefore it was called Hormah.[c]** [18]**The men of Judah also took[d] Gaza, Ashkelon and Ekron—each city with its territory.**

[19]**The LORD was with the men of Judah. They took possession of the hill country, but they were unable to drive the people from the plains, because they had iron chariots.** [20]**As Moses had promised, Hebron was given to Caleb, who drove from it the three sons of Anak.** [21]**The Benjamites, however, failed to dislodge the Jebusites, who were living in Jerusalem; to this day the Jebusites live there with the Benjamites.**

[a]*16* **That is, Jericho**　　[b]*17* **The Hebrew term refers to the irrevocable giving over of things or persons to the LORD, often by totally destroying**

[14]Daniel Block, "Unspeakable Crimes: The Abuse of Women in the Book of Judges," *SBJT* 2 (Fall 1998): 48.

them. ᶜ*17 Hormah* means *destruction.*   ᵈ*18* **Hebrew; Septuagint** *Judah did not take*

1:16 Since it lay within Judah's territory, the city of Jericho provides an ideal settlement for the tribe. The city had a fresh water supply and had already been destroyed in the opening phase of the Conquest (Joshua 6). The Kenites — the descendants of Jethro — take possession of Jericho, becoming a *de facto* part of Judah.

1:17-20 Judah attacks and destroys **Zephath**; in fact, **they totally destroyed the city.** "Destroy" is the translation of חָרַם (*ḥāram*), used to describe the placing of an "off-limits" status on something — banning it and devoting it to destruction. The verb is used in reference to the cities Joshua destroys (Josh 6:21; 10:1,37,39). The noun form, *ḥērem*, describes the off-limits status given to Jericho in Joshua 6:18, which Achan later violates. The city is renamed **Hormah**, a variation of the root, in order to make a permanent monument to things set aside to the LORD. Simeon participates in the campaign in exchange for the assistance Judah will provide later. **Gaza, Ashkelon and Ekron** are also captured, **each city with its territory.** The target in the conquest is not only the power centers represented by the cities but the valuable regional farmland that each city controls. Although Judah is able to capture these territories, the success is short lived. By the time of Samson, they are firmly back in Philistine hands (Judg 16:21; 14:19; 1 Sam 5:10) and will remain so until their subjugation by Solomon (1 Kgs 4:24).

Judah is effectively able to subdue the foothills where their numbers give them dominance in hand-to-hand combat. In the lower plains however, Judah's inability to remove the inhabitants of the plain is due to the Canaanite possession of iron chariots. The iron chariots are the same problem Ephraim and Manasseh face in Joshua 17.[15] Because chariots are limited to flat areas where they are militarily effective, Israel is able to dominate the hill country where foot soldiers are more effective.

---

[15]The iron chariots were not solid iron and were unlikely to be iron plated. The weight of a chariot constructed of iron would have been prohibitive to being drawn by a horse. Iron plating would have lightened the weight but made the frame unstable. Robert Drews ("The 'Chariots of Iron' of Joshua and Judges," *JSOT* 45 [1989]: 15-23) limits the options for iron chariots to either iron-wheeled or iron-scythed (having sharp iron protrusions). Both are known technologies of the later Assyrian empire.

The NIV appropriately corrects the ambiguity of the KJV that reads as if Yahweh is incapable of driving out the Canaanites because of their iron chariots. Translated literally, verse 19 reads "and the LORD was with Judah, and he possessed the hill country, but not possessing the valley dwellings because they had iron chariots." "He" refers to Judah, not Yahweh.[16] The inability to conquer the lowlands rests squarely on Judah's shoulders. To further clarify Judah's responsibility, the Targum makes a theological addition to the text. "Afterwards, when they had sinned . . ." is added to the text to remove any culpability from Yahweh.[17]

1:21 notes that the **Benjamites** were unable to conquer **Jerusalem**. Verse 1:8 mentions that Judah had already captured the city during their military campaign through the area. Judah's conquest was evidently incomplete in some way; perhaps the slaughter of the inhabitants was unfinished, allowing enough of the population to escape that they had sufficient numbers to reoccupy the city after Judah's departure. Another perspective suggests that Judah "captured and conquered the lower city but [was] unable to conquer the citadel."[18] Ultimately, the **Jebusites** will cohabitate with the Benjamites, with the irony of Benjamin's spiritual weakness reaching its climax in chapters 19–21. The failure of the Benjamites to dislodge the inhabitants of Jebus comes back to bite them when the Levite feels compelled to pass by the non-Israelite city because lodging there would be unsafe. And whereas Joshua 15:63 places the failure to capture Jebus on the tribe of Judah, Judges places the failure to capture the city on Benjamin, further foreshadowing the difficulty with the tribe at the end of the book.[19]

4. The Capture of Bethel (1:22-26)

[22]Now the house of Joseph attacked Bethel, and the LORD was with them. [23]When they sent men to spy out Bethel (formerly called Luz), [24]the spies saw a man coming out of the city and they said to

---

[16]The anti-apologetic Web site www.ironchariots.org utilizes this mistranslation of the KJV as evidence of the Bible's admission that Yahweh is not omnipotent; hence, their namesake.

[17]Willem F. Smelik, *The Targum of Judges* (Leiden: E.J. Brill, 1995), p. 343.

[18]Cohen, *Joshua and Judges*, p. 156.

[19]Wong, *Compositional Strategy*, pp. 29-31.

him, "Show us how to get into the city and we will see that you are treated well." ²⁵So he showed them, and they put the city to the sword but spared the man and his whole family. ²⁶He then went to the land of the Hittites, where he built a city and called it Luz, which is its name to this day.

1:22-26 Ephraim and Manasseh, the two half-tribes of **Joseph**, are initially treated together. **Luz**, located on the central ridge some twelve miles north of Jerusalem, is the first target. Capturing a citizen of the city, Israelite **spies** coerce information from the man with the promise of safety during the imminent attack. As was done with Rahab (Joshua 2; 6:22-23), **the man and his family** are **spared** when Israel moves against the city. This Canaanite traitor is unnamed, but is inserted by the author of Judges to explain the name of the city of Luz. The Israelites adopt the name of the city given by Jacob in Genesis 27:19: Bethel (House of God). The man who betrayed his city is surely welcome to live among the Hebrews — Rahab has done so, but he instead opts to move north to the **Hittite** empire[20] and start a new settlement, which he names **Luz**. Retaining the name of his former home would serve both as a memorial to the city and people he betrayed and as a reminder of his Canaanite ethnic identity.

5. Israel's Incomplete Conquest (1:27-36)

²⁷**But Manasseh did not drive out the people of Beth Shan or Taanach or Dor or Ibleam or Megiddo and their surrounding settlements, for the Canaanites were determined to live in that land. ²⁸When Israel became strong, they pressed the Canaanites into forced labor but never drove them out completely. ²⁹Nor did Ephraim drive out the Canaanites living in Gezer, but the Canaanites continued to live there among them. ³⁰Neither did Zebulun drive out the Canaanites living in Kitron or Nahalol, who remained among them; but they did subject them to forced labor. ³¹Nor did Asher drive out those living in Acco or Sidon or Ahlab or Aczib or Helbah or Aphek or Rehob, ³²and because of this the people of**

---

[20]The New Hittite Kingdom (1430–1180 B.C.) controlled the area of modern-day Turkey north of Canaan.

**Asher lived among the Canaanite inhabitants of the land. [33]Neither
did Naphtali drive out those living in Beth Shemesh or Beth Anath;
but the Naphtalites too lived among the Canaanite inhabitants of
the land, and those living in Beth Shemesh and Beth Anath
became forced laborers for them. [34]The Amorites confined the
Danites to the hill country, not allowing them to come down into
the plain. [35]And the Amorites were determined also to hold out in
Mount Heres, Aijalon and Shaalbim, but when the power of the
house of Joseph increased, they too were pressed into forced
labor. [36]The boundary of the Amorites was from Scorpion[a] Pass to
Sela and beyond.**

[a]*36 Hebrew Akrabbim*

1:27-36 The remainder of the chapter is a litany of Israelite failure during the conquest. The Canaanites were understandably
unwilling to relinquish their homes and livelihood, and were too
large in number for military conquest. The majority of cities listed
in verses 27-36 lay in the fertile growing areas of the coastal plain.
When push came to shove, it was the fertile growing region that was
the most difficult to surrender. In the arid climate, productive land
was the lifeblood of a people, and the Canaanites did not relinquish
it easily.

The Israelite interaction with the Canaanites progressed through
four levels. The first level was to achieve military victory. During the
earliest part of the Conquest, the united Israelite army created dread
in the Canaanite peoples. Theologically, the God of the Hebrews had
defeated the Egyptians and was now proving his might over Canaanite deities. The Canaanites had every reason to be afraid.

The second level of Israelite interaction with the Canaanites
relied on the fear created by Hebrew military capacity. Terrorizing
Canaan's inhabitants, the Hebrews used their prowess to drive various people groups from the land. While military conquest was certainly easier for larger tribes like Judah, it was not always feasible for
smaller tribes. Once the tribes split up to possess their allotted
inheritance, it was up to the individual tribe to remove any remaining Canaanite occupants. Smaller tribes did not possess the clout
necessary to defeat the inhabitants militarily, so the next best solution was to drive the inhabitants out of the area. This forced reloca-

tion minimized Israelite deaths due to hostilities, and was more merciful toward the Canaanites.

The third level of interaction was to subject the Canaanites to forced labor. After a few generations, the Israelite population expansion would produce enough of a demographic shift that the Hebrews could force slavery on the surrounding inhabitants. That the Israelites would impose involuntary servitude on another people group is especially ironic in light of their own experiences in Egypt.

Of the six tribes mentioned at the end of Judges 1, three are not described as subjecting Canaanites to forced labor. **Ephraim**, however, does force **Gezer** to servitude in the parallel passage in Joshua 16:10. **Asher** and Dan likely had insufficient numbers to dominate the local Canaanite groups enough to elicit forced labor from them.

The final aspect of Hebrew-Canaanite interaction is cohabitation. When tribes did not have the population and power to militarily defeat, evict, or enslave the inhabitants, living with them was the only alternative short of abandoning their inheritance altogether. Dan nearly does lose its allotted inheritance, as Amorite pressure confines them to the rougher mountain terrain along the central ridge. Dan was the second largest tribe behind Judah, and its failure against the inhabitants of its territory reveals both the larger Canaanite population in the area and the tenacity of the inhabitants to hold onto their land. Dan's inability to capture its inheritance will figure prominently in the apostasy in chapters 17 and 18.

Israel's interaction with the Canaanites reflects a progressive decrease in the use of power against the people groups of Canaan:

Kill the inhabitants

Drive out the inhabitants

Subject the inhabitants to forced labor

Cohabit with the inhabitants

Each level of this progression increases the tolerance for inhabitants whose way of life was diametrically opposed to Israel's identity as the people of Yahweh. As Christians, we also balance on the tightrope of intimacy with the world. Much of the Christian life involves learning not just to exist, but to thrive living among a world that opposes the Kingdom. Living too close to the world has the potential to blur faith and undermine a believer's identity as a follower of Christ (Jas 4:4). Isolation from the world, on the other hand, permanently dooms women and men made in God's image to life and eternity without him (1 Cor 5:9-10).

Hamlin lists three models for Christians in society. The first is a society where Christianity controls culture. The history of the West after the decline of the Roman Empire reflects this kind of culture. As civil authority disintegrated, the organizational structure of the church easily replaced it, controlling culture for more than a millennium. The second kind of society is pluralistic, but has a "dominant Christian tradition" that heavily affects culture. The West is currently this kind of culture. Pluralism is the predominant nature of culture, but Christianity still maintains deep roots in language, art, and history. In the third kind of society, Christianity is a minority in a culture that is structured on a paradigm not derived from the Christian tradition.[21] The issue for followers of Christ is not to create a particular system of government or culture. Because the culture of the Kingdom is transcultural, believers have a responsibility to represent Christ well in whatever culture they find themselves, whether that culture is post-, non-, or anti-Christian.

Christians often assume the Israelite posture of holy war against the kingdom of the Enemy. Christians have no business persecuting unbelievers. In fact, a Christian's inheritance is the Kingdom of God (Col 1:12), and the Kingdom is comprised of people. Cultural battles certainly need to be fought over morality, genocide, abortion, and poverty; but believers must never lose sight of the fact that every opponent embodies the divine motivation for the cross of Christ.

---

[21]Hamlin, *At Risk in the Promised Land*, p. 20.

CHAPTER 2

B. VISIT FROM THE ANGEL OF THE LORD (2:1-5)

¹**The angel of the LORD went up from Gilgal to Bokim and said, "I brought you up out of Egypt and led you into the land that I swore to give to your forefathers. I said, 'I will never break my covenant with you, ²and you shall not make a covenant with the people of this land, but you shall break down their altars.' Yet you have disobeyed me. Why have you done this? ³Now therefore I tell you that I will not drive them out before you; they will be ⌐thorns⌐ in your sides and their gods will be a snare to you."**

⁴**When the angel of the LORD had spoken these things to all the Israelites, the people wept aloud, ⁵and they called that place Bokim.^a There they offered sacrifices to the LORD.**

^a*5 Bokim means weepers.*

2:1-2 The mysterious **angel of the LORD** makes his first of four appearances in 2:1.[1] The messenger's journey originated in **Gilgal**, the location of the memorial of twelve stones Joshua set up after the people had successfully crossed the Jordan (Josh 4:19-24). The name Gilgal (rolled away) was given to the area after the second circumcision Joshua performed on those who had been born after the Exodus. Between the memorial and God's removal of Israel's reproach through circumcision, Gilgal was a significant spiritual location for the Israelites.

The angel's destination was **Bokim** (weeping), a location that may have been the site of an annual ritualized mourning expressing concern over the harvest.[2] At this time, however, Bokim becomes the cause of a new reason for weeping. At Bokim, the angel announces that

---

[1]See the discussion of the angel of the LORD at 6:11.
[2]Hamlin, *At Risk in the Promised Land*, p. 55.

God has withdrawn his support against the Canaanite inhabitants of the land. Bokim is the beginning of God's distance from his people, and the Israelites rightfully agonize over their disobedience. The angel's journey from Gilgal to Bokim is more than just physical; the author uses it to show the vast spiritual distance that the Israelites have descended in just a short time. In Gilgal, the Spirit of the LORD is present to sanctify his people. In Bokim, Yahweh removes part of his blessing from the people.

God states that he has promised **never** to **break** his **covenant** with Israel, and he offers as proof his deliverance of the people from Egypt and his bringing them to the land of their inheritance that he had promised to their ancestors generations before.[3] Yahweh does not simply assert his reliability; he proves it. His only stipulation was for the Hebrews to resist assimilation into Canaanite culture through avoiding covenants with the inhabitants and eliminating non-Yahwistic worship from the region.

God's command to the Israelites has not been merely personal. He desires relationship with his people, and false worship interferes with that relationship. Intimacy with God is in the best interests of his people. God understood that the absence of that relationship would result in all kinds of consequences, not the least of which is the anarchy that is described throughout the remainder of Judges.

2:3 God's refusal to aid Israel against the Canaanites may seem to produce results that God does not want. The Canaanite inhabitants will certainly be a negative influence on Israel. The noun used for **snare** in 2:3 refers to a net used to trap birds, figuratively used for things that entrap people spiritually. It is the same term used to describe the entrapment Gideon inadvertently springs on his family with his creation of a golden ephod (Judg 8:27). If God desires relationship with his people, then leaving a contaminating influence in their midst appears counterproductive. The Israelites no doubt perceive God's withdrawal of assistance to be a limitation of their inheritance of the physical land as punishment for their disobedience. Without his help, they will never fully possess the land. But Yahweh

---

[3]God's self-identification as the one who brought the Israelites "out of Egypt" occurs several times in Judges (2:12; 6:8,13) and is common throughout the Old Testament (Exod 20:2; 29:46; Lev 11:45; Num 15:41; Deut 5:6; Ps 81:10; Hosea 13:4).

has a deeper lesson in mind than mere obedience. He is intent on teaching his people that they are better off with him than without him, even if the lesson takes generations to learn.

2:4-5 The angel's pronouncement causes weeping among the people and at least a momentary devotion to the LORD as they offer sacrifices in worship. Their motives at this point are probably mixed. Repentance and humble worship are likely combined with the hope that God will change his mind. This is the only corporate sacrifice in Judges until chapter 20. At best, the people have a difficulty with repentance throughout the book. They easily cry out because of their suffering, but less often demonstrate repentance by changing their behavior. Throughout the book, God in his generosity often responds to his people's suffering even without their repentance. God's graciousness serves as a reminder that repentance cannot "buy" anything from God. Believers repent because God is worthy of our holiness and because we desire uninhibited relationship with our maker, but not because it somehow forces God to act on our behalf.

II. THE SECOND PROLOGUE (2:6–3:6)

A. THE DEATH OF JOSHUA (2:6-9)

⁶**After Joshua had dismissed the Israelites, they went to take possession of the land, each to his own inheritance. ⁷The people served the LORD throughout the lifetime of Joshua and of the elders who outlived him and who had seen all the great things the LORD had done for Israel.**

⁸**Joshua son of Nun, the servant of the LORD, died at the age of a hundred and ten. ⁹And they buried him in the land of his inheritance, at Timnath Heresᵃ in the hill country of Ephraim, north of Mount Gaash.**

ᵃ**9 Also known as *Timnath Serah* (see Joshua 19:50 and 24:30)**

2:6-9 Here begins the double prologue. Joshua has already died in 1:1, yet has just finished addressing the people in 2:6. Verses 6-9 are a summary of Joshua 24:28-31. The statement regarding Israel's loyalty to God during the life of **Joshua** and **the elders** who outlived him becomes a dark foreshadowing of what is to come in the book of Judges. Judges, in effect, is the story of what happens to the people's faithfulness when godly leadership disappears.

Some suggest that because the material from the first chapter is repeated in a modified form here, that the author simply cobbles together different traditions of the conquest. Rather than being understood as a later insertion of a second account, the second repetition of introductory information in Judges 2 may be seen as a clarification of the first account. This is not unknown in the Old Testament. Genesis immediately repeats the creation account with additional detail, and the songs of Miriam and Deborah do the same in poetic form.

This repetition of material in chapters 2:6-3:5 serves a twofold purpose. First, the section is a theological interpretation of the events described in chapter 1. The physical details, positive and negative, of the conquest have been described. The author uses the second prologue to comment on the reason behind the limited success he previously describes.

B. THE CYCLE OF JUDGES DESCRIBED (2:10-19)

[10]After that whole generation had been gathered to their fathers, another generation grew up, who knew neither the LORD nor what he had done for Israel. [11]Then the Israelites did evil in the eyes of the LORD and served the Baals. [12]They forsook the LORD, the God of their fathers, who had brought them out of Egypt. They followed and worshiped various gods of the peoples around them. They provoked the LORD to anger [13]because they forsook him and served Baal and the Ashtoreths. [14]In his anger against Israel the LORD handed them over to raiders who plundered them. He sold them to their enemies all around, whom they were no longer able to resist. [15]Whenever Israel went out to fight, the hand of the LORD was against them to defeat them, just as he had sworn to them. They were in great distress.

[16]Then the LORD raised up judges,[a] who saved them out of the hands of these raiders. [17]Yet they would not listen to their judges but prostituted themselves to other gods and worshiped them. Unlike their fathers, they quickly turned from the way in which

their fathers had walked, the way of obedience to the LORD's commands. [18]Whenever the LORD raised up a judge for them, he was
with the judge and saved them out of the hands of their enemies
as long as the judge lived; for the LORD had compassion on them
as they groaned under those who oppressed and afflicted them.
[19]But when the judge died, the people returned to ways even more
corrupt than those of their fathers, following other gods and serving and worshiping them. They refused to give up their evil practices and stubborn ways.

[a]16 Or leaders; similarly in verses 17-19

The second prologue also provides the outline for the remainder
of the book. As the people's sin and indifference toward God
increase, he abandons them to the natural consequences of their
decisions.

Judges has been traditionally understood to be a cycle—sin by the
people, followed by God delivering them into servitude. The oppression results in repentance and supplication, and is answered by God
with salvation. While this scheme describes the individual instances
of disobedience, oppression, repentance, and deliverance, the cycles
progress downward toward chaos.

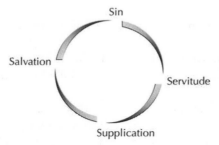

Judges may perhaps be better understood as a downward spiral.
Judges portrays an ever-increasing separation and distance from God
as the spiritual status of the people degenerates. The Hebrew society
degrades from loyalty to Yahweh at the beginning of Judges to near
anarchy at the end of the book. Even the judges themselves are not
immune from the downward slide. Idolatry, disobedience, and even
human sacrifice will occur at the hands of the judges themselves.

2:10 Verse 10 begins to fill in the details regarding the difficulty
facing the Israelites only hinted at in verse 6. The people retained

their loyalty to Yahweh for as long as godly leadership remained, but now, with Joshua and the elders absent from the scene, the people immediately depart from the unadulterated devotion to their God.

Although Scripture expects faith to be transmitted from parents to children (Deut 6:6-7; Prov 22:6), it also acknowledges that faith is not merely intellectual. Faith must be personalized, and that personalization often comes only after an encounter with the Living God.

2:11-14 The Israelites do evil **in the eyes of the LORD**. The phrase is common in the Bible, particularly in the Old Testament. In Judges, however, the phrase will find contrast with both the people and Samson as the standard of "the eyes of the LORD" is abandoned for individuals choosing to do what their own eyes prefer (14:3,7; 17:6; 19:24; 21:25). Unfortunately, the NIV opts not to translate these passages using the literal translation of עַיִן (*'ayin*) and misses a theme that the author of Judges carefully crafts into his book.

The **evil** the Israelites commit is the worship of the Canaanite deity **Baal**. Baal, whose name simply means "husband" or "master," makes his first Judges appearance in 2:11, and his consort **Ashtoreth** first appears in 2:13. Baal was the Canaanite god of the storm and fertility of the land and the head of the pantheon in the area. His prominence in ancient Canaan was no doubt due to the uncertainty concerning the arid climate. Any deity possessing power over weather would appeal to an agrarian society relying on livestock and farming for sustenance.

Ancient Near Eastern deities exhibited all the traits of humanity, both positive and negative. Deities exhibited admirable traits such as courage, cleverness, and generosity. At the same time, the gods in ancient polytheistic systems displayed the same evils present in humanity: deceit, petty jealousy, fear, rape, and murder. The problem with the deities in the ancient world was that they reflected the limitations of humanity. The Canaanite deities were incapable of creating the world from nothing, but they could die. They were powerful beings, but possessed limited spheres of influence. Baal, for instance, was believed to have engaged in a seven-year cycle in which he battled the deity Death for control over the fertility of the land. Baal would be temporarily defeated before he emerged victorious over Death.

Yahweh's difficulty with the polytheism prevalent in Canaan is obvious. First, there are no other gods. God alone is the ruler of the universe. He does not need to compete for or share his throne. Second, polytheism creates a very small definition of the Divine. A belief in multiple deities is always accompanied by a specific limitation on the power of any particular god. Yahweh alone exists, and his power is not fragmented among multiple beings. Third, polytheism remakes the Divine in the image of humanity, the opposite of God's design (Gen 1:26-27). When the glory, power, and morality of God are diminished, it also diminishes the status of humanity, his crowning achievement. Canaanite theology was too limited because it undermined both God and people. The holy God of Israel has no desire to be made in the image of flawed human beings and therefore commanded the images of Baal to be removed as part of the Conquest. Unfortunately, the Israelites, unable and unwilling to conquer the land thoroughly, became susceptible to the theological influence of the Canaanites they had failed to remove from the land.

While God is not human and does not possess human limitations or flaws, he still is a being who experiences emotion. Anger is his natural response to the disobedience of the Israelites, and it motivates him to strike at the Israelites where they care most: the land. The southern tip of the Fertile Crescent which Israel occupied had the capacity for high agricultural productivity. Losing the produce of the land would make everyday life a struggle for the Israelites.

God wisely does not utilize weather to punish the Israelites, which would likely reinforce Baal as a god with power over the weather. Instead, God allows the Hebrews to be vulnerable to marauders. Raiding bands were common in the decentralized power structure of ancient Canaan. The plunder of grain and livestock by such groups would reduce the victims to a subsistence level.

2:15 Such raiding groups operated either on behalf of the surrounding nations or with their tacit approval and protection. When the Israelites attempted to confront political entities militarily that harbored the raiders, they were repulsed, verse 15 states, because of Yahweh's active intervention on behalf of their enemies. Throughout the book of Judges, whenever the Israelites abandon their loyalty to God, they find themselves in a no-win situation. The end of verse 15 presents the great understatement: **They were in great distress**. The verb צָרַר (*sārar*) refers to being bound up or restricted, as well as the emotional reaction to being confined. Whenever the

Israelites disobey, they suffer at the hands of their enemies with no options except to return to Yahweh.

2:16-17 In verse 16 the author introduces the **judges**, leaders whom God raises up specifically for the purpose of providing deliverance from military oppression by Canaanite nations. Verse 17 implies that the judges also provided spiritual instruction on some level. That instruction is repeatedly ignored by the people as they refuse to abandon Canaanite polytheism. The verb זָנָה (*zānāh*), referring to prostitution, is emotionally reminiscent of the object lesson God later gives Israel through the prophet Hosea's marriage to the unfaithful Gomer. The Israelites' infidelity is a severe violation of a sacred relationship. Believers do well to keep in mind that their actions have the capacity to affect the heart of God.

2:18-19 Verses 18-19 echo the same difficulty as verse 10: people follow the leadership that is available. If godly leadership exists, it will be reflected in the character of a community. If wicked leadership, or worse, as in the case of Judges, no leadership is present, individuals pursue their own desires. Jesus' referral to members of the community as sheep was not accidental. Sheep are thoughtless, stubborn, mob-minded animals. Such characteristics are easily directed by the attributes of a leader. As in the time of Judges, the contemporary world needs leaders with integrity to wisely, humbly, and powerfully direct God's people in a positive way.

The downward spiral is alluded to in verse 19. The presence of an individual judge restrains the people during that judge's lifetime. After the death of the **judge**, however, the people return to practices **even more corrupt than those of their fathers**. Judges clearly reflects this trend toward progressive societal depravity. The earliest communal sins recorded are the people's failure to drive out the inhabitants and Baal worship. By the end of the book, however, gang rape, murder, kidnapping, and genocide are all justified as the reasonable expectations of a less than ideal world. One component of evil is its powerful potential to desensitize. Desensitization is a crucial enemy in our culture as media capabilities deliver with ever-increasing frequency material that is evil when contrasted with God's purity. When followers of Christ lose the capacity to detect evil, they also lose the capacity to perceive good. The two are inseparable. Sensitivity to the Spirit of God decreases as indifference to evil becomes commonplace.

C. THE TESTING OF ISRAEL EXPLAINED (2:20–3:6)

[20]Therefore the LORD was very angry with Israel and said, "Because this nation has violated the covenant that I laid down for their forefathers and has not listened to me, [21]I will no longer drive out before them any of the nations Joshua left when he died. [22]I will use them to test Israel and see whether they will keep the way of the LORD and walk in it as their forefathers did." [23]The LORD had allowed those nations to remain; he did not drive them out at once by giving them into the hands of Joshua.

2:20-21 The Israelites have failed to evict the Canaanites from the Promised Land, and in response God refuses to participate in the removal of the land's inhabitants. God's graciousness is revealed in verses 22ff. Yahweh reveals that he will adapt to the Israelites' new circumstances and act on Israel's behalf even in *and through* their punishment. The Canaanite presence in the land is now a permanent reality for the Israelites, one that God will utilize for his people's benefit.

2:22 God reveals two ways he will use the Canaanites to benefit Israel. First, the surrounding nations are left to **test** Israel. נָסָה (nāsāh), translated "test," refers to the revealing and proving of something's nature. This discovery often involves hardship and difficulty.[4] God is interested in revealing and proving the character of Israel, and he will accomplish it by sharpening Israel through conflict with her neighbors. God has invested himself in the descendants of Abraham, and he is certain he has made a good choice for his own people. Honing Israel through conflict will continue throughout Scripture. Each adversity — oppression, invasion, exile — will eventually produce a people that understands fealty to Yahweh. By the time of Jesus, the Jews are thoroughly monotheistic, having permanently abandoned idolatry and polytheism during the suffering of the Assyrian and Babylonian Exiles.

This testing also presupposes that there will be enough spiritual leadership to keep the people educated regarding the Law. The judges will perform this function in the short term, although the author has already noted that they will be ignored. In Judges, the

---

[4]Marvin Wilson, "נָסָה (nāsâ)," *TWOT*, 2:581.

issue for the people is not a general ignorance of the Law, but the people's unwillingness to acknowledge and obey it.

2:23 Verse 23 places the ultimate responsibility for the lingering presence of the Canaanites squarely on God's shoulders. The God of the universe certainly could remove any people group if he should so desire. Yahweh's power is not limited by his people's disobedience. But God has chosen to punish his people by leaving competition for land and resources in their midst, while at the same time using that very punishment to bless them.

God's willingness to adapt and use the consequences of sin for the benefit of his people demonstrates his overwhelming love and grace. Promiscuity may result in an unplanned child who grows to be a source of delight and comfort for her mother. A man with a marriage destroyed by pornography may find healing and become a source of ministry to others. A criminal's life may be changed through a prison ministry. A teenager comes to Christ as a refugee against the ravages created by a broken family. God meets us for healing and instruction in the midst of our sin. What is the Incarnation, except God coming in human form to engage us where we need it most: the depths of our sinfulness?

CHAPTER 3

C. THE TESTING OF ISRAEL EXPLAINED
(2:20–3:6, continued)

[1]These are the nations the LORD left to test all those Israelites who had not experienced any of the wars in Canaan [2](he did this only to teach warfare to the descendants of the Israelites who had not had previous battle experience):

3:1-2 Chapter 3 opens with the second goal God plans to achieve through continued Canaanite presence: Israel's education regarding warfare. Yahweh knows that the reality of multiple people groups inhabiting the same area and competing for the same limited resources will inevitably result in military conflict. God does not want his people to be unprepared to fight should they be required to do so, and the ongoing presence of hostile communities within Israel will ensure that combat experience becomes commonplace for the men of Israel. Gideon will lose 72,000 troops to their fear (7:3), suggesting that the courage to fight is a slowly learned lesson for Israel.

God's expectation that his people develop a capacity for war may seem to fly in the face of Psalm 20:7, "Some trust in chariots and some in horses, but we trust in the name of the LORD our God," but military preparedness is not incompatible with trust in God. There is, however, a marked difference between possessing a skill that God utilizes and relying on that skill for security. God clearly intends to be the protector of Israel, but he desires to be able to use his people's military skill to achieve that protection whenever he chooses.

[3]the five rulers of the Philistines, all the Canaanites, the Sidonians, and the Hivites living in the Lebanon mountains from Mount Baal Hermon to Lebo[a] Hamath. [4]They were left to test the Israelites to

see whether they would obey the LORD's commands, which he had
given their forefathers through Moses.

⁵The Israelites lived among the Canaanites, Hittites, Amorites,
Perizzites, Hivites and Jebusites.

ᵃ3 Or *to the entrance to*

3:3 The text lists the specific nations that the Israelites were
unable to remove from the region. **The Philistines** are described as
having **five rulers**. The Philistine society functioned as a confederation of five political regions controlled by a joint leadership. This
structure is the same as that described in Joshua 13:3. These five
Philistine rulers will show up again in 16:5, the likely number of
rulers who each offered Delilah eleven hundred pieces of silver for
her betrayal of Samson. In 1 Samuel 6, after the Philistines suffer
physically because of capturing the ark, they respond with an offering of five gold tumors and five gold rats from each of the rulers and
their subjects. As a confederation, the Philistine political structure
was decentralized enough that the Israelites would find it difficult to
conquer them — there was no single king to depose. On the other
hand, the close cooperation among the rulers and their respective
cities increased the power and security of each fivefold.

The Philistines are believed to have been seafaring immigrants
from the Aegean area who settled on the western coast of Palestine.
After resisting the Israelite conquest, the Philistines remain a constant source of trouble for Israel as the two peoples compete for
control of the fertile lowlands. It will be Solomon's empire that permanently curbs Philistine power in the area. In Judges, the Philistines are the foes Samson engages.

While most of the people groups remaining in Canaan are in the
lowlands, 3:3 mentions the **Hivites** living in the rugged mountain-
ous terrain north of the Sea of Galilee. The Hivite presence overlapped the territories of Naphtali and Dan. Judges 1:34 states that
the Amorites also pressured Dan, forcing the tribe into the hill country. Unable to settle in its allotted territory, Dan will later attack the
Sidonite colony at Laish, a settlement too distant from its mother
city to allow rescue (Judg 18:27-28).

3:4-5 God reiterates his purpose for leaving Canaanites in the
land. The Israelites' interaction with the foreign peoples among
them would expose the character of the Hebrew people. God knows

that exposure to evil reveals and shapes character. God's decision is risky, because exposure to evil is also capable of shaping character in undesirable ways. God is evidently confident enough in the long-term results that he is willing to take that risk.

⁶They took their daughters in marriage and gave their own daughters to their sons, and served their gods.

3:6 With such close interaction with the people groups around them, as is often the case, Israel develops a problem with intermarriage. Judges 3:6 is a direct reference to Deuteronomy 7:1-6 where the specific groups are off limits as marriage partners for the Israelites. Moses clearly warns the people that the result of intermarriage will be syncretism with the people of Canaan. Judges is simply the story of how Moses' warning plays out.

Beyond the Law, leaders in the Old Testament recognize the wisdom of not marrying outside of the Israelite faith. In rebuking the people for foreign marriages after the Exile, Nehemiah invokes the example of Solomon as devastating proof of the damage wrought by marrying a foreign spouse. No other human relationship affects a man or woman as deeply as marriage. The shared intimacy is designed by God in part to establish a stable foundation from which intimacy with God might be pursued. When only one spouse has an interest in serving God, the divided loyalties can produce conflict in both spouses. The interpretation of 2 Corinthians 6:14 has often been understood to include marriage to unbelievers as spiritually imbalanced and therefore inappropriate.

It should be noted that interracial marriage itself was not the issue for the Israelites, nor should it be for Christians. The issue is one of spiritual compatibility. Moses' marriage to Zipporah (Num 12:1), Rahab's marriage to Salmon (Matt 1:5), and Boaz's marriage to Ruth were all interracial. But all three marriages were between followers of Yahweh — there was no spiritual compromise. While society makes race an issue in marriage, God does not (Gal 3:28).

III. THE CENTRAL SECTION (3:7–16:31)

A. THE FIRST JUDGE: OTHNIEL (3:7-11)

[7]The Israelites did evil in the eyes of the LORD; they forgot the LORD their God and served the Baals and the Asherahs. [8]The anger of the LORD burned against Israel so that he sold them into the hands of Cushan-Rishathaim king of Aram Naharaim,[a] to whom the Israelites were subject for eight years. [9]But when they cried out to the LORD, he raised up for them a deliverer, Othniel son of Kenaz, Caleb's younger brother, who saved them. [10]The Spirit of the LORD came upon him, so that he became Israel's judge[b] and went to war. The LORD gave Cushan-Rishathaim king of Aram into the hands of Othniel, who overpowered him. [11]So the land had peace for forty years, until Othniel son of Kenaz died.

[a]8 That is, Northwest Mesopotamia   [b]10 Or leader

3:7 The first judge enters the scene in 3:7, and the author introduces the standard literary formula used for all the judges: the people sin, God punishes them through oppression, the people cry out to God, and he delivers them.

3:8 Cushan-Rishathaim is the leader responsible for this first specific instance of Israelite oppression. He is unknown outside this passage. The meaning of his name is uncertain, but may possibly be a wordplay by the author on the root רָשַׁע (*rāšaʿ*), meaning "Cushan the Doubly Wicked." He rules **Aram Naharaim** (Aram of the Two Rivers), an area to the northeast of Palestine in modern day Syria. His pressure on Israel likely includes heavy levies of property and produce. The **eight-year** oppression causes the people to cry out to Yahweh. As is usually the case, the text makes no mention of the people's repentance,[1] which serves to enhance God's grace toward his people. God acts out of love for his people, not merely as an exchange for correct behavior.

3:9 Cushan-Rishathaim's dominion over Israel is ended by the first judge, **Othniel**. Caleb's younger brother has already demonstrated his military prowess after conquering Kiriath Sepher in 1:12-13, and he represents the last of the righteous leadership of the old generation under Moses.

---

[1]See the exception in 10:16.

3:10-11 The text is clear that Othniel's position as judge is determined by God, who raises Othniel up for the task. God's personal involvement is further exhibited in this first of seven passages where the **Spirit of the LORD** comes on the **judge** (6:34; 11:29; 13:25; 14:6,19; 15:14). The phrase indicates a temporary empowering of the Spirit for a specific task. In Judges, these tasks include leadership (6:34; 11:29), emotional motivation (13:25), and acts of physical prowess (14:6,19; 15:14). Outside of Judges, the Spirit of the LORD in the Old Testament is also responsible for visions and prophecy, and is even believed to be responsible for the miraculous transportation of prophets (2 Kgs 2:16)!

In the case of Othniel, the specific activity of the Spirit of the LORD is vague. After receiving the Spirit, he becomes a judge and goes to war. Presumably the Spirit's empowerment is similar to Gideon and Jephthah's and supernaturally fuels Othniel's leadership capabilities. Othniel successfully breaks the rule of Cushan-Rishathaim, and leads Israel during the subsequent **peace** for four decades.

B. THE SECOND JUDGE: EHUD (3:12-30)

[12]**Once again the Israelites did evil in the eyes of the LORD, and because they did this evil the LORD gave Eglon king of Moab power over Israel.** [13]**Getting the Ammonites and Amalekites to join him, Eglon came and attacked Israel, and they took possession of the City of Palms.**[a] [14]**The Israelites were subject to Eglon king of Moab for eighteen years.**

[a]*13* That is, Jericho

3:12 The cycle of sin, oppression, crying out, and deliverance repeats itself after the death of Othniel. This time, the oppressor is the Moabite king **Eglon**. The nation of **Moab** is descended from the product of an incestuous relationship between Lot and his oldest daughter (Gen 19:30-38). While most scholarship rejects the existence of a cohesive group known as the Moabites,[2] nothing precludes the Genesis 19:37 account of Moab's ancestry being the product of Lot's drunken encounter with his daughter.

---

[2]Marc Zvi Brettler, *The Creation of History in Ancient Israel* (London: Routledge, 1995), p. 83.

3:13-14 Eglon convinces the **Ammonites** and the **Amalekites** to participate with him against the Israelites. Ammon was descended from Lot's younger daughter with the same circumstances as Moab, and the two peoples were cousins. Amalek represented an older nation that had been in Canaan prior to Abraham (Gen 14:7). God especially detested this loosely organized group of nomads for their aggression and exploitation of Israel's vulnerabilities (Deut 25:17-19). Together, the Moabites, Ammonites, and Amalekites capture Jericho.

[15]Again the Israelites cried out to the LORD, and he gave them a deliverer—Ehud, a left-handed man, the son of Gera the Benjamite. The Israelites sent him with tribute to Eglon king of Moab. [16]Now Ehud had made a double-edged sword about a foot and a half[a] long, which he strapped to his right thigh under his clothing. [17]He presented the tribute to Eglon king of Moab, who was a very fat man. [18]After Ehud had presented the tribute, he sent on their way the men who had carried it. [19]At the idols[b] near Gilgal he himself turned back and said, "I have a secret message for you, O king."

The king said, "Quiet!" And all his attendants left him.

[20]Ehud then approached him while he was sitting alone in the upper room of his summer palace[c] and said, "I have a message from God for you." As the king rose from his seat, [21]Ehud reached with his left hand, drew the sword from his right thigh and plunged it into the king's belly. [22]Even the handle sank in after the blade, which came out his back. Ehud did not pull the sword out, and the fat closed in over it. [23]Then Ehud went out to the porch[d]; he shut the doors of the upper room behind him and locked them.

[24]After he had gone, the servants came and found the doors of the upper room locked. They said, "He must be relieving himself in the inner room of the house." [25]They waited to the point of embarrassment, but when he did not open the doors of the room, they took a key and unlocked them. There they saw their lord fallen to the floor, dead.

[26]While they waited, Ehud got away. He passed by the idols and escaped to Seirah. [27]When he arrived there, he blew a trumpet in the hill country of Ephraim, and the Israelites went down with him from the hills, with him leading them.

[28]"Follow me," he ordered, "for the LORD has given Moab, your enemy, into your hands." So they followed him down and, taking

**possession of the fords of the Jordan that led to Moab, they
allowed no one to cross over. [29]At that time they struck down about
ten thousand Moabites, all vigorous and strong; not a man
escaped. [30]That day Moab was made subject to Israel, and the land
had peace for eighty years.**

[a]*16* Hebrew *a cubit* (about 0.5 meter)   [b]*19* Or *the stone quarries*; also in
verse 26   [c]*20* The meaning of the Hebrew for this phrase is uncertain.
[d]*23* The meaning of the Hebrew for this word is uncertain.

When the Israelites cry out to God because of Eglon's oppression, God provides another deliverer. The Ehud narrative reveals
the Hebrew belief that a story about God's activity doesn't have to
be boring. The story, like much of Judges, is filled with wordplay,
clever subtleties, and crass humor. The ancient audience certainly
found the sexual innuendo and scatological remarks humorous.[3]
The Ehud story is first and foremost an entertaining story about
God's deliverance for his people.

Not only does Scripture portray Israel's enemies as soundly
defeated by God, it presents them as laughable. This treatment may
seem unkind by contemporary standards, but for the ancient reader, it enhanced communal identity. One method of building a community's identity is to provide it with a common object of derision.
Through an entertaining story that ridicules Israel's enemies, the
power of God not only to defeat but to humiliate his enemies was
embedded in the Hebrew psyche.

3:15 As the story unfolds, all the necessary details for the amus-
ing ending are inserted along the way. The **Israelites**, responsible to
provide the ruling **Eglon** with monetary **tribute**, send the levy in the
hand of an assassin. The first detail is the mention of Ehud's lefthandedness. Two other instances of lefthandedness appear in Scripture (Judg 20:16 and 1 Chr 12:2), both describing the tribe of
Benjamin. Benjamin was known as the tribe of the southpaw.

The NIV's description of **Ehud** as **left-handed** may be a bit of a
misnomer. The Hebrew term is אִטֵּר יַד־יְמִינוֹ (*'iṭṭēr yad-yᵉmînô*), literally "bound in his right hand." The phrase is used only twice in the
Old Testament (here and in Judg 20:16). The normal term for the
left hand is שְׂמֹאל (*śᵉmō'l*). Some suggest that "bound in his right

---

[3]Ibid., p. 84.

hand" indicates that Ehud was handicapped.[4] That Ehud is crippled is unlikely in light of Judges 20:16 and 1 Chronicles 12:2. Benjamin is a tribe of skilled lefties. Baruch Halpern suggests that in order to train an ambidextrous military, Benjamin bound the right hand of its youth to force them to learn to fight with their left hands. A left-hander would have a tactical advantage in hand-to-hand combat. The ancient Spartans were similarly trained.[5] Even after the decimation Benjamin suffers in Judges 20, by the time of David, Benjamin still has a population of lefthanders who provide military support for David during his exile. Ehud, rather than having the trait of having been born lefthanded, is likely a trained warrior, making him well suited for assassination. Ehud's lefthandedness will soon figure prominently in Eglon's demise.

3:16 The next detail is the reference to the short **sword** that Ehud makes. The sword is described as **about a foot and a half long**, the standard measure for a cubit. The sword is more a large dagger than a sword. Ehud, with premeditation, has designed the dagger for thrusting.

The third detail describes how Ehud smuggles the sword into Eglon's presence. Men carrying the tribute to be presented to Eglon accompany Ehud. A guard would likely check emissaries for arms, but because the short sword has been tightly strapped to Ehud's right thigh, an examiner easily dismisses Ehud with just a cursory evaluation. Ehud can easily brush back the folds of his robe to reveal he is carrying nothing on his left side (where a righthanded person would access it). Since Ehud's companions are unarmed, the entourage is allowed into Eglon's presence.

3:17 The fourth detail is presented in verse 17. **Eglon** is **a very fat man**. Eglon's name is similar to the Hebrew word for calf, עֶגֶל (*ʿēgel*). The wordplay is obvious: the calf is fat and ready for the slaughter.[6] Eglon's size is also commentary on his status. Assuming he has no medical conditions, Eglon's size indicates that he does not have to perform physical labor, and his diet in an agrarian society is rich enough for him to maintain his heavy weight.

---

[4]Hamlin, *At Risk in the Promised Land*, p. 73.
[5]Baruch Halpern, "The Assassination of Eglon: The First Locked-room Murder Mystery," *BR* 4 (December 1988): 33-41.
[6]Lindars, *Judges 1–5*, p. 138.

3:18-19 Having **presented the tribute**, the Israelite entourage leaves. Reaching Gilgal, Ehud **turns back** and returns to Eglon. Verse 19 mentions that Ehud reached **the idols at Gilgal**. Previously, Gilgal has been a symbolic spiritual location for the Hebrews.[7] By the time of Ehud, it has become a center for idol worship. Perhaps part of Ehud's impetus to follow through with the assassination was motivated by the pagan worship that had overtaken the area around Gilgal.

3:20-21 When **Ehud** reaches Eglon's presence, he announces that he has a surprise for the ruler. Like any bored ruler, Eglon is unwilling to turn down a surprise. Ehud makes a second play on words understood by the reader, but not by the unfortunate Eglon. Ehud says he has a **message** for the king. The text uses דָּבָר (*dᵊbar*), which can mean either "word" or "thing." So while Eglon hears, "**I have a** [word] **from God for you**," the reader hears the humorous, "I have a *thing* from God for you," referring to the sword. The message Eglon receives from Yahweh is a **belly** full of bronze as Ehud delivers the killing blow.

3:22 Eglon is obese enough that his fat completely engulfs the blade. If Ehud's sword is eighteen inches long, then Eglon's girth is likely in excess of a hefty size 60. Any reader winces with gleeful disgust at such an image.

The NIV sanitizes the text by omitting from the translation the last two words of verse 22. The phrase וַיֵּצֵא הַפַּרְשְׁדֹנָה (*wayyēṣē' happaršᵊdōnāh*) is uncertain, and is often translated, "and out came the dirt" or "out came the excrement." *Paršᵊdōn* is a *hapax legomenon* — a word appearing only once in the Bible. English translations vary on the exact meaning of the phrase. The NKJV uses "entrails" and most other translations use either "dirt" or "excrement," but the scatological meaning is clear. Ehud's sword pops the bloated king.

3:23-25 With Eglon dead, Ehud needs to make good his escape. Halpern argues against Ehud using some side exit from the **upper** chamber where Eglon is relieving himself and instead suggests that Ehud locks the doors to the outer room (from which there was no exit to the outside). Having **locked** himself inside, Ehud returns to the inner chamber (the restroom), removes the stone used as a toilet seat, and drops down through the latrine! The latrine was regu-

---

[7]See comment on 2:1-5.

larly emptied, so Ehud is able to exit through the janitor's closet.[8] After the sword puncture, Eglon's bodily waste, *parš°dōn*, comes out. In his escape, Ehud comes out the מִסְדְּרוֹן (*misd°rôn*), another *hapax legomenon*. If Halpern is correct, the reader understands the humor of verse 24 when Ehud had "gone out."

The humor continues as Eglon's **servants**, tired of waiting for their master, check his restroom door and find it **locked**. They wait "until ashamed" before unlocking the door and finding Eglon dead. The reader laughs as Ehud is safely out of reach of Moabite retribution.

3:26-29 Upon arriving **in the hill country of Ephraim**, Ehud uses a horn as a military summons. With Eglon dead, the leaderless Moabite troops head toward the Jordan River in order to cross over and retreat to Moabite territory. By capturing **the fords of the Jordan**, Ehud is able to cut off the Moabite retreat while also preventing troops from crossing the Jordan to reinforce the stranded troops.[9] Jephthah will use the same strategy against the Ephraimites in chapter 12. Trapped between the river and the Israelite army, the Moabite troops are easily picked off by the Israelites as they try to flee. The Moabite body count is 10,000 troops, which the text mentions are able warriors.

3:30 Ehud's assassination of Eglon and leadership of Israel eliminates **Moab** as a threat, eliminating their ability to pressure Israel for several generations. Moab will not become a problem again for Israel until the time of Saul.

Ehud is a shrewd trickster. The clever deceit he demonstrates makes him an admirable hero for the reader. The custom-made and concealed dagger, his secret lefthandedness and warrior training, the enticement of Eglon with a promised secret, and Ehud's sneaky escape all give the reader reason to cheer the underdog Israelite turned sneaky deliverer. The trickster theme is also seen in the narratives of Gideon and Samson.[10] God is willing to utilize a diverse range of skills for his purposes, including cunning.

---

[8]Halpern, "Assassination of Eglon," pp. 37-41.
[9]Cohen, *Joshua and Judges*, p. 184.
[10]Matthews, *Judges*, p. 60.

C: THE THIRD JUDGE: SHAMGAR (3:31)

[31]**After Ehud came Shamgar son of Anath, who struck down six hundred Philistines with an oxgoad. He too saved Israel.**

3:31 The third judge mentioned is a minor judge, significant only because of the manner in which he delivers Israel. **Shamgar** uses an unusual weapon to battle the **Philistines**. Like Ehud's dagger, Shamgar's **oxgoad** provides a small surprise for the reader, communicating that Yahweh does not require national military capabilities to accomplish his ends. God just as easily uses a man or woman wielding a strange weapon to provide salvation for his people.

Some consider the Shamgar narrative to be a fabrication because of the improbability of killing 600 men with a farm implement. But massive slaughters committed by a single individual empowered by God are not unknown in Scripture (2 Sam 23:8-12; Judg 15:15-16).

Not only does God deliver the Israelites through unexpected weapons, he also uses unexpected people. Shamgar himself is probably not an Israelite. His name is not a Hebrew name, and the description as the "son of Anath" has been used to describe an individual devoted to the service of the Canaanite deity Anat.[11] Lindars notes that because Anat was a war goddess, Shamgar may very well be a Canaanite mercenary leader whom God uses against the Philistines.[12] If Shamgar is indeed a Canaanite, he is unlikely interested in the Israelite cause. In that case, God uses an individual who is not part of the Covenant to bring salvation to his people. God does this very thing with Xerxes in the book of Esther and Cyrus's release of the Jewish exiles. God expresses no hesitation in utilizing whomever he desires to fulfill his purposes, even if they are not on his side.

This perspective certainly speculates beyond the information provided by the text. The only specifics provided by the text are Shamgar's name, parentage, and the manner in which he saves Israel. His name also shows up in the song of Deborah (Judg 5:6) as a chronological marker for an era in Israel's past in which daily life was uncertain and unsafe.

---

[11]Peter C. Craigie, "Reconsideration of Shamgar Ben Anath (Judg 3:31 and 5:6)," *JBL* 91 (1972): 239-240.

[12]Lindars, *Judges 1–5*, p. 158.

Absent from the account is the cyclical formula applied to the major judges. The people's apostasy, suffering, and crying out are not mentioned, and Yahweh plays no overt role in the account. God's involvement is made clear, however, from the description of the cycle in chapter 2. For the author of Judges, one verse becomes an adequate testimony to Yahweh's faithfulness.

CHAPTER 4

D. THE FOURTH JUDGE: DEBORAH (4:1–5:31)

1. Deborah Presents the Task (4:1-10)

[1]After Ehud died, the Israelites once again did evil in the eyes of the LORD. [2]So the LORD sold them into the hands of Jabin, a king of Canaan, who reigned in Hazor. The commander of his army was Sisera, who lived in Harosheth Haggoyim. [3]Because he had nine hundred iron chariots and had cruelly oppressed the Israelites for twenty years, they cried to the LORD for help.

[4]Deborah, a prophetess, the wife of Lappidoth, was leading[a] Israel at that time. [5]She held court under the Palm of Deborah between Ramah and Bethel in the hill country of Ephraim, and the Israelites came to her to have their disputes decided. [6]She sent for Barak son of Abinoam from Kedesh in Naphtali and said to him, "The LORD, the God of Israel, commands you: 'Go, take with you ten thousand men of Naphtali and Zebulun and lead the way to Mount Tabor. [7]I will lure Sisera, the commander of Jabin's army, with his chariots and his troops to the Kishon River and give him into your hands.'"

[8]Barak said to her, "If you go with me, I will go; but if you don't go with me, I won't go."

[9]"Very well," Deborah said, "I will go with you. But because of the way you are going about this,[b] the honor will not be yours, for the LORD will hand Sisera over to a woman." So Deborah went with Barak to Kedesh, [10]where he summoned Zebulun and Naphtali. Ten thousand men followed him, and Deborah also went with him.

[a]4 Traditionally *judging* [b]9 Or *But on the expedition you are undertaking*

4:1-2a The death of **Ehud** again initiates the downward spiral in the status of Israel. Without righteous leadership to restrain their inclination toward **evil**, the people's finicky spiritual appetites once more result in God's chastisement. This time, God delivers the Israelites **into the hands of** a regional power in northern Palestine, **Jabin** of Hazor.[1] His name, meaning "wise one," may be a title rather than a personal name.

Once Canaanites and Israelites shared the land in the Galilee region, peaceful coexistence between the two groups was likely frayed by trade inequities and the increasing power of the Canaanite city-states like those mentioned in Judges 1.[2] Canaanite emphasis focused on the lower fertile farmland regions, and Jabin possessed the military might to establish control over the area.

4:2b-3 Jabin's military **commander** is **Sisera**, a resident of **Harosheth** at the foot of Mount Carmel by the Wadi Kishon. Sisera commands a force that has **900 iron chariots**, a force easily capable of controlling the lowlands, but not useful in the rugged forest terrain of the central ridge. Sisera's chariots represent an overwhelming military presence utilized by the Canaanites to maintain their dominance. Further accentuating Israel's suffering is the long duration of Jabin's oppression. Only the Philistine oppression of chapter 13 will last longer than Sisera's twenty-year domination of the Israelites. For the Hebrews, the prowess and success of Jabin's general Sisera likely undermines Hebrew confidence in Yahweh, driving them deeper into the quest for divine salvation in foreign gods. But the oppression of a foreign nation once again becomes too much for the people of Israel. Receiving no deliverance from pagan deities, the people cry out to God for deliverance, which God provides through the second powerful female character in the book.

4:4 When considering the significance of important female characters within Judges, one invariably turns first to Deborah. Deborah has been described as the solitary "positive image of a woman in the Hebrew Bible."[3] With the arrival of Deborah in the narrative, the reader's expectations are overturned. Until Deborah, the reader has

---

[1]Hazor was located in northern Canaan, about ten miles north of the Sea of Galilee. The city is mentioned in multiple ancient extrabiblical documents, including the Mari letters, texts from Amarna, and various Egyptian texts.

[2]Hamlin, *At Risk in the Promised Land*, p. 84.

[3]Mieke Bal, "Introduction," in *Anti-covenant: Counter-Reading Women's Lives in the Hebrew Bible*, ed. by Mieke Bal (Sheffield: Almond, 1989), p. 21.

encountered Acsah's assertiveness in obtaining her own independence, but this is nothing new to the reader of the Hebrew Bible. The five daughters of Zelophehad have already set the precedent by assertively engaging the Israelite leadership for the rights to their father's inheritance in Numbers 27:1-11, and Miriam is already known as a prophetess. So while Acsah's self-interest in obtaining a better portion from her father is new in Judges, it is hardly surprising.

The author of Judges playfully toys with gender models of his day. Deborah and Barak essentially invert their cultural gender roles in the text. Acting like a male, Deborah is the strong, decisive leader while Barak assumes the passive, subservient role of a woman. This gender inversion will also occur in the interaction between Jael and Sisera, as well as Samson and Delilah.

In the first three chapters of Judges, the author quietly shapes the reader's expectations toward a traditionally masculine solution to the problems in the narrative. First, the writer of Judges juxtaposes Israel's communal disobedience with the strong, righteous, individualistic presence of stereotypical masculine leadership. Joshua, the mighty conqueror and godly leader, lives to the age of 110. During his watch and the watch of the elders who survive him, the people are loyal. After their deaths, the community abandons Yahweh. And the cycle of Judges is initiated. With the onset of oppression, the people return to Yahweh, and he raises up a judge as a mechanism of deliverance.

That deliverance also expects stereotypical masculine traits to be displayed by the judge; the reader expects a military victory over oppressive enemies. Men, naturally adept at violence, will be looked for to lead the Israelites. Early on, the reader expects masculine deliverers. The early chapters of Judges are replete with stereotypical examples of men as brave warriors.[4] The first judge is Othniel, younger brother of loyal and righteous Caleb. Othniel is presented briefly as a successful warrior. The second judge, Ehud, is masculinity personified. He acts as a stealthy maverick, relying first on trickery and assassination before gathering the army and leading as a successful general. The brief reference to Shamgar in 3:21 exhibits a masculine prowess rivaling Samson, slaying 600 Philistines with an oxgoad. By chapter 4, the reader expects a masculine warrior to produce delivery for the Israelites.

[4]J. Cheryl Exum, "Feminist Criticism: Whose Interests Are Being Served?" in *Judges and Method*, pp. 71-72.

Deborah, however, upends the expectations in a threefold way. First, the text emphasizes Deborah's status as a female **prophetess**. "Deborah, a woman prophetess" emphasizes that the person serving in the role of prophet is female. Israel has had some experience with prophetesses before; Miriam, the sister of Moses, is mentioned as a prophetess in Exodus 15:20. In Miriam's case, however, the text notes that only the women followed her. Deborah, as soon shall be seen, is different.

Deborah's second identification is filled with images of flame. As **the wife of Lappidoth**, Deborah is married to "the torch." Although her name means "swarm of bees," it may also be understood to mean "Woman of flames," a fitting associate for Barak, a man with a name meaning "Lightning."[5] Beyond the identification as the wife of Lappidoth, Deborah does not function in the role of wife in the narrative.[6]

4:5 The text also emphatically stresses Deborah's sex in regard to her third identification: judge. The text literally reads, "She herself judged Israel," drawing attention to the unusual function of a woman as a Judge over the Israelites. The narrator twice emphasizes the unique nature of this fourth judge. Deborah is unexpectedly female. Matthews argues that Deborah is a postmenopausal woman, making her gender irrelevant to her role as prophetess and judge.[7] This perspective is contradicted by the grammar of the text. The author of Judges calls special attention to the woman who will deliver Israel from Jabin.

Another distinction made about Deborah is her relationship to the typical power structures of the day. The text mentions she set up judicial shop under a tree **between Ramah and Bethel**.[8] Deborah is not affiliated with any city or its judicial system. Rather, residents seek out a woman sitting under a tree for judgment instead of seeking justice from the elders sitting at their own gates. As a judge,

---

[5]Freema Gottlieb, "Three Mothers," *Judaism* 30 (1981): 195.

[6]Danna Nolan Fewell and David M. Gunn, "Controlling Perspectives: Women, Men, and the Authority of Violence in Judges 4 and 5," *JAAR* 58 (1990): 391.

[7]Matthews, *Judges*, p. 64.

[8]Tammi J. Schneider sees a connection to Rebekah's nurse, also named Deborah, buried in the same area around Bethel and under a significant tree (*Judges*, 69).

COLLEGE PRESS NIV COMMENTARY

Deborah is superior to the judicial systems of local cities. Both as a woman and as a judge, Deborah operates outside the normal boundaries of her day.

4:6-7 Deborah sends for **Barak** and orders him to recruit forces from the tribes of **Zebulun** and **Naphtali** to confront Jabin's army. Zebulun and Naphtali are at the forefront of suffering because of Canaanite pressure, and it is appropriate that they provide the military troops to be used to deliver them. Barak himself has been in a good position to experience the subjugation of Jabin first hand. Barak is a Naphtalite from **Kedesh**, a town scarcely eight miles north of Hazor. The Israelite settlement is located close enough to Hazor that it is the first to suffer and is tightly controlled.

Deborah provides Barak with substantial information. She gives him the number of troops to gather, the rallying point of **Mount Tabor**, and even the military strategy that will be used: the Wadi **Kishon** will work against Sisera's chariot forces. Her pronouncement is provided not as a decision as the leader of Israel, but as a direct command from Yahweh. Barak has been given a direct and specific command from **the Lord** to follow.

Deborah, the surprise female leader of Israel, summons a man, Barak. Barak, like Deborah, is a gendered surprise for readers. Whereas Deborah steps into a stereotypical masculine role, Barak abandons the masculine and resists both the command of God given through Deborah and his part in Yahweh's upcoming plans. Barak refuses to go into battle unless the woman goes with him. This reluctance may simply affirm his belief in Deborah's power as a prophetess or her potential as a morale booster for the troops, but the implication is clear. The expected powerful warrior needs the presence of a woman to find the confidence to lead.

4:8 Barak's refusal is an act of cowardly disobedience; he places parameters on his willingness to obey the command of Yahweh given through Deborah.[9] Barak may believe that his success will be ensured through the presence of Yahweh's representative,[10] but his stubbornness is a sinful response to God's command.

4:9 The consequence for Barak's disobedience is not extreme. Deborah agrees to accompany Barak, but predicts that he will lose

---

[9]Fewell and Gunn, "Controlling Perspectives," p. 398.

[10]Matthews, *Judges*, p. 64.

the honor of capturing the Canaanite general **Sisera**. Honor for defeating Sisera would appropriately be given to the victor. Deborah uses a precise phrase that emphasizes both Yahweh's activity in the battle and the fact that it will be **a woman** who achieves the victory: literally, "Into the hand of a woman the LORD will sell Sisera."

God's "handing over" (literally, "selling into the hand") of a group to its enemy is always a military term.[11] In the Hebrew of 4:9, the phrase occurs at the beginning of the clause, indicating the author's highlight of the victor *as female*. The implication for Barak is not that he will simply lose the glory of victory as a result of his reluctance, but rather that he as a man will lose the honor *to a woman*. The writer of Judges here provides an insight into the mind of Barak and the culture of the day. There is more shame attached to publicly losing face to a woman than merely losing face.

Does the narrator intend Deborah or Jael as the woman usurping Barak's honor? Deborah does not function in the narrative of the battle, whereas Jael personally assassinates Sisera. Jael, then, is the more likely candidate. Whether the narrator intends Jael or Deborah is irrelevant, however. Both women receive honor for a military victory that should have gone to Barak, and Barak's status is diminished as a result of his disobedience.

4:10 With Deborah accompanying him, Barak proceeds through the plan God has laid out. He rallies 10,000 troops from **Zebulun and Naphtali** and encamps at Mount Tabor, some ten miles east of the Wadi Kishon and plain of Jezreel.

2. Israel's Victory over Sisera (4:11-16)

[11]**Now Heber the Kenite had left the other Kenites, the descendants of Hobab, Moses' brother-in-law,[a] and pitched his tent by the great tree in Zaanannim near Kedesh.**

[12]**When they told Sisera that Barak son of Abinoam had gone up to Mount Tabor, [13]Sisera gathered together his nine hundred iron chariots and all the men with him, from Harosheth Haggoyim to the Kishon River.**

[14]**Then Deborah said to Barak, "Go! This is the day the LORD**

[11]Lindars, *Judges 1-5*, pp. 189-190.

has given Sisera into your hands. Has not the LORD gone ahead of you?" So Barak went down Mount Tabor, followed by ten thousand men. ¹⁵At Barak's advance, the LORD routed Sisera and all his chariots and army by the sword, and Sisera abandoned his chariot and fled on foot. ¹⁶But Barak pursued the chariots and army as far as Harosheth Haggoyim. All the troops of Sisera fell by the sword; not a man was left.

ᵃ*11 Or father-in-law*

4:11 Verse 11 is inserted by the author to lay a foundation for the action at the end of the chapter. The **Kenite** clan is descended from **Moses'** Midianite father-in-law, Jethro. They were cousins of Israel, but an independent people. They held territory in southern Palestine in the Judah and Simeon tribal areas. **Heber** lives in the region of **Kedesh**, placing his residence in the geographic center of the narrative's resolution.

4:12-13 The Kenites, loyal to Jabin, inform **Sisera** of the Israelite assembly at **Mount Tabor**. In response, Sisera gathers his chariot troops from his hometown of **Harosheth** and creates a front along the **Kishon**. The chariots would easily command the flat terrain of the valley. Archers were typically mounted in chariots, providing an army with an advantage in speed, weight, and striking distance. The Israelite foot troops and stationary archers would essentially be useless against chariots in open country. Fortunately for Barak and his army, chariots prove much less effective against the God of Israel.

4:14-16 **Deborah**, present among the Israelite army, initiates the attack. At Deborah's command, **Barak** and his troops emerge from the safety of Mount Tabor and descend into the Jezreel Valley to confront Sisera's front line. The author credits God with the victory over Sisera's forces. Yahweh acts as a force in conjunction with Barak's advance, successfully routing the Canaanite army.

Chapter 4 does not describe the method by which God achieves victory over Sisera's army. Although more detail will be provided in the Song of Deborah in chapter 5, the hints in 4:15-16 should suffice for the reader to infer the physical source of Canaanite defeat. As soon as God acts and Sisera's forces are routed, **Sisera abandon[s] his chariot** and escapes **on foot**. Fleeing on foot rather than in a speedy horse-drawn chariot would be foolish on Sisera's part unless it provided a better opportunity for survival than did remaining in the chariot. Sisera was forced to abandon his chariot, a vehicle useless only when it cannot move. The seasonal torrents flooding through the Wadi Kishon quickly flood the floor of the Jezreel Valley, depositing sediment and creating a mucky soil easily capable of immobilizing both horses and chariots. Sisera, with his chariot wheels and horses' legs buried in mud, is vulnerable to Israelite archers and foot soldiers, and has no choice but to escape on foot.

Sisera's chariot forces suffer a similar fate. Fleeing toward **Harosheth**, they are overcome first by the muck, and then by the Israelite forces. As the Canaanites struggle against the deep mud, fresh Israelite troops easily take control of the solid ground above the valley floor, killing the exhausted Canaanites as they emerge from the mud.

3. Jael Murders Sisera (4:17-24)

[17]Sisera, however, fled on foot to the tent of Jael, the wife of Heber the Kenite, because there were friendly relations between Jabin king of Hazor and the clan of Heber the Kenite.

[18]Jael went out to meet Sisera and said to him, "Come, my lord, come right in. Don't be afraid." So he entered her tent, and she put a covering over him.

[19]"I'm thirsty," he said. "Please give me some water." She opened a skin of milk, gave him a drink, and covered him up.

[20]"Stand in the doorway of the tent," he told her. "If someone comes by and asks you, 'Is anyone here?' say 'No.'"

[21]But Jael, Heber's wife, picked up a tent peg and a hammer and went quietly to him while he lay fast asleep, exhausted. She drove the peg through his temple into the ground, and he died.

[22]Barak came by in pursuit of Sisera, and Jael went out to meet him. "Come," she said, "I will show you the man you're looking for." So he went in with her, and there lay Sisera with the tent peg through his temple—dead.

[23]On that day God subdued Jabin, the Canaanite king, before the Israelites. [24]And the hand of the Israelites grew stronger and stronger against Jabin, the Canaanite king, until they destroyed him.

4:17 The Israelites control the Jezreel Valley from Tabor to Harosheth, making escape to his hometown impossible for Sisera. He manages to pass through the Israelite lines, avoids capture, and heads north in the direction of **Hazor**, running for his life. His closest safe haven is the home of **Heber the Kenite**, previously mentioned in verse 11.

4:18 Sisera heads for the tent of Heber's wife **Jael**. Since women possessed their own tents,[12] a man would not be sought out in a woman's tent. At the same time, Sisera's presence as a nonrelative inside a woman's tent is an unacceptable violation of societal norms.[13] Victor Matthews and Don Benjamin go further in suggesting that Sisera's violation of hospitality protocol is the lens through which to understand the story. Sisera's approaching Jael's tent infringes on Heber's hospitality: the male head of the family is the only one with the right to offer Sisera the status of guest. Sisera, according to this view, approaches Jael's tent ostensibly for the purpose of rape. Raping Jael, they argue, would enable Sisera to take over the household.[14]

This perspective ignores two details in the text. First, Sisera does indeed approach Jael's tent, but the reader does not encounter nefarious motives on Sisera's part. Sisera flees to Jael's tent because he is counting on the presumed safety available because of the amicable relationship between Jabin and Heber. Fleeing on foot, Sisera is not looking to destroy his master's friendship through a foolish act of sexual assault. Sisera simply chooses the safest location with the best proximity and runs there for safety. Sisera's flight to Heber's property may not even be his destination; he may simply be fleeing through an area where he is not likely to be attacked.

The second textual detail suggesting Sisera is not breaching hospitality etiquette is Jael's assertiveness in her interactions with Sisera. It is Jael, not Sisera, who initiates the hospitality. She goes **out to meet** him, giving him the invitation to turn aside. The verb for "turn aside," סוּר (sûr), indicates a turning away from the intended course, strengthening the idea that Sisera was merely passing through what he considered to be safe territory. But Jael's encouragement to turn aside causes Sisera to abandon his flight and enter her tent for safety.

---

[12]See Genesis 31:33-34.
[13]Cohen, *Joshua and Judges*, p. 191.
[14]Victor H. Matthews and Don C. Benjamin, "Jael: Host or Judge?" *TBT* (September 1992): 291-296.

Matthews's assertion that Jael's treatment of Sisera is a violation of Ancient Near Eastern hospitality codes is far-fetched.[15] Jael, as a woman, has no right to offer hospitality at all, nor does Sisera have the right to accept. Instead, Jael's treatment of Sisera relies on her ability to hoodwink and manipulate him. The vocabulary is about seduction as Jael lulls Sisera to his death with a false sense of security. Hospitality is secondary to Jael's craftiness and Sisera's foolishness.

Jael is the perfect hostess: by doing more than expected, she seduces Sisera through her magnanimity. Sisera enters the tent and the narrative notes twice that Jael covered Sisera, hiding him under a rug or blanket. Some suggest that Jael slept with Sisera to exhaust him, making him easy prey for her homicidal proclivities,[16] but the narrative at this point in chapter 4 reveals little more about a possible sexual interaction between them than Jael's assertive solicitation for hospitality. Fewell and Gunn suggest that "in biblical literature, a man seldom enters a woman's tent for purposes other than sexual intercourse. The woman's tent is symbolic of the woman's body."[17] This argument is at its best unconvincing. Occurrences of men entering a woman's tent at all are rare in the Hebrew Bible, and several have nothing to do with sexuality. Abraham entered *a tent* simply to issue instructions to Sarah (although the tent is not specifically identified as Sarah's). Laban entered Leah's, Rachel's, Zilpah's, and Bildad's tent for the purpose of searching. Isaac is the only clear example of entering a tent for sex when he consummates his marriage to Rebekah. Even then, the tent is identified as Sarah's, not Rebekah's, although it is reasonable to assume that Rebekah would be assuming the residence of Sarah as matriarch of the family. Much more common is the use of the simple phrase, "he went (in) to her" to describe sexual contact. Judges 4:18 uses the phrase "he turned aside to her." The same construction is used elsewhere only in Genesis 19:3 when the angels accept Lot's offer of lodging. That a woman's tent in the Hebrew Bible is symbolic of her body is unrealistic. When looking for missing idols, Laban refuses to search Rachel's body because of her clever excuse, but he still searches her tent. This is obviously not an invasion of her body.

---

[15]Matthews, *Judges*, pp. 68-73.
[16]Gottlieb, "Three Mothers," p. 199.
[17]Fewell and Gunn, "Controlling Perspectives," p. 392.

Nevertheless, the text may still be using a slight double entendre for sexuality. When Jael approaches Sisera to murder him, the text describes Jael as "coming to him" in verse 21. This phrase is a common way to describe sexual intercourse. But the entendre for the reader stops with the next word. Jael came quietly — hardly an adjective used in relation to sexual seduction. The word is used in a possible sexual context elsewhere only in Ruth 3:7, although it is not used to refer to sex itself. The word translated "quietly" (בַּלָּאט, *ballā'ṭ*) refers to secret information or stealthy acts rather than sexual interaction. That Ruth 3:7 has a similar reading is coincidental.

4:19-20 Once inside Jael's tent, an exhausted Sisera asks Jael for **water**. Jael, fulfilling the stereotypical female role of nurturer for Sisera, instead brings him a much more satisfying drink/meal of **milk**.[18] After feeding Sisera, Jael again covers him, calling to mind an image of a mother tucking in a child. Sisera, comfortable in his role as the servant of Jabin, friend of Jael's husband Heber, easily assumes and attempts to assert authority over Jael and commands her to stand guard at the door. Rather than speaking from a position of power, the portrait of Sisera is comical. Like a child afraid of the dark needing a mother's presence to ward off monsters, Sisera, with a full tummy, tucked into bed, hides with the covers pulled up over his head as he asks Jael to guard the door. The narrator has rendered Sisera powerless, his life in the hands of a woman. Sisera will soon die because he foolishly expects to be nurtured by his murderer.

4:21-22 Sisera, hidden under cover of rug, soon falls **asleep**. It is then that the reader encounters Jael's treachery. A **tent peg** and a few blows from a mallet put a quick end to this enemy of Israel. Sisera's humiliation is complete. Jael's status as clever assassin is established. Rather than expressing any regret at murdering a guest, she triumphantly goes out to meet **Barak** to lead him to Sisera's corpse. **Sisera**, the mighty Canaanite general, has lost his status as Canaanite warrior to a tent-dwelling woman who knows how to wield a hammer and **tent peg**. Similarly, Barak stands over the body of Sisera, but cannot claim the honor for defeating the head of the Canaanite army. The honor, as prophesied by Deborah, will go to the woman Jael.

4:23-24 The clever narrative concludes with a reminder of the true source of the Israelite victory: God himself has defeated **Jabin**

---

[18]Gottlieb, "Three Mothers," pp. 197-200.

and his army. Verse 24 apparently observes multiple generations, as
the demographic power between the two people groups shifts in
favor of the **Israelites**, and they are ultimately able to permanently
remove this Canaanite nuisance from their midst.

Barnabas Lindars suggests that the Deborah/Jael narrative avoids
raising moral issues and instead concentrates on entertaining the
reader.[19] The story of Deborah and Jael certainly delivers. The reader's expectations are twisted by gender inversion, innuendo,
intrigue, and comeuppance. Like much of Judges, moral instruction
is not the focus of the Deborah narrative; the sovereignty and faithfulness of God are.

[19]Barnabas Lindars, "Deborah's Song: Women in the Old Testament,"
BJRL 65 (Spring 1983): 165.

CHAPTER 5

D. THE FOURTH JUDGE: DEBORAH (4:1–5:31, continued)

The Song of Deborah has long presented difficulty for commentators. The poem's date, structure, and vocabulary are all debated and have achieved little in the way of scholarly consensus. Manuscript evidence is somewhat murky, and the difficulty in understanding the passage is compounded by often uncertain vocabulary presented in poetic form.[1] Phrases such as "notoriously difficult to translate" and "mutilated text" are not uncommon in describing the difficulties in pinpointing the textual details of the chapter.[2]

The Hebrew text of the chapter is often assumed to be early, both because of its obscure vocabulary and the assumed corruption of the text.[3] These factors lead scholars to the commonly held position that the song was composed at the time of the events it describes. The self-testimony of Scripture should be satisfactory; verse 1 describes the song as sung by Deborah and Barak.

The early date of the chapter also undermines the common suggestion that Israel's monotheistic theology developed over time. The song indicates that Israel clearly considers itself to be a people existing in a distinct relationship with Yahweh. Within the song, Yahweh is already firmly established as the God who works miracles and delivers his people.

Judges 5 provides a retelling of the Deborah-Barak/Jael-Sisera account in poetic form. Hebrew poetry is complex, and is arguably

---

[1]See J. Alberto Soggin, *Judges, A Commentary* (Philadelphia: Westminster Press, 1981), pp. 84-101.

[2]Robert G. Boling, *Judges* (Garden City, NY: Doubleday, 1975), p. 109.

[3]Peter Craigie offers the possible alternative that the text of chapter 5 represents "an early northern dialect of Hebrew." Peter C. Craigie, "Song of Deborah and the Epic of Tukulti-Ninurta.," *JBL* 88 (1969): 254.

not well understood.[4] At the most basic level, the Song of Deborah, like all Hebrew poetry, rhymes ideas in parallel lines. Music is a powerful communication tool in an oral culture. Combining information with a melody allows an event to be easily remembered across generations. The Song of Deborah is most easily understood as a victory hymn celebrating God's deliverance of his people. The song is composed in the style of other ancient victory hymns.[5] The song also may have been intended as a riposte — a musical response to the Canaanites mocking their defeat.[6] Marc Zvi Brettler suggests that the song served as a call to war for future generations — a testimony about God's faithfulness that could be utilized to rally troops in times of war.[7]

The song's structure can be divided into four sections.

The Need for Deliverance	5:2-11a
The Call to Arms	5:11b-18
The Battle	5:19-22
The Humiliation of Sisera	5:23-31

4. The Song of Deborah (5:1-31)

Introduction (5:1)

[1]On that day Deborah and Barak son of Abinoam sang this song:

5:1 After the final defeat of the Canaanite troops with the death of Sisera, **Deborah and Barak** express their praise to God in the form of a **song**. The verb for **sang** is a feminine singular, referring to Deborah as the primary singer. As a Levite, Barak was likely skilled in music and probably accompanied Deborah in the song.

---

[4]See Alan J. Hauser, "Judges 5: Parataxis in Hebrew Poetry," *JBL* 99 (March 1980): 23-41, and Mark A. Vincent, "The Song of Deborah: A Structural and Literary Consideration," *JSOT* 91 (2000): 61-82, for two examples that argue for a cohesive unity of the poem based on the complexities of the poetry in chapter 5.

[5]Boling, *Judges*, p. 117.

[6]Geoffrey Miller, "A Riposte Form in the Song of Deborah," in *Gender and Law in the Hebrew Bible and the Ancient Near East*, ed. by Victor H. Matthews, Bernard M. Levinson, and Tikva Frymer-Kensky (Sheffield: Sheffield Academic, 1998), pp. 113-127.

[7]Brettler, *Creation of History*, pp. 69-74.

Songs are not an uncommon response to God's deliverance. Judges 5, along with the Song of Moses in Exodus 15, is unique in that it is a song that narrates a specific event. The Psalms arise out of specific circumstances and often allude to particular events, but Judges 5 is a poetic retelling of an event.

The Need for Deliverance (5:2-11a)

[2]"When the princes in Israel take the lead,
  when the people willingly offer themselves—
  praise the LORD!

[3]"Hear this, you kings! Listen, you rulers!
  I will sing to[a] the LORD, I will sing;
  I will make music to[b] the LORD, the God of Israel.

[4]"O LORD, when you went out from Seir,
  when you marched from the land of Edom,
the earth shook, the heavens poured,
  the clouds poured down water.

[5]The mountains quaked before the LORD, the One of Sinai,
  before the LORD, the God of Israel.

[6]"In the days of Shamgar son of Anath,
  in the days of Jael, the roads were abandoned;
  travelers took to winding paths.

[7]Village life[c] in Israel ceased,
  ceased until I,[d] Deborah, arose,
  arose a mother in Israel.

[8]When they chose new gods,
  war came to the city gates,
and not a shield or spear was seen
  among forty thousand in Israel.

[9]My heart is with Israel's princes,
  with the willing volunteers among the people.
  Praise the LORD!

[10]"You who ride on white donkeys,
  sitting on your saddle blankets,
  and you who walk along the road,
consider [11]the voice of the singers[e] at the watering places.
  They recite the righteous acts of the LORD,
  the righteous acts of his warriors[f] in Israel.

[a]3 Or of   [b]3 Or / with song I will praise   [c]7 Or Warriors   [d]7 Or you

95

e11 **Or** *archers*; **the meaning of the Hebrew for this word is uncertain.**
f11 **Or** *villagers*

5:2-3 Undergirding the Israelite war effort against the Canaanites has been the voluntary cooperation of the individual tribes. The unity of the tribes is essential to their individual survival. Aligning with the theme of Judges, the song touts skilled leadership as the basis for Israel's unity. The effectiveness of Israel's unity has resulted in the defeat of the Canaanites and becomes a source of celebration and praise to God.

5:4-5 The LORD is described in parallel terms as going **out from Seir** and marching **from Edom**. Both people groups and their territories were off limits for Israelite conquest. Both the people of Seir and the Edomites were descendants of Jacob's brother Esau. Because they were kin, the Israelites were not allowed to attack them or possess their land (see Gen 36:6-8; Deut 2:2-8,12; Josh 24:4). Both groups would later be conquered by the "Scepter of Israel" (Num 24:15-19).

Verses 4-5 recall the miraculous activity surrounding God's presence after the Exodus of Israel from Egypt. The bizarre atmospheric conditions surrounding the giving of the Law — thunder, lightning, and smoke — are seen here. The verses also sound remarkably like Psalm 68:8. The **God of Israel** is the God of the heavens, not the storm god Baal of Canaan. Yahweh also possesses power over the earth, causing earthquakes by his very presence.

Water will be a recurring motif throughout Deborah's song.[8] Beyond just the provision of water, God repeatedly demonstrates to his people his power to manipulate water. The flood, the turning of the Nile to blood, the crossing of the Red Sea, the splitting of the waters at the Jordan — all reveal the God of Israel as capable of bending the power of water to his will. The song will elaborate more in verse 21 how water under the control of Yahweh fights on behalf of Israel.

5:6 The song shifts to describe the unstable conditions at the time Deborah assumes leadership over Israel. A time of anarchy existed in the oxgoad-wielding **days of Shamgar**. The description of abandoned roads[9] and villages expresses the common feeling of

---

[8]Vincent, "The Song of Deborah," pp. 65-66.

[9]Cundall (*Judges*, p. 95) suggests that a vocalization change in the Hebrew word for road in verse 6 (אֳרָחוֹת *'ŏrāḥôth*) will shift the meaning to caravans,

insecurity and lack of safety in basic travel. Without the presence of a stable regional power, major trade routes were controlled by marauders and bandits. Similarly, small villages also were exposed to aggressive exploitation by nomadic raiders.

5:7 Israel's survival in the face of these groups necessitated a unified resistance. Community offers significant advantages in the pursuit of an agenda. Individually, Israelite clans and tribes could mount little opposition to the stronger Canaanite people groups. Deborah's role is significant because she motivates the various self-interested tribes to unite for the sake of national self-preservation.

5:8 Deborah does not lapse in stating the root cause of Israel's difficulties. The source of their dilemma, as is often the case in Judges, is their abandonment of fidelity to Yahweh in favor of the worship of the Canaanite deities of the people groups around them. The immediate consequence is that **war came to the city gates**. Without obedience to God, the Israelites have no divine protector and are at the mercy of their oppressors.

Oppressive powers maintained their superiority over Israel by limiting the possession of weaponry. Rebellion is difficult without the military technology to instigate it. The Canaanites prevented significant opposition by preventing Israelite access to weapons.[10] Deborah's reference to 40,000 "may be an indication of the available manpower of the tribes at that time."[11] A force of 40,000, properly armed, represents a substantial fighting force. Without weaponry, such a force is ineffective against heavily armed opponents. Fortunately for Israel, the presence of God and Deborah's leadership will provide the people with overwhelming military power.

5:9 Verse 9 echoes verse 2, praising God for the presence of leadership and unity among the people. The willingness of the leaders and people who participated against the Canaanites is especially commendable in light of verse 8 and the lack of sufficient arma-

---

(*'ōrªḥôth*) which fits the parallel structure better. The text would then read, "The caravans ceased, and travelers took the winding paths."

[10]The Israelites will experience a similar absence of weapons under the early reign of Saul (1 Sam 13:19-22). The Philistines prevent the Israelites from working in iron to prevent opposition. Saul and Jonathan's possession of swords is symbolic of their position and poses no military threat to the Philistines.

[11]Cundall, *Judges*, p. 96.

ment. To engage in a military conflict with a superiorly armed enemy is rooted in either foolishness or faith. The peoples' willingness to trust God is yet one more example of the theme permeating Scripture that God does not wage the same kind of war the world does, nor is it waged in the same way (2 Cor 10:1-5; Eph 6:12).

5:10-11a The riders of **white donkeys** are likely wealthy merchants who stand to gain financially from the defeat of the Canaanites. The Israelite victory would immediately provide stability on the major trade routes, enabling larger and quicker-moving caravans. It is these wealthy beneficiaries whom Deborah encourages to pay attention to the songs about God's victory sung at the **watering** holes as they water their caravan animals along the trade routes.

The Call to Arms (5:11b-18)

"Then the people of the LORD
    went down to the city gates.
[12]"Wake up, wake up, Deborah!
    Wake up, wake up, break out in song!
Arise, O Barak!
    Take captive your captives, O son of Abinoam.'
[13]"Then the men who were left
    came down to the nobles;
the people of the LORD
    came to me with the mighty.
[14]Some came from Ephraim, whose roots were in Amalek;
    Benjamin was with the people who followed you.
From Makir captains came down,
    from Zebulun those who bear a commander's staff.
[15]The princes of Issachar were with Deborah;
    yes, Issachar was with Barak,
    rushing after him into the valley.
In the districts of Reuben
    there was much searching of heart.
[16]Why did you stay among the campfires[a]
    to hear the whistling for the flocks?
In the districts of Reuben
    there was much searching of heart.
[17]Gilead stayed beyond the Jordan.

> And Dan, why did he linger by the ships?
> Asher remained on the coast
>   and stayed in his coves.
> [18]The people of Zebulun risked their very lives;
>   so did Naphtali on the heights of the field.

[a]16 Or *saddlebags*

5:11b-13 Under the leadership of Deborah, the people rally to the cause. This next section functions as a role call of the tribes and their willingness to participate in the battle. The southern tribes of Judah and Simeon are not mentioned in the poem. Levi is not mentioned because they did not participate in war. Gad's presence is assumed to be included in the reference to the region of Gilead, and Manasseh's presence occurs through the participation of a clan from the city of Makir.

5:14-15a Ephraim is the first tribe to be mentioned as a participant. Judges portrays Ephraim as hotheaded, quickly willing to jump into conflict. It is no surprise that when the call to battle is announced, Ephraim stands at the front of the line.

The phrase about Ephraim having its **roots in Amalek** is probably a reference to Balaam's oracle in Numbers 24:20. Amalek is "first among nations," strong and prominent in its military prowess. Ephraim is also a group with a substantial military capacity. And, like Amalek, Ephraim will also foolishly cause Israel trouble.

5:15b-18 While Ephraim, Benjamin, Manasseh, Zebulun, and Issachar are commended for their willingness to join the Israelite army, four tribes — **Reuben**, Gad, Dan, and Asher — are criticized for their refusal to participate. Deborah describes Reuben sarcastically as undergoing **much searching of heart**, portraying the tribe as wrestling with the soul-searching decision. In the end, Reuben opts to tend their **flocks** rather than help their brothers during war. Gad stays in its territory of **Gilead beyond the Jordan**. Ironically, Jephthah will later assemble an Israelite army to assist the Gileadites against the Ammonites. **Dan** and **Asher** also avoid the conflict, opting to remain in their oceanside territories.

Each of the reluctant tribes is pictured as enjoying its inheritance and presence in the Promised Land. The Reubenites enjoy sitting around the campfire while they tend their sheep. The Gileadites will not put forth the effort to ford the Jordan. The Danites work at their shipbuilding trades and the Asherites live with their heads buried in the beach sand of their coastal **coves**. Deborah's song is intended to publicly shame these tribes for their enjoyment of their comfort while their fellow Israelites risk their very lives for the betterment of the community.

The attitude demonstrated by these four tribes can be spiritually toxic to a healthy community. When self-interest dominates an individual or group within the larger congregation, vital resources are withheld from the church. Service should not be determined by personal relevance to the individual. Being part of the church demands thinking at the community level. Such community-level thinking will joyfully find a way to serve the larger community of the church, whether that involves serving the elderly, children, the poor, or in missions, especially when there seems to be no immediate personal connection or relevance.

The Battle (5:19-22)

> [19]"Kings came, they fought;
> the kings of Canaan fought
> at Taanach by the waters of Megiddo,
> but they carried off no silver, no plunder.
> [20]From the heavens the stars fought,
> from their courses they fought against Sisera.
> [21]The river Kishon swept them away,
> the age-old river, the river Kishon.
> March on, my soul; be strong!
> [22]Then thundered the horses' hoofs—
> galloping, galloping go his mighty steeds.

5:19-20 Deborah's poetic description of the battle at **Megiddo** elaborates on the prose version in chapter 4. Multiple kings over small regions in Canaan united to oppose Israel at Megiddo. Their intention of looting the defeated Israelites goes unfulfilled. Verse 20 uses the **stars** as a metaphor for divine aggression against the Canaanite forces. Sisera has been opposed by the heavens, and his fate has not been created by a lucky stroke from the Israelites. Sisera has been divinely destined to be defeated.

5:21-22 The mechanism of Sisera's defeat is the **Kishon** River. Rains and torrents have caused the river to flood the floor of the

COLLEGE PRESS NIV COMMENTARY

Jezreel Valley. Sisera's chariots are quickly mired in mud, useless to the Canaanite troops. The Israelite victory is not the focus in the poem. Deborah's song reflects God's use of water to achieve the victory. As with Pharaoh's army in Exodus 14–15, God uses water to destroy Israel's enemies.[12] The thundering of Sisera's warhorses is no match for the power of the ancient Kishon.

The Humiliation of Sisera (5:23-31)

> [23]'Curse Meroz,' said the angel of the LORD.
>   'Curse its people bitterly,
> because they did not come to help the LORD,
>   to help the LORD against the mighty.'
>
> [24]"Most blessed of women be Jael,
>   the wife of Heber the Kenite,
>   most blessed of tent-dwelling women.
> [25]He asked for water, and she gave him milk;
>   in a bowl fit for nobles she brought him curdled milk.
> [26]Her hand reached for the tent peg,
>   her right hand for the workman's hammer.
> She struck Sisera, she crushed his head,
>   she shattered and pierced his temple.
> [27]At her feet he sank,
>   he fell; there he lay.
> At her feet he sank, he fell;
>   where he sank, there he fell—dead.
> [28]"Through the window peered Sisera's mother;
>   behind the lattice she cried out,
> 'Why is his chariot so long in coming?
>   Why is the clatter of his chariots delayed?'
> [29]The wisest of her ladies answer her;
>   indeed, she keeps saying to herself,
> [30]'Are they not finding and dividing the spoils:
>   a girl or two for each man,
>   colorful garments as plunder for Sisera,
>   colorful garments embroidered,
>   highly embroidered garments for my neck—
> all this as plunder?'

---

[12]O'Connell, *Rhetoric of the Book of Judges*, pp. 134-137.

[31]**"So may all your enemies perish, O LORD!**
    But may they who love you be like the sun
    when it rises in its strength."
Then the land had peace forty years.

5:23-24 Verse 23 is an appropriate introduction to the account of
Jael. Jael, as the blessed Canaanite deliverer of Israel is the perfect
contrast to the stubborn city of **Meroz**, known in the Bible only as
the town cursed by the angel of the LORD for its refusal to participate against the Canaanite armies. **Jael** is **most blessed of women**, a
title applied to Mary in Luke 1:42. Jael, in providing deliverance to
Israel, stands in good company.

Deborah's poem is part of the narrator's entertaining storytelling. In perhaps the most noticeable gender inversion in the book,
Jael will gain prominence over two men. The reader expects Barak
to be the powerful hero who defeats the Canaanites, but he is obviously not that hero. Deborah has already demonstrated more masculine prowess than Barak. The reader might anticipate Barak's
redemption by his personal capture and defeat of Sisera, but the
wait is in vain. As the battle concludes, Sisera, his army defeated, is
forced to abandon his chariot and make a run for safety on foot
toward the property of Heber the Kenite. Barak pursues and
destroys the Canaanite army, and is hot on the heels of Sisera. But
by the time Barak tracks Sisera to the tent in which he is hiding,
Sisera is already dead. Stepping forward in the text to claim the
honor is the real warrior and victor: the woman, Jael.

The Song of Deborah communicates more than just Sisera's
death and defeat. The song enshrines his humiliation at the hands
of a woman. Sisera's complicity in his own demise becomes Sisera's
biggest debasement. Not only are the gender roles between Jael and
Sisera inverted, but Sisera is the one who obediently plods the path
of making his masculinity subservient to Jael. The narrative focuses
on Sisera's reliance on Jael as a nurturer. Jael lures Sisera inside the
tent, but it is Sisera who follows, subject to his own naïve assumptions about Jael's femininity. He lies down, he asks for help, he covers up, he goes to sleep. He trusts Jael to nurture him, and it is that
very trust that ultimately costs him his life.

5:25-26 Not only does the text utilize expected feminine nurture to
invert the gender roles of Jael and Sisera, it employs sexuality as a

mechanism to capsize gender expectations in the text. The Song of Deborah revels in the inversion of sexual imagery that occurs in the murder of Sisera. Whereas the narrative of chapter 4 emphasizes Sisera as a victim of his reliance on feminine nurture, the Song of Deborah in chapter 5 portrays Sisera's death as Jael's sexual conquest. This is perhaps the most significant aspect of gender inversion occurring in the text of Judges. In 5:25-26, the lines simply recount the narrative, exalting Jael for luring **Sisera** into a false sense of security with her hospitality. Easy pickings, Sisera's **head** is pinned to the ground with a **hammer** and **tent peg**. Nothing significant in these two verses occurs but a poetic expression of delight at the irony amidst the victory.

5:27 Judges 5:27-30, however, presents a different image altogether. Many commentators have noted the sexual imagery implied by the passage. Sisera's death at **her feet** is more accurately "her legs," a sexual image rooted in the translation of בֵּין רַגְלֶיהָ (*bên raglêhā*). Referring to Jael's murder of Sisera, Niditch writes,

> Double meanings of violent death and sexuality emerge in every line. He is at her feet in a pose of defeat and humiliation; he kneels between her legs in a sexual pose. He falls and lies, a dead warrior assassinated by a warrior better than he; he is a supplicant and a would-be lover. This one verse [Judges 5:27] holds an entire story. The final twist and nuance of the tale awaits the last line, which nevertheless retains the doubleness of meaning. He is despoiled/destroyed. The woman Jael becomes not the object of sexual advances . . . and not the complacent responder to requests for mercy, but herself is the aggressor, the despoiler.[13]

Because of the sexual imagery in the Song of Deborah, some see the need to hypersexualize the rest of the text. Since the sexual inversion is so overwhelming in 5:27, that same inversion is read back into the narrative, treating the tent peg as a phallic symbol and the milk Jael brings as butter intended for use as a sexual lubricant.[14]

---

[13]Susan Niditch, "Eroticism and Death in the Tale of Jael," in *Gender and Difference in Ancient Israel*, ed. by Peggy Day (Minneapolis: Fortress Press, 1989), p. 50.

[14]Thalia Gur-Klein, "Sexual Hospitality in the Hebrew Bible?" *Lectio Difficilior – European Electronic Journal for Feminist Exegesis* (February 2003), http://www.lectio.unibe.ch/03_2/gur.htm.

This interpretation is tenuous at best. Sexual symbols are a modern conception of Western psychological and literary schools,[15] and butter as an element of foreplay in the Ancient Near East is without support.[16]

Modern commentators are not the only ones hypersexualizing the text. The Babylonian Talmud suggests that Jael's primary mechanism to lure Sisera inside the tent is sexual: "Rahab inspired lust by her name; Jael by her voice."[17] One Jewish thinker suggested that Jael was innocent and righteous in her interaction with Sisera: "That wicked wretch [Sisera] had sevenfold intercourse [with Jael] at that time, as it says, *At her feet he sunk, he fell, he lay*; etc. But she derived pleasure from his intercourse?"[18]

Nevertheless, without hypersexualizing the text, the author does use sexual imagery to convey a gender inversion between Sisera and Jael. Barnabas Lindars says it best when he notes the possible double meaning in the vocabulary of death and sexuality, but that the "primary intention of the narrative, and the subtlety of the dynamic irony is lost if the sexual overtones are overemphasized."[19] In other words, the narrator uses deliberately vague language both to convey Sisera's execution and suggest sexual interaction between Jael and Sisera.

Geoffrey Miller adds an additional gender inversion to the entire text. Arguing that the Song of Deborah represents a riposte — an insulting reply to another insult — Miller states "the insult that the Israelites are led by women — and, implicitly, that Israelite men are emasculated and feminine — is returned back to the Canaanites with a vengeance. Jael drives a tent peg into Sisera's skull, a violent parody of the sexual act in which the woman wields the phallic object and

---

[15]See Z. Bahrani, "Sex as Symbolic Form: Erotism and the Body in Mesopotamian Art," in *Sex and Gender in the Ancient Near East, Proceedings of the 47th Rencontre Assyriologique Internationale, Helsinki, July 2-6, 2001* (Helsinki: Neo-Assyrian Text Corpus Project, 2002), pp. 53-58, for the interaction between modern criticism and ancient sexuality.

[16]Gur-Klein cites a reference to Job 29:6 as having his feet "washed in butter" as indicative of sexual activity, but that text is better understood as Job's recollection of his prosperity than of his sexual satisfaction.

[17]*Megillah, Babylonian Talmud* (London: Soncino Press, 1938), p. 87.

[18]*Nazir, Babylonian Talmud* (London: Soncino Press, 1936), p. 84.

[19]Lindars, *Judges 1–5*, p. 280.

the man is feminized and raped . . . Sisera is condemned to the ultimate warrior's humiliation — to be killed by a woman."[20] Miller understands the Song of Deborah as an Israelite poetic polemic of national masculinity, mocking the Canaanites for a general who is clearly not man enough to avoid being killed by a woman. If truly a riposte, the song demonstrates the composer's deliberate utilization of gender for the purpose of asserting national pride.

Ultimately, it is Sisera's perception of women that proves fatal to him.[21] Perceiving Jael as a nurturer and possibly as a sexual opportunity places Sisera in the unexpected role akin to a vulnerable female. Because Sisera enters into Jael's presence with androcentric presuppositions, he falls victim to those same biases. His unexpected plight rooted in his own prejudices is what makes the narrative entertaining. Sisera's reliance on his stereotypes makes him easy prey for a female assassin with a tent peg.

5:28-31 Deborah's song makes a further satirical comment about the traditional gender roles in the final section. In 5:29 the wise women attending **Sisera's mother** speak to his delay at returning from battle. In increasing fear and denial, his mother agrees with her attendants and provides a mantra of excuses, centered on the army's loot of the spoil. The image Sisera's mother and her attendants use pictures the expected rape of war victims. רַחַם רַחֲמָתַיִם לְרֹאשׁ (raḥam raḥămāthayim lᵊrōʾš) is a "rare term . . . actually derived from

---

[20]Miller, "A Riposte Form in the Song of Deborah," p. 126.

[21]Considering the horrible implications for Sisera, Mordecai Levine ("A Polemic: In the Days of Jael: Reclaiming the History of Women in Ancient Israel," in *Immaculate and Powerful: The Female Sacred Image and Social Reality*, ed. by C.W. Atkinson, C.H. Buchanan, and M.R. Miles [Boston: Beacon, 1985], pp. 15-38) argues that the writer of Judges must be a female offering a polemic critical of rape. This perspective would extend, of course, to the narrative of Judges 19–21 as well. Even if a polemic were the intention of the narrative (which is doubtful), this conclusion fallaciously assumes that only a woman could be opposed to rape. Levine's suggestions once again reflect the modern bias that men in the ancient world were so homogeneously androcentric as to be unaware of their prejudices and consequently incapable of critiquing them. The narrator of Judges, however, wields the power of gender like an artist, penning subtle nuances rather than blundering scrawls. It stands to reason that the narrator of Judges understood the gender model of the day well enough to utilize it for literary purposes.

the word for 'womb,' and so might in ancient usage have meant something much coarser than 'damsel.'"[22] The NIV reading, **a girl or two for each man**, reads far more crassly in Hebrew. More literally, the text reads, "a womb, two wombs, to each leading man [head]." Sisera's mother also expects him to remember a gift for her as he sifts through the plunder (5:30). Sisera's mother expects him to fulfill the expected male role of conqueror and plunderer, but her expectations are overturned by Jael's actions.

Deborah's portrayal of Sisera's mother is filled with irony. Sisera's mother expects her son and his male army to capture and rape young women as the rightful spoil of their victory when it is Sisera himself who has been violated by a woman. "The spoils of war expected by the women in [Judges 5] stands in shocking contrast to the still lingering . . . image of the Canaanite general felled by the hand of a woman, lying shattered between her legs in a hideous parody of soldierly sexual assault on the women of a defeated foe."[23] Deborah's song exalts God and his people at the expense of their enemies. Israelite women, who were considered weak in the ancient world, are still more powerful than the most powerful Canaanite men. God specializes in negating power with weakness (1 Cor 1:27; 1 Pet 5:5).

From a practical standpoint, it is crucial for followers of Christ to be aware of and combat their inappropriate prejudices. Lurking in the background of the humorous account of Jael and Sisera are the dark undertones of bigotry and sexual violence. Prejudices invariably diminish other human beings who have been crafted in the image of God. And whenever prejudice objectifies a person, it also becomes easier to mistreat the victim. Rape and sexual abuse, slavery, torture, and most of human sin directed at others is rooted in the failure to perceive another person as being made fully in the likeness of God. Christians must be distinguished by their ability to reflect the heart of God, valuing and treating everyone equally (Acts 10:34; Gal 3:28).

---

[22]Alter, *Art of Biblical Poetry*, p. 46.
[23]Ibid.

CHAPTER 6

E. THE FIFTH JUDGE: GIDEON (6:1–8:35)

1. The Midianite Oppression of Israel (6:1-10)

¹Again the Israelites did evil in the eyes of the LORD, and for seven years he gave them into the hands of the Midianites. ²Because the power of Midian was so oppressive, the Israelites prepared shelters for themselves in mountain clefts, caves and strongholds. ³Whenever the Israelites planted their crops, the Midianites, Amalekites and other eastern peoples invaded the country. ⁴They camped on the land and ruined the crops all the way to Gaza and did not spare a living thing for Israel, neither sheep nor cattle nor donkeys. ⁵They came up with their livestock and their tents like swarms of locusts. It was impossible to count the men and their camels; they invaded the land to ravage it. ⁶Midian so impoverished the Israelites that they cried out to the LORD for help.

⁷When the Israelites cried to the LORD because of Midian, ⁸he sent them a prophet, who said, "This is what the LORD, the God of Israel, says: I brought you up out of Egypt, out of the land of slavery. ⁹I snatched you from the power of Egypt and from the hand of all your oppressors. I drove them from before you and gave you their land. ¹⁰I said to you, 'I am the LORD your God; do not worship the gods of the Amorites, in whose land you live.' But you have not listened to me."

6:1 The seven-year Midianite oppression against the Israelites is the shortest in Judges. The **Midianites** were descended from Abraham and his second wife, Keturah (Gen 25:1-2). The Midianites were not spiritually helpful to Israel, and God had commanded their destruction. In the incident in Numbers 25 a Midianite woman and Israelite man were killed by Phinehas for their idolatrous immorality.

The woman was not merely engaging in a sexual encounter — she was the daughter of the Midianite leader, likely sent as part of an effort to consummate Israelite and Midianite religions through sexual activity. As a result, God commanded the Israelites to treat the Midianites as enemies (Num 25:17-18). By the time of Judges 6, Midianite activity against Israel involves thee brutal exploitations of Israelite resources.

6:2 Verse 2 provides a window into the status of Israelite society during the early Iron Age. The Hebrews did not control fortified cities that were useful defensively — they were not firmly established and were too loosely organized. Consequently, when pressured by **Midian**, they were forced to improvise a defense by withdrawing to natural **strongholds**. The topography of Palestine provides many such areas to which small farming settlements might retreat and hide. The Israelites prepared **caves** and refuges in the rugged terrain by stocking them with supplies in order to wait out Midianite attacks.

6:3-4 The text indicates the malicious nature of the Midianite oppression of Israel. Rather than merely looting excess Israelite produce at the time of harvest, **the Midianites** invade the land *at the time of planting*. By camping on land that had been tilled and planted, the crops are destroyed, eliminating the Hebrews' livelihood. Further, any grain that the Midianites plunder is grain that cannot be used for planting.

Ancient agrarian societies needed adequate grain both to eat and to plant for the following year. Famine or plunder by enemies created a multiyear impact. In lean times, a minimum amount of grain is required for a subsistence-level existence. Any excess amounts are withheld for planting during the following season. If there is not enough excess grain to provide seed beyond subsistence needs, the following year's crops will be small, repeating the problem for the following year. Midian was apparently leaving Israel with a subsistence-level existence, annually looting the excess produce.

The Midianites also take Israelite livestock, eliminating the source of much of the Israelite diet and economy. Dairy, meat, wool, and labor were all provided by livestock, and their absence would make life much more difficult for the struggling Hebrews.

6:5 Another component of the annual Midianite invasion is the presence of **their livestock**. Not only did the nomadic group take Israel's livestock, they brought their own. The description offered in verse 5 compares their arrival to a **swarm of locusts**, covering and eating everything. The simile is reminiscent of the locust plague that struck Israel described by the prophet Joel. The image presented is one of an innumerable and irresistible force that sweeps the land clean. The meaning of the Hebrew root for locust comes from a word meaning "to multiply," an apt choice to describe the Midianite activity in the land. Livestock would strip the spring grasses from the hills, leaving little edible supply for any Israelite livestock managing to avoid Midianite detection and capture. In every way, the Midianite presence strips the land bare.

This Midianite behavior is particularly savage in that it does not care about the long-term effects of exploiting Israelite resources. Not only do their actions condemn Israel to immense suffering, the Midianite actions — even regarding their own self-interests — are shortsighted. By reducing the Israelites to a subsistence level, the Midianites will produce a diminishing amount of resources for their own future exploitation.

The Midianite model certainly serves as a negative example for the modern world. While God's provision through the earth he has made is limitless, it still requires stewardship to avoid depletion and maximize productivity. Part of the purpose for Adam's creation was to steward the environment in which he was placed (Gen 2:15). Similarly, part of Christian responsibility is appropriate stewardship of the environment in which we have been placed. While we rightly resist attempts by some to worship the creation and ignore the Creator (Rom 1:21-25), we honor God well when we gratefully demonstrate gratitude to him by caring for the gifts he has given.

6:6 The annual Midianite presence and exploitation quickly become too much for the weary **Israelites. Impoverished** and broken, they once again **cry out** to God for deliverance. There is again no mention of Israelite repentance, either here or after Yahweh's response in the following verses. Judges again elevates God's graciousness to his people. The Israelites are flawed and imperfect, and yet God loves them enough to respond in spite of their blemishes.

6:7-10 God's initial response to the people's cry is not to send a judge to deliver them, but **a prophet** who instead confronts them. In the midst of suffering, people desire both relief and comfort. When suffering is the result of sin, however, the cause itself must be treated. Unfortunately, the last thing the sufferer desires is to be confronted with his sin. God, however, does not play by the rules of theological decency to which we try to limit him. God desires to treat the symptom *and* the disease. When asked by his audience about a bloody injustice committed by Pilate, Jesus responds not with a message of comfort or hope, but with a challenge to repent (Luke 13:1-5). Because the Israelites are shortsighted, having forgotten their culpability in their own suffering, God gives them first what they need most: confrontation over their sin.

This appearance by a prophet to confront Israel is unique in Judges. Although Deborah prophetically announces and orchestrates God's deliverance, she does not challenge the people regarding their sin. Confrontation and conversation with God throughout the rest of the book is accomplished either through the angel of the LORD (2:1-3), or through an undetermined means, communicated through the simple formula, "The LORD said" (10:11). This formula allows for prophets, judges, or the angel of the LORD to be the source of confrontation.

The prophet's proclamation to the people provides fuller detail about God's activity than the angel of the LORD's speech in 2:1-3. Both speeches mention deliverance from **Egypt**, but chapter 6 includes the reminder about slavery the people experienced there. Chapter 6 also includes the components of God's protection and his active involvement in driving out the Canaanite peoples. The further Israel gets from the time of the Exodus, the cloudier their memory becomes. The cure will always be the voice of the prophets, calling the people to remembrance.

2. The Angel of the LORD Appears to Gideon (6:11-24)

[11]The angel of the LORD came and sat down under the oak in Ophrah that belonged to Joash the Abiezrite, where his son Gideon was threshing wheat in a winepress to keep it from the Midianites. [12]When the angel of the LORD appeared to Gideon, he said, "The LORD is with you, mighty warrior."

[13]"But sir," Gideon replied, "if the LORD is with us, why has all this happened to us? Where are all his wonders that our fathers told us about when they said, 'Did not the LORD bring us up out of

Egypt?' But now the LORD has abandoned us and put us into the hand of Midian."

¹⁴The LORD turned to him and said, "Go in the strength you have and save Israel out of Midian's hand. Am I not sending you?"

¹⁵"But Lord,ᵃ" Gideon asked, "how can I save Israel? My clan is the weakest in Manasseh, and I am the least in my family."

¹⁶The LORD answered, "I will be with you, and you will strike down all the Midianites together."

¹⁷Gideon replied, "If now I have found favor in your eyes, give me a sign that it is really you talking to me. ¹⁸Please do not go away until I come back and bring my offering and set it before you.

And the LORD said, "I will wait until you return."

¹⁹Gideon went in, prepared a young goat, and from an ephahᵃ of flour he made bread without yeast. Putting the meat in a basket and its broth in a pot, he brought them out and offered them to him under the oak.

²⁰The angel of God said to him, "Take the meat and the unleavened bread, place them on this rock, and pour out the broth." And Gideon did so. ²¹With the tip of the staff that was in his hand, the angel of the LORD touched the meat and the unleavened bread. Fire flared from the rock, consuming the meat and the bread. And the angel of the LORD disappeared. ²²When Gideon realized that it was the angel of the LORD, he exclaimed, "Ah, Sovereign LORD! I have seen the angel of the LORD face to face!"

²³But the LORD said to him, "Peace! Do not be afraid. You are not going to die."

²⁴So Gideon built an altar to the LORD there and called it The LORD is Peace. To this day it stands in Ophrah of the Abiezrites.

ᵃ15 Or sir   ᵃ19 That is, probably about ⅗ bushel (about 22 liters)

6:11-12 The enigmatic **angel of the LORD** makes his second appearance in Judges when he encounters **Gideon**. The nature of the angel has been the source of some debate. The grammatical choice would be to link the angel in 6:11 to the prophet in 6:8, making the angel merely a human messenger. מַלְאָךְ (mal'ak) simply means "messenger" and is used throughout the Old Testament to refer to both humans and supernatural beings. The prophet in 6:8 merely delivers the message with which he is sent.

The angel of the LORD in Judges and elsewhere seems to be more than human, however. The second option for the term is that it describes an angelic being. An angel would certainly account for the miraculous disappearance seen in 6:21 and his ascension in 13:20. But some additional details lead to the third and better option, that the identity of the angel of the LORD is that he is a theophany — a physical manifestation of God. First, people who interact with the angel of the LORD assume he is God. Gideon makes this assumption (6:22), as do Manoah and his wife (13:22-23). Their human assumption is not necessarily accurate theology, but it is a perception that the angel himself does not correct. Second, the text repeatedly uses the terms "angel of the LORD," "angel of God," and "the LORD" interchangeably, as if the angel is a physical manifestation of Yahweh himself.

The angel of the LORD is certainly not Jesus of Nazareth, but may well be a physical representation of the preincarnate Christ. The text does not focus on the nature and substance of the angel of the LORD, and it is wise to follow the lead of Scripture. What is important about the angel of the LORD is the same thing that is important about God walking the earth as Jesus of Nazareth: God goes far beyond what may be expected of him by providing his people with himself — his very presence in physical form as a comforter, confronter, challenger, and deliverer.

The angel finds the next judge and Israelite hero **threshing wheat in a winepress**. Gideon need not be understood as cowardly and hiding from his enemies. He is performing what by now is a common practice in Israel under the Midianite oppression. By stashing grain in a winepress, Gideon attempts to hide a portion of his family's produce from Midianite theft. Although more labor was no doubt required to keep food supplies safely hidden from Midianite eyes, the extra effort allowed the Israelites to survive the annual incursions.

The angel meets Gideon and gives him a two-part greeting. The first is **"the LORD is with you."** This powerful statement immediately suggests God's abundant blessing in any endeavor. Abraham and Joseph prospered financially (Gen 26:3; 39:2), Moses led the people from Egypt (Exod 3:12) and the Israelite hero Joshua achieved military success because of God's presence (Josh 6:27). The simple statement by the angel of the LORD both singles out Gideon for the task ahead and provides him the assurance that he will have the divine support necessary to accomplish it.

The second part of the angel's greeting is his reference to Gideon as **"mighty warrior."** The phrase lets Gideon know immediately that the kind of blessing he will receive is military in nature. God will deliver his people through Gideon's leadership as a warrior.

6:13 Gideon's response to the angel questions not Yahweh's justice in allowing the Midianite oppression, but his power. **Gideon** mentions the miracle stories accompanying the Exodus he has grown up hearing about but has never seen. Gideon claims that rather than using that power, God has **abandoned** Israel. Gideon is not trying to be obstinate. He simply has not personally seen the God of Israel demonstrate power superior to that of the Canaanite deities. Gideon will soon put God's power to the test in order to validate the power and authority behind God's commands. Gideon believes that either God does not have the power to deliver Israel, or he is choosing not to use it.

6:14 The angel does not bother to address Gideon's theological dilemma. He answers Gideon's question with the command to destroy the altar of Baal. The angel's implied answer is that the answer to Gideon's question should be self-evident. The people are suffering because they have abandoned the worship of Yahweh for the worship of idols. The altar to Baal on his own father's property should have come to Gideon's mind.

6:15-16 Like Moses, **Gideon** begins to rattle off a list of excuses as to why he is unqualified to lead. The best excuse he can muster is the significance of his family. Gideon was an Abiezrite, a descendant of Manasseh. He says that his clan is **weakest in Manasseh**, indicating a **family** that has not experienced the same level of population growth as that of the rest of the tribe. Similarly, Gideon's immediate family is the smallest in his clan. He expresses his doubts to God that such societal insignificance can translate into effective leadership. God responds by again emphasizing that he **will be with** Gideon, providing a partnership against the Midianites.

6:17-18a Gideon's doubts about God's presence and power among the Israelites is demonstrated again when he asks God for **a sign**. Gideon does not specify what the sign should be, but asks the angel to wait until he returns with an **offering**. At this stage, Gideon is content to allow Yahweh to determine the sign. Before long, he receives the specific sign he wishes to see. Gideon's doubt stems from the fact that he has never personally seen the miraculous acts of Yahweh. He has heard the stories, and he has even seen the results and the status of his people's presence in the Promised Land. But in the face of Midianite oppression, the testimony of older generations is not sufficient to satisfy his desire for faith. Gideon desires to experience the power of Yahweh firsthand, especially before committing to such radical activity as engaging the Midianites in military conflict.

6:18b Verse 18b uses the word LORD in place of the term "angel of the LORD." When Gideon proposes an offering, the God of the universe in human form agrees to **wait**. Gideon's preparation of the offering and God's patient waiting are both part of the sign that God will soon perform. Gideon honors God with an offering, and God honors Gideon by being willing to accept the offering and grant the request for a sign.

6:19 Gideon's offering is an appropriate expression of Middle Eastern hospitality. Considering the scarcity of resources due to the Midianite oppression, Gideon provides a particularly lavish feast of goat meat for his guest. He makes **bread without yeast**, allowing him to prepare the meal more quickly. Gideon completes the meal and presents it to the angel of the LORD **under the oak**.

Eliyahu Assis suggests that the location of the oak tree Gideon chooses for the presentation of the offering indicates that Gideon was thoroughly saturated with the Canaanite religious culture. The tree is often a focus in Baal worship.[1] If Assis's suggestion is correct, Gideon suffers from the same syncretism common in the rest of Israelite culture. While syncretism on Gideon's part is not surprising given the later apostasy for which he is responsible, it is not the driving force of Gideon's activity here. Trees are often the location for significant spiritual or political activities (Gen 21:33; Judg 4:5; 1 Sam 10:3; 1 Chr 10:12). Further, Gideon does not choose the tree as a location for the offering; the LORD himself comes to the oak and sits under it. Gideon merely meets him there. If anything, God is accommodating the syncretistic belief that trees possessed a spiritual significance. Within the pages of Scripture, God commonly reveals himself in pagan theological contexts. God used the expectations of

---

[1]Eliyahu Assis, *Self-interest or Communal Interest: An Ideology of Leadership in the Gideon, Abimelech, and Jephthah Narratives (Judg. 6–12)* (Leiden: Brill, 2005), pp. 37-38.

Egyptian theology to dismantle it through the Ten Plagues. In Acts 17, Paul utilized idols in Athens and Greek poetry as a foundation for the gospel. While God certainly expects accurate belief in worship (John 4:23; Acts 17:30), he repeatedly demonstrates his graciousness by accommodating inaccurate beliefs until such a time as truth can be learned.

6:20-21 The sign the angel of the LORD performs is twofold. First, God commands Gideon to place **the meat and bread** on a **rock and pour out the broth**. Gideon does so, the angel of the LORD touches the food with **the tip of** his **staff**, and **fire** springs **from the rock** and consumes the offering. The second sign God performs is his miraculous departure. The angel's arrival has been nondescript, as was his journey from Gilgal to Bokim in 2:1. In this instance, however, the angel "went from his eyes," suddenly disappearing from view.

6:22-24 Gideon has received the sign for which he asked. He is no doubt convinced by the signs, for he knows that he has seen God face to face, and is certain that he will die. Exodus 33:20 fueled the popular belief that such an encounter with God would result in a human being's death.[2] The fear of death after seeing God appears again in Judges with Manoah in 13:22. God reassures Gideon that his life is safe, and Gideon responds in worship by building **an altar** in his hometown.

3. Gideon Tears Down His Father's Altar (6:25-32)

[25]**That same night the LORD said to him, "Take the second bull from your father's herd, the one seven years old.[a] Tear down your father's altar to Baal and cut down the Asherah pole[b] beside it. [26]Then build a proper kind of[c] altar to the LORD your God on the top of this height. Using the wood of the Asherah pole that you cut down, offer the second[d] bull as a burnt offering.**

[27]**So Gideon took ten of his servants and did as the LORD told him. But because he was afraid of his family and the men of the town, he did it at night rather than in the daytime.**

[28]**In the morning when the men of the town got up, there was Baal's altar, demolished, with the Asherah pole beside it cut down and the second bull sacrificed on the newly built altar!**

---

[2]Cohen, *Joshua and Judges*, p. 210.

²⁹**They asked each other, "Who did this?"**

When they carefully investigated, they were told, "Gideon son of Joash did it."

³⁰**The men of the town demanded of Joash, "Bring out your son. He must die, because he has broken down Baal's altar and cut down the Asherah pole beside it."**

³¹**But Joash replied to the hostile crowd around him, "Are you going to plead Baal's cause? Are you trying to save him? Whoever fights for him shall be put to death by morning! If Baal really is a god, he can defend himself when someone breaks down his altar."**

³²**So that day they called Gideon "Jerub-Baal,ᵉ" saying, "Let Baal contend with him," because he broke down Baal's altar.**

ᵃ25 Or *Take a full-grown, mature bull from your father's herd*   ᵇ25 That is, a symbol of the goddess Asherah; here and elsewhere in Judges   ᶜ26 Or *build with layers of stone an*   ᵈ26 Or *full-grown*; also in verse 28   ᵉ32 *Jerub-Baal* means *let Baal contend*.

6:25-26 God has provided a sign of confirmation at Gideon's request and can now reasonably expect Gideon to obey his commands. The command for the evening is simple: using two bulls from his **father's herd**, Gideon is to **tear down** his **father's altar to Baal** and replace it with an altar to Yahweh. The cultic site is located on a high place (6:26), a common setting for cultic activity in ancient Palestine.

Of all the judges, only Gideon receives the command to combat idolatry. Other judges deliver the people immediately after being raised up as deliverers.[3] Unlike other judges, Gideon is not a trained warrior or supernaturally strengthened hothead.

Rather than thrusting Gideon immediately into military hostilities, Yahweh assigns Gideon a simple and seemingly safe task. The Baalic altar and **Asherah pole** Gideon is to destroy are located on the property of Joash, Gideon's father. Gideon knows both his family and Ophrah's inhabitants will oppose the destruction of the cultic center, but as the son of Joash, he likely hopes the repercussions to be limited.

The two bulls used by Gideon have not been taken by the Midianites, likely indicating the wealth of Joash's house as well as his influence and skill in resisting Midianite looting. Even so, the sacrifice of a bull represents an extremely costly act of vandalism.

---

[3]Assis, *Self-interest or Communal Interest*, p. 41.

God's command to sacrifice a seven-year-old bull may have little to do with the completeness of the number seven and more to do with the time Israelites have spent under Midianite oppression. The seven-year-old bull is as old as the term of subjection to the Midianites, and as such, it represents an ideal sacrifice. The beginning of deliverance is marked by the slaughter of the symbol of the seven-year oppression.

6:27 Intimidated by the unpopularity of his actions, **Gideon** opts to perform the destruction **at night**. He is undoubtedly aware that the **ten servants** assisting him will also compromise his secrecy. Nevertheless, Gideon obeys the LORD and leaves for the local worshipers of Baal a sunrise surprise.

6:28-29 Daylight in Ophrah brings the wrath of the residents. Not only have the Baal and Asherah cultic objects been destroyed, the site has been defiled by the construction of an altar to a competing deity. The use of the wood from the Asherah pole to fuel the fire of Yahweh's altar is symbolic of the living God of Israel's superiority and further insults the Canaanite deities. The Baal worshipers are not about to allow this act of blasphemy to go unpunished. The Hebrew text uses two verbs where one would do in order to emphasize that the Baal worshipers' investigation is meticulous. They probably apply enough pressure to enough people that Gideon's identity as saboteur is quickly established.

6:30 To avenge blasphemy against Baal, **the men of the town** show up on Joash's doorstep and demand that he deliver his **son** Gideon over for execution. Cohen suggests that the demand to **bring out** Gideon avoids the inevitable blood feud that will surely result if they captured Gideon by force. This view, however, overlooks the same "request" being made in Judges 19 of the man hosting the Levite and his entourage. An edgy mob feels it has the liberty to make a request, because the use of force is obviously standing behind the request.

6:31 Joash's response to the crowd is emphatic in the Hebrew, stressing the pronoun: "*You* will plead Baal's case?" Joash's challenge to the men of the town is not so much a delightfully clever maneuver as it is a response birthed from his strong personal faith in Baal. For those who would punish Gideon for the destruction of Baal's altar, **Joash** shrewdly places their faith at the center of their indignation. **Baal**, Joash argues, should be powerful enough to defend his own interests. The implication is clear: if Baal is a real deity, then Gideon will be adequately punished for his blasphemy. Joash's call for death to those who would harm Gideon forces Baal's followers to wait for their deity to act against Gideon. Baal is nonexistent, and of course can do nothing.

6:32 Joash's maneuver is perhaps the most theologically consistent response he can make, and it has the added benefit of preserving the life of his son. The incident is permanently embedded in a name change for Gideon. Gideon's name means "the hacker," a fitting name for one who cuts down idols and Israel's enemies. The Hebrew text indicates that it is Joash who renames his son **Jerub-Baal**, "let Baal strive." Gideon has been renamed as a testimony to the god Baal. When he drops dead, Baal is vindicated. As long as he lives, Baal either does not care or does not have the power to do anything about the blasphemy.

In his response, Joash refers to the altar as belonging to Baal. Schneider suggests that Joash distances himself from the altar, referring to it as **Baal's altar** when it was previously Gideon's "father's altar."[4] Schneider overlooks the nuance created by two different speakers. Joash is a worshiper of Baal, and as far as he is concerned, the altar belongs to the deity. In 6:25, it is Yahweh himself who refers to the altar as belonging to Gideon's father. God does not recognize Baal or his altar, but he does recognize the source of blasphemy and disobedience it represents. After having revealed himself to Gideon and validated his identity and power with two signs, God has commanded Gideon to begin the purification of Israel by starting at home. Leading God's people necessitates having the smaller arena of one's home in good spiritual working order (1 Tim 3:4-5).

4. Israel Battles Midian (6:33–8:35)

God Provides Assurance through Signs (6:33-40)

³³**Now all the Midianites, Amalekites and other eastern peoples joined forces and crossed over the Jordan and camped in the**

[4]Schneider, *Judges*, p. 109.

Valley of Jezreel. **³⁴Then the Spirit of the LORD came upon Gideon,
and he blew a trumpet, summoning the Abiezrites to follow him.
³⁵He sent messengers throughout Manasseh, calling them to arms,
and also into Asher, Zebulun and Naphtali, so that they too went
up to meet them.**

**³⁶Gideon said to God, "If you will save Israel by my hand as you
have promised— ³⁷look, I will place a wool fleece on the threshing
floor. If there is dew only on the fleece and all the ground is dry,
then I will know that you will save Israel by my hand, as you said."
³⁸And that is what happened. Gideon rose early the next day; he
squeezed the fleece and wrung out the dew—a bowlful of water.**

**³⁹Then Gideon said to God, "Do not be angry with me. Let me
make just one more request. Allow me one more test with the
fleece. This time make the fleece dry and the ground covered with
dew." ⁴⁰That night God did so. Only the fleece was dry; all the
ground was covered with dew.**

6:33 The tension in the narrative increases as the author describes a federation of powers gathering to oppose Israel. Gideon and
Israel have apparently already made overtures of war that elicit the
Canaanite armies. As Eglon did in 3:13, **the Midianites** combine
forces with the **Amalekites** to strengthen their military ability. **Other
eastern peoples** are also mentioned, culled from many of the semi-
nomadic groups in the Transjordan that had a grudge against Israel.

The location where the Canaanite armies gather is **the Valley of
Jezreel**. The area has long been referred to as "the battlefield of
Palestine."⁵ Deborah and Barak fought Sisera's army there, and
David will later battle the Philistines in the same location. Bordered
by Mount Carmel on the south and Mount Tabor and Mount Gilboa
to the east, the fertile plain provides a well-defined field of battle
with access routes for military forces. The level valley floor proved
useful for chariots, though only while it was dry, as Sisera discovered. The biblical stories are historically reasonable stories in part
because they are rooted in real geography.

6:34-35 For the second time in Judges, **the Spirit of the LORD**
comes upon the judge. The Hebrew verb used for "come upon" is
לָבַשׁ (*lābaš*), a word meaning "to wear." The text translated literally

---

⁵Cohen, *Joshua and Judges*, p. 213.

reads, "The Spirit of the LORD clothed Gideon."[6] Being clothed by Yahweh's Spirit is an effective metaphor for being enveloped and empowered by God himself.

As he does with Jephthah in chapter 11, the Spirit of the LORD empowers **Gideon** with supernaturally fueled leadership. Gideon blows **a trumpet** and summons **the Abiezrites**, his clan in the tribe of Manasseh. Four of the five tribes near the Jezreel Valley — **Manasseh, Asher, Zebulun and Naphtali** — are also recruited. The reason Issachar is not summoned is unknown. Issachar's territory borders the Jezreel Valley, and they would provide ready reinforcements. They may have been involved in other military activities in the unstable region.

6:36-40 Prior to engaging the Canaanite forces in battle, Gideon asks God for confirmation of his promise to deliver the Israelites. During his encounter with the angel of the LORD, Gideon simply asked for a sign, which God provided. In this instance, Gideon decides to specify the sign he wishes to receive from the LORD. Gideon asks God to demonstrate his sovereignty over weather by saturating **a fleece** with **dew**, leaving the surrounding ground dry. When God grants Gideon's request, Gideon, worried that he is pressing his luck, asks God to invert the sign by leaving **the fleece dry and the ground covered with dew**. God again grants Gideon this fourth sign.

The popular image of Gideon picking up a wet fleece from the threshing floor has long been embedded in children's songs and Sunday school lessons. The story is often presented as a prayer of a man of faith that is answered by God. Considered against the broader context of Judges' account of his life, however, Gideon's faith is less than stellar. Gideon "was not using the fleece to obtain guidance, but to confirm guidance already given . . . hardly a robust faith."[7]

Gideon asks for these two signs after the Spirit of the LORD has clothed him. While the Spirit's presence is temporary, and the text does not indicate Gideon was aware of the Spirit's presence and influence, Gideon has already encountered God and seen his power first hand. Even so Gideon feels the need to personally experience a supernatural verification of Yahweh's promise.

---

[6]The same terminology is used in 1 Chr 12:18 and 2 Chr 24:20.
[7]Jackman, *Judges*, p. 120.

The desire for supernatural confirmation runs deep in a society where pluralism dominates. Which deity should be believed and trusted? Which deity has the most power? Contemporary society differs little from the time of Gideon's day.

Unfortunately, signs seem to have little ability to render permanent changes in the lives of observers. Scripture is filled with stories of women and men who have been faithless after seeing firsthand some of God's most impressive miracles. After his victory over the prophets of Baal on Mt. Carmel, Elijah is able to command the people's hearts for an afternoon, but their loyalty exists only for the moment. Even Elijah himself seems to have forgotten the power of the victory as the text follows him running for his life in fear! The Israelites see the power of Yahweh over the gods of Egypt in the ten plagues and they walk through a divided sea only to wander away spiritually for the next four decades. Miraculous signs do not have a good record of producing faithfulness. Jesus said that a wicked generation looks for a sign. Jesus' rebuke of the religious leaders (Matt 16:1-4) is in part a criticism for demanding a sign when the available evidence is too obvious to ignore.

The request of a sign often represents a test — a challenge — to God. After all, a person has to acknowledge God to demand a sign *from* him. If belief is present, then a sign is not needed. If a sign is asked for, it is often a subtle challenge to God rooted in a stubborn heart.

There is no need to be unnecessarily harsh in the evaluation of Gideon. In a pluralistic, syncretistic culture, Gideon encounters the God of Israel. The works God has performed in history seem too good to be true, and Gideon wants a reason to choose Yahweh over the gods of his father. In his graciousness, God patiently reveals himself to Gideon as the deliverer grows in his faith. Similarly, modern ministry should diligently impart grace and patience to those struggling with issues of faith (Jude 22). Faith that is certain for some is often elusive for others. Fortunately, God is always perfect, even when our faith is not.

121

CHAPTER 7

4. Israel Battles Midian (6:33–8:35, continued)

Gideon Reduces His Army (7:1-8a)

¹Early in the morning, Jerub-Baal (that is, Gideon) and all his men camped at the spring of Harod. The camp of Midian was north of them in the valley near the hill of Moreh. ²The LORD said to Gideon, "You have too many men for me to deliver Midian into their hands. In order that Israel may not boast against me that her own strength has saved her, ³announce now to the people, 'Anyone who trembles with fear may turn back and leave Mount Gilead.'" So twenty-two thousand men left, while ten thousand remained.

⁴But the LORD said to Gideon, "There are still too many men. Take them down to the water, and I will sift them for you there. If I say, 'This one shall go with you,' he shall go; but if I say, 'This one shall not go with you,' he shall not go."

⁵So Gideon took the men down to the water. There the LORD told him, "Separate those who lap the water with their tongues like a dog from those who kneel down to drink." ⁶Three hundred men lapped with their hands to their mouths. All the rest got down on their knees to drink.

⁷The LORD said to Gideon, "With the three hundred men that lapped I will save you and give the Midianites into your hands. Let all the other men go, each to his own place." ⁸So Gideon sent the rest of the Israelites to their tents but kept the three hundred, who took over the provisions and trumpets of the others.

7:1 Gideon's forces assemble for battle and camp **at the spring of Harod**, south of the Midianite troops. Gideon has managed to amass an army of 32,000, a force of sufficient size to confront the Canaanite troops. God is aware that Israel may well be the winner if the two armies are left to themselves, and he is unwilling to allow that to happen. Yahweh wants to teach his people to rely on him rather than their own military might (Ps 20:7). Further, Israel has not personally experienced God's deliverance during Gideon's generation. God's involvement will be much more immediate for that generation after having witnessed it firsthand. Parents will be much more earnest about communicating God's saving activity to their children. In a sense, God refreshes Israel's experience of his deliverance periodically to embed a personal knowledge of him in their hearts. For Israel and for modern believers, the Gideon story supplements the many stories passed down through the generations, constantly reaffirming God's faithfulness to his people.

7:2-3 To prevent Israel from obtaining a military victory through numerical superiority, God commands Gideon to release any soldier **who trembles with fear**. The fearful are given the option of turning back and **leaving Mount Gilead**. Since Mount Gilead is located in the Transjordan, Cohen suggests that the term is an idiom for "slink away from the battlefield."[1] Two-thirds of the men leave, leaving a still formidable force of 10,000 ready to confront the Canaanite armies. The remaining troops likely represented a mixture of the courageous, the bravado-filled, and the dim-witted.

7:4 God decides that 10,300 is 10,000 more than he needs for his purposes, so he commands Gideon to move his men to a source of drinking water where he **will sift them**. The verb the NIV translates "sift" is צָרַף (*srp*), a term related to removing the impurities during the processing of precious metals. God will refine the army, removing soldiers inadequate for the task ahead.

7:5-6 God commands Gideon to **separate** the men who **lap the water with their tongues like a dog from those who kneel down to drink**. Only **three hundred men** lap the water from **their hands**, leaving 10,000 who kneel down and plunge their faces into the water to drink.

Discussion about the nature of the separation remains uncertain. Some suggest that the kneeling drinkers were the prepared warriors and the most timid drank by hand in order to keep watch. God then delivers through the most inadequate soldiers.[2] Others suggest the soldiers' lapping from their hands demonstrates alertness, making

---

[1]Cohen, *Joshua and Judges*, p. 216.
[2]Ibid., p. 217.

them the cream of the crop. Still others think that the three hundred
are the most reckless, too stupid to know their cause is hopeless.
The purifying terminology, though, implies a progressive removal of
impurities — God's selective refinement of the troops. Regardless,
the military capability and the character of the groups of 10,000 and
three hundred troops are irrelevant. The focus of the text is not on
what kind of men these are, but on the God who can produce a military rout with a mere 300 troops.

7:7-8a God informs Gideon that he will deliver the victory with
the smaller group of **three hundred men**. The larger group is dismissed **to his own place**, a term used to designate something's proper location. Gideon does not send the 10,000 home, but to their del-
egated **tents** at the camp. They are available for battle if needed, but
will not be utilized for the immediate mission.

Israel Defeats Midian (7:8b-25)

[8b]Now the camp of Midian lay below him in the valley.

[9]During that night the LORD said to Gideon, "Get up, go down
against the camp, because I am going to give it into your hands. [10]If
you are afraid to attack, go down to the camp with your servant
Purah [11]and listen to what they are saying. Afterward, you will be
encouraged to attack the camp." So he and Purah his servant went
down to the outposts of the camp. [12]The Midianites, the Amalekites and all the other eastern peoples had settled in the valley, thick
as locusts. Their camels could no more be counted than the sand
on the seashore.

[13]Gideon arrived just as a man was telling a friend his dream.
"I had a dream," he was saying. "A round loaf of barley bread
came tumbling into the Midianite camp. It struck the tent with
such force that the tent overturned and collapsed."

[14]His friend responded, "This can be nothing other than the
sword of Gideon son of Joash, the Israelite. God has given the Midianites and the whole camp into his hands."

[15]When Gideon heard the dream and its interpretation, he worshiped God. He returned to the camp of Israel and called out,
"Get up! The LORD has given the Midianite camp into your
hands." [16]Dividing the three hundred men into three companies,
he placed trumpets and empty jars in the hands of all of them,
with torches inside.

¹⁷"Watch me," he told them. "Follow my lead. When I get to the edge of the camp, do exactly as I do. ¹⁸When I and all who are with me blow our trumpets, then from all around the camp blow yours and shout, 'For the LORD and for Gideon.'"

¹⁹Gideon and the hundred men with him reached the edge of the camp at the beginning of the middle watch, just after they had changed the guard. They blew their trumpets and broke the jars that were in their hands. ²⁰The three companies blew the trumpets and smashed the jars. Grasping the torches in their left hands and holding in their right hands the trumpets they were to blow, they shouted, "A sword for the LORD and for Gideon!" ²¹While each man held his position around the camp, all the Midianites ran, crying out as they fled.

²²When the three hundred trumpets sounded, the LORD caused the men throughout the camp to turn on each other with their swords. The army fled to Beth Shittah toward Zererah as far as the border of Abel Meholah near Tabbath. ²³Israelites from Naphtali, Asher and all Manasseh were called out, and they pursued the Midianites. ²⁴Gideon sent messengers throughout the hill country of Ephraim, saying, "Come down against the Midianites and seize the waters of the Jordan ahead of them as far as Beth Barah."

So all the men of Ephraim were called out and they took the waters of the Jordan as far as Beth Barah. ²⁵They also captured two of the Midianite leaders, Oreb and Zeeb. They killed Oreb at the rock of Oreb, and Zeeb at the winepress of Zeeb. They pursued the Midianites and brought the heads of Oreb and Zeeb to Gideon, who was by the Jordan.

7:8b-12 God has already decided on the size of the Israelite company, and he now designates the timing of the attack as well. The predetermined outcome will be assisted by the darkness of night. God commands Gideon to attack the Canaanite camp. Gideon would reasonably be intimidated by the poor odds of attacking such a vast army with such a paltry-sized contingent. God, ever gracious, makes an allowance for Gideon's fear. God encourages Gideon to simply sneak down to the Midianite camp and listen in on enemy conversations, promising him that what he overhears will provide him with the fortitude necessary to attack. Sharing the brazen mission with his **servant Purah**, Gideon descends the hill toward the Midianite camp, approaching close enough to eavesdrop.

The Valley of Jezreel is covered with the federated army, described as being as **thick as locusts** — too numerous to count. Similarly, the enemy's **camels** — used to transport both the nomadic peoples and their goods — are as easy to count as beach sand. Their massive numbers dwarf the militarily irrelevant Israelite force.

7:13-14 In a divinely maneuvered encounter, Gideon and Purah listen in on a conversation in which a Midianite soldier relates a **dream** to his friend. The only dream occurring in the book of Judges is a prophecy given by God through a Canaanite warrior. As the two concealed Israelites listen, the soldier relates how a round **barley** cake barrels through **the Midianite camp**. The camp in the dream, symbolized by a **tent**, is **struck** and **collapsed** by the impact of the barley cake.

The friend immediately supplies an interpretation for the dream, limiting the meaning to Gideon's victory over the Canaanite armies. The friend also makes the theological statement that God will be the one providing the victory to Israel at Midianite expense. The Midianite forces would be aware of who Gideon is. **Gideon** is identified as **the son of Joash**, likely known for his role in the destruction of his father's altar to Baal and Asherah pole. Gideon is also the commander of the Israelite army camped out against them above the valley. The Midianites are unlikely to know that 22,000 troops have been sent home and another 10,000 will be sitting out the battle. With such a significant force, Yahweh might well upset the intended outcome.

7:15 The dream seems to be what finally removes all doubt for Gideon. The fire's consuming the offering and the disappearance of the angel of the LORD, the double sign with the fleece, and the fact that Gideon still has his head attached to his shoulders after destroying the altar to Baal should all indicate to him that God is powerfully on his side. Yet all of these experiences are inadequate to calm Gideon's uncertainty and unease. Gideon does not ask for this final miraculous validation, but God generously provides another sign to bolster Gideon's confidence.

The dream and the interpretation convince Gideon that Yahweh is directing the events and their outcome. His initial response is appropriate: he worships. The works of God — creation, miracles, redemption through his Son on the Cross — should always move the

Christian toward genuine worship. Gideon has not even returned to the Israelite camp before he expresses the praise God is due. Gideon finally believes that God alone controls the destiny of Israel.

7:16-18a By the time he arrives back at the Israelite camp, Gideon has his plan well in mind. He kicks sleeping bags and rouses his slumbering army, encouraging them with the LORD's deliverance of the Midianite army into their hands. He divides **the three hundred** troops **into three companies**, equipping each man with an earthenware **jar**, a **torch**, and a **trumpet**. The trumpets were collected from the company heads of the larger army after its reduction in size (7:8). The plan with which Gideon provides his men is simple: The three companies will surround the Canaanite camp, and follow Gideon's lead. A trumpet blow and a shout will result in the defeat of the Canaanite armies.

7:18b Gideon's cry of "**For the LORD and for Gideon**" need not be thought of as an attempt by Gideon to narcissistically link his name to Yahweh. Rather, Gideon likely took the dream he overheard at face value, and reasonably included his name in the cry. The sound of his name being shouted from multiple directions would cause further fear among the spooked Midianites, increasing their panic. Gideon overheard one man relate his dream, but many more Canaanite troops may have had the same or a similar dream. Gideon's identity as divinely appointed victor may have already saturated the enemy camp, linking the sound of his name to the dread of their imminent defeat.

7:19-20 Every viewer of a good bank heist movie knows that the best time to pull a job is when the guard changes shifts. The small force of **three hundred** has been able to move both quickly and stealthily, and the three groups take their positions **at the beginning of the middle watch**, about midnight. All three objects each man carries are unwieldy. The most likely scenario is that while moving into position, one hand carries the concealing jar and the other the torch inside. The jars are carried for the concealment of the light from the torches, not for the sound they make when broken. The sound of **trumpets** and shouting voices will be much louder and more sustained than any noise from the jars. The trumpets would be slung until needed. Upon receiving Gideon's signal, the jars are smashed on the ground, freeing up a hand to blow the trumpet.

7:21 Boling finds the battle to be a "contrived unreality," unwilling to accept that noise and light could cause a self-destructive panic among the Midianites.[3] Hamlin simply allegorizes the text finding a deeper meaning.[4] But such perspectives are unwarranted. The Canaanites are already edgy after the dream, and are nervous about their impending fate at the hands of Yahweh and Gideon. The noise of shattering pitchers quickly draws drowsy attention to the torchlight. Men quickly rouse from sleep at the sound of the trumpets and shouting, springing into action without the benefit of discussion, communication, and orders. Terror and darkness isolate every man from his comrades. As the Midianites assume that each torch and trumpet blast represents the leader of a separate company, wild panic sets in, and on a dark night with the only light supplied by the torches of the enemy, the Canaanite troops run aimlessly, their terrified cries adding to the noise and confusion.

7:22a In a company of thousands, each man panics under the weight of his own isolated terror. Individual survival becomes paramount in such a situation. Snatching up **their swords**, the Canaanite troops hastily and blindly hack at any perceived threat, condemning themselves to defeat. Working in the midst of the chaos is God himself, who augments the confusion and terror, causing these enemies of Israel to **turn** their swords on themselves.

7:22b Eventually, the defeated Canaanite army is apparently able to coalesce sufficiently enough to mount a retreat. They flee east toward the Jordan in an attempt to retreat to their home territories.

7:23-24a Israel's acceptance of Gideon's leadership over the tribes is demonstrated as his simple summons and command are followed.[5] The army of three hundred has performed the rout of the Canaanite forces. It will be the larger army Gideon has assembled that performs the cleanup: troops from **Naphtali, Asher, and Manasseh**. The fear has likely evaporated from fearful Israelite soldiers in the wake of the Midianite defeat, and Gideon is likely able to muster a considerably sizeable army.

7:24b-25 Gideon utilizes the same strategy against the fleeing Canaanites that Ehud uses against the Moabites. He summons the

---

[3]Boling, *Judges*, p. 147.
[4]Hamlin, *At Risk in the Promised Land*, p. 97.
[5]Assis, *Self-interest or Communal Interest*, pp. 83-84.

Ephraimites to capture the fords **of the Jordan**, preventing both the Midianites' retreat across the river and the possibility of any reinforcements arriving from the other side. The Israelites also capture two Midianite leaders. **Oreb** means "raven," and **Zeeb** means "wolf." Each leader is captured and executed independently of the other. The sites of the leaders' executions become "Raven Rock" and "Wolf Winepress," minor memorials of Israel's victory over Midian.

Judges 7 is a remarkable account of God's ability — and even desire — to produce success not dependent on human resources. We have the tendency to act as if God is only able to succeed when his people provide him with adequate resources with which he can work. Time, skill, money, labor, people, planning, and education are all worshipfully placed before the throne of God in order to accomplish his purposes. Human self-sufficiency, however, too often masquerades as God's provision and has the propensity to interfere with our perception of God's activity. While God is worthy of our best efforts at excellence, he does not need human achievements to fulfill his purposes.

The story of Gideon also traces God's immense patience as Gideon's faith gets up to speed. Gideon begins as the son of a Baal worshiper and ultimately becomes a confident warrior and worshiper of Yahweh. God works with Gideon to overcome uncertainty and doubt. God must experience delight as an individual increasingly perceives who he is. God reveals himself so that we might know him.

CHAPTER 8

4. Israel Battles Midian (6:33–8:35, continued)

Conflict with Ephraim (8:1-3)

[1]Now the Ephraimites asked Gideon, "Why have you treated us like this? Why didn't you call us when you went to fight Midian?" And they criticized him sharply.

[2]But he answered them, "What have I accomplished compared to you? Aren't the gleanings of Ephraim's grapes better than the full grape harvest of Abiezer? [3]God gave Oreb and Zeeb, the Midianite leaders, into your hands. What was I able to do compared to you?" At this, their resentment against him subsided.

8:1 When Gideon was assembling an army to fight against the Midianites, he recruited forces from the tribes whose territory was closest to the field of battle in the Valley of Jezreel. Gideon does not send messengers to Ephraim's territory, located south of Manasseh in central Palestine. As the Canaanite troops haphazardly retreat eastward, however, Gideon utilizes the Ephraimites to control the fords of the Jordan, allowing the larger Israelite army to perform cleanup operations against the scattered enemy army.

Ephraim, not recruited for the initial battle, is incensed and severely castigates Gideon. Part of the Ephraimite contention may be rooted in the fact that Gideon's actions have occurred on their turf.[1] Matthews makes the more reasonable suggestion that the **Ephraimites** are upset over the loss of plunder and the loss of honor.[2] Ephraim will later make a similar complaint to Jephthah in Judges 12, even though in that instance they had been summoned to battle and had ignored the call.

---

[1]Cohen, *Joshua and Judges*, p. 223.
[2]Matthews, *Judges*, p. 94.

The Ephraimite complaint is the first clear tribal confrontation in the book.[3] In the heat of the moment, the reader waits with bated breath to see how Gideon will choose to respond. After hearing his diplomatic and conciliatory reply, the Ephraimites, somewhat surprisingly, are easily satisfied and leave. This sets the scene for another narrative thread woven into the pattern of degeneration occurring in Judges. Tribal confrontations will happen again in the book, first with the Ephraimites in chapter 12, and then with the tribe of Benjamin in chapter 20. These next occurrences of tribal conflict, however, will not end so well.

8:2-3 Gideon assuages Ephraimite anger by taking a diplomatic approach. He points out to the honor-obsessed tribe that their contribution to the overall war effort has been greater than anything he has personally accomplished. Gideon compares his own military accomplishments to a full grape crop, while he compares Ephraim's capture of Oreb and Zeeb to the gleanings left for the poor after the harvest (Lev 19:10; Ruth 2:2-3). Gideon humbly plays to the ego of the offended tribe, asserting that Ephraim's unwanted leftovers are more valuable than the entire harvest of the Abiezrite clan. Gideon's shrewd response removes the motivation for Ephraimite reprisal, and the tribe gets over its indignation. Jephthah's response to Ephraim's indignation in chapter 12 will not be so conciliatory.

Demise of the Midianite Kings (8:4-21)

⁴Gideon and his three hundred men, exhausted yet keeping up the pursuit, came to the Jordan and crossed it. ⁵He said to the men of Succoth, "Give my troops some bread; they are worn out, and I am still pursuing Zebah and Zalmunna, the kings of Midian."

⁶But the officials of Succoth said, "Do you already have the hands of Zebah and Zalmunna in your possession? Why should we give bread to your troops?"

⁷Then Gideon replied, "Just for that, when the LORD has given Zebah and Zalmunna into my hand, I will tear your flesh with desert thorns and briers."

⁸From there he went up to Peniel[a] and made the same request of them, but they answered as the men of Succoth had. ⁹So he said

---

[3]In Judges 5, Deborah does criticize some of the tribes for their lack of participation, but no conflict threatens to erupt.

to the men of Peniel, "When I return in triumph, I will tear down this tower."

¹⁰Now Zebah and Zalmunna were in Karkor with a force of about fifteen thousand men, all that were left of the armies of the eastern peoples; a hundred and twenty thousand swordsmen had fallen. ¹¹Gideon went up by the route of the nomads east of Nobah and Jogbehah and fell upon the unsuspecting army. ¹²Zebah and Zalmunna, the two kings of Midian, fled, but he pursued them and captured them, routing their entire army.

¹³Gideon son of Joash then returned from the battle by the Pass of Heres. ¹⁴He caught a young man of Succoth and questioned him, and the young man wrote down for him the names of the seventy-seven officials of Succoth, the elders of the town. ¹⁵Then Gideon came and said to the men of Succoth, "Here are Zebah and Zalmunna, about whom you taunted me by saying, 'Do you already have the hands of Zebah and Zalmunna in your possession? Why should we give bread to your exhausted men?'" ¹⁶He took the elders of the town and taught the men of Succoth a lesson by punishing them with desert thorns and briers. ¹⁷He also pulled down the tower of Peniel and killed the men of the town.

¹⁸Then he asked Zebah and Zalmunna, "What kind of men did you kill at Tabor?"

"Men like you," they answered, "each one with the bearing of a prince."

¹⁹Gideon replied, "Those were my brothers, the sons of my own mother. As surely as the LORD lives, if you had spared their lives, I would not kill you." ²⁰Turning to Jether, his oldest son, he said, "Kill them!" But Jether did not draw his sword, because he was only a boy and was afraid.

²¹Zebah and Zalmunna said, "Come, do it yourself. 'As is the man, so is his strength.'" So Gideon stepped forward and killed them, and took the ornaments off their camels' necks.

ᵃ8 Hebrew *Penuel*, a variant of Peniel; also in verses 9 and 17

8:4 Gideon and his band of **three hundred** cross **the Jordan** in pursuit of Midianite troops that had survived the battle and had successfully retreated across the river. The Jordan River lies twenty miles to the east of the Valley of Jezreel over rugged ground. Four miles per hour would be a difficult pace over the difficult terrain.

The Israelite attack began near midnight, and the pursuers would have reached the Jordan by early morning after a tiring journey. The town of Succoth was located another twenty miles and another six-hour journey to the south. Gideon and his troops probably arrive at the city in the late afternoon, exhausted and not having eaten in nearly a day.

8:5-6 Gideon appropriately expects that the city of **Succoth**[4] will assist their fellow Israelites by providing a meal for his troops. The Midianite leaders **Zebah and Zalmunna** are still on Gideon's hit list, and their capture should provide the town sufficient motivation to assist. The leaders of Succoth are not convinced, however, that Gideon will be victorious. His ragged troupe of three hundred is pursuing a Midianite army of 15,000. **The officials of Succoth** respond, revealing their opinion about Gideon's slim chances for success. Because Gideon has not yet captured **Zebah and Zalmunna**, any assistance Succoth renders to Gideon will prove to be a liability if Gideon fails in his quest. The Midianites will surely punish any town that aids the Israelite judge. The leaders of Succoth are not about to take the risk, and refuse Gideon any assistance.

8:7-9 Unlike the leaders of Succoth, Gideon carries no doubts about his success. God himself will deliver the remaining Midianite leaders into his hands. Irate with the city officials, Gideon promises that he will use thorny bushes to **tear your flesh**. Gideon's bold retaliation will be rooted in his military success. He perceives his victory as giving him the right to punish these stubborn men so severely. Gideon similarly metes punishment when the city of **Peniel** denies him aid: he will **tear down the tower** stronghold of the city.

8:10 In the battle's aftermath, the Midianite army has been reduced to 15,000, a loss of 120,000. The army has fled into the desert area in the southern Transjordan, and is likely just as tired and hungry as Gideon's forces, but far more dejected. By now the Midianites are petrified by the name of Gideon, and the fifty-to-one odds against the Israelites will matter little in the upcoming battle.

8:11-12 Gideon's primary purpose is to decapitate his enemy's effectiveness by capturing its remaining leaders. Strategically, Gideon only needs to scatter the army enough to allow his troops a

---

[4]The exact location of Succoth is uncertain, probably located just north of the Jabbok River in the territory of Gad.

clear path to the two kings. He approaches the Midianite army **by the route of the nomads,**[5] taking them by surprise. Gideon captures **Zebah and Zalmunna** and returns to Succoth to keep his promise.

8:13-14 The entire narrative of Gideon at this point takes a turn as the judge begins to assert his newly established power. The city of Succoth will be the first to suffer. Nearing **Succoth**, Gideon captures a youth from the city. **The young man** is likely a trained servant of the city leaders, which explains his ability to write down the names of Succoth's leaders. The **seventy-seven** men are probably the family heads in the city, all equally culpable in Gideon's eyes for their stubborn refusal to support him in his divinely appointed task. Gideon and his troops, not easily resisted by a small town like Succoth, occupy the city and gather the leaders.

8:15 Gideon has delayed in killing **Zebah and Zalmunna** in order to present them captive as an object lesson to the leaders of **Succoth**. Gideon feels the need not only to punish Succoth, but also to validate his authority to do so. God has successfully provided victory over the Midianites, and the men of Succoth deliberately hindered Gideon's task.

8:16 The scourging Gideon delivers the leaders of **Succoth** is as humiliating as it is painful. Verse 16 says that he **taught** them **with thorns and briers**. The text does not specify what kind of an education Gideon provides. Presumably, the public scourging teaches the elders of Succoth the foolishness of resisting Gideon's authority.

8:17 Gideon intensifies the punishment at **Peniel**. His promise to the city was to tear **down** their **tower**, leaving them without a stronghold to which they could retreat in times of attack. Gideon not only tears down this defensive component of the city, he kills all the men. His actions leave the women and children of the town susceptible to the nomadic marauders in the area. Gideon has ensured the demise of the city.

Gideon has not yet completed the victory over the Midianites. He delayed the execution of Zebah and Zalmunna while he retaliated against Succoth and Peniel. Gideon's response toward the two cities seems to indicate that he has crossed a line from just punish-

---

[5]The current road of the nomads lies between the "SW spurs of the Havram and the broken hills in which the river Zerka has its source" (Cohen, *Joshua and Judges*, p. 226).

ment to revenge. "Gideon represents a paradigm shift where personal revenge becomes the prime motivation for subsequent leaders."[6] Revenge does not appear in Judges before this incident, but occurs several times afterward: Abimelech, Samson, and perhaps Israel's response toward Benjamin demonstrate a further decline in the spiritual character of Israel's leaders.

This incident is the first indication of Gideon allowing power to go to his head. By brutally chastising the leaders of Succoth and killing the men of Peniel, he begins the transition from fearful, reluctant servant of God to overconfident ruler. People take revenge when they believe they have the power to act. After Gideon's successes and his experience of divinely provided signs, it would be very natural for Gideon to assume his status gives him the right to retaliate against Succoth and Peniel. Sadly, his exploitation of his status and power will not stop with revenge.

The popular expectation of heroes is that their retaliation should be measured and appropriate — we desire our heroes to be *just*. Gideon's overreaction tarnishes his image as a righteous follower of God and relegates him to the much more human status common in judges: a flawed tool used by God for divine purposes.

Gideon's reaction to the two cities represents well the difficulty with revenge. God's exhortation against seeking personal revenge (Rom 12:17-21) is appropriate in part because human beings seeking revenge easily lose the ability to make a proportionate response (Jas 1:20). Cycles of revenge escalate, as bitter divorces, murders, inner-city gang wars, and tribal conflicts all attest. Christ calls his followers to think differently about responding to offenses. A believer can "overcome evil with good" by demonstrating love when the world expects revenge.

8:18 After Gideon exacts his revenge from Succoth and Peniel, the scene shifts to his confrontation with **Zebah and Zalmunna**. Gideon refers to a previously unmentioned incident occurring at **Tabor**. The two had been responsible for the deaths of an unknown number of men. Gideon asks the two kings **what kind of men** they had killed. The kings' mocking response indicates that they knew the slain men are connected to Gideon: they were, like Gideon, "likened in form to the sons of the king."

---

[6]Schneider, *Judges,* p. 124.

8:19 The men Zebah and Zalmunna had killed were Gideon's **brothers**. Gideon emphasizes that the men were the **sons of my mother**, specifying full-blooded relatives in relationship, not half-siblings. Scripture nowhere states how many brothers Gideon had, but at least some of them were dead because of the two Midianite kings. Gideon's desire to execute the men goes beyond the final act delivering Israel. Gideon in this instance is the avenger of blood (Num 35:19). As the closest blood relative, Gideon is responsible to kill his brothers' murderers.[7]

8:20-21 Gideon commands **his oldest son** to slay Zebah and Zalmunna. Having a youth slay the kings was intended to add to the humiliation in death.[8] **Jether**, however, is young and hesitates, emotionally reluctant to perform the execution. The two leaders begin to mock Gideon, challenging him to perform the execution himself. Matthews suggests that the two men preferred an efficient and quick death to the sloppy one that a young boy would deliver.[9] They may simply want to taunt Gideon. Their death is a certainty anyway, and their false bravado saves face. The text provides no elaboration as Gideon, without compunction or hesitation, steps forward and executes the two.

The text notes in verse 21 that Gideon takes **the ornaments** hanging from the necks of the two leaders' camels. These ornaments were the symbols of leadership, marking the authority of the kings.[10] Gideon will not be using the golden ornaments as a symbol of leadership — he has a different purpose in mind for the gold.

Gideon's Apostasy (8:22-27)

[22]**The Israelites said to Gideon, "Rule over us—you, your son and your grandson—because you have saved us out of the hand of Midian."**

[23]**But Gideon told them, "I will not rule over you, nor will my son rule over you. The LORD will rule over you." [24]And he said, "I do have one request, that each of you give me an earring from your share of the plunder." (It was the custom of the Ishmaelites to wear gold earrings.)**

---

[7]Cohen, *Joshua and Judges*, p. 228.
[8]Ibid.
[9]Matthews, *Judges*, p. 96.
[10]Ibid., p. 97.

[25]They answered, "We'll be glad to give them." So they spread out a garment, and each man threw a ring from his plunder onto it. [26]The weight of the gold rings he asked for came to seventeen hundred shekels,[a] not counting the ornaments, the pendants and the purple garments worn by the kings of Midian or the chains that were on their camels' necks. [27]Gideon made the gold into an ephod, which he placed in Ophrah, his town. All Israel prostituted themselves by worshiping it there, and it became a snare to Gideon and his family.

[a]**26 That is, about 43 pounds (about 19.5 kilograms)**

8:22 Gideon's success is significant in the eyes of the Israelites. He has not only delivered the people from the Midianites, but from an entire federation of Canaanite powers. He has performed this feat with only three hundred men. His position as judge has been designated and validated by Yahweh himself. In the elation of the moment the Israelites look to Gideon as a natural to fill the role of king. Their request carries significant implications for Gideon. Not only are the people offering him a kingship, they are proposing a dynasty — the opportunity for multigenerational power and significance.

8:23 Gideon wisely refuses the offer and instead advances Yahweh as the appropriate ruler of Israel. Gideon knows that a human monarchy is incompatible with the rule of God,[11] and for this moment, he makes the right decision. The temptation will later taint him, however, as he makes monarchical decisions, acting like a king.

8:24-25 Although Gideon decides to turn down the kingship, he is more than willing to exploit the people's good will toward him by requesting a cut from **the plunder** taken from the Midianites. Gideon specifies the plunder: a gold **earring** taken from the bodies of slain Midianites. The gold comes from the ears of **Ishmaelites**, a term seemingly out of place here. The expression is not a reference to a particular ethnic group, but more likely used to refer to a nomadic way of life.[12] The troops are grateful for their freedom from oppression and happily agree to Gideon's request. They collect about forty pounds of gold in the form of earrings for their leader.

---

[11]Assis, *Self-interest or Communal Interest*, p. 103.
[12]Cohen, *Joshua and Judges*, p. 229.

8:26-27 Gideon combines **the gold** he collects from his troops with the substantial amounts of gold taken from the trappings of the Midianite kings and the **purple** fabric from their robes to fashion **an ephod**. Ephods were garments worn by priests while performing religious service and occasionally worn by nonpriests (1 Chr 15:27). Exodus 28 describes the details for the construction of the ephod of the high priest. The completed garment worn by Aaron is an intricately crafted and beautiful garment. The total weight of gold adorning the garment Gideon makes is probably in excess of fifty pounds, making for a stunning yet heavy garment.

Gideon may have constructed the ephod as a victory monument, putting the captured gold and fabric on permanent display as a sign of victory and Yahweh's deliverance. If so, Gideon makes a poor choice of objects to construct. An ephod is expected to be worn by priests while receiving oracles,[13] and even though no one wears the ephod, it becomes the focus of religious worship. The people's gratitude to God and admiration of Gideon very quickly morph into idolatry.

Assis considers the worship developing around the ephod to be still centered on Yahweh, but performed in a forbidden way.[14] The law certainly provided specifics regarding the expression of worship, from which the people were not to deviate. In a violation of God's command in Exodus 30:37, the priests Nadab and Abihu were killed for their freestyle formulation of incense (Num 3:4). Gideon's ephod may well be intended as an imitation of — or even a replacement for — Aaron's ephod. The ephod itself, without a high priest to wear it and communicate God's will, becomes the focus of Israelite worship. Even Gideon and his family are sucked into the heresy.

Gideon's error, even though well intentioned, clearly reveals the danger of acting as a theological maverick. Ideas regarding God, how he is worshiped, and what he expects from his people should be viewed suspiciously when they deviate from Scripture and the understanding of the saints accumulated over the centuries. An interpretation held by only one individual is certain to be problematic. Both regular study and regular participation in a community of faith act as safeguards against rogue theology.

---

[13]Burney, *Judges*, p. 243.
[14]Assis, *Self-interest or Communal Interest*, p. 116.

The Death of Gideon (8:28-35)

²⁸**Thus Midian was subdued before the Israelites and did not raise its head again. During Gideon's lifetime, the land enjoyed peace forty years.**

²⁹**Jerub-Baal son of Joash went back home to live.** ³⁰**He had seventy sons of his own, for he had many wives.** ³¹**His concubine, who lived in Shechem, also bore him a son, whom he named Abimelech.** ³²**Gideon son of Joash died at a good old age and was buried in the tomb of his father Joash in Ophrah of the Abiezrites.**

³³**No sooner had Gideon died than the Israelites again prostituted themselves to the Baals. They set up Baal-Berith as their god and** ³⁴**did not remember the LORD their God, who had rescued them from the hands of all their enemies on every side.** ³⁵**They also failed to show kindness to the family of Jerub-Baal (that is, Gideon) for all the good things he had done for them.**

8:28 Gideon's defeat of the Midianites results in the group's permanent demise. While not completely destroyed as a people, defeat at the hands of **the Israelite**s leaves them far enough behind demographically that they will never again reach a significant enough population size to present a threat to Israel. The Midianites have been permanently **subdued**. **Midian** does not show up again in the pages of the Old Testament except as the name of a location or as a reflection on Gideon's victory (Ps 83:9; Isa 10:26). Gideon's victory over the Midianites removes the threat and preserves Israel's security for **forty years**.

8:29 To conclude the story of Gideon, the narrator switches to calling him **Jerub-baal**. The unexpected name change is the author's way of mocking Baal a final time. At the beginning of life as a judge, Gideon is renamed by his Baal-worshiping father Joash in a way that reflects a contest between Gideon and Baal. Gideon's new name challenges Baal to a confrontation. In 8:29, "Let Baal Strive" goes **home** in peace after having torn down Baal's altar and defeated Canaanite armies. In every way, Gideon is successful, and Baal has been proven impotent. Baal has striven with Gideon and has lost. The name "Jerub-baal" is now a source of pride for the people of Israel.

8:30 Gideon's life is summarized with several additional details. First, Gideon has **seventy sons**. Like Jacob's seventy descendants that migrated to Egypt, seventy is the ideal number from which to begin a nation and a dynasty. The judge Abdon and Israel's King Ahab are also described as having seventy sons or descendants (Judg 12:13-14; 2 Kgs 10:1). The possession of seventy sons reflects a royal and powerful status for Gideon. His legacy seems certain. Only treachery will later derail Gideon's dynasty.

The second detail of Gideon's life is his possession of **many wives**. Although the detail is obvious, the text presents the multiple marriages as the reason for Gideon's seventy sons. Polygamy generally foreshadows problems in the Bible, and Gideon's marriages are no exception. Abraham, Jacob, Samson, David, and Solomon all reap havoc in their personal lives and families because of their choice to maintain more than one intimate relationship. Gideon's family will be destroyed because of his polygamous choices, although he will not live to see it.

Polygamy, adultery, promiscuity, and divorce all run against the grain of human design (Mark 10:6-8). Difficult emotional development in the children of divorced parents, economic difficulties experienced by abandoned spouses, the objectification of women and men, loneliness, and guilt are just a few of the many struggles encountered by those who step outside the boundaries of monogamous relationships. Adhering to God's design provides the most freedom simply because it creates the most positive results.

8:31 The third detail that complicates Gideon's life is the **concubine** he maintains at **Shechem**. The concubine is legally his wife, though of a lesser status.[15] She lives separately from Gideon twenty-five miles to the south of Ophrah, likely with her family. The woman is significant because of the son she bears. Gideon names the child **Abimelech**, literally, "My father is king." Although God is occasionally referred to as "father" in the Old Testament (Ps 68:5; Isa 9:6; Mal 2:10), that is not likely the meaning intended by Gideon. Gideon has already made some regal decisions, and the name of his son represents one more. Gideon rejected an official kingship, but as a judge with seventy sons, he is a *de facto* king. For forty years, the people defer to his leadership. "My father is king" is a rather ironic name for a man who resists being made king to give his son, but may

---

[15]See the discussion of פִּילֶגֶשׁ (*pîlegeš*) at 19:1.

merely be Gideon's comment on the reality with which he lived. Regardless of Gideon's intent in naming his son, Abimelech will soon assume the role of king, and many will suffer.

8:32 Gideon dies **at a good old age**, literally, "With good gray hair." In his death, he joins some distinguished company. Only Abraham and David are described as reaching the grave in the same way (Gen 25:8; 1 Chr 29:28). From the perspective of Judges' author, Gideon dies as a significant figure in Israelite history and faith. His burial is described in typical fashion as occurring in the tomb of his father in his hometown.

8:33-34 Immediately after Gideon's death, the people abandon Yahweh in favor of Baal worship. The deity **Baal-Berith**, literally, "lord of the covenant," replaces Yahweh. Such a deity likely reflects the attempt to merge Baal and Yahweh. Such syncretism allows the worshipers to choose the best of both deities. Yahweh is all-powerful and delivers a special covenant to his chosen people. Baal seems more real — he can be physically seen, and his demands are simpler. The resulting divine hybrid is a humanlike god who graciously provides a covenant yet demands little from his people.

Not only do the people forget God, they forget the works that he has just performed. The Israelites take forty years of peace for granted, shuffling God to the side. Gideon is also forgotten. After all, at the time of his death, he was probably revered more as legend than deliverer. Four decades had passed since Gideon's exploits, and the people's ever-wandering appetites were just waiting for a new flavor of worship.

8:35 The text notes that the people fail **to show kindness** to Gideon's family, again referring to the judge as **Jerub-baal**. The author again expresses the people's shortsightedness and fickleness in their loyalties. Gideon's life and new name prove that Baal is powerless, and yet the people return wholeheartedly to idol worship. Memory and tradition have yet to become more powerful than immediate experience for the people. The continuing chaos ahead of Israel will be a harsh teacher.

CHAPTER 9

F. THE USURPER: ABIMELECH (9:1-57)

Gideon's son Abimelech should not be considered a judge. He is thoroughly evil, is never used by God, and does not deliver Israel. The Abimelech narrative is a continuation of the Gideon account. Gideon has been portrayed as an uncrowned king, and he has seventy sons to carry on his dynasty. The Abimelech story is bracketed by those seventy sons: Abimelech murders them, and then experiences divine retribution for their murder (9:56-57).

1. Abimelech's Conspiracy (9:1-6)

¹Abimelech son of Jerub-Baal went to his mother's brothers in Shechem and said to them and to all his mother's clan, ²"Ask all the citizens of Shechem, 'Which is better for you: to have all seventy of Jerub-Baal's sons rule over you, or just one man?' Remember, I am your flesh and blood."

³When the brothers repeated all this to the citizens of Shechem, they were inclined to follow Abimelech, for they said, "He is our brother." ⁴They gave him seventy shekels^a of silver from the temple of Baal-Berith, and Abimelech used it to hire reckless adventurers, who became his followers. ⁵He went to his father's home in Ophrah and on one stone murdered his seventy brothers, the sons of Jerub-Baal. But Jotham, the youngest son of Jerub-Baal, escaped by hiding. ⁶Then all the citizens of Shechem and Beth Millo gathered beside the great tree at the pillar in Shechem to crown Abimelech king.

^a*4 That is, about 1¾ pounds (about 0.8 kilogram)*

9:1-2 The text draws a distinction between **Abimelech** and his half-brothers. His brothers were born to Gideon's "many wives."

143

These wives possessed the higher status within the household, as would their sons. Jotham will later identify Abimelech's mother as a maidservant (אָמָה, *'āmāh*) in 9:18, an even lower term for her position among Gideon's many women. Jotham publicly implies that Abimelech is of lower status because of the lower status of his mother. Abimelech, however, although of lesser status, was apparently a member of Gideon's household. He goes *to* **Shechem** to promote his reign, and is easily familiar enough with his father's household to identify and murder his brothers.

Whereas Gideon seems to struggle with motives mixed between humility and the desire for dynasty, Abimelech shows no wavering in his ambitions: he clearly intends to install himself as king over the people and initiates a careful strategy designed to make him ruler of Shechem. Abimelech approaches his uncles and his mother's extended family in order to convince them of the desirability of his rule. With them on his side, he then enlists them to promote his rule over the rule of Gideon's dynasty.

Gideon's prominence and his seventy sons allowed him to control a significant area, including the region around Shechem. With his death, his sons continue to rule the territory. Abimelech presents himself as more closely related to the inhabitants of Shechem than his seventy half-brothers. Ultimately, he appeals to them based on their relationship to his mother. Native to Shechem and possibly still living in the city, Abimelech's mother becomes his link to a throne at Shechem. Her status as a native resident makes Abimelech a full-blooded Shechemite alternative to the rule externally imposed by Gideon and his sons.

9:3-4 Abimelech's family successfully communicates his appeal to the residents of **Shechem**, and they agree to follow **Abimelech**. Abimelech, half Jewish and half Canaanite, is preferable to Jewish rule by Gideon's sons. The city opts to fund the assassination of Gideon's brother and supplies him with **seventy shekels** taken **from the temple of Baal-Berith**. The source of the funds implies an official religious sanction for Abimelech's role and actions.

9:5 Abimelech uses the seventy shekels to hire **reckless adventurers** — literally, "empty men." The evil and shallow nature of these mercenaries is revealed by the low price — only a shekel — for which they will commit murder. Abimelech and his band of thugs capture

Gideon's sons and slaughter them **on one stone**. The single stone is probably not a site for official executions as Burney suggests,[1] nor does Abimelech utilize the location for some kind of perverted sacrifice. Abimelech never displays loyalty to any deity, and it is doubtful he does so here. The stone simply becomes notorious as the location Abimelech selects to complete the murders. Unlike the rock where Oreb was slain, the stone remains unnamed.

Gideon's **youngest son Jotham** hides and is able to escape undetected by Abimelech's henchmen. Jotham's escape has little relevance to Abimelech's takeover of the region. Jotham is the youngest brother and lacks any remaining family to support him in an armed retaliation. Abimelech's mercenaries provide the self-appointed ruler with enough power to intimidate that few are likely to immediately rise and oppose him. From the divine perspective of Scripture, however, Jotham's escape will prove fatal to Abimelech. Jotham will deliver a powerful curse against Abimelech and Shechem, and God will ensure that it is fulfilled.

9:6 The people **of Shechem and Beth Millo** gather at a large oak for Abimelech's coronation. The location was "a natural spot from which to proclaim a new king."[2] Abimelech has achieved his heart's desire, and it has only cost him the blood of sixty-nine men.

2. Jotham's Fable (9:7-21)

[7]**When Jotham was told about this, he climbed up on the top of Mount Gerizim and shouted to them, "Listen to me, citizens of Shechem, so that God may listen to you. [8]One day the trees went out to anoint a king for themselves. They said to the olive tree, 'Be our king.'**

[9]**"But the olive tree answered, 'Should I give up my oil, by which both gods and men are honored, to hold sway over the trees?'**

[10]**"Next, the trees said to the fig tree, 'Come and be our king.'**

[11]**"But the fig tree replied, 'Should I give up my fruit, so good and sweet, to hold sway over the trees?'**

[1]Burney, *Judges*, p. 271.
[2]Cohen, *Joshua and Judges*, p. 235.

¹²"Then the trees said to the vine, 'Come and be our king.'

¹³"But the vine answered, 'Should I give up my wine, which cheers both gods and men, to hold sway over the trees?'

¹⁴"Finally all the trees said to the thornbush, 'Come and be our king.'

¹⁵"The thornbush said to the trees, 'If you really want to anoint me king over you, come and take refuge in my shade; but if not, then let fire come out of the thornbush and consume the cedars of Lebanon!'

¹⁶"Now if you have acted honorably and in good faith when you made Abimelech king, and if you have been fair to Jerub-Baal and his family, and if you have treated him as he deserves— ¹⁷and to think that my father fought for you, risked his life to rescue you from the hand of Midian ¹⁸(but today you have revolted against my father's family, murdered his seventy sons on a single stone, and made Abimelech, the son of his slave girl, king over the citizens of Shechem because he is your brother)— ¹⁹if then you have acted honorably and in good faith toward Jerub-Baal and his family today, may Abimelech be your joy, and may you be his, too! ²⁰But if you have not, let fire come out from Abimelech and consume you, citizens of Shechem and Beth Millo, and let fire come out from you, citizens of Shechem and Beth Millo, and consume Abimelech!"

²¹Then Jotham fled, escaping to Beer, and he lived there because he was afraid of his brother Abimelech.

9:7-15 Jotham hears of Abimelech's coronation and climbs **Mount Gerizim** to brazenly proclaim a curse upon Abimelech and Shechem. Mount Gerizim is the location where the Israelites were to speak the blessings promised them by God for obedience. Mount Ebal was the location for the pronouncement of the curses (Deut 11:29). Shechem was situated between the two. Speaking a curse from Mount Gerizim is symbolic for Jotham — no trace of a blessing will fall on Abimelech or Shechem. The conspirators have acted treacherously, and the young son of Gideon utters a curse intended to bring guilty retribution.

Jotham introduces his curse with a fable structured around the central agricultural products of Palestine.[3] The fable follows trees as

---

[3] Burney, *Judges*, p. 273.

they seek a ruler. **The trees** approach three different producing plants, and all are valuable for their niche in an agricultural economy. **The olive tree** yields **oil** for anointing rulers and provides oil for lighting and baking, the **fig** yields enjoyable **fruit**, and the **vine** is the source of **wine**. The cycle repeats three times as the trees approach the source of produce to rule, and the fruit-bearing source rejects leadership as inferior to producing fruit. During the fourth cycle, the trees approach a useless **thornbush**. With nothing to lose, the valueless plant accepts the offer and places harsh conditions on the trees as terms of its rule.

Jotham's parable denigrates both Shechem and Abimelech's character as a leader. The people of Shechem are portrayed as unproductive trees, with nothing to offer that would entice a man of quality to lead them. Abimelech is the worthless thornbush, demanding and cruel. The words of the thornbush reveal exactly how Abimelech will treat the people he rules.

9:16-20 Jotham explains his parable in the second section of his speech. He addresses Shechem first, linking the curse he will soon pronounce to the city's motives. He sarcastically blesses the city and **Abimelech** with a mutual **joy** in their relationship if they are blameless in their actions. If they are guilty, however, Jotham calls for Shechem and Abimelech to destroy each other through **fire**. The metaphor of fire will soon become a reality for the people of the city.

Jotham is specific in his accusations toward Shechem. They have **made Abimelech king,** have **been** un**fair to [Gideon] and his family** in spite of Gideon's deliverance of the city from **Midian**. Jotham accuses the city of rebelling against Gideon and murdering his brothers. They have been more than complicit in the murders — they have personally funded the assassinations and rewarded Abimelech with a crown after he had slaughtered his half-brothers. Shechem is the killer; Abimelech is the murder weapon.

Many scholars suggest a disconnect between Jotham's parable and its moral. The fable promotes Abimelech's ambition to be king (8-15), while the second section calls for justice over Abimelech and Shechem's treachery (16-20).[4] The two sections, however, represent Jotham's unified response to the murder of his brothers. The parable explains the cruelty of Abimelech, and the curse presents the

---

[4]Assis, *Self-interest or Communal Interest*, pp. 141-153.

treachery of Shechem. The leaderless trees and the cruel thornbush deserve each other. The curse invokes their reciprocal annihilation — each will destroy the other.

Jotham's speech is more than just a public statement or criticism of Abimelech and Shechem. His words have been well thought out and are spoken in the belief that they will come true. The Hebrews firmly believed in the power of blessings and curses to shape the future (Gen 27:1-40; Exod 21:17). Jotham's words carry the force of a prayer which Yahweh is more than ready to answer. The curse prepares the reader for the divine retribution soon to be coming Abimelech's way.

9:21 After uttering his curse, **Jotham** flees to the town of **Beer**, a common Hebrew word meaning "well." His fear of his half-brother will cause him to live there until **Abimelech** dies. Jotham will not wait long.

3. Conflict with Shechem (9:22-57)

[22]**After Abimelech had governed Israel three years,** [23]**God sent an evil spirit between Abimelech and the citizens of Shechem, who acted treacherously against Abimelech.** [24]**God did this in order that the crime against Jerub-Baal's seventy sons, the shedding of their blood, might be avenged on their brother Abimelech and on the citizens of Shechem, who had helped him murder his brothers.** [25]**In opposition to him these citizens of Shechem set men on the hilltops to ambush and rob everyone who passed by, and this was reported to Abimelech.**

[26]**Now Gaal son of Ebed moved with his brothers into Shechem, and its citizens put their confidence in him.** [27]**After they had gone out into the fields and gathered the grapes and trodden them, they held a festival in the temple of their god. While they were eating and drinking, they cursed Abimelech.** [28]**Then Gaal son of Ebed said, "Who is Abimelech, and who is Shechem, that we should be subject to him? Isn't he Jerub-Baal's son, and isn't Zebul his deputy? Serve the men of Hamor, Shechem's father! Why should we serve Abimelech?** [29]**If only this people were under my command! Then I would get rid of him. I would say to Abimelech, 'Call out your whole army!'"**[a]

[30]**When Zebul the governor of the city heard what Gaal son of Ebed said, he was very angry.** [31]**Under cover he sent messengers to**

Abimelech, saying, "Gaal son of Ebed and his brothers have come to Shechem and are stirring up the city against you. [32]Now then, during the night you and your men should come and lie in wait in the fields. [33]In the morning at sunrise, advance against the city. When Gaal and his men come out against you, do whatever your hand finds to do."

[34]So Abimelech and all his troops set out by night and took up concealed positions near Shechem in four companies. [35]Now Gaal son of Ebed had gone out and was standing at the entrance to the city gate just as Abimelech and his soldiers came out from their hiding place.

[36]When Gaal saw them, he said to Zebul, "Look, people are coming down from the tops of the mountains!"

Zebul replied, "You mistake the shadows of the mountains for men."

[37]But Gaal spoke up again: "Look, people are coming down from the center of the land, and a company is coming from the direction of the soothsayers' tree."

[38]Then Zebul said to him, "Where is your big talk now, you who said, 'Who is Abimelech that we should be subject to him?' Aren't these the men you ridiculed? Go out and fight them!"

[39]So Gaal led out[b] the citizens of Shechem and fought Abimelech. [40]Abimelech chased him, and many fell wounded in the flight—all the way to the entrance to the gate. [41]Abimelech stayed in Arumah, and Zebul drove Gaal and his brothers out of Shechem.

[42]The next day the people of Shechem went out to the fields, and this was reported to Abimelech. [43]So he took his men, divided them into three companies and set an ambush in the fields. When he saw the people coming out of the city, he rose to attack them. [44]Abimelech and the companies with him rushed forward to a position at the entrance to the city gate. Then two companies rushed upon those in the fields and struck them down. [45]All that day Abimelech pressed his attack against the city until he had captured it and killed its people. Then he destroyed the city and scattered salt over it.

[46]On hearing this, the citizens in the tower of Shechem went into the stronghold of the temple of El-Berith. [47]When Abimelech heard that they had assembled there, [48]he and all his men went up Mount Zalmon. He took an ax and cut off some branches, which

he lifted to his shoulders. He ordered the men with him, "Quick! Do what you have seen me do!" [49]So all the men cut branches and followed Abimelech. They piled them against the stronghold and set it on fire over the people inside. So all the people in the tower of Shechem, about a thousand men and women, also died.

[50]Next Abimelech went to Thebez and besieged it and captured it. [51]Inside the city, however, was a strong tower, to which all the men and women—all the people of the city—fled. They locked themselves in and climbed up on the tower roof. [52]Abimelech went to the tower and stormed it. But as he approached the entrance to the tower to set it on fire, [53]a woman dropped an upper millstone on his head and cracked his skull.

[54]Hurriedly he called to his armor-bearer, "Draw your sword and kill me, so that they can't say, 'A woman killed him.'" So his servant ran him through, and he died. [55]When the Israelites saw that Abimelech was dead, they went home.

[56]Thus God repaid the wickedness that Abimelech had done to his father by murdering his seventy brothers. [57]God also made the men of Shechem pay for all their wickedness. The curse of Jotham son of Jerub-Baal came on them.

[a]*29 Septuagint; Hebrew him." Then he said to Abimelech, "Call out your whole army!"*   [b]*39 Or Gaal went out in the sight of*

9:22 After **three years**, the relationship between Abimelech and Shechem deteriorates. The relationship sours, the narrator notes, as a divinely produced hostility intended to result in vengeance against Abimelech and Shechem for their conspiracy against Gideon's sons.

9:23-24 The text claims that God himself is the source of animosity and division **between Abimelech and Shechem**. Yahweh sends **an evil spirit** to divide the two allies. A spirit sent by God that brings evil consequences is not unknown in the Old Testament. Such a spirit fuels Saul's dark moods (1 Sam 16:14) and attempts to lead Ahab to his doom (1 Kgs 22:22). In each of these instances, the spirit is a part of God's punishment — the evildoer has already been condemned, and the spirit God sends drives the wicked down the preordained path to destruction.

Abimelech is the first leader mentioned within Judges whose length of rule is mentioned independently of his benefit to Israel. He is not described as providing Israel with a period of peace, nor are any of the subsequent judges. As apostasy in Israel grows, so does societal anarchy. While God will use the later judges to strike against Israel's oppressors, seasons of peace will not be the result.

9:25 Shechem's insurrection against Abimelech begins when the city initiates a program to loot travelers passing through their territory. The rugged terrain surrounding Shechem provides multiple locations to station squads of bandits. By positioning lookouts on peaks, Shechem is able to effectively **ambush** travelers over a large area.

The text mentions that Shechem's banditry is **reported to Abimelech**, but it does not specify why their activity should be considered rebellious. Abimelech certainly controls more than Shechem, and the city's oppression of the surrounding area would cause other jurisdictions to question Abimelech's leadership and pressure him for relief. Shechem knows full well the consequences for their actions, and they deliberately create the difficult situation for their king.

9:26 Abimelech's competition for leadership is introduced in verse 26. The name **Gaal** is Arabic for a "small, ugly, or contentious person."[5] The Hebrew root simply means "to loathe." In his name is embedded the trouble he will be to Abimelech. Gaal and his clan move into the city and gain the popular support of the leading men of the city.

9:27-29 After the harvest and wine production season, a religious thanksgiving feast is held in the temple of the local deity. Cohen suggests that the celebration represents an open defiance of Abimelech by the people of Shechem.[6] The people **curse Abimelech** as part of the celebration. Gaal's remarks are not unrestrained words spoken by a drunken partyer, but a campaign speech by the city's new would-be ruler. Gaal is presenting his case for the rejection of Abimelech and for his own inauguration as king.

Abimelech's argument to the Shechemites for becoming king has become his own undoing. Abimelech previously convinced the city that Gideon and his dynasty should be rejected as foreign rulers. His mother provides his blood connection to the city, and they install him as king. When they finally get around to considering his father, Abimelech does not appear nearly as desirable. Gaal's rhetor-

---

[5]Burney, *Judges*, p. 278.
[6]Cohen, *Joshua and Judges*, p. 239.

ical question, **"Isn't he Jerub-baal's son?"** is rooted in resistance to Abimelech's half-blooded heritage.[7]

Abimelech has created the very environment in which he can be resisted and deposed. Abimelech is the one who has taught Shechem that undesirable rulers are disposable. He is simply the next in line to be ousted by an ambitious politician.

Gaal's speech concludes with a politician's bravado. He claims not only to have the ability to render Abimelech powerless, but to defeat his army as well. And like any foolish politician, he underestimates the opposition and assumes his own charisma will produce the desired results.

9:30-31 Gaal feels comfortable bragging, as long as Abimelech is out of earshot. **Zebul**, Abimelech's appointed ruler in Shechem, however, is not about to allow such an affront to go unanswered. He secretly smuggles a communiqué to Abimelech informing him of the situation. Zebul also provides the strategy with which Abimelech should respond.

9:32-33 Zebul proposes that Abimelech station troops around Shechem under cover of darkness. When daylight arrives, Abimelech should advance against Shechem and attack Gaal's troops as they exit the city. Zebul is certain that **Gaal** will leave the city to engage Abimelech's forces. He is certain because he will personally be the one to prod Gaal out of the city.

9:34-38 Abimelech follows Zebul's advice and stations his troops in **four companies** around Shechem. In the dim light of early morning, **Gaal** sees the advancing companies, but is uncertain. He attempts to verify his observations with **Zebul**, but the governor tells him the **shadows** are playing tricks on his eyes. Gaal continues to observe Abimelech's forces, and again tries to confirm their presence with Zebul. By now, Abimelech's army is positioned to attack, allowing Zebul to reveal the truth. Zebul mocks Gaal for his boasting. Gaal has publicly bragged that he can beat Abimelech, and Zebul challenges him to back up his boasting. This braggart has been cornered and goaded into a fight.

9:39-41 Abimelech's troops are able to force Gaal's men back into the city, leaving injured Shechemites strewn **to the entrance** of the city. Gaal's leadership has proven inferior to Abimelech, and his

---

[7]Burney, *Judges*, p. 280.

surviving followers are insufficient to maintain his status in Shechem. No longer hindered by Gaal's supporters, **Zebul** drives **Gaal** and his surviving clan members from the city. **Abimelech** lingers in the area, determined to reassert his power. Eliminating Gaal as competition is not enough for Abimelech. He wants to punish the city for betraying him.

9:42-44 The day after Abimelech's first attack, **the people of Shechem** return to life as normal as if nothing has happened. Without Gaal's presence in the city, the people believe they have nothing to fear from Abimelech. Abimelech plans to teach them otherwise. When he receives word that the inhabitants of Shechem are working in the fields, he ambushes them. One of Abimelech's companies positions itself between the laborers and the city gates, while the two other companies complete the pincer movement. Surrounded and without weaponry, the people of Shechem are easy targets for Abimelech's forces.

9:45 Having slain the day laborers, Abimelech shifts his focus to the city itself. Abimelech spends just one day annihilating the city. Because most of the population has been killed outside the walls, Shechem lacks adequate troops with which to defend itself. Without defense, the city is easily breached and captured. Most of the day is probably spent locating and slaughtering all of the inhabitants.

Large quantities of salt in the soil ensured "enduring desolation" for a community.[8] The surrounding land was rendered unsuitable for farming. The action would not prevent eventual resettlement, but would certainly limit the immediate resettlement of the area before weather and time had purified the soil. Sowing with salt was a "symbolic action, apparently intended to indicate that nothing thereafter was to live and flourish there."[9] The action demonstrated that the winner of the battle had achieved a permanent victory over the enemy.

9:46-49 Shechem apparently had two locations to which refugees could flee during armed conflict. The first refuge is a **tower**, which the people abandon after being made aware of Abimelech's determination. Believing the tower will not ultimately protect them, the people abandon the structure in favor of an alternative sanctuary.

---

[8]Cohen, *Joshua and Judges*, p. 243.
[9]Burney, *Judges*, p. 285.

The meaning of the word used for **stronghold** is uncertain. צְרִיחַ (ṣᵉrîaḥ) occurs elsewhere only in 1 Samuel 13:6. The word probably refers to some kind of excavated stronghold. This particular stronghold was attached to **the temple of El-Berith**, literally, "god of the covenant." The Canaanite deity was powerless to protect its followers. Abimelech and his troops gather timber, pile it around the opening of the stronghold, and light a fire. Heat and smoke inhalation kill the refugees. Abimelech has now repaid Shechem for their treachery against him, although the reader knows their deaths are divine retribution for their part in the slaughter of Abimelech's brothers.

9:50 Abimelech seems to take his newfound success as a warrior a little too seriously. With no provocation, he marches thirteen miles north toward **Thebez**, ostensibly to expand his rule over the area. He captures Thebez, again driving refugees into the city's defensive tower.

9:51 Judges again inverts the reader's expectations about gender in relating Abimelech's death. The author sets the scene for Abimelech's death at Thebez by noting that both **men *and* women** had **fled** into the tower. In the account of the attack on Shechem, only "the lords," בַּעֲלֵי (ba'ălê), are mentioned as fleeing into the El-Berith temple stronghold, an inner chamber within the tower.[10] The description of the victims of the massacre is expanded to include men and women in verse 49. When Abimelech mounts a similar siege at Thebez, men and women are mentioned as fleeing into the tower.

9:52-53 After capturing Thebez, Abimelech utilizes the same strategy against the tower stronghold as he did in Shechem; he gathers and surrounds the tower with fuel in order to burn the inhabitants. The narrator mentions that the inhabitants have taken refuge on the tower roof. The text singles out a "certain woman" who relies on an **upper millstone** and gravity. The millstone was the upper half of a handmill. Millstones were circular and could be a foot wide, several inches thick, and weigh as much as 25 pounds.[11] The certain woman drops the millstone on Abimelech, cracking **his skull**.

The only weapons the woman has are her ingenuity, her aim, and a millstone in her hand. These are hardly the tools of a warrior.

---

[10]Block, *Judges*, p. 332.
[11]Cohen, *Joshua and Judges*, p. 245.

By the time Abimelech steps up to the tower, the reader of Judges is well prepared for the inversion about to take place. The nonpowerful, nonskilled woman turns the tables and murders the male oppressor.

9:54-55 Recognizing his wound as fatal, Abimelech commands **his armor-bearer** to strike first, achieving his death before the head wound can do so. The armor bearer complies, but the narrative humorously taunts Abimelech in the background, because the reader already realizes that Abimelech's death has been caused by **a woman**, in spite of the *coup de grâce* from his attendant.

The only other example of would-be suicide-by-armor-bearer occurs when archers on Mount Gilboa heavily wound Saul. The command is similar — to kill with the sword — but the motive behind the request is different. In Saul's case, he is trying to avoid physical mistreatment at the hands of the Philistines — a common fate captive leaders were certain to suffer. Abimelech, on the other hand, is not concerned about his impending death. Rather, his concern rests with his historical legacy. In such a situation, a leader — especially a man named "My father is king" — might be expected to express concern over how conquests or characteristics might be remembered. Abimelech is self-centered, so it comes as no surprise that his interests in his death would focus on himself. Abimelech's concern, however, is not with the remembrance of his life, but with how the cause of his death is remembered. With his dying words, Abimelech seeks to control the propaganda that might spread after his demise. He commands his armor-bearer to kill him with a sword, **"so that they cannot say, 'A woman killed him.'"** Abimelech's biggest concern as he bleeds out is avoiding a historical stigma of being a man killed by a woman.

Abimelech is surely familiar with the story of Sisera and Jael. Abimelech's city of Shechem was located between Mount Tabor where Sisera was defeated and Bethel where Deborah prophesied. After the battle, the song Deborah composed surely made its rounds in the region. So the same gender inversion with which Deborah's song played also plays with Abimelech as he lies dying. Surely he thinks himself to be a warrior in the mold of Sisera. And surely he can see the parallels between Sisera's demise and his own. For the second time, the skilled hand of a woman fells a powerful warrior. It is his death at the hands of a woman that Abimelech acknowledges, but refuses to accept.

Ironically, Abimelech is remembered in the very way he tries to avoid. In 2 Samuel 11:18-21, in arranging Uriah's assassination, Joab prepares a messenger for David's response about the army's close proximity to the city wall during a siege. Joab anticipates the king's retort to be, "Why did you get so close to the city to fight? Didn't you know they would shoot arrows from the wall? Who killed Abimelech son of Jerub-besheth? Didn't a woman throw an upper millstone on him from the wall, so that he died in Thebez? Why did you get so close to the wall?" The author of 1 Samuel obviously sees the humor in visiting justice on Abimelech through the very vehicle in which he did not wish to ride: a woman's killing hand.[12]

Abimelech's concern at death reveals his prejudice. Only where women are viewed as unpowerful and unskilled in warfare would such a death as Abimelech's be a humiliation. His strong bias against women overpowers the desire for any other legacy. Abimelech's potential disgrace exists only in his own mind, yet he is willing to die sooner if it means saving face.

God's punishment of Abimelech reaches beyond his death. The pages of Scripture have enshrined Abimelech's self-perceived disgrace as a permanently mocking memorial of his wickedness. Abimelech has received retribution from God in the form he least desires: becoming a permanent memorial of a warrior who is bested by a woman.

9:56-57 The Abimelech narrative does not tell the story of a deliverer in Israel. If anything, Abimelech's life reflects an ill-conceived attempt to be a king. Within Judges, only Abimelech rules as a king.[13] One may wonder about the relevance of the Abimelech narrative. Abimelech is not a judge, nor properly a king. He is not righteous and he does not save Israel.

---

[12]Joab's remarks reflect the availability of Judges as a text during the writing of 2 Samuel. The connection may even indicate the link between authorship of the two books. The author of 2 Samuel makes a jab at Abimelech through what is by Joab's time a well-known story containing its own warning. The author of 2 Samuel likely had the Judges account at hand in order to make the statement about Abimelech being a victim of his own prejudice.

[13]Gideon may have named Abimelech to reflect Yahweh as the king, but Gideon's self-centered nature more likely made Abimelech's name an opportunity for self promotion. See Daniel Block, *Judges,* pp. 303-304.

COLLEGE PRESS NIV COMMENTARY

The story of Abimelech is rightfully seen as both a continuation of the Gideon narrative and a reflection on the lack of righteous leadership within Israel. Evil leadership can be just as damaging as the absence of leadership.

T.A. Boogart suggests that the narrative is about the theme of retribution,[14] and the last two verses of the chapter support that conclusion. **Abimelech** has been killed, and the only legacy he leaves behind is to be remembered for his own prejudices. **Shechem**, too, has been destroyed in return for its participation in the murders of Gideon's sons. The text treats the curse of Jotham as divinely delivered retribution, not just an angry protest. Jotham's curse has been prophetic, and Abimelech and Shechem have devoured one another.

The lengthy narrative is a testimony of God's faithfulness in judgment. Murder and injustice deserve to be punished harshly. Abimelech and Shechem receive what they deserve, delivered by the hand of God. Even in times of anarchy, God cares passionately about justice.

---

[14]T.A. Boogaart, "Stone for Stone: Retribution in the Story of Abimelech and Shechem," *JSOT* 32 (1985): 45-56.

CHAPTER 10

G. THE SIXTH AND SEVENTH JUDGES: TOLA AND JAIR
(10:1-5)

¹After the time of Abimelech a man of Issachar, Tola son of
Puah, the son of Dodo, rose to save Israel. He lived in Shamir, in
the hill country of Ephraim. ²He led[a] Israel twenty-three years;
then he died, and was buried in Shamir.

³He was followed by Jair of Gilead, who led Israel twenty-two
years. ⁴He had thirty sons, who rode thirty donkeys. They controlled thirty towns in Gilead, which to this day are called Havvoth
Jair.[b] ⁵When Jair died, he was buried in Kamon.

[a]2 Traditionally *judged*; also in verse   [b]4 Or *called the settlements of Jair*

10:1-2 Chapter 10 opens with two short records of minor judges.
Tola, the first, has a name that means "a dark red worm." His grand-
father and father are the son and grandson of **Issachar**. Although
Tola is from the tribe of Issachar, he lives in the hill country of
Ephraim, thirty miles south of his tribe's territory. The hill country of
Ephraim plays a prominent role in Judges. Mentioned twelve times,
the area is central to much of the action occurring in the book. Tola
is described as saving **Israel**, although the specific group oppressing
Israel is not mentioned. He is simply presented as leading Israel for
twenty-three years. His death is abnormal in that he is buried in the
town in which he lives and not in his home territory of Issachar.

10:3-5 Jair of Gilead is the next minor judge briefly mentioned.
Jair is a Manassehite from the region of Gilead, a region that will
also feature prominently in the upcoming Jephthah narrative. He
leads **Israel** for **twenty-two years**, and like Tola, the text does not
mention a particular people group from which he delivers Israel.
The most significant aspect of Jair's description is his family. Jair is

a significant regional power in the Transjordan area of Gilead. His **thirty sons** ride **donkeys** as a status symbol, and each controls a city in the region. As the patriarch of the leaders of thirty cities, Jair has access to significant military power through his ruling family.[1]

The Ammonites held territory to the east of Gilead and represented the most likely immediate threat. The thirty towns are designated as **Havvoth Jair**, or, simply, "Jair's Villages." Jair captured the towns during the initial Israelite settlement of the area and names the group of cities after himself (Num 32:41). After he dies, Jair is **buried in Kamon** in northern Gad. Both Tola and Jair are from Transjordan Gilead, the same place the action surrounding Jephthah will occur.

H. THE EIGHTH JUDGE: JEPHTHAH (10:6–12:7)

1. Oppression of the Ammonites (10:6-17)

[6]**Again the Israelites did evil in the eyes of the LORD. They served the Baals and the Ashtoreths, and the gods of Aram, the gods of Sidon, the gods of Moab, the gods of the Ammonites and the gods of the Philistines. And because the Israelites forsook the LORD and no longer served him, [7]he became angry with them. He sold them into the hands of the Philistines and the Ammonites, [8]who that year shattered and crushed them. For eighteen years they oppressed all the Israelites on the east side of the Jordan in Gilead, the land of the Amorites. [9]The Ammonites also crossed the Jordan to fight against Judah, Benjamin and the house of Ephraim; and Israel was in great distress. [10]Then the Israelites cried out to the LORD, "We have sinned against you, forsaking our God and serving the Baals."**

[11]**The LORD replied, "When the Egyptians, the Amorites, the Ammonites, the Philistines, [12]the Sidonians, the Amalekites and the Maonites[a] oppressed you and you cried to me for help, did I not save you from their hands? [13]But you have forsaken me and served other gods, so I will no longer save you. [14]Go and cry out to the gods you have chosen. Let them save you when you are in trouble!"**

---

[1]Schneider, *Judges,* p. 156.

¹⁵But the Israelites said to the LORD, "We have sinned. Do with us whatever you think best, but please rescue us now." ¹⁶Then they got rid of the foreign gods among them and served the LORD. And he could bear Israel's misery no longer.

¹⁷When the Ammonites were called to arms and camped in Gilead, the Israelites assembled and camped at Mizpah. ¹⁸The leaders of the people of Gilead said to each other, "Whoever will launch the attack against the Ammonites will be the head of all those living in Gilead."

ª*12* Hebrew; some Septuagint manuscripts *Midianites*

10:6 The next major judge section opens with a rather lengthy introduction. The introductory formula is present, portraying the people as doing **evil in the eyes of the LORD**. But in this section, the author expands on the idolatry of the people to encompass the entire range of Canaanite cultic theology and practice. Seven entities or groups of entities are mentioned, demonstrating Israel's total abandonment of Yahweh. "The number seven is probably typological, and expresses totality. It shows Israel as adopting foreign cults of all types, and the forsaking of God is more serious than in any other account in the book."[2] The list of deities is also arranged in order of their first appearance in Judges.[3]

10:7-9 God responds to the people's unfaithfulness by raising up a twofold source of oppression: **the Philistines** on the west **and the Ammonites** on the east. The text notes emphatically that the Philistines and Ammonites **shattered and crushed** the people *that year*. The pressure put on Israel by its enemies takes an immediate toll and continues for **eighteen years**. Whatever the influence of Jair's control in the region, Gilead is no match for Ammonite pressure from the south. Ammon also regularly crosses **the Jordan** River to attack the southern tribes of **Judah, Benjamin and Ephraim**. As the Midianites had done in Gideon's day, the Ammonite and Philistine marauders are quickly able to deplete the Israelite economy. Hamlin suggests that Ammon has had an interest in bolstering

---

[2]Assis, *Self-interest or Communal Interest*, p. 176.

[3]W. Richter, *Die Bearbeitungen des "Retterbuches" in der Deuteronomischen Epoche* (Bonn: Bonner Biblische Beiträge, 21, 1964), p. 16.

its trade interests by securing various east-west trade routes from Jericho to the west.[4]

10:10 In despair because of the suffering caused by their enemies, **the Israelites** cry out to Yahweh. Until now, the Israelites have not repented when they cry out to God, nor do they initially in this instance. They do not turn away from their idolatry until after God has rejected their pleas. The people have confessed that they have forsaken **God and serv[ed] the Baals**. Although the text makes no mention of the people's attempts at deliverance, it would be well within the pluralistic characteristics of Israel to seek deliverance from whatever source can provide it. A military solution is infeasible against the superior Philistine and Ammonite armies, and the ravages of oppression leave little in the way of economic resources with which the Israelites might pay a tribute and bribe their way out of trouble. The next logical step would be to appeal to the gods. From which god to seek help is the question. The Israelites hedge their metaphysical bets by worshiping a wide range of deities; Yahweh is one among many. As is the case for many in our modern era, God often represents the last resort rather than first. Israel has likely already appealed to Baal for deliverance by the time they seek out Yahweh. It is only after nearly two decades of failure by every other deity to provide deliverance that the Israelites turn to God.

While the polytheistic system in ancient Canaan accommodates the worship of a plurality of deities, Yahweh does not. God desires his people to worship him to the exclusion of any other deity. The people's confession acknowledges this reality by acknowledging what the reader already knows: Yahweh alone must be worshiped. While the people's statement seems on the surface like a heartfelt confession, the text carefully places their action after the wounded refusal of God to do anything for them. The people say the appropriate words, admitting their misplaced fealty to Baal, but they do nothing. Then as now, God is unimpressed with rhetoric unsupported by the action that springs from faith (Jas 2:14-26).

10:11-12 God responds to the people's confession with a history lesson. He recounts seven instances of deliverance and concludes with his unwillingness to deliver them again. The seven nations from which he has delivered Israel are symbolic of his perfect deliverance

---

[4]Hamlin, *At Risk in the Promised Land*, p. 109.

of Israel. Whereas the people have been completely faithless, God has been completely faithful. The list of "seven enemy nations may well have been intended to recall all of Yahweh's deliverances — not just those portrayed in Judges.[5] God claims to have reliably delivered Israel in its times of stress, and yet the people have not reciprocated with commitment to him.

10:13-14 Like a man suffering from the repeated unfaithfulness of his wife, God tells Israel he is finished delivering them. The emotional tone of God's response should be heard clearly. These words are spoken by someone who has received a stinging wound from one he cares about. God is appealing to more than the suzerain-vassal treaty reflected by Deuteronomy.[6] He is interested in more than holiness or religious fidelity. At the core of the God of the Hebrews is a desire for relationship with his people. Christianity easily makes the same mistake as the Israelites by relegating God to merely a discussion of his attributes or activities. God desires intimacy with his people rather than a mechanical exchange between a deity and his subjects, as was so often reflected in the religions surrounding Israel. And, like the Israelites, Christians seldom realize their capacity to wound God emotionally. Love cannot exist without a vulnerability to betrayal, and the immense love of God has often been cut deeply.

10:15 The people's statement in 10:10 mentions that they have sinned "against you," a phrase omitted in verse 15. There, they simply say, **"we have sinned."** In verse 10, they understand their sin as against Yahweh relative to Baal, but after God's rebuke, they realize their sin is much larger in scope. Idolatry has not been a misstep or misjudgment into which the Israelites have temporarily fallen, but a long-term lifestyle that Yahweh will no longer accommodate. God points out that the sin of the people is multigenerational and has become a part of the fabric of Israelite society. Their sin is a part of their identity, and a deeper problem than they can easily admit.

The people acknowledge God's divine right to treat them in whatever way he deems appropriate. The appeal to God for punish-

---

[5]O'Connell, *Rhetoric of the Book of Judges*, p. 42.
[6]Meredith G. Kline (*Treaty of the Great King: The Covenant Structure of Deuteronomy* [Grand Rapids: Eerdmans, 1963]) describes how Deuteronomy fits the structure of second-millennium-B.C. treaties between a suzerain (the ruler) and the vassal (the subordinate party).

ment may seem like theological hair splitting, since God's punishment often involves oppression by enemies. The perspective taken by Israel is similar to David's attitude after disobediently taking a census. When God offers David a choice of punishments, David resists his enemies as vehicles of that punishment (2 Sam 24:14). For both David and the Israelites, the direct but restrained application of God's hand of judgment is preferable to the unrestrained oppression of a human enemy. The free-will choices of an occupying power very easily will cause more pain than the choices of a merciful God.

10:16 After confessing God's right to punish them, with nothing to lose, the people ask for deliverance from their Ammonite and Philistine oppressors. They attempt to demonstrate their sincerity to God by abandoning their non-Yahwistic cultic practices. Hamlin suggests that even the removal of the idols does not signify true repentance on the people's part. "Many infer that Israel's confession (10:10b) and their removal of foreign gods (10:16a) reflect the genuineness of this, the first explicit instance of true repentance in the book. However the use of the same words in Yahweh's rebuke (10:12b-13a) indicates" that removing the foreign gods from their midst had simply become a routine activity in times of crisis.[7]

The text avoids stating that God is moved by the people's act of repentance. Instead, it is the suffering of the people he loves that moves God to action. Verse 10:16 reads literally, "and his soul was short with Israel's trouble." The phrase "short in soul" is used in the Old Testament to describe severe impatience and exasperation over circumstances (Num 21:4; Judg 16:16; Zech 11:8). God himself has become frustrated and impatient with Israel's suffering. Yahweh, as deeply hurt as he is by his people's betrayal, anguishes just as deeply over his people's suffering. While human disloyalty can affect God emotionally, so does human pain. God is not indifferent to suffering, even suffering caused by the consequences of sin. It is God's faithfulness and commitment to relationship that motivates him to act, even on behalf of those whose loyalty is unstable.

It is the statement in verse 16 about the LORD's unwillingness to allow Israel to suffer any longer that provides the segue into the Jephthah narrative. Jephthah will soon be introduced at the beginning of chapter 11, and the remainder of the text of chapter 10 sets the scene for his arrival.

---

[7]O'Connell, *Rhetoric of the Book of Judges*, p. 187.

10:17 The Ammonite empire to the east of the Transjordan assembles its army and makes camp against the Israelite army near **Mizpah**. Ben-Ammi, a son of Lot, was the father of the Ammonites (Gen 19:38). Because the Ammonites were close relatives to the Israelites, God forbade conquering their territory (Deut 2:19). However, by the time of Judges, the Ammonites are demanding the return of territory taken by Israel from the Amorites. The setting for the Jephthah narrative is in the Trans-Jordan area of Gilead, in the area of Gad and Manasseh. Ammon's territory is south of Manasseh and east of Gad. The sites listed as conquered by Jephthah are uncertain,[8] but it is likely that the twenty cities Jephthah captured are conquests of Ammon's western defensive fortifications.[9]

Ammon controls part of the King's Highway, the central north-south trade route through Canaan, allowing it to have a larger level of prosperity and power than other local political entities. The Ammonites are strong enough to cross the Jordan and pressure Israelite tribes in Cis-Jordan. This is likely due to Gideon's defeat of Moab, which "allowed Ammon to consolidate and rise to power."[10] Ultimately, the power of both the Philistines and Ammonites over Egypt is facilitated by the power vacuum created by the decline of the Egyptian empire, finalized by Tiglath-Pileser I's influence in the area.[11] Mayes suggests Judges 10 is an introduction to both the Jephthah and Samson narratives because both the Philistines and Ammonites are introduced.[12]

10:18 Needing symbolic and psychological leadership, the Israelite leaders in **Gilead** offer regional leadership to anyone who will **attack the Ammonites**. A successful attack is implied in the offer, since survival is an obvious prerequisite to assuming leadership. A promise of reward in exchange for military victory has already been seen in the case of Caleb's giving his daughter Acsah as a bride to Othniel for his successful conquest of Kirath Sepher (Judg 1:12-13). With the offer made, and an enemy to engage, all that is needed now is for a deliverer to step forward.

---

[8]Burney, *Judges*, p. 320.

[9]Benjamin Mazar, *Judges, The World History of the Jewish People: Ancient Times*, 1st ser., v. 3 (Tel-Aviv: Jewish History Publications; New Brunswick: Rutgers University Press, 1971), pp. 156-157.

[10]Ibid., p. 156.

[11]John Garstang, *Joshua Judges* (Grand Rapids: Kregel, 1978), pp. 329-331.

[12]A.D.H. Mayes, *Judges* (Sheffield: Sheffield Academic, 1995), p. 29.

The narrative of 10:6 through 12:7 is one of the major judge stories in the book. Chapter 10 lays the formulaic groundwork for the need for a judge: Israel's forsaking Yahweh, Yahweh's delivering them over to their enemies (the Philistines and Ammonites, in this instance), the people's repentance, and Yahweh's relenting and deliverance. The reader encountering this formula knows that a judge will be entering the scene shortly. Not to disappoint, Jephthah arrives in 11:1.

CHAPTER 11

2. Jephthah's Agreement with Gilead (11:1-11)

¹Jephthah the Gileadite was a mighty warrior. His father was Gilead; his mother was a prostitute. ²Gilead's wife also bore him sons, and when they were grown up, they drove Jephthah away. "You are not going to get any inheritance in our family," they said, "because you are the son of another woman." ³So Jephthah fled from his brothers and settled in the land of Tob, where a group of adventurers gathered around him and followed him.

⁴Some time later, when the Ammonites made war on Israel, ⁵the elders of Gilead went to get Jephthah from the land of Tob. ⁶"Come," they said, "be our commander, so we can fight the Ammonites."

⁷Jephthah said to them, "Didn't you hate me and drive me from my father's house? Why do you come to me now, when you're in trouble?"

⁸The elders of Gilead said to him, "Nevertheless, we are turning to you now; come with us to fight the Ammonites, and you will be our head over all who live in Gilead."

⁹Jephthah answered, "Suppose you take me back to fight the Ammonites and the LORD gives them to me—will I really be your head?"

¹⁰The elders of Gilead replied, "The LORD is our witness; we will certainly do as you say." ¹¹So Jephthah went with the elders of Gilead, and the people made him head and commander over them. And he repeated all his words before the LORD in Mizpah.

11:1 Judges 11:1 provides two pieces of information about **Jephthah**. The first description of the judge is that he is a **mighty warrior**. Literally "a mighty strength," the NIV appropriately chooses "mighty warrior" for the translation. The term can refer to individuals of significant social standing and wealth as well as to per-

sonal military prowess (1 Sam 9:1; 1 Kgs 11:28; Ruth 2:1). As will
shortly be revealed by the narrative, Jephthah clearly fits in the latter category. As a man of mighty strength, Jephthah represents the
typical hero expected by the reader. Although Jephthah throughout
the narrative displays an affinity for diplomacy and leadership
before engaging in conflict, he proves to be an able warrior.

The second description of Jephthah involves his lineage. He is
presented with parentage some consider a mixed blessing. He is the
son of the reputable man **Gilead**, and yet at the same time the son of
a prostitute.[1] His positive attribute, however, is that he is a "mighty
warrior." But Jephthah's parentage represents a more dubious lineage than a well-known father. A derogatory double meaning is probably intended at this point. Rather than being the son of a particular
man, the entire region of Gilead is probably being referred to.[2] In a
society where parentage signifies social status, Jephthah's father is
said to be all of Gilead, a rather crass way to indicate that because of
his mother's profession, no one knew who his father was.

11:2 Jephthah's uncertain parentage diminishes his status even
further when the offspring of the legitimate relationships within
Gilead refused to allow Jephthah an **inheritance** within the clan.
Jephthah is disallowed an inheritance in verse 2 by the entire community, not from their *father's* house but from their *fathers'* house, a
possessive plural. Jephthah should receive a share of inheritance as
his "father's" son, but no one is willing to allow an inheritance to be
passed down through his particular family. The community readily
acknowledges that Jephthah possesses Gileadite lineage, but no one
is ready to diminish their own wealth on behalf of a prostitute's son.

Jephthah's expulsion may also be related to an initial acquiring
of wealth and power. If he has gained status in the community, he
may well be able to assert a greater claim to an inheritance. Whatever the reason for his exile, the Gileadites treat their kinsman with
petty disdain.

Jephthah is apparently an older member of his generation, since
the text describes the legitimate children as needing to grow old
enough to drive Jephthah out of the area over the issue of inheritance. This is a slight reversal of the Abimelech story — Abimelech

---

[1]Assis, *Self-interest or Communal Interest*, p. 192.
[2]Burney, *Judges*, p. 308.

conspires against his brothers; Jephthah's brothers conspire against him. Unable to choose his parents, Jephthah becomes a victim of Gilead's prejudices against his maternal lineage.

11:3 Jephthah flees from his Gileadite relatives and **settle[s] in the land of Tob** (Good). There he is joined by a group of men the NIV has optimistically sanitized by describing them as "**adventurers who followed**" Jephthah. The literal translation is "worthless men gathered to Jephthah and went out with him." The NIV translates the same term referring to Abimelech's mercenaries as "reckless adventurers" (Judg 9:4). Jeroboam's "associates" in 2 Chronicles 13:7 are presented as "worthless scoundrels." The men with whom Jephthah forms community are not merely pioneers who enjoyed the outdoors; they are outcasts who live as thieves and mercenaries.

The implications of this blunt interpretation are uncomfortably obvious. Jephthah and the community surrounding him live nomadically, but their subsistence comes from the kind of enterprise in which worthless men engage. Raids and theft are a part of this community's way of life, likely committed with the ethics thuggery commonly possesses.

That Jephthah leads a group of bandits is unsettling for those who resist major imperfections in God's servants. First, it should be remembered that this is not the most significant of Jephthah's character deficiencies, nor is it the first or last occurrence of significant character flaws in God's servants in the book of Judges.

Secondly, while Jephthah built his wealth and reputation as a bandit, there is no reason to think that he preyed specifically on Israelites. While he certainly possessed a motive for revenge against the region of Gilead, the adjacent territory of Ammon likely proved a more attractive target. Repercussions from the Ammonites directly against Jephthah would be less severe and more difficult to enact against a mobile group. Part of the impetus for Ammonite pressure against Gilead may have been the irritation caused by Jephthah and his men. By exerting pressure against Gilead, perhaps the Ammonites hoped to force the Hebrews to solve their problem for them.

11:4-6 Having completed the introduction of Jephthah, the author returns to the arrival of the **Ammonite** army at Mizpah mentioned in 10:17. Faced by a daunting enemy, **the elders of Gilead** make their way to **Jephthah in Tob** in order to elicit his aid in the

upcoming battle against the Ammonites. Jephthah, having surrounded himself with mercenaries, has suddenly become a valuable com-
modity to the region of Gilead. Jephthah has troops that are ready to
engage an enemy, and the elders of Gilead offer him leadership over
the army. "That the elders of Gilead called Jephthah back from the
land of Tob so that he could lead Israel against the Ammonites shows
that he must have been an extremely capable commander."[3]

11:7 Jephthah presents a legitimate complaint to Gilead's leaders.
They actively drove Jephthah from his home and yet are willing to
seek his assistance in desperate times. His response to the elders is
similar to Isaac's response to Abimelech in Genesis 26:27. After being
sent away, the power the exile amasses becomes both a threat and an
asset to the ones doing the exiling. Both Isaac and Jephthah are better allies than enemies. In Jephthah's case, it is ironic that the very elders begging Jephthah for help are the ones who could have intervened
to prevent his earlier expulsion at the hands of his brothers.

11:8 The elders seemingly ignore the question concerning their
previous injustice, but they have come fully prepared to bargain with
Jephthah. In return for leading the military against Ammon and providing troops, **the elders of Gilead** are prepared to offer Jephthah
leadership over the entire region.

The offer of rule to Jephthah may merely be a ploy by the
Gileadite elders to eliminate two problems at once. The entire
region of Gilead is surely not without resources, and Jephthah's
troops could hardly have supplemented the Gileadite forces enor-
mously. If Jephthah's banditry is causing Ammonite pressure on
Gilead, or if Jephthah's activities are taken directly against Gilead,
the elders may simply have been trying to ensure that two enemies
(both the Ammonites and Jephthah's forces) would be sufficiently
depleted enough to ensure Gilead's survival in the conflict.

11:9-11 Jephthah is not an idiot and verifies the elders' promise
by eliciting an oath. He realizes there are really two conditions necessary to claim leadership over Gilead — fighting and victory.
Jephthah cannot assume leadership if he fails and is killed in battle.
The elders swear, by Yahweh, a serious oath considered to bind
them under the very nature and name of God. But for all Jephthah's
problems, he demonstrates a simple faith in Yahweh. Any victory

---

[3]Goslinga, *Joshua, Judges, Ruth*, p. 381.

achieved against the Ammonites will be the result of God's provision. Assuming that God will be on his side as a deliverer, Jephthah accepts the offer too good to refuse.

Verse 11:11b presents Jephthah as repeating **all his words before the LORD at Mizpah**. What words are being referred to? Jephthah has only spoken in his dialogue with the elders of Gilead. There would be no need to repeat this conversation to God. What Jephthah likely repeats to God is the vow he takes in verses 29-31. Verses 12-31 are the expanded account of 11b, describing Jephthah's journey that culminates with the vow to the LORD at Mizpah.

3. Jephthah Attempts Diplomacy (11:12-28)

¹²**Then Jephthah sent messengers to the Ammonite king with the question: "What do you have against us that you have attacked our country?"**

¹³**The king of the Ammonites answered Jephthah's messengers, "When Israel came up out of Egypt, they took away my land from the Arnon to the Jabbok, all the way to the Jordan. Now give it back peaceably."**

¹⁴**Jephthah sent back messengers to the Ammonite king,** ¹⁵**saying:**

"This is what Jephthah says: Israel did not take the land of Moab or the land of the Ammonites. ¹⁶**But when they came up out of Egypt, Israel went through the desert to the Red Sea**ᵃ **and on to Kadesh.** ¹⁷**Then Israel sent messengers to the king of Edom, saying, 'Give us permission to go through your country,' but the king of Edom would not listen. They sent also to the king of Moab, and he refused. So Israel stayed at Kadesh.**

¹⁸**"Next they traveled through the desert, skirted the lands of Edom and Moab, passed along the eastern side of the country of Moab, and camped on the other side of the Arnon. They did not enter the territory of Moab, for the Arnon was its border.**

¹⁹**"Then Israel sent messengers to Sihon king of the Amorites, who ruled in Heshbon, and said to him, 'Let us pass through your country to our own place.'** ²⁰**Sihon, however, did not trust Israel**ᵇ **to pass through his territory. He mustered all his men and encamped at Jahaz and fought with Israel.**

²¹**"Then the LORD, the God of Israel, gave Sihon and all his**

men into Israel's hands, and they defeated them. Israel took over all the land of the Amorites who lived in that country, ²²capturing all of it from the Arnon to the Jabbok and from the desert to the Jordan.

²³"Now since the LORD, the God of Israel, has driven the Amorites out before his people Israel, what right have you to take it over? ²⁴Will you not take what your god Chemosh gives you? Likewise, whatever the LORD our God has given us, we will possess. ²⁵Are you better than Balak son of Zippor, king of Moab? Did he ever quarrel with Israel or fight with them? ²⁶For three hundred years Israel occupied Heshbon, Aroer, the surrounding settlements and all the towns along the Arnon. Why didn't you retake them during that time? ²⁷I have not wronged you, but you are doing me wrong by waging war against me. Let the LORD, the Judge,ᶜ decide the dispute this day between the Israelites and the Ammonites."

²⁸The king of Ammon, however, paid no attention to the message Jephthah sent him.

ᵃ16 Hebrew *Yam Suph*; that is, Sea of Reeds   ᵇ20 Or *however, would not make an agreement for Israel*   ᶜ27 Or *Ruler*

11:12 Jephthah initially attempts diplomacy to resolve the dispute with Ammon. While some have suggested Jephthah is a wise diplomat for attempting to negotiate with the king of Ammon, others have understood his negotiations as a shrewd, stalling tactic or as an attempt to goad Ammon into a fight.

Appealing directly to the king, Jephthah dispatches messengers to Ammon in order to ask for a defense of Ammon's imminent attack against Israel. Jephthah's comments to the Ammonite King take the form of actual royal covenant disputations used in the Ancient Near East. The royal disputer form included a summons to dispute, accusation toward the offender and defense of alleged wrongs by the offended, and an ultimatum.[4]

11:13 The Ammonite **king** replies with a history lesson, presented from the Ammonite perspective. During the Exodus, Israel captured an 800-square-mile swath of land in the Transjordan.[5] This

---

[4]O'Connell, *Rhetoric of the Book of Judges*, pp. 193-200.

capture of land mitigated Ammon to the less productive desert area to the east. Ammon is interested in reclaiming land that had been uncontestedly theirs prior to the Israelite arrival.

11:14-22 The Israelite perspective of history differs, of course, and Jephthah readily counters with a different version of history. Jephthah's version does not change the details of Israel's possession of the Transjordan; rather, it adds additional details and provides the crucial divine perspective with which Ammon will have difficulty arguing. Since the Ammonites were inhospitable to the Israelites after the Exodus, Yahweh drove the Ammonites out of their own land and gave it to the Israelites. The interjection of Moab into the discussion has caused scholars some uncertainty. Likely, the "king of Ammon was claiming Moabite territory which had been conquered by the Amorites before passing into Israel's possession."[6]

Jephthah's long recount is designed to demonstrate two realities to the Ammonites. First, Ammon needs to understand that during the Exodus, the Israelites went out of their way to accommodate Ammonite sovereignty. While Israel possessed the military capacity to remove Ammon forcibly from its territory, they merely requested passage through Ammon. Ammon refused and attacked Israel, and Israel appropriately abandoned courtesy and implemented a military solution. The second and more significant fact that shaped the reality of the two nations is the power of their gods. Israel defeats Ammon because Yahweh is more powerful than the Ammonite god Molech. The real battle that Ammon loses is theological, and Jephthah claims a divine right for Israel's presence in the Transjordan (Judg 11:23).

11:23-24 Jephthah makes a subtle dig at Ammonite theology when he suggests that Ammonite territory represents the limits of the sovereignty of **Chemosh** in 11:24. His exhortation to trust in Chemosh is a sarcastic statement that demeans Chemosh as an impotent deity.

Jephthah's reference to Chemosh remains puzzling. Jephthah sarcastically encourages the king of Ammon to appeal to the Moabite god Chemosh, not to Ammon's national deity, Molech. The *BHS* attempts to correct this difficulty by suggesting the reading of

[5]Burney, *Judges*, p. 310.
[6]Cohen, *Joshua and Judges*, p. 253.

מוֹאָב (Mô'āb) in this instance and throughout the chapter as opposed
to עַמּוֹן ('Ammôn). One solution suggests that Jephthah is actually
interacting with the Moabites as well, but the territory of Jephthah's
activities suggests Ammon is the focus and location of his efforts.
Goslinga solves the dilemma by suggesting the Ammonites had previously conquered the Moabite territory, adopting the deity of the
area.[7] It is not unreasonable to expect the Ammonites to have suffered from the same religious pluralism as the Israelites. Especially in
the face of a defeat by Yahweh, the Ammonites may be more willing
to explore theological alternatives to the powerless Molech.

11:25-27 Jephthah's final assertion is that Ammon has failed to
act before now. Ammon has tacitly accepted Israel's presence because
they have been unwilling to do anything about it. The land in the
Transjordan is effectively Israelite, making Ammon's attempted re-
possession unjust.

11:28 The Ammonites, of course, disagree with Jephthah's evaluation of the state of affairs and ignore his message.

4. Israel Defeats Ammon (11:29-33)

[29]**Then the Spirit of the LORD came upon Jephthah. He crossed
Gilead and Manasseh, passed through Mizpah of Gilead, and from
there he advanced against the Ammonites.** [30]**And Jephthah made a
vow to the LORD: "If you give the Ammonites into my hands,
[31]whatever comes out of the door of my house to meet me when I
return in triumph from the Ammonites will be the LORD's, and I
will sacrifice it as a burnt offering."**

[32]**Then Jephthah went over to fight the Ammonites, and the
LORD gave them into his hands.** [33]**He devastated twenty towns from
Aroer to the vicinity of Minnith, as far as Abel Keramim. Thus
Israel subdued Ammon.**

11:29 It is now that **the Spirit of the LORD** moves on **Jephthah**.
The Spirit's presence apparently aids him in rallying an army from
Gilead and Manasseh.[8] The Spirit of the LORD here comes upon

---

[7]Goslinga, *Joshua, Judges, Ruth*, pp. 385-387.
[8]Burney, *Judges*, pp. 317-318.

Jephthah without the text giving a clear idea of what he is empowered to do. In the book of Judges, the Spirit of the LORD enables the judges to wage war. Samson's wars are always personal, but Ehud, Gideon, and Jephthah all have the Spirit of the LORD come upon them before they conduct a military campaign.

The Spirit of the LORD is representative of God's presence and activity in the narrative. An interesting detail is that even though Jephthah receives the Spirit of the LORD to rally the troops, and he himself speaks his vow to the LORD, God's speaking to Jephthah is notoriously absent from the text. God speaks *to* people in the cases of the other major judges receiving lengthy treatment in the book — through Deborah to Barak, to Gideon, and to Samson's parents. The narrative does not record God speaking *to* Jephthah.

Mizpah again is presented as the staging ground for the impending battle. Various manuscripts make alterations in verse 29 to allow for a smoother reading. The first occurrence of **Mizpah of Gilead** is absent in several manuscripts, and the Vulgate adds the preposition "to" to "the sons of Ammon" at the end of the verse — both changes to make Jephthah's movements in collecting an army clearer.

11:30 Judges 11:30-31 and the subsequent narrative is one of the most debated and discussed incidents in the book. Jephthah makes **a vow** to God that, in exchange for victory, he will burn in offering the first thing exiting his house on his return. One wonders why Jephthah, after being filled with the Spirit of God, still needs to make a vow in order to assure victory.[9] Jephthah may simply be faithless. Although he is filled with the Spirit of God, the text makes no mention of his awareness of that fact. Either way, Jephthah makes a vow in attempt to manipulate God.[10] "Jephthah's vow in itself violates a deeply held Israelite norm in regard to the prohibition of gifts or bribes to judges."[11] Whether or not an aversion to bribery was "a deeply held Israelite norm" is debatable. The issue is how much Jephthah is aware of the law, and how much he cares about it. The law forbids stealing, but Jephthah is a bandit. He is either unaware of the law, or ignores it.

---

[9]Matthews, *Judges*, p. 124.

[10]Phyllis Trible, *Texts of Terror* (Philadelphia: Fortress Press, 1984), pp. 93-116.

[11]Dennis T. Olson, "Dialogues of Life and Death," in *Postmodern Interpretations of the Bible*, ed. by A.K.M. Adam (St. Louis: Chalice Press, 2001), p. 49.

The word used for vow is the noun נֶדֶר (*neder*). The term is used
for an oath sworn to God in which the one making the pledge commits to some specific service or activity. A vow may be to present an
offering, abstain from something, or to perform a specific task. In
Numbers 30:3 the term is used for swearing "to God with an oath . . .
and to bind one's self with what proceeds from one's mouth. . . . In
most cases the context shows that the vow implies a promised gift or
sacrifice, not merely a course of action as is implied by the English
word 'vow.'" Later Hebrew use of the word is linked with abstinence,
refusing communal benefits, or abstaining from cooked foods.[12]

The vow Jephthah makes is not merely a promised action, but
includes "a promised gift or sacrifice."[13] Numbers 30:2ff. discusses
the binding nature of a spoken vow. The phrase used in Numbers
30:2 is "He shall do according to all that proceeds out of his mouth."
Jephthah does not need to be one who righteously clings to the law
in order to keep his vow. In fact, Jephthah's relationship to the law
seems to be one of inconsistent convenience. Jephthah is part of a
society that takes oaths seriously. Regardless of his relationship to
the law of Moses, Jephthah is not about to break a vow he makes
with a deity. The Talmud notes that Jephthah is one of three men
who framed a vow carelessly.[14] Even though his vow is vague regarding the identity of the offering, Jephthah fully intends to keep it.

11:31 Because the ending of the story apparently results in a man
of God performing a human sacrifice, it is necessary to treat the vow
with some detail. The text narrates Jephthah as not only engaging in
the horrific activity of human sacrifice, but of sacrificing his own
daughter. The alternative interpretation is that Jephthah merely forbids his daughter to marry, dedicating her to a life of celibacy. While
this second interpretation has the advantage of making Jephthah
appear less monstrous, it is unsupported by the text.

In order to understand how Jephthah fulfills his vow, it is important to understand what he intends when he makes the vow.
Jephthah vows to religiously offer up something. That something is
an עוֹלָה (*'ôlāh*) — *a burnt offering*. The root means to go up, ascend,

---

[12]Marcus Jastrow, *A Dictionary of the Targumim, the Talmud Babli and Yerushalmi, and the Midrashic Literature* (Peabody, MA: Hendrickson, 2005).

[13]Leonard Copes, "נֵדֶר (*nēder*), נֶדֶר (*neder*)," *TWOT*, 2:557.

[14]Or, "thoughtless request," *Ta'anit*, 4a.

or climb. The same term is used in Genesis 22:2 for God's command to sacrifice Isaac, and it occurs in 2 Kings 3:27 when the king of Moab offers his son as a burnt offering. Jeremiah 19:4-5 mentions that human sacrifice as a burnt offering is not an expectation that ever enters his mind. All lexical treatments offer "burnt offering" as the only definition for 'ōlāh.[15] It is difficult to conceive how 'ōlāh can mean anything *but* "burnt offering." The word is never used in the Old Testament in a metaphorical way. The simple phrase **[it] will be the LORD's** is combined with **and I will offer it up as a burnt offering** is clear: Jephthah intends to fulfill his vow with a burnt offering.

Jephthah vows that he will offer **whatever comes out of the door of my house** as the burnt offering. The phrase "from my door" (מִדַּלְתִי, *middalthê*) is straightforward. This is the door to Jephthah's house, hinged on a single post set in sockets top and bottom. Some suggest the Hebrew word for door — דֶלֶת (*deleth*) — is relevant to understanding what Jephthah thought might exit from his house. In response to the argument that only a person can come out of the door of a house, Boling presents the archaeological record of an Iron Age house that accommodated animals.[16] Boling assumes animals would have been the natural focus of the vow, and only Jephthah's foolishness forced him to sacrifice his daughter.

Others understand the grammar to imply that Jephthah was offering God a human sacrifice. Burney treats the "comer-forth that cometh forth" as "a phrase which implies that from the first a *human* sacrifice is contemplated."[17] Moore concurs: "That a human victim is intended is, in fact, as plain as words can make it; the language is inapplicable to an animal, and a vow to offer the first sheep or goat that he comes across — not to mention the possibility of an unclean animal — is trivial to absurdity. It is not, therefore, a rash vow to sacrifice *whatever* first meets him . . . but a deliberate one."[18] But Moore extrapolates the Talmudic argument that criticizes Jephthah for his foolishness in not anticipating an unclean animal. Jephthah is con-

---

[15]Richard Avebeck, "עָלָה ('ōlâ)," *NIDOTTE*, 3:405-415.

[16]Boling, *Judges*, p. 179.

[17]Burney, *Judges*, p. 319.

[18]G.F. Moore, *The Book of Judges: A New English Translation Printed in Colors Exhibiting the Composite Structure of the Book: with Explanatory Notes and Pictorial Illustrations* (New York: Dodd, Mead, and Company, 1898), p. 299.

sequently punished by the appearance of his daughter, but his error is not the intention of a human sacrifice.[19] Cundall suggests Jephthah assumes he would be sacrificing one of his household servants.[20] Human sacrifice is not unknown among the Israelites, (2 Kgs 16:3; 17:17; Deut 12:31; 18:9-10),[21] and it is also a familiar practice among the Babylonians and Greeks.[22]

To some extent, the nature and intent of the spoken vow is irrelevant. How the vow is *fulfilled* is the issue. Trible makes the commonsense statement about the ambiguity of the vow: "The story fails to clarify the precise meaning of his words; we shall know it by the fruits." Jephthah's character will be revealed in the fulfillment of his vow.

11:32-33 The negotiations with the Ammonites having failed, the two armies collide, and the Israelites are victorious. God again is the victor over the Ammonites, and gives them **into [Jephthah's hands]**. **Twenty** separate villages are attacked, devastating the enemy enough that they will not be able to exert pressure against Israel again until the early reign of Saul. Ammon is "subdued," or humbled, before Jephthah and Israel.

With the foreshadowing of the vow in the reader's mind, the actual military victory Jephthah achieves over the Ammonites is almost a tangent to where the narrative is heading. God apparently answers Jephthah's earlier prayer and gives Jephthah's troops success. God should not be understood here as being susceptible to Jephthah's attempt at bribery with a vow of sacrifice. Rather, God has already determined to free the Israelites and has raised up Jephthah to do it (Judg 10:16). Ironically, Jephthah does not need to make a vow at all. God is already in the process of responding positively to Israel's repentance.

5. Jephthah Sacrifices His Daughter (11:34-40)

[34]When Jephthah returned to his home in Mizpah, who should come out to meet him but his daughter, dancing to the sound of tambourines! She was an only child. Except for her he had neither

[19]Cohen, *Joshua and Judges*, p. 256.
[20]Cundall, *Judges*, p. 147.
[21]Burney, *Judges*, pp. 329-331.
[22]Ibid., pp. 332-334.

son nor daughter. [35]When he saw her, he tore his clothes and cried, "Oh! My daughter! You have made me miserable and wretched, because I have made a vow to the LORD that I cannot break."

[36]"My father," she replied, "you have given your word to the LORD. Do to me just as you promised, now that the LORD has avenged you of your enemies, the Ammonites. [37]But grant me this one request," she said. "Give me two months to roam the hills and weep with my friends, because I will never marry."

[38]"You may go," he said. And he let her go for two months. She and the girls went into the hills and wept because she would never marry. [39]After the two months, she returned to her father and he did to her as he had vowed. And she was a virgin.

From this comes the Israelite custom [40]that each year the young women of Israel go out for four days to commemorate the daughter of Jephthah the Gileadite.

11:34 Jephthah encounters a big surprise upon returning home after the successful military campaign. Jephthah's **only child — his daughter** — in the tradition of Miriam goes out to welcome the hero. The celebration of women after battle is common in Israel (see Exod 15:20), only Jephthah's victory turned celebration quickly to tragedy as he realizes he must sacrifice his daughter.[23] The text heavily emphasizes that she is Jephthah's only child. Like Abraham, Jephthah is now faced with sacrificing his only child.

Nothing is known of Jephthah's daughter outside of the immediate narrative. Eagerly, apparently, she greets her father after his victory with celebratory **dancing** and music. She is evidently a young woman of marriageable age, hence, her lament concerning her virginity. She voluntarily submits to her father's vow, yet does seek a brief respite to mourn the life that she will never know. She joins a larger cast in the wider Judges narrative of both women and daughters addressed by sometimes distressing narratives (Caleb's daughter, Deborah, Jael, Abimelech's killer, Manoah's wife, Samson's Timnite wife and Delilah, Micah's mother, the Levite's concubine, and the daughters of Shiloh).

11:35 Jephthah's reaction in verse 35 indicates that he has not been expecting his daughter to be the first one to greet him. When Jephthah

---

[23]Boling, *Judges*, p. 208.

sees his daughter, he expresses his anguish in the typical Jewish fashion by tearing his clothing, acting like a man grieving the loss of his only child. Marcus, arguing that Jephthah is delivering his daughter to perpetual celibacy, asserts that Jephthah is actually grieving the loss of his family line. Many commentators follow suit. However, modern interpreters who argue for the end of Jephthah's line fail to acknowledge that lineage is not passed through daughters. The most Jephthah could have then been grieving would be the loss of grandchildren and his daughter's unhappiness, but not the loss of his lineage. If this is so, rending his clothes seems a vast overreaction.[24]

Jephthah tells his daughter that her arrival has made him **miserable and wretched**. The literal translation of the Hebrew is more emphatic. Jephthah tells his daughter, "Oh, my daughter! You have forced me to my knees and you are my agony!" Jephthah's love for his daughter will be the source of his suffering.

Jephthah's daughter has become a source of pain to Jephthah because he has **made a vow** that he cannot retract. The Hebrew makes a wordplay at this point. Jephthah says that he has opened his mouth to the LORD: פָּצִיתִי־פִּי (*pāṣîthî-phî*). Jephthah's name, יִפְתָּח (*yiphthāḥ*), comes from the root פָּתַח (*pāthaḥ*), meaning "He [God] opens."[25] The verb is usually linked to the opening of the mouth.[26] Jephthah, "God Opens," has opened his mouth to the detriment of his own family. The sense of the narrative is "If only *He Opens* had not opened his mouth!"

11:36 Strangely, Jephthah's daughter supports his intention to fulfill his vow. She, too, attributes her father's victory to Yahweh and will willingly participate in the sacrifice. The reason for her willingness is uncertain. Reis suggests that Jephthah's daughter is not a victim, but a presumptuous and rebellious teen who, aware of her father's vow, deliberately interjects herself into the situation. Reis suggests that Jephthah intended to vow and redeem one of his servants for the LORD and that Jephthah's daughter deliberately interferes. Jephthah's daughter would then be a young teen with a sense

---

[24]David Marcus, *Jephthah and His Vow* (Lubbock: Texas Tech Press, 1986), p. 31. Marcus's work provides a thorough survey of the arguments for and against the literal sacrifice of Jephthah's daughter.

[25]"פָּתַח," *BDB*, pp. 834-835.

[26]Victor Hamilton, "פָּתַח (*pātaḥ*)," *TWOT*, 2:743.

of drama who wants to be immortalized, which she achieves with the annual festival in her honor.[27]

11:37-38 The only request Jephthah's daughter makes is that she be allowed to mourn her fate with her **friends** for **two months**. The time away in the mountains around Mizpah is a "time to be filled with lamentation, not for death, but for unfulfilled life."[28] The text later emphasizes her virginity (11:39), leaving Jephthah's daughter bereft of every young woman's hope at the time: husband and family.

11:39a The author's summary of Jephthah's fulfillment of the vow is vague. Jephthah is described as doing **to her as he had vowed**. The narrator's omniscient perspective in Judges 11:29-40 often seems to shroud details and obscure information, as two millennia of debate over the interpretation of this passage have aptly demonstrated. The narrator provides no insight into the specific activity of the Spirit of the LORD's coming on Jephthah — no miraculous activity is seen on Jephthah's part. Further, the language of the vow leaves its details open to confusion. Perhaps the biggest ambiguity in the passage is the exact nature of the vow fulfillment. Ehud's bowel-spilling endeavors and the Levite's dismembering of his concubine are presented in gory detail. Why the ambiguity here? Olson insightfully suggests,

> The effect of the ambivalence is to heighten suspense, to draw the reader into wrestling with the moral dilemmas and ambiguities of the story, and to increase the sense of horror at a possibility so repulsive that it is not described but left only as an imagined potentiality. This central ambiguity of the entire story — whether Jephthah killed his daughter or not — reflects the overall ambiguity of Jephthah's [foolishness].[29]

Several inclusions and clarifications omitted from the text would also have proven useful. In what activity is the Spirit of the LORD involved? Is Jephthah intending a human sacrifice? Does Jephthah's daughter know about the vow? Is the commemoration ceremony Jewish or Canaanite in nature?

---

[27]Pamela Tamarkin Reis, "Spoiled Child: A Fresh Look at Jephthah's Daughter," *Proof* (Spring 1997): 279-298.

[28]Trible, *Texts of Terror*, p. 104.

[29]Olson, "Dialogues of Life and Death," pp. 43-54.

The biggest question surrounding the passage regards the nature of the vow's fulfillment. Does he or doesn't he? Jephthah makes a vow to sacrifice "whatever comes out of the door" of his house to greet him should he return successfully from battle. His daughter greets him, and the text concludes with the vague statement that Jephthah "did to her as he had vowed." The difficulty over interpretation stems from the lack of certainty about the exact nature and fulfillment of Jephthah's vow.[30] Suggestions for resolution are many, although two in particular dominate the discussion. The simplest reading of the text indicates that Jephthah fulfills his vow by sacrificing his daughter. If this is true, then reconciling the Judges 11 account with Hebrews 11:32 where Jephthah is presented as a definitive example of faith becomes difficult. Another option is that Jephthah does not sacrifice his daughter at all, but instead forbids her to marry, dedicating her to a life of celibacy. Below is a summary of some of the most popular arguments for both positions.

Arguments that Jephthah Sacrifices His Daughter	Response
This interpretation is the plainest reading of the text.	The text is deliberately ambiguous.
'ōlāh has no other meaning than a literal burnt offering.	Jephthah intends a burnt offering for an animal *OR* a dedication for human being.
The text was understood as describing a literal sacrifice until the Middle Ages.	An early interpretation is not necessarily correct.
Jephthah's reaction to his daughter demonstrates his sorrow over his vow.	Jephthah is mourning the loss of his line and descendants, not his daughter's sacrifice.
The text heavily emphasizes that Jephthah has only one child.	Jephthah's vow leaves him with no children to carry on his line.
In the Old Testament, tearing clothes usually symbolizes grief over death or impending death.	Tearing clothes may symbolize grief over the end of a line (1 Kgs 21:20-29).
There are many ancient stories similar to the Jephthah account in which a hero's daughter is tragically sacrificed.	Myth is a poor standard through which to evaluate Scripture.
Connection between Jephthah's daughter and Isaac; both are only children, only with Jephthah's daughter, there is no angel to intervene.	This is conjecture; the text nowhere makes an overt connection between Judges 11 and Genesis 22.

[30]D.M. Gunn, *Judges* (Malden, MA: Blackwell, 2005), p. 134.

Arguments that Jephthah Dedicates His Daughter to Celibacy	Response
Human sacrifice is unthinkable for the Hebrews (Deut 12:31).	Gen 22:2; 2 Kgs 3:27
Human sacrifice is forbidden by the Law of Moses.	Jephthah is demonstrably ignorant of or indifferent to the Law.
Jephthah's daughter is too willing to submit to being sacrificed.	The daughter may be as foolish as her father.
The Spirit of the LORD is on Jephthah, and so he is incapable of disobeying God's law.	The Spirit of the LORD is not a permanent manifestation and assisted in accomplishing feats, not righteousness; see the life of Samson.
God apparently approves Jephthah's vow by delivering victory over the Ammonites.	The text makes no mention of God's response to Jephthah; God's activity is not mentioned again in the life of Jephthah.
The text nowhere condemns Jephthah's actions.	Nor does it condemn Samson's or the Levite's in Judges 19; a lack of condemnation does not demonstrate the presence of morality.
11:39 adds the phrase, "And she was a virgin," suggesting that she remained that way.	Jephthah's daughter's virginity is linked in the text to the festival that grew up in her memory, not to her sacrifice.
The Israelites would have reacted strongly against human sacrifice.	Perhaps Ephraim's complaint against Jephthah in chapter 12 is a smokescreen to do just that.

The debate about how Jephthah actually fulfilled his vow dates back to the twelfth century A.D., when it was first suggested that Jephthah shut his daughter up in a house, forcing on her a celibate life. Earlier Christian and Jewish sources all attested to literal human sacrifice.[31] Richard Rogers acknowledges the virginity-sacrifice debate in the seventeenth century, and responds that a vow of virginity is unheard of in Scripture (no doubt betraying his Protestant paradigm). Rogers also mentions argument of the limitations of the definition of *'ôlāh*, as well as the focus of the text on Jephthah's daughter being an only child.[32]

Human sacrifice is uncommon in Iron Age Israel, but not unknown.[33] Soggin bluntly says, "Here we have one of the very rare

---

[31]Ibid., pp. 134-142.

[32]Richard Rogers, *A Commentary on Judges* (Edinburgh: Banner of Truth, 1983), pp. 584-585.

[33]Burney, *Judges*, p. 330.

cases of human sacrifice attested in the Old Testament, which not only is not censured in any way, but is even considered necessary as the fulfillment of a vow." Israel would have had the burnt offering of human sacrifice embedded in their very identity, with the sacrifice of Isaac in Genesis 22. The echo narrative on the part of the author is difficult to miss: both Isaac and Jephthah's daughter are the only children of their parents. The difference in Isaac's case is, the sacrifice is initiated by God, and God ultimately intervenes.[34]

Some have argued that Jephthah is an upright servant of God who could not have performed human sacrifice. Jephthah's character actually does allow him to fulfill this vow. He kills 42,000 of his own countrymen, after all.[35] Although Leviticus 18:21 and 20:2 prohibit human sacrifice, Jephthah's awareness of and compliance with the law are a separate issue (to be discussed below).

Extrabiblical sources also contain multiple references to a father's sacrifice of his daughter.

> It is often supposed that the story of Jephthah's vow is purely etiological, a tale originally told to rationalize a defunct lamentation festival (vs. 40). There is a number of parallels to the tragic sacrifice of the hero's daughter in comparative folklore, and so the question of the shaping of the record must remain an open one. That there is no other trace of such a "festival" suggests that the tale is told for other than etiological purpose. It heightens the tragic dimension of the story of Jephthah. . . .[36]

It should be noted that the presence of mythological parallels do not necessarily negate the historicity of the Judges account.

One interesting argument against literal sacrifice is the anticipated reaction of Jephthah's fellow Israelites who would have strongly resisted and opposed human sacrifice. Goslinga notes that in 1 Samuel 14:45 the people resist Saul's attempt to kill Jonathan in fulfillment of his oath.[37] Judges 20 demonstrates what Israelites opposed to human sacrifice are prepared to do. The people's strong reaction to the Levite who dismembers his concubine might also be

[34]Soggin, *Judges,* p. 215.
[35]Samuel Ridout, *Judges and Ruth* (Neptune, NJ: Loizeaux Brothers, 1981), pp. 174-176.
[36]Boling, *Judges,* p. 210.
[37]Goslinga, *Joshua, Judges, Ruth,* p. 392.

considered as an example of what could happen to someone who acts outside the bounds of appropriate Israelite law and culture. Would not the people of Israel react violently against human sacrifice? Perhaps they do. Interestingly, chapter 12 begins in much the same way as chapter 20 — with a group of Israelites assembled to punish someone who commits a heinous act. In Judges 20, the Levite has not only dismembered his concubine, but he has proactively advertised his actions. In Judges 12, the Ephraimites show up, ostensibly to execute Jephthah for his failure to include them in the fight against Ammon. Perhaps Ephraim, aware of Jephthah's sacrifice of his daughter, decides to act. They are in a difficult position to punish a vague vow that Jephthah has obediently fulfilled, because God would be understood to be the one who caused his daughter to walk out the door. With a needed smokescreen to conceal their desire to remove such a brutal man from their midst, Ephraim arrives at Jephthah's doorstep with a lame excuse. Perhaps adding to Ephraim's offense is the implication that Jephthah's vow would not have been necessary had they been included in the war party.

In the debate between sacrifice and celibacy, Marcus represents the definitive work. "The text, as it stands now, admits the possibility of either conclusion." Ultimately, Marcus suggests that the narrator deliberately obfuscates the truth to allow for either conclusion.[38] But surely biblical Hebrew has easier ways to express a vow than with a concrete term like 'ōlāh.

Ridout cuts through the debate best: "I must confess, that with all I have read on the subject, I have never been able to disabuse my mind of the fact that Jephthah did what every simple soul who reads the passage believes he did."[39] The best way to understand the text is the plainest reading: Jephthah offers his own daughter as a burnt offering as a fulfillment of the vow he made at Mizpah.

But even the way the vow is fulfilled is not the most crucial aspect in understanding the text. "The fact of human sacrifice in Jephthah's story is secondary to the theme of the irrevocability of the vow."[40] Jephthah makes a vague and subsequently difficult vow, and he keeps it anyway.

---

[38]Marcus, *Jephthah and His Vow*, pp. 52-53.
[39]Ridout, *Judges and Ruth*, p. 173.
[40]Boling, *Judges*, p. 209.

11:39b-40 Jephthah's daughter is commemorated through an annual celebration that is mentioned in Scripture only here. The text provides little information regarding the nature of the celebration. The annual event is more than a "custom." It is in some way given an official legal status. The NIV's translation of בְּיִשְׂרָאֵל חֹק־וַתְּהִי (watt³hî-ḥōq b³yiśrā'ēl) is better translated, "It was a statute in Israel." The annual event surrounding the fate of Jephthah's daughter is more akin to legislation than custom.

Since there is no known Jewish celebration linked to the event, James Martin is likely correct when he suggests (along with Pamela Tamarkin Reis) that the four-day festival is likely linked to a fertility religion.[41] Although Reis's suggestion of the daughter's manipulation of Jephthah's vow is questionable,[42] her suggestion regarding the ascendance of a fertility cult in connection with Jephthah's daughter is a likely possibility. There are no other references to the festival in the Hebrew Bible, and the festival itself is limited to women, itself suggestive of a fertility cult. Unfortunately, the narrator does not provide more information since the original audience was surely familiar with both the ceremony and the statute-festival.

The existence of a fertility cult that undermines Israel's loyalty to Yahweh as a result of Jephthah's foolishness fits with similar occurrences throughout the book. Gideon's ephod becomes a snare to Israel, as do Samson's indiscretions, as does the Levite's dismembering of his concubine that leads to the near elimination of a tribe,

[41]James D. Martin, *The Book of Judges* (Cambridge: Cambridge University Press, 1975), p. 146. Also see Pamela Tamarkin Reis, "Spoiled Child," pp. 279-298.

[42]Pamela Reis's argument is predicated on understanding the nature of the vow to be related to perpetual celibacy rather than sacrifice. Reis suggests that Jephthah's intention is to dedicate a slave as a burnt offering, rather than to be a burnt offering. She argues that Jephthah's daughter not only imposes herself onto Jephthah's vow, but disrespects him as an elder through the use of imperatives rather than the proper entreating of an elder, and she manipulates Jephthah to allow her to pursue non-Hebrew religious intervention of the vow and initiate a pagan fertility celebration. Although this perspective is intriguing, it relies heavily on a metaphorical understanding of 'ôláh, which, if true, occurs nowhere else in the Old Testament. If his daughter is a victim, then Jephthah is a foolish, cruel father. If she is a manipulator, Jephthah is a spineless, indecisive, ineffectual man subject to the machinations of a teenage daughter.

as does this fertility cult. The successful warrior Jephthah making and keeping his foolish vow leads to heresy in Israel. Jephthah causes all Israel to suffer in the form of false worship. A blasphemous fertility cult is the result of Jephthah's well-intentioned and thoughtless vow. Ironically, Jephthah's lack of discretion undermines the very things he hopes to preserve: the life of his daughter and the community of Israel.

Much of the argument about the entire narrative revolves around Israelite culture and Law. If the Israelites were ignorant of the Law, a human sacrifice wouldn't be out of place. With a syncretistic religious context, almost anything goes. Many commentators, however, assume Jephthah and his culture possessed the ideal in both understanding *and* implementing the Law. As has already been noted, however, Jephthah has spent his life neglecting the Law through theft. Following the narrative in Judges 11, he will oversee the murder of his fellow Israelites *after* a battle. Considering Jephthah's activities, his knowledge and/or practice of the Law is safely questionable.

Another barrier to interpreting this passage is the erroneous attempt to eliminate tension. Many have a strong desire to reconcile the apparent conflict between Judges 11 and Hebrews 11:32. How can a man sacrifice his own daughter in violation of the Law and still be held up as an example of faith? Jephthah is much more easily esteemed as a man of faith if he has shed no innocent blood. But Jephthah is only one of many imperfect men of faith. One need look no further than David, a man after God's own heart who committed adultery and murder. Tension in Scripture is not problematic. It forces us to wrestle with our small, limited understanding of God and our relationship with him. Wrestling with paradox will always reveal that our actions and existence are much less significant and the grace of God far more vast than we ever imagined. The narrative of Jephthah's daughter in Judges 11:29-40 is more than a story about a reckless warrior who attempts to manipulate God with a vow that backfires. The narrative is not about Jephthah's foolishness, but about the larger story running through the book of Judges: God is faithful, active, and sovereign among a faithless and disobedient people. Jephthah's lack of faith is somehow faith enough for God. Rather than undermining Jephthah, the narrative actually exalts God for his graciousness.

In seeking application from the narrative of Jephthah's daughter, stepping away from the debate swirling around the text is important. Richard Rogers in his 1615 sermon commentary on Judges focuses on the individual responsibility to God and others in spite of injustice. Jephthah wanted to please God in his limited understanding, which doesn't excuse his ignorance, but it is still important to be faithful with the amount of knowledge one possesses. Similarly, Rogers understands Jephthah's daughter as an example of submitting to authority even in the face of injustice. His simple application is refreshing after being bogged down in the debate over the text.[43]

Application derived from this passage tends to ruffle modern sensibilities. Even so, the Jephthah narrative provides some valuable instruction. First, followers of Christ must labor against syncretism. Jephthah's religious expression is amazingly inconsistent. He refuses to break a vow, but he will steal. He is generous granting his daughter two months more of life, but mercilessly kills his fellow countrymen. It remains debatable whether Jephthah's religious understanding is some kind of syncretism — Yahweh worship blended with cultic practices around him — or whether he simply chooses those elements of religious expression he deems significant. Either way, Jephthah represents a self-centered approach to theology. Those filling churches in the current era are no less susceptible to a syncretized belief system, obtaining beliefs about grace from Romans, marriage from television soap operas, and politics from talk radio. Syncretism is often rooted in ignorance, but it also arises from stubbornness — thriving in the hearts of those who are unwilling to bow the knee all the way to the ground before the throne of God.

Second, enthusiasm must be tempered with wisdom. Enthusiasm is a wonderful motivator. It has the advantage of providing emotional security ("I'm zealous, so my theology is correct") and is useful in accomplishing tasks. The enthusiastic dreamer achieves. Jephthah's faith is actually proven by his willingness to keep his vow (no matter the interpretation of the nature of the vow). So sacrificing his daughter could really have been the greatest expression of his faith. On the one hand, the same could be said of Abraham. On the other hand, Jesus' words in John 16:2, "An hour is coming for

[43]Rogers, *Commentary on Judges*, pp. 575-588.

everyone who kills you to think that he is offering service to God," suggests that zeal is not the only qualification for obedience to God. If it were, radical religious extremists would likely possess the correct theology. Enthusiasm is the most effective when it is tempered with understanding and the wisdom from above spoken about in James 3.

To temper enthusiasm, wisdom is a must. In Judges, the Spirit of God shows up sporadically, fills a man to perform a task, and then moves on. Fortunately for followers of Christ, a different arrival of the Spirit of God is present. Within the Christian paradigm is the belief that access to the heart and mind of God is available through the ongoing indwelling presence of his Spirit. So the supernatural wisdom described in James 3, Galatians 5, and John 16 cannot help but modify and mature enthusiasm to avoid foolishness like Jephthah's. The discussion about Jephthah's faith-vow connection is only a discussion about degree. Forcing celibacy on his daughter or her actual burnt offering — *both* are foolish because his vow was not thought out. The Christian perspective is that God himself provides the guidance to the believer, enabling that believer to serve God appropriately.

On the flip side, God paradoxically seems often to honor ignorant enthusiasm. This does not provide an excuse for indifference or ignorance. But growing in faith can be a messy, dirty, and confused process, and faith is often held strongly by messy, dirty, and confused people. The Jephthah narrative is yet one more of the many beautiful examples that demonstrate that faith is not determined by singular and even significant failures. God's perspective on human faith seems to be transtemporal, stretching beyond individual incidents, looking at the faith represented by an entire lifetime. A perusal of the great men of faith in Hebrews 11 reveals sin and foolishness similar to those in Jephthah's life. Noah is an exhibitionist drunkard. Abraham tries to disguise his wife as his sister, and he attempts in his own wisdom to father a son. Isaac learns from dad, and lies about Rebekah. Jacob "the Supplanter" steals his brother's birthright. Joseph is arrogant and practices divination. Moses is a murderer. The Israelite people cross the Red Sea on faith, Hebrews 11 tells the reader, but those same people die in the desert because of their disobedience. Barak is a coward. Gideon is an idolatrous coward. David is a murdering adulterer. And Jephthah sacrifices his only daughter.

Christians tend to equate faith with perfect performance. Reaching some ideal seems deeply entrenched in our minds and hearts, so much so that we're uncomfortable considering the alternative: that immoral people might just be people of powerful faith. This is not to suggest that we are free to ignore character, but rather to remind us that God's activity does not depend on holiness. It depends on faith.

Third, God is impossible to bribe. Bribing or bargaining with a particular deity is common in the ancient world, and Jephthah gives it a try. But a bribe is only effective when the superior values the object of the bribe. We often attempt to manipulate God in the way we manipulate others. But God has no need to respond to vanity, or being liked, the monetary value of an offering, or our holiness. Perhaps a better way to think about God is with a parent-child metaphor. Most children do not attempt to offer anything to their parents in exchange for a granted request. Children might attempt to behave for Santa's arrival, but they ultimately lack the attention span and capacity. Gifts are given from love, not for an exchanged value.

Finally, speech has the power to affect reality, so speak well. Without agreeing with the theologically unorthodox who claim reality may be spoken into existence by human beings, spoken words do have the power to *affect* reality. The Tower of Babel, Proverbs, the Prophets, the Incarnation, Pentecost, the Epistles — all testify to the power words have. Language is God's chosen vehicle for specific revelation. Scripture is filled with encouragement to speak wisely, whether in keeping silent or keeping vows, the spoken word carries spiritual implications. Consequently, believers are responsible for what and how they speak. And believers' speech should reflect the nature of God — all the love, all the optimism, and all the holiness of the Giver of language.

Jephthah is a flawed man with an imperfect faith whom God uses anyway. Christians can easily relate to him, even as God draws them into a deeper faith through his Spirit.

CHAPTER 12

6. Conflict with Ephraim (12:1-7)

¹The men of Ephraim called out their forces, crossed over to Zaphon and said to Jephthah, "Why did you go to fight the Ammonites without calling us to go with you? We're going to burn down your house over your head."

²Jephthah answered, "I and my people were engaged in a great struggle with the Ammonites, and although I called, you didn't save me out of their hands. ³When I saw that you wouldn't help, I took my life in my hands and crossed over to fight the Ammonites, and the LORD gave me the victory over them. Now why have you come up today to fight me?"

⁴Jephthah then called together the men of Gilead and fought against Ephraim. The Gileadites struck them down because the Ephraimites had said, "You Gileadites are renegades from Ephraim and Manasseh." ⁵The Gileadites captured the fords of the Jordan leading to Ephraim, and whenever a survivor of Ephraim said, "Let me cross over," the men of Gilead asked him, "Are you an Ephraimite?" If he replied, "No," ⁶they said, "All right, say 'Shibboleth.'" He said, "Sibboleth," because he could not pronounce the word correctly, they seized him and killed him at the fords of the Jordan. Forty-two thousand Ephraimites were killed at that time.

⁷Jephthah led* Israel six years. Then Jephthah the Gileadite died, and was buried in a town in Gilead.

ª7 Traditionally *judged*; also in verses 8-14

12:1 Chapter 12 opens with the temperamental Ephraimites gathering their military forces and making the significant move of crossing the Jordan River from their territory and camping out in the Gadite town of **Zaphon**.

The Ephraimites had previously answered the military summons of Gideon in 7:24. There, Gideon had successfully defeated the Midianites, and requested Ephraimite help only in preventing the Midianite escape. The Ephraimites were incensed with Gideon's belated call to action. Gideon, through a humble and diplomatic response, was able to diffuse the situation.

In the instance with Jephthah, the Ephraimites are again enraged over being slighted and ignored for the united Israelite army. This time, however, they have no intentions of cooling down. They boldly announce their plan to **burn down [Jephthah's] house** with him in it.

Ephraim has previously demonstrated the inability to be content with their circumstances. In Joshua 17:14-18, the tribe complains to Joshua that their allotted inheritance is too small for their large population. Because the Canaanites in the plains possess iron chariots, the Ephraimites are confined to the hill country. Joshua tells them to clear the forests and take over territory belonging to the Perizzites and Rephaimites. When the Ephraimites protest, Joshua uses their own argument against them: the large Ephraimite population will allow them to capture both more forest territory and the plains, in spite of resistance from chariot-equipped opposition. Joshua and Judges portray the tribe as cowards with an easily wounded pride, and it is this pride that motivates them to murder a fellow Israelite.

12:2-3 Jephthah's response to the Ephraimites provides a fuller picture of the tribe's desire to be engaged in the battle against the Ammonites. Jephthah reminds the Ephraimites that he had indeed summoned them for assistance against the Ammonites, but they had refused to come to the aid of their fellow Israelites. Jephthah's comments cut through to the cowardice of the Ephraimites. He says in 12:3 that he **took my life in my hands**, indicating that he had no assurance of success before the battle. Yahweh, not superior military numbers, provided the victory. Jephthah's response can easily be understood as a criticism of both Ephraim's cowardice and lack of faith. It is only when hindsight clearly proves that a military victory is possible and easily obtained that they resent the fact that they had not participated. Rather than acknowledge their own cowardice and lack of faith, the Ephraimites target Jephthah for failing to include them.

12:4 Like the Ephraimites, Jephthah and the Gileadite army also have their pride issues. Verse 4 describes the battle and slaughter before it presents the motive. While Jephthah has attempted to be conciliatory in the past, his patience ends with the Ephraimites' final insult.

Ephraim has the population to bolster Jephthah's army significantly, but has refused Jephthah's request for assistance. Then, when the battle with the Ammonites is successful, Ephraim complains that Jephthah has slighted them. Already annoyed with the flaky tribe, Jephthah and the Gileadites will not stomach the Ephraimite insult.

The Ephraimites called the Gileadites **renegades from Ephraim and Manasseh.** פָּלִיט (*pālîṭ*) is a term used to refer to refugees escaping from war.[1] Without a battle, the large Ephraimite army is branding the smaller Gileadite army as defeated at their hands. The battle-hardened Gileadites are not about to accept the label of "loser" by cowards who sat safely on the sidelines during the battle with the Ammonites. The Ephraimite insult combined with the tribe's stubborn refusal to aid in the battle against Ammon is enough for Gilead to slaughter their kin with no remorse.

12:5-6 In light of the familial ties between the Ephraimites and Gileadites, the Gileadite execution of the fleeing Ephraimites seems cruel.[2] Presumably at the command of Jephthah, the **Gileadites** capture and control **the fords of the Jordan.** The Jordan carried much more water in ancient times than it does now and presented a formidable obstacle to travelers. Crossing was possible only at locations where the water was shallow enough to permit passage. After being defeated in battle, fleeing Ephraimite troops head toward the ford where they can cross the river back to Ephraimite territory. There, the Gileadites rely on the Ephraimite dialect to betray fugitives. A traveler's inability to correctly pronounce an *sh* sound betrays him as an Ephraimite and gains him an immediate execution at the hand of the Gileadites. There is a certain irony in the fall of the Ephraimites to the Gileadite control of the fords. The Ephraimites themselves employed the same strategy against the Midianites at Gideon's behest (7:24).

---

[1]Victor Hamilton, "פָּלִיט (*pālîṭ*)," *TWOT*, 2:725.
[2]Assis, *Self-interest or Communal Interest*, p. 231.

Jephthah's reaction is cruel in the sense that he is slaughtering his own countrymen. From a military perspective, however, his actions are strategic and effective. Jephthah is simply engaging in well-performed warfare, which seeks to remove both an enemy's ability and desire to engage in war. Fewer surviving enemies leave fewer opportunities for future retaliation. Ephraim twice has assumed a threatening posture against a judge, and by slaughtering 42,000, Jephthah heavily decimates the tribe and prevents any possibility of aggression against fellow Israelites for several generations. Numbers 1:33 lists the preconquest number of the fighting men of Ephraim at 40,500. Just a few generations later, their numbers would not have been much larger. Although not as heavily decimated as the tribe of Benjamin will be in chapter 20, Ephraim's military capacity has been severely curtailed.

12:7 The Jephthah narrative ends with the standard formula describing the judge's duration of leadership, death, and burial. Jephthah's leadership over Israel lasts only **six years**. Jephthah's character is not evaluated, but it is certainly mixed. He is an outcast who becomes a skilled warrior and leader. At the same time, he is rash and foolish. One Targum manuscript contains a marginal note at 12:7 condemning Jephthah for not seeking to be absolved from his vow.[3] Beyond all his accomplishments and inadequacies, Jephthah will always be most remembered for his foolish vow.

The final note on Jephthah is his burial in **a town** in the region of **Gilead**. In spite of his negotiation with the Gileadites for leadership of the clan, he has not obtained their respect. The fact that a specific place of burial is not mentioned for Jephthah suggests that his death and burial are unremarkable. He dies and is buried. He has no family to be united with in death, and no hometown to warrant mention as a gravesite.

I. THE NINTH JUDGE: IBZAN (12:8-10)

Chapter 12 concludes with a brief summary of three minor judges, the last judges before Samson. The three judges mirror the two minor judges Tola and Jair mentioned at the beginning of chap-

[3]Smelik, *Targum*, p. 557.

ter 10. The two groups of minor judges sandwich the Jephthah narrative. The five minor judges rule for a total of seventy years, a number indicating completeness. Jephthah has only ruled for six years, a year short of the ideal number seven. The stories of all six judges have been structured in a way that emphasizes Jephthah's story. The minor judges are wealthy and powerful. Jephthah is neither. The minor judges have family, influence in the clan, and a proper burial place. Jephthah is an outsider who lives and dies without family connections. Jephthah is not the typical judge of Israel, but God powerfully uses him nevertheless.

None of these three final minor judges is described as "saving" Israel. They apparently functioned in a nonmilitary capacity, providing leadership and its accompanying stability to Israel. The three territories of the judges cover southern, central, and northern Israel, representing God's provision of leadership for all the people.

⁸After him, Ibzan of Bethlehem led Israel. ⁹He had thirty sons and thirty daughters. He gave his daughters away in marriage to those outside his clan, and for his sons he brought in thirty young women as wives from outside his clan. Ibzan led Israel seven years. ¹⁰Then Ibzan died, and was buried in Bethlehem.

12:8-10 Ibzan from **Bethlehem** in the territory of Judah leads Israel for **seven years**. His significance in the text is not because of his leadership, but because of his use of marriage as a tool to bolster his power in the region. Ibzan arranges marital relationships for his **thirty sons and thirty daughters** with spouses from **outside his clan**. "Outside the clan" is mentioned twice, in regard to his giving his daughters to husbands and in seeking wives for his sons. Ibzan would have arranged such marriages in order to consolidate his power base in the region around Bethlehem.[4]

Three primary options exist for the term "outside." The Hebrew word is הַחוּצָה (*haḥûṣāh*), simply meaning "the outside." The word may refer, as the NIV translates, to "outside the clan." In this case, the large size of Ibzan's family may necessitate reaching out to other clans in Judah for spouses for his children. The NIV's translation is

---

[4]Alan J. Hauser, "Unity and Diversity in Early Israel before Samuel," *JETS* 22 (December 1979): 301.

based on similar usage concerning Levirate marriage in Deuteronomy 25:5.

A second option for "outside" is the KJV and ASV translation of "abroad," meaning that Ibzan looks for marriage partners in a larger territorial region than just the area surrounding Bethlehem. This perspective certainly overlaps the first: reaching outside the clan means reaching out to other areas as well.

The third option is somewhat unflattering for Ibzan. "Outside" may refer to "outside Israel." As many translators and scholars do with Jephthah, the tendency is to assume the best about the judge. It is possible, however, that the author of Judges is commenting on Ibzan's seeking marriage partners for his children from outside Israel, something expressly forbidden by the Law (Deut 7:1-4). Judges 1:19 indicates Judah's failure to conquer all of their allotted territory, leaving a significant Canaanite population within the region. The double mention of "outside" reinforces the idea that Ibzan's actions are inappropriate. If Ibzan has arranged marriages for his children with non-Israelites, he has furthered the Canaanization of the judges and Israel.

J. THE TENTH JUDGE: ELON (12:11-12)

¹¹After him, Elon the Zebulunite led Israel ten years. ¹²Then Elon died, and was buried in Aijalon in the land of Zebulun.

12:11-12 Of **Elon**, little is said. He is from the tribe of **Zebulun** and leads Israel for **ten years**. He is the judge with the most northerly location. He leads Israel for ten years, dies, and is **buried in Aijalon**, where God stopped the sun to aid the Israelites in their battle against the Amorites (Josh 10:12-14).

K. THE ELEVENTH JUDGE: ABDON (12:13-15)

¹³After him, Abdon son of Hillel, from Pirathon, led Israel. ¹⁴He had forty sons and thirty grandsons, who rode on seventy donkeys. He led Israel eight years. ¹⁵Then Abdon son of Hillel died, and was buried at Pirathon in Ephraim, in the hill country of the Amalekites.

12:13 Abdon, like Jair and Ibzan, is both well known and well off. He is twice described as **the son of Hillel**. Although Hillel is nowhere else known in Scripture, the double mention in verses 13 and 15 indicates that the earliest readers of Judges were certainly familiar with the name. Similarly, nothing is known about Abdon's hometown of **Pirathon**. David's loyal mighty man Benaiah would later come from the town.

12:14 Abdon's power base is provided by two generations of his male descendants. His **forty sons and thirty grandsons** are a powerful status symbol, allowing him to control a substantial region. Similarly, the **seventy donkeys** his sons and grandsons ride are a further symbol of power and wealth (Gen 12:16; Job 42:12). Donkeys were primarily cargo vehicles — the jeep of the ancient Near East. Abdon's sons are high enough in status that they have no need to lead donkeys carrying cargo — they *are* the valuable cargo.

12:15 After his death, Abdon is buried in the territory allotted to **Ephraim**, but in the hill country controlled by the Amalekites. The Ephraimites have been unable to displace them, and the Canaanite group will later be battled by both Saul and David. Abdon's burial in Amalekite territory speaks to his influence even over the Canaanite group.

Ibzan, Elon, and Abdon do not receive the attention of judges like Gideon and Samson. The minor judges seem like little more than a footnote in the text. Nevertheless, they still serve as examples of people used by God, even though they are given little recognition. The minor judges are a reminder to labor for God's purposes irrespective of acknowledgment and gratitude.

CHAPTER 13

L. THE TWELFTH JUDGE: SAMSON (13:1–16:31)

1. Samson's Birth Promised (13:1-25)

¹Again the Israelites did evil in the eyes of the LORD, so the LORD delivered them into the hands of the Philistines for forty years.

²A certain man of Zorah, named Manoah, from the clan of the Danites, had a wife who was sterile and remained childless. ³The angel of the LORD appeared to her and said, "You are sterile and childless, but you are going to conceive and have a son. ⁴Now see to it that you drink no wine or other fermented drink and that you do not eat anything unclean, ⁵because you will conceive and give birth to a son. No razor may be used on his head, because the boy is to be a Nazirite, set apart to God from birth, and he will begin the deliverance of Israel from the hands of the Philistines."

⁶Then the woman went to her husband and told him, "A man of God came to me. He looked like an angel of God, very awesome. I didn't ask him where he came from, and he didn't tell me his name. ⁷But he said to me, 'You will conceive and give birth to a son. Now then, drink no wine or other fermented drink and do not eat anything unclean, because the boy will be a Nazirite of God from birth until the day of his death.'"

⁸Then Manoah prayed to the LORD: "O LORD, I beg you, let the man of God you sent to us come again to teach us how to bring up the boy who is to be born."

⁹God heard Manoah, and the angel of God came again to the woman while she was out in the field; but her husband Manoah was not with her. ¹⁰The woman hurried to tell her husband, "He's here! The man who appeared to me the other day!"

¹¹Manoah got up and followed his wife. When he came to the man, he said, "Are you the one who talked to my wife?"

"I am," he said.

¹²So Manoah asked him, "When your words are fulfilled, what is to be the rule for the boy's life and work?"

¹³The angel of the LORD answered, "Your wife must do all that I have told her. ¹⁴She must not eat anything that comes from the grapevine, nor drink any wine or other fermented drink nor eat anything unclean. She must do everything I have commanded her."

¹⁵Manoah said to the angel of the LORD, "We would like you to stay until we prepare a young goat for you."

¹⁶The angel of the LORD replied, "Even though you detain me, I will not eat any of your food. But if you prepare a burnt offering, offer it to the LORD." (Manoah did not realize that it was the angel of the LORD.)

¹⁷Then Manoah inquired of the angel of the LORD, "What is your name, so that we may honor you when your word comes true?"

¹⁸He replied, "Why do you ask my name? It is beyond understanding.ᵃ" ¹⁹Then Manoah took a young goat, together with the grain offering, and sacrificed it on a rock to the LORD. And the LORD did an amazing thing while Manoah and his wife watched: ²⁰As the flame blazed up from the altar toward heaven, the angel of the LORD ascended in the flame. Seeing this, Manoah and his wife fell with their faces to the ground. ²¹When the angel of the LORD did not show himself again to Manoah and his wife, Manoah realized that it was the angel of the LORD.

²²"We are doomed to die!" he said to his wife. "We have seen God!"

²³But his wife answered, "If the LORD had meant to kill us, he would not have accepted a burnt offering and grain offering from our hands, nor shown us all these things or now told us this."

²⁴The woman gave birth to a boy and named him Samson. He grew and the LORD blessed him, ²⁵and the Spirit of the LORD began to stir him while he was in Mahaneh Dan, between Zorah and Eshtaol.

ᵃ18 Or is wonderful

13:1 Chapter 13 opens with the refrain, **Israel did evil in the sight of the LORD**. This is the final occurrence of the phrase in the book. The Hebrew term includes the definite article and is singular. The Israelites have been doing "the evil," or "the bad thing." This singular evil thing they have been doing throughout the book is apostasy in the form of Baal worship (2:11; 3:7; 10:6). For the final time in the book, Yahweh delivers **them into the hand** of their enemies for a specific period of time. In this case, the wandering hearts of the people result in a forty-year oppression by their arch nemesis, **the Philistines**. With a generation-long oppression, the stage has once again been set for the people's delivery through the ministry of a judge.

Chapter 13 serves as a prelude to the activities of Samson. The amount of material dedicated to the birth of Samson is significant in understanding the author's intention for the section. Samson is not just another judge who happens upon the scene and whom God raises up. Samson is the result of divinely provided birth.

13:2 The reader is introduced to the Danite **Manoah**. Manoah is from **Zorah**, a small town on the edge of Philistine territory. God chooses a town for the birth of Israel's deliverer that is strategically located to strike at the heart of the enemy.

Manoah has an unnamed **wife** who will figure prominently in the immediate context. Though the detail of her name is not provided, the description of the woman as childless is emphatic. The Hebrew phrase אִשְׁתּוֹ עֲקָרָה וְלֹא יָלָדָה (*'ištô 'āqārāh w⁰lō' yālādāh*) accentuates this woman's inability to bear children. The translated Hebrew reads, "his wife was barren and she did not conceive," repeating the same concept in order to emphasize that the birth that will take place will certainly be supernatural in origin. The addition of the concept of "not having borne children" to the term "barren" is used descriptively elsewhere only of Sarah (Gen 11:30). As is typical for the era, the sterility is assumed to originate with the woman. And because a woman's social status in the ancient Near East is linked to childbearing, the upcoming angel's promise of a child will naturally elevate her standing in the community.

13:3 The **angel of the LORD** makes a surprise appearance to Manoah's wife.[1] This cycle of oppression lacks any appeal on the

---

[1]See discussion at Judges 6:11.

part of the people for deliverance. God simply appears on the scene to rescue his people. The method for deliverance will be a divine birth. Although other characters in the book have had births relevant to their lives, the birth the angel of the LORD announces in chapter 13 is the only birth in Judges that is divinely instigated. This divine birth places Samson at the forefront of significance.

13:4-5 The angel addresses Manoah's wife, stating her inability to have children, and promising her **a son**. Although she is not given a name for the child, she is given a list of prohibitions that are to be permanently applied to her son. The condition being imposed on Samson will be the **Nazirite** attributes described in Numbers 6:1-21. The prohibition of alcoholic beverages and unclean foods is also extended to his mother during the pregnancy. While the entire Nazirite code will apply to Samson, the angel singles out the prohibition against hair cutting. Long hair, not muscles, will be the most visible trait of Samson's Nazirite status. And of all the Nazirite prohibitions Samson violates, shaving his hair will be the last of them.

The angel's visit is unique in that the angel appears to Manoah's wife and not to Manoah. Jewish tradition made clear that *both* parents are responsible for the training of a child (Prov 1:8). In Samson's case, however, the instructions for his identity as a Nazirite are given only to his mother. During the pregnancy, she is to be bound to the Nazirite dietary standards that Samson will later follow. Beyond issuing the commands, the angel also predicts Samson's role in delivering Israel. It could reasonably be expected that the angel will visit with Manoah as well, but the reader has to wait.

The angel of the LORD sidelines Manoah by speaking to Manoah's wife and not to Manoah. Matthews argues that with the exception of Isaac, in all similar angelic-foretold births in Scripture (Ishmael, John the Baptist, and Jesus), the angel speaks to the mother first.

> Few men in the Bible are singled out as chosen from their mother's womb to become a pivotal character in the life of a people. Only Ishmael (Gen 16:7-16), Isaac (Gen. 17:16-21; 18:10-15), John the Baptist (Luke 1:5-25, 57-66), and Jesus (Luke 1:26-45; 2:1-7) are announced to their mothers and fathers in quite the same way that Samson is to Manoah and his wife (Judg 13:3-14). Each of these annunciations, except for that of Isaac, involves an angel speaking to the mother first and then to the father, and each signifies the beginning of a special

relationship between YHWH and the child. The only major departure in the pattern between the Samson narrative and these other theophanies is that the angel does not name the child of Manoah and his wife. These variations may simply reflect poetic license on the part of the storyteller since the annunciation type-scene often allows for flexibility of detail.[2]

Matthews' "pattern," however, is inconveniently unsupported by facts. In the case of Hagar, the angel of the LORD announces not Ishmael's birth, but his significance; Hagar is already pregnant with Ishmael. Nor does the angel of the LORD announce Ishmael's birth to Abraham at all. The angel of the LORD speaks to Hagar to command her to return and submit to Sarah. In the case of Elizabeth and Zechariah, Matthews is simply incorrect. John's birth was first announced to Zechariah, and not announced to his mother Elizabeth at all. Although the angel of the LORD spoke to Mary before Joseph chronologically, only Luke records the angel's words to Mary. Matthew ignores Mary's encounter with the angel and focuses on the angel's command to Joseph. Two of the women Matthews mentions (Elizabeth and Sarah) are barren, while the births in all four cases are to be significant for God's purposes.

The common denominator, then, for these miraculous births is not the fertility or barrenness of the mother, nor is it the order of parent with whom the birth announcement takes place. Rather, it is the presence of the angel of the LORD and the prediction of God's activity through the life of the child. A second commonality between all these births is the command(s) of the angel of the LORD to the parent; each birth is to be accompanied by certain acts of obedience on either the parents' part or the child's part, or both. That obedience may be simply what to name the child (Ishmael or Jesus), or it may involve strict rules for behavior (Abraham and the covenant of circumcision, John's abstinence from liquor, or Samson's Nazirite status).

13:6-7 As would be expected, Manoah's wife relates to him the angel's visit and the commands issued. The testimony of Manoah's wife revolves around the intimidating presence of the **angel** of the LORD. She describes the angel as **awesome**, the NIV's translation of the participle form of the common Hebrew word for fear, ‏ירא‎ (yr').

---

[2]Matthews, *Judges*, p. 139.

The angel's physical manifestation is fear inspiring, and no credentials are needed. She tells Manoah that she did not ask the angel for his origin and was not offered **his name**. She reiterates the **Nazirite** status of her offspring, omitting the specific command regarding the prohibition of a razor touching the child's head. Curiously, she also omits the status their child will have as the deliverer of Israel.

13:8 After hearing his wife's account of the visit, Manoah accepts her testimony as far as his belief that he and his wife will have a son. But he apparently ignores his wife's account of the angel's commands. The reader might reasonably wonder why **Manoah** prays and asks for instructions on how to raise his son. Manoah's ignorant prayer, along with the angel's initial appearance to his wife, suggests that Manoah is far from being the brightest bulb in the chandelier. The narrative is beginning to sideline him as insignificant and ignorant in comparison with his wife. This marginalization of Manoah will continue for the remainder of the chapter.

13:9-11a In spite of Manoah's ignorance, **God** still graciously answers his prayer and returns for a second visit. But rather than appear to Manoah, the **angel** of the LORD again appears to Manoah's wife, bypassing him entirely. Manoah's wife quickly fetches him, and he follows her to the angel's presence.

13:11b-14 Manoah now begins to quiz the angel regarding his future son. With his first question, Manoah asks for validation that the angel is the same being who has previously spoken to his wife. The angel answers with a minimalistically elusive answer: **"I am."** Manoah follows up with another question concerning **the boy's life and work**. Manoah is inquiring not only about Samson's future but about his upbringing. The angel, far from accommodating Manoah, simply states, **"Your wife must do all that I have told her."**

The angel has snubbed Manoah for the third time. Rather than repeating the information concerning Samson's Nazirite status and upbringing to Manoah, the angel merely refers to Manoah's wife as the viable source of information regarding his question. With his succinct answer, the angel has validated the testimony of Manoah's wife, and perhaps included in that validation is an implicit rebuke of Manoah for not believing her.

13:15-16 After the useless query and quick brush-off by the angel, Manoah makes an offer of hospitality, suggesting a typical feast of

goat meat. Verse 16 reveals that Manoah assumes the angel is merely a "man of God" — a prophet. Manoah is apparently ignorant
about the messenger's angelic nature. Either the **angel of the LORD**
has not manifested himself in an impressive way, or Manoah lacks
the acuity to perceive it. The angel refuses the offer of food, but is
willing to accept a **burnt offering**.

13:17 Manoah's ignorance continues as the narrative progresses.
Manoah asks the angel his **name**, in order to have a basis for hon-
oring him when the prediction comes true. Manoah's wife's

> actions reveal that she accepts the Israelite tradition and that
> she knows better than to ask the name of the divine or his mes-
> senger. In contrast, her husband, Manoah, asks, **"What is your
> name, so that we may honor you when your word comes
> true?"** (13.17). His question initially seems either ignorant or
> skeptical or both. That it is not ignorant is revealed shortly
> when Manoah fears death after the messenger has disappeared
> in the flame of the altar.[3]

13:18 The angel replies that his name is beyond Manoah's capacity to experience. This response again sounds like a reply from God
himself, and not from a messenger sent on Yahweh's behalf. Yahweh
is distancing himself from Manoah's human customs and expectations, but Manoah is slow to catch on.

13:19-20 Manoah prepares the **goat** not for a meal but for an
offering, placing the meat and a **grain offering on a rock** while the
LORD does **an amazing thing**. The NASB uses the plural "wonders,"
while the KJV translates the phrase as the adverb "wondrously."
Both are verbs in Hebrew, וּמַפְלִא לַעֲשׂוֹת (*ûmaphli' la'ăśôth*) making it
difficult to determine whether the miracle is an independent display or
connected to the angel's disappearance. Followed in the context immediately by the angel's ascension, the NIV offers the best reading.

13:21-23 Only when the **angel** ascends to heaven in the flame of
the altar does Manoah realize the divine nature of the messenger.
But here the text draws a crucial distinction between Manoah and
his wife. Both fall on their faces in fear of the angel, but their
responses are quite different. **Manoah** fears for his life because he
has gazed upon God. Gideon exhibits similar fears in Judges 6:22

---

[3]Klein, *Triumph of Irony*, p. 26.

and is reassured by the angel that he will not die from the incident. Manoah's comment might be perceived as reasonable in that context, except for the next comment by his wife. Manoah's quick-thinking wife rapidly dismantles his unfounded fears. She points out the logic of the situation, noting that had the angel's intentions been malevolent, then his acceptance of the offering and revelation of the coming pleasant circumstances would not have been forthcoming. Next to the acuity of his wife, Manoah is clearly obtuse.

This entertaining of an angelic host for a birth announcement echoes Genesis 18. Manoah, though, is no Abraham. Like Thomas's unwillingness to believe in the resurrection without personally observing Jesus, so Manoah is unwilling to accept testimony concerning the activity of God. Manoah reflects the very human desire to know God experientially — through the five senses. Miracles can only be believed and God only known if personally experienced. The faith advantage, however, as Jesus gently reminds Thomas in John 20:29, goes to those whose faith moves past the need for validation through direct experience.

The narrative of Manoah and his wife represents the fourth major gender inversion in the book of Judges. Similar to Sisera, Manoah lacks an awareness of what is happening to him. Deborah directly informs Barak that he will lose to a woman the honor of personally defeating Sisera. Likewise, Abimelech is painfully aware as he dies that his posthumous reputation relies on no one being aware of his death at the hands of a woman. Sisera, on the other hand, is not presented as being aware of the gender inversion that is not only forced upon him, but to which he willingly succumbs. Similarly, the text portrays Manoah's marginalization as leaving him no wiser to its occurrence. The text gives prominence not to Manoah (as the reader expects) but to his wife. The narrative portrays Manoah "as somewhat of a schlemiel, whereas his unnamed wife emerges as the clear protagonist of the scene."[4]

The sidelining of Manoah is unique in Judges in that it occurs at the hands of the angel of the LORD; Yahweh himself imposes the inversion on Manoah. The angel of the LORD figures prominently throughout Judges, appearing in three narratives (the confrontation

[4]Esther Fuchs, "The Literary Characterization of Mothers and Sexual Politics in the Hebrew Bible," *Semeia* 46 (1989): 130-131.

of the people in chapter 2, the encounter with Gideon in chapter 6, and the interaction with Samson's parents in chapter 13), as well as the Song of Deborah. The angel of the LORD is also prominent in Judges 11 by his conspicuous absence.[5] But only in chapter 13 do the angel's actions and words serve to diminish a character.

Feminist critic Cheryl Exum admits that the status of Manoah's wife is superior to Manoah, but still understands the text as demeaning to her.

> Manoah's wife, who is portrayed more favorably than her husband, is shown not to be trustworthy. She, after all, does not tell Manoah the whole message concerning Samson's future. Nor does Manoah really trust her, since he is not content with her account of the visitation but prays that the messenger come "to us". Even though Manoah never gets as much information as the woman about his son's future, he does get confirmation of the woman's story from the (male) messenger.[6]

Although Exum is correct that Manoah's wife does not communicate the whole of the angel's message, that hardly translates into her untrustworthiness. In speaking with Manoah, the angel tells him that not only has his wife received the full story, but that *she* should pay attention to it, in essence sidelining Manoah in the upbringing of his son. The angel's comments place Manoah's wife in the prominent position as the source of knowledge and responsibility concerning Samson's instruction.

Further, Exum's assertion that Manoah does not trust his wife because he prays that the messenger would come to them both is unwarranted. Manoah *does* believe his wife concerning both the arrival of a divine messenger and the nature of the message. He prays specifically for divine guidance relating to Samson's upbringing. Even if Exum is correct about Manoah's disbelief of his wife's recitation of the angel's message, his skepticism does not reflect a negative portrayal of the woman. Rather, it is an assessment of Manoah's stupidity. He trusts his wife's account of the visit enough

---

[5]Because of the similarities of the sacrifice of Jephthah's daughter and the sacrifice of Isaac in Genesis 22, the reader notes the *absence* of the angel of the LORD, who is not present to intervene on behalf of the young girl.

[6]J. Cheryl Exum, *Fragmented Women: Feminist (Sub)versions of Biblical Narratives* (Valley Forge, PA: Trinity, 1993), p. 90.

to pray for a return visit. He clearly believes his wife received a divine visitor, and he believes that he has been promised a son. The oddity is that he needs the message of Samson's Nazirite upbringing repeated. John the Baptist's father, Zechariah, is struck mute because of his disbelief toward the angel's message. The text of Judges, however, indicates no such disbelief on Manoah's part. Worse than a lack of faith, Manoah is simply a dullard, slow to comprehend the situation. He apparently knows the divine nature of the angel, and yet is unwilling to settle for his wife's testimony regarding the message.

Much of the difficulty commentators encounter in assigning Manoah's wife an elevated position within the text centers on her lack of identification. Anonymity, it is argued, is often a literary tool for dehumanizing characters.[7] Adele Reinhartz suggests that while the typical plot expectations of an angelic presence, the annunciation of a child, and the promised birth are fulfilled for the reader, the character portrayal of the narrative flows against the stream of reader expectations. Typically one would expect an unnamed protagonist like Manoah's wife to fade from the narrative rather than slowly increase her esteem in the plotline.[8] Reinhartz goes on to suggest that Manoah's wife's anonymity, far from portraying her as diminished in some sense, serves to link her to the angel.[9] "The characterization of the angel draws a direct connection between his anonymity and his identity. It is because he is an angel of God that humans are not to know his name. This must be impressed upon Manoah, although it is recognized intuitively by the woman."[10] Reinhartz suggests,

> This story may serve as a basis for challenging the assumption that woman's anonymity in biblical narrative is necessarily and in every case symbolic of her lesser status, her powerlessness and her role as victim. . . . Only by examining the anonymity of

---

[7]Corrine L. Patton, "From Heroic Individual to Nameless Victim: Women in the Social World of the Judges," in *Biblical and Humane: A Festschrift for John F. Priest*, ed. by Linda Bennett Elder, David L. Barr, Elizabeth Struthers Malbon (Atlanta: Scholars Press, 1996), pp. 33-46.

[8]Adele Reinhartz, "Samson's Mother: An Unnamed Protagonist," *JSOT* 55 (1992): 26.

[9]Ibid., p. 27.

[10]Ibid., p. 29.

a character as an element of characterization, in the context of the specific narratives in which she or he appears, should conclusion concerning the significance of anonymity be drawn.[11]

If Reinhartz is correct, then the anonymity of Manoah's wife enhances her position in the text. Manoah's wife is unnamed as a literary technique connecting her to the angel of God. If Reinhartz is incorrect and anonymity is a means of debasing a character, then a nameless woman still has a higher status than a dim-witted Manoah! The text effectively inverts the gender expectation between Manoah and his wife. The typically informed and wise male is ignorant, while the wife not only has knowledge, but a quick wit to enhance it.

An intelligent woman is only a problem for a man viewing her through an androcentric paradigm. In Manoah's case, the text gives no indication that he is androcentric, only dense. At the same time, the text leaves little doubt that Manoah is clearly inferior to his wife.

The society in which Manoah and his wife live is undoubtedly androcentristic, as were the earliest readers of the text. The comparison of Manoah to his wife presents an entertaining inversion of the gender expectations of the reader. Manoah is ignored by the angel for a visit, and ignored when he asks the angel a question. Manoah is slow to catch on, and does not think clearly or quickly. His wife does. The angel visits with her, converses with her, and does not confuse her. The narrative cleverly exalts Manoah's wife at his expense. It is the juxtaposition of Manoah and his wife in the text that present the contrast. The reader would be unfazed by reading the account of only one of them. An angel visiting a woman in the biblical text is not unprecedented, nor is a man's fear at encountering a divine messenger. But when Manoah's reactions are contrasted to those of his wife, Manoah emerges as inferior.

Turning the tables on a reader's expectation makes for good storytelling. In Judges God not only reveals himself, but does so in an enjoyable way through entertaining literature.

13:24 Chapter 13 ends with the birth of the last judge and hero of the book, **Samson.** His name shares the common Hebrew root meaning sun, leading some to suggest that Samson was named after the Canaanite sun-god Chemish. If so, Samson's mother may ulti-

---

[11]Ibid., p. 37.

mately have been confused about the identity of the angel of the LORD when she named her son. However, it is not unreasonable that Samson was simply named in connection with the sun independently of any religious or cultic connotations. This understanding fits with the spiritually astute nature of his mother portrayed earlier in the chapter.

Samson is described as growing and being **blessed** by **the LORD**. This may be a truncated version of the formula used to describe Samuel (1 Sam 2:26) and later Jesus (Luke 2:52). Samson is not described as growing in "favor with men." This omission is appropriate, since his reputation will make him odious to both the Philistines and his own people.

13:25 While Samson grows in Danite territory, **the Spirit of the LORD began to stir him**. The word used for "stir" is לְפַעֲמוֹ (*lᵉpha'ămô*), a term of force not used in connection with any of the other judges. The word carries the idea of impelling, suggesting that Samson will be powerfully motivated and utilized in his role as Israel's deliverer by Yahweh.

CHAPTER 14

2. Samson's Marriage (14:1-19)

Few narratives in the book of Judges draw more attention than that of Samson. The story of the man who pursues his passions to his own detriment at the hands of Delilah has captured imaginations for centuries. Samson is portrayed as a pursuer of his passions, and his unbridled lust and his impulsive anger are directed by God at Israel's enemy, the Philistines.

Instrumental in God's activity against the Philistines, Samson well represents the symbolic zenith of Yahweh's power in the book of Judges. Samson's birth is divinely predicted and orchestrated, and his abilities are superhuman. The last of the judges in the book, Samson never leads an army and always acts alone. He is the ultimate hero of Israel standing against Israel's greatest foe.

The Philistines are certainly not the most powerful of Israel's opponents during Hebrew history. Rather, they are the primary enemy during the era in which Israel forms its identity. The development of the early monarchy occurs in the context of Israelite resistance to the Philistines. Samson's exploits and David's victory over Goliath form the framework for Israelite self-definition during the Iron Age. Every hero needs an archenemy, and Israel finds its prototypical nemesis in the Philistines.

The Philistine presence in Palestine is older than Israel's during the Iron Age, and is therefore more entrenched and stable in every respect. The Philistines hold major advantages over the Israelites that have until now prevented their expulsion from the Promised Land. Philistine political organization is a cooperative confederation of powerful city-states that protects the population through superior military discipline and technology.[1] The Philistines have a monop-

---

[1] Hamlin, *At Risk in the Promised Land*, p. 129.

oly on iron in the region, making it difficult for anyone to mount an armed opposition (Judg 1:19; 1 Sam 13:19-21). In every physical way conceivable, Israel is at a military disadvantage to the Philistines. Fortunately, military prowess does not stop God from throwing a muscle-bound wrench into the Philistine works.

¹Samson went down to Timnah and saw there a young Philistine woman. ²When he returned, he said to his father and mother, "I have seen a Philistine woman in Timnah; now get her for me as my wife."

³His father and mother replied, "Isn't there an acceptable woman among your relatives or among all our people? Must you go to the uncircumcised Philistines to get a wife?"

But Samson said to his father, "Get her for me. She's the right one for me." ⁴(His parents did not know that this was from the LORD, who was seeking an occasion to confront the Philistines; for at that time they were ruling over Israel.) ⁵Samson went down to Timnah together with his father and mother. As they approached the vineyards of Timnah, suddenly a young lion came roaring toward him. ⁶The Spirit of the LORD came upon him in power so that he tore the lion apart with his bare hands as he might have torn a young goat. But he told neither his father nor his mother what he had done. ⁷Then he went down and talked with the woman, and he liked her.

⁸Some time later, when he went back to marry her, he turned aside to look at the lion's carcass. In it was a swarm of bees and some honey, ⁹which he scooped out with his hands and ate as he went along. When he rejoined his parents, he gave them some, and they too ate it. But he did not tell them that he had taken the honey from the lion's carcass.

¹⁰Now his father went down to see the woman. And Samson made a feast there, as was customary for bridegrooms. ¹¹When he appeared, he was given thirty companions.

¹²"Let me tell you a riddle," Samson said to them. "If you can give me the answer within the seven days of the feast, I will give you thirty linen garments and thirty sets of clothes. ¹³If you can't tell me the answer, you must give me thirty linen garments and thirty sets of clothes."

"Tell us your riddle," they said. "Let's hear it."

[14]He replied,

> "Out of the eater, something to eat;
> out of the strong, something sweet."

For three days they could not give the answer.

[15]On the fourth[a] day, they said to Samson's wife, "Coax your husband into explaining the riddle for us, or we will burn you and your father's household to death. Did you invite us here to rob us?"

[16]Then Samson's wife threw herself on him, sobbing, "You hate me! You don't really love me. You've given my people a riddle, but you haven't told me the answer."

"I haven't even explained it to my father or mother," he replied, "so why should I explain it to you?" [17]She cried the whole seven days of the feast. So on the seventh day he finally told her, because she continued to press him. She in turn explained the riddle to her people.

[18]Before sunset on the seventh day the men of the town said to him,

> "What is sweeter than honey?
> What is stronger than a lion?"

Samson said to them,

> "If you had not plowed with my heifer,
> you would not have solved my riddle."

[19]Then the Spirit of the LORD came upon him in power. He went down to Ashkelon, struck down thirty of their men, stripped them of their belongings and gave their clothes to those who had explained the riddle. Burning with anger, he went up to his father's house. [20]And Samson's wife was given to the friend who had attended him at his wedding.

[a]15 Some Septuagint manuscripts and Syriac; Hebrew *seventh*

14:1-2 In 14:1 Samson travels a few miles from his home in Zorah to the Philistine town of **Timnah** where he meets a woman. The text uses ראה (*r'h*), a word used elsewhere for a man seeing a woman for the first time (see Gen 34:2 and 38:2). Upon his return, Samson directs his parents to arrange a marriage with the woman. The first words from Samson that the reader encounters hint about how shallow the hero will be. Samson reveals his character when he emphasizes to his parents that he has **seen a woman**. Rather than address them respectfully, he demands that they immediately obtain the woman for him as a wife. The reader has barely encountered Samson but has already been made aware of his impulsive attitude.

14:3a Samson's *seeing* a woman provides him with sufficient motive for marriage. His parents respond with the desire that he marry from within the tribes of Israel. Deuteronomy 7:3 forbids marriage to foreigners. Whatever the pluralistic tendencies of the people at the time, Samson's parents cling tightly to the mark of the Covenant. The cultural dividing line between Jew and Canaanite is circumcision. Samson's parents recommend two alternatives to a bride from an **uncircumcised** people: Samson should select a bride from within his tribe of Dan or from the larger pool of available women within the nation of Israel. A wife from either group would have been acceptable to Samson's parents, and easily arranged.

14:3b Samson is uninterested in the nationality of the wife he chooses, and, by extension, the issue of personal fidelity to the Covenant. Any such concern on his part is secondary to his primary and superficial interest: the appearance of the woman. The NIV translates Samson's response to his parents as **She's the right one for me.** This unfortunate translation overlooks the Hebrew word-play in Samson's statement. The Hebrew reads, יָשְׁרָה בְעֵינָי (*yāšrāh bə'ênāy*), "she is right in my eyes." The root יָשָׁר (*yšr*), meaning "right" or "straight," appears four times in Judges; here in 14:3, again in verse 7, and in the refrain that brackets the final section of the book in 17:6 and 21:25. Samson chooses what is right in his own eyes in his initial appearance in the text. The Samson narrative immediately precedes the final section of the book (ch. 17–21). Samson's eye problems foreshadow the same problems the people as a whole have. In the early sections of the book, God's eyes provide the evaluation of the people's conduct. In the final section, the people's eyes provide that evaluation. Samson's use of his own eyes as a standard marks a turning point in the book. Samson is God's man, and yet an extremely flawed character who pursues his passions. More than any other character in the book, Samson is double-minded, engaged in serving God while continually compromising God's expectations.

14:4 God's eyes evaluate the evil of the people in the earlier sections of the book, and in the final section, the people do what is right in their own eyes. In the middle section and Zenith of the book, Samson alone is the standard of his own conduct. And what is right in Samson's eyes is his lust for an inappropriate woman. His Gomer-like cravings prefigure the very thing the people will do in the final section. Israel commits spiritual adultery against Yahweh by choosing what looks right in their own eyes, in opposition to the very thing Moses warned them against (Deut 12:8,28). Eyes tend to be a problem throughout Judges. Samson's troubles (and the Philistines!) start with the description of a woman who looked "good in my eyes." When God's eyes see evil, the oppression of Israel by its enemies follows. When the people do what is right in their own eyes, anarchy results.

While Samson is often criticized for pursuing his shallow desires, the structure of the text is crucial to understanding the surprising theology occurring at this point. Verse 14:1 is not the introduction to Samson; 13:24 is. Verse 13:25 clearly states that the Spirit of the LORD is motivating Samson. In the cases of other judges, the Spirit of the LORD endows and motivates the deliverer with leadership (3:10; 6:34; 11:29). But in Samson's case, the Spirit of the LORD seems to motivate him to impulsive acts. In every instance of the phrase in Judges, the presence of the Spirit of the LORD on the judge results in a specific action within the text.

The Spirit of the LORD stirs Samson in 13:25. In 14:1-3, Samson stubbornly follows his shallow urges and pursues a Philistine wife. Verse 14:4 provides the behind-the-scenes of Samson's motivations: Yahweh is behind them. Samson's parents are unaware that Samson's desire for a Philistine wife is "from Yahweh." The author's description of Samson following his one-track mind is carefully positioned between two statements about Yahweh's involvement in Samson's motivation.

That God would foment Samson's lust is theologically unjustifiable. The very passions that cause Samson to suffer would be unjust if they are artificially induced by Yahweh. God cannot be the source for Samson's inappropriate proclivities and desires (Jas 1:13). Rather, God utilizes Samson's drives and channels them for his divine purposes.

The best solution is that God's Spirit stirred Samson *to go to Timnah.* God, fully aware of Samson's appetites, knows that a Philistine woman Samson will find attractive resides in Timnah, so he motivates Samson to make the journey there. The Spirit of the LORD similarly motivated Jephthah to make a journey in Judges 11:29. God desires to create circumstances in which the Philistines can be confronted and harassed, and he uses his Spirit to strategically position an impulsive womanizer and temperamental Nazirite to do it. The narrator weaves the story around Samson skillfully to present him as both a tool of Yahweh and a victim of his own passions. Yahweh is the ultimate source behind the slaughter and vandalism wrought by Samson. Although Samson's passions will ultimately cost him his life, Yahweh exploits them for Israel's benefit.

14:5 Having won over his parents, Samson journeys with them **to Timnah**. The mention of **the vineyards of Timnah** is not an irrelevant detail, but likely a reference to Samson's Nazirite status. Nazirites are prohibited not only from alcoholic beverages, but also from grapes and raisins (Num 6:3). By mentioning the vineyards, the narrator is reminding the reader of Samson's Nazirite status, hinting that Samson may be violating his Nazirite status in the vineyards near Timnah.

Samson's mother is given the divine charge to make Samson a Nazirite. Samson's Nazirite status is not a vow Samson himself takes in keeping with Numbers 6. Rather, Samson is designated by God as a Nazirite from birth. So while the components of the vow — abstinence from alcohol and grapes, never cutting hair, and avoiding touching the dead — are present in Samson's life, it is not of his own volition. Consequently, it should come as no surprise to the reader when the sensuous Samson violates each of these.

14:6 Apparently traveling some distance from his parents, Samson is confronted by a lion and quickly kills it without their knowledge. **The Spirit of the LORD** empowers him for this supernatural task, and the ease with which Samson performs it is likened to the easy separation of a goat. To emphasize the secrecy of the riddle Samson will soon offer his wedding guests, the text notes that Samson does not inform his parents about his miraculous kill. Samson's omission also serves to avoid any confrontation of his parents over further violation of his Nazirite status.

14:7 After killing the lion, Samson arrives in Timnah and talks **with the woman** he has previously entreated his parents to obtain for him as a bride. For a second time, the woman is described as being "right in Samson's eyes." Presumably, Samson's parents arrange the marriage at this time.

14:8 An undetermined gap of time occurs between verses 7 and 8. In the interim Samson and his parents have returned home. On a later trip back to Timnah, Samson makes a detour to observe **the lion's carcass**. Inside the carcass is a beehive, a hive old enough to produce enough **honey** for Samson to eat and share with his parents. Many have suggested that this story (if not the larger narrative) is entirely fictional, since bees naturally avoid decaying flesh. Although bees will avoid a rotting carcass, they will not avoid a dried one. Arab travelers in the Middle East commonly report that the summer months can dry the moisture from a corpse in a single day.[2] A dried, hollowed-out carcass would easily provide a desirable location for a colony, especially in an agricultural area where trees are few.

14:9 That Samson has been trained in keeping the commitments of a Nazirite is evident in 14:9. When Samson kills the lion, he violates the cleanliness laws by removing honey from the lion's carcass (Num 6:6). Although he shares the honey with his parents, he carefully avoids telling them about the lion or the tainted and unclean nature of the honey. The text subtly presents Samson's small compromises on his Nazirite status. Samson is not portrayed as drinking, but as being in proximity of the vineyards. He kills the lion, later retrieving the honey from the carcass without being described as touching it. As the narrative progresses, the reader encounters the ongoing deterioration of Samson's Nazirite status.

14:10 Samson's **father** travels to Timnah to interact with the young Philistine **woman**, likely to finish marriage negotiations and participate in wedding preparation. Samson, for his part, holds a **customary** bridegroom **feast**.

14:11 Because he is in Philistine territory, his groomsmen are provided for him. These are not merely warm bodies, but at least acquaintances and perhaps some friendships that Samson has cultivated throughout the period of marriage negotiations with his fiancée and her family. Judges 14:20 indicates that there is at least one attendee at the feast that had a closer relationship to Samson.

C.F. Burney suggests that the wedding feast is a "drinking bout."[3] If so, Samson's wedding celebration has further implications for Samson's Nazirite status. The Nazirite lifestyle was undertaken as a tem-

[2]Cohen, *Joshua and Judges*, p. 270.
[3]Burney, *Judges*, p. 344.

porary vow of devotion, and consequently was a matter of choice. Samson is never mentioned as having taken a Nazirite vow. On the contrary, it is clear that his Nazirite status has been assigned to him, before birth, by Yahweh. Samson did not choose to be a Nazirite, which makes it somewhat easier to understand his flippant attitude toward it described in the text. He did not have a personal, emotional investment and commitment to his Nazirite condition. Samson represents one more example of the dangers of externally imposed morality. A person's behavior can certainly be controlled, but an internal moral gyroscope is a far superior regulator of righteousness. An externally applied righteousness cannot guarantee a righteous heart, but a righteous heart produces righteous behavior. Unfortunately, Samson lacks both an internal righteousness and an external motivator to restrain his behavior. His parents are the only ones who attempt to point him in a moral direction when they encourage him to marry an Israelite, but their influence is insufficient. Without restraint, the maverick Samson follows his unrestrained passions.

14:12-13 The author selects details surrounding the wedding relevant to God's intentions toward the Philistines. The first detail is a riddle proposed by Samson that will result in thirty Philistine deaths at the hands of the hotheaded groom. As part of the feast's entertainment, Samson offers **a riddle** to his guests. He offers them **the seven days of the feast** to solve the riddle, wagering **thirty** changes of clothing on the solution. Thirty changes of clothing are likely more clothing than Samson can use, but represent a costly price for his thirty guests. Eager to demonstrate his intellectual superiority and wit, Samson makes the offer, never considering that he might lose the wager.

Riddles in the ancient Near East were poetic creations that focused on the resolution of paradox.[4] The Hebrew word חִידָה (ḥîdāh) occurs nine times in the Old Testament outside of its eight appearances in Judges. The word often indicates speech in which information is hidden.[5] Only in its Judges use does it function as a riddle requiring an answer.[6] Samson is, of course, uninterested in

---

[4]Karl McDaniel, "Samson's Riddle," *Did* 12 (Spring 2001): 47.

[5]Num 12:8; 2 Chr 9:1; 1 Kgs 10:1; Ezek 17:2; Hab 2:6; Ps 49:4; 78:2; Prov 1:6 and Dan 8:23.

[6]Othniel Margalith, "Samson's Riddle and Samson's Magic Locks," *VT* 36 (April 1986): 226.

his guests solving the puzzle. He provides them with the riddle with hopes that they are unable to solve it, since he stands to gain substantially from their failure.

14:14 Samson's riddle is a chiastic parallel between two couplets. The audience for the riddle knows that **the eater** and **the strong** are the same, as are **to eat** and **sweet**. In Hebrew, it is not the words that rhyme in chiastic poetry, but the ideas. Samson's listeners were looking for a source of enjoyable food that was also powerful. The reader of the narrative has already encountered and knows the solution to the riddle. The Philistines, however, are at a loss as to the solution. Part of the difficulty Samson's guests have in solving the riddle is their lack of a context with which to solve the puzzle. Some suggest that the guests' natural inclination would tend to view the riddle within the context of the wedding feast. The guests would therefore interpret the riddle in terms of the food and drink present during the feast, or perhaps as sexual innuendo, which would be common at such an event.[7]

14:15 Unable to solve the riddle after three days, Samson's wedding guests resort to discovering the answer through alternative means. Threatening to **burn** Samson's fiancée and her **father's household to death**, they effectively coerce the woman into obtaining the solution. Their relationship with Samson is beginning to sour as they blame the bride for their problems, asking, **"Did you bring us here to rob us?"**

14:16-17 Samson's bride manipulates Samson by playing on his affections, suggesting that he must not love her since he has not revealed to her the solution to the riddle. She cries and nags Samson throughout the seven-day feast, ultimately becoming enough of a nuisance to Samson that he gives in and tells her the riddle's answer. Samson tells his wife in verse 16 that he has not revealed the solution of the riddle even to his parents. His parents also have not been privy to the context of the lion and honey that provide the basis for the riddle. Only Samson and his wife now know the answer, leaving no doubt as to how the Philistines will learn the answer.

The timeline regarding the riddle poses some difficulty. Samson proffers the riddle with an allowance of the seven days of the feast in which to solve it (14:12). The Philistines have not solved it after

---

[7]McDaniel, "Samson's Riddle," pp. 53-54.

three days (14:14) and approach Samson's wife **on the fourth day** for the solution (14:15). The difficulty arises with the statement in verse 17 that Samson's wife **cried** the entire week **of the feast**. She apparently has been crying for three days for the answer before she is threatened.

The likely solution to this dilemma is that Samson's wife was encouraged to seek the answer from her husband as soon as the riddle was asked at the beginning of the feast. She begins crying in her attempt to manipulate Samson, to no avail. The death threat against her and her father is made on the fourth day. She does not change the method of her appeal to Samson, but very likely increases the intensity in order to wear him down. Her machinations are successful, and Samson acquiesces.

14:18 Learning the answer to the riddle, Samson's bride passes the solution on to her people. Samson's bride, although deceitful, has operated under duress. She serves in the narrative to reveal Samson's vulnerability to female manipulation. The reader will experience no surprise in chapter 16 when Delilah employs the same mechanisms to elicit information from the tight-lipped Samson.

The Philistines only learn of the solution to the riddle on the last day of the feast. The text notes the impending deadline of **sunset on the seventh day.** Within the allotted time period, Samson's Philistine wedding guests offer their solution to the riddle. Without an awareness of Samson's killing the lion in the vicinity of Timnah and his later finding a honeycomb in the carcass, the Philistines nevertheless are able to provide the correct answer to the riddle.

Samson immediately knows the source of their information. He responds by placing the blame on the guests and acknowledging his wife's complicity. He refers to her as a **heifer** used for plowing, a derogatory term indicating that she had been sexually promiscuous.[8]

14:19a His wager lost, Samson is responsible to provide a change of clothes to each of his thirty guests. The task will be accomplished through his slaughter of thirty Philistines. Empowered by **the Spirit of the Lord**, Samson makes a day's journey to the Philistine harbor and population center at **Ashkelon**. There he kills **thirty men** and loots their belongings in order to pay off his debt. Because Samson

---

[8]J.L. Crenshaw, "Samson Saga: Filial Devotion or Erotic Attachment?" *ZAW* 86 (1974): 493-494.

goes to the trouble of travel and murder to fulfill his obligation, it is reasonable to assume that he desires to provide the garments in good shape. Consequently, he needs to kill the men barehandedly, avoiding weapons that spill blood. Samson never does use a sword in any of the instances in which he kills, because he himself is the weapon and is able to make use of whatever he finds in a battle environment: a jawbone, stone pillars, or his bare hands.

When the Spirit of the LORD comes on Samson, he does not simply impel Samson to make the journey to Ashkelon as he did in motivating Samson to go to Timnah. The Spirit comes on Samson *in power,* shown by the author's use of תִּצְלַח (*tiṣlaḥ*) in verse 19. *Tiṣlaḥ* refers to the powerful accomplishment of success, prosperity or victory. The Spirit has powerfully come over Samson for more than just the twenty-mile journey to Ashkelon. The Spirit of God is again utilizing Samson's natural passions. Samson is angry at his guests and his wife for making him look foolish, and he also has to pay off an expensive wager debt. God does not motivate Samson to murder the thirty Ashkelonites, but he does provide Samson with the supernatural strength to do it. The combination of Samson's temper and God's power is lethal to the Philistines.

That God empowers Samson to commit violence is as unnerving as the idea that God incites Samson to lust. While God does not create the tendencies within Samson's heart, he does supply Samson with the means to act on them. It should be remembered that God does not need a morally pure-hearted warrior to strike at the Philistines. Samson's impulsive nature will strike out at the Philistines with what may be considered random acts of terror. It is the Spirit of the LORD that will provide Samson with the ability to express his carnal motivations in a supernatural way. God's purpose — always the foundation for his activity — is to loosen the Philistine grip on his people.

Samson's guests may well wonder how Samson is so quickly able to pay off his wager with Philistine clothing. They are unlikely to inquire too deeply, however. Samson is still infuriated when he leaves for home after paying his debts. Although news of Samson's actions in Ashkelon would quickly reach Timnah, the Philistines make no attempt at reprisal. They may be unwilling to risk an outburst from Samson after they learn of his capabilities.

14:19b-20 Samson's marriage, apparently unconsummated, is put on hold as he returns home **burning with anger**. The Hebrew uses the phrase אַפּוֹ חָרָה יִ (*yiḥar 'appô*), a common Hebrew term to emphatically express extreme anger. Translated literally, Samson's "nose burned." Samson is so hotheaded that killing thirty men does little to assuage his fury. Samson's bride, technically married but without a husband, is given by her father to one of Samson's wedding guests.

CHAPTER 15

3. Samson's Vengeance on the Philistines (15:1-20)

¹Later on, at the time of wheat harvest, Samson took a young goat and went to visit his wife. He said, "I'm going to my wife's room." But her father would not let him go in.

²"I was so sure you thoroughly hated her," he said, "that I gave her to your friend. Isn't her younger sister more attractive? Take her instead."

³Samson said to them, "This time I have a right to get even with the Philistines; I will really harm them." ⁴So he went out and caught three hundred foxes and tied them tail to tail in pairs. He then fastened a torch to every pair of tails, ⁵lit the torches and let the foxes loose in the standing grain of the Philistines. He burned up the shocks and standing grain, together with the vineyards and olive groves.

⁶When the Philistines asked, "Who did this?" they were told, "Samson, the Timnite's son-in-law, because his wife was given to his friend."

So the Philistines went up and burned her and her father to death. ⁷Samson said to them, "Since you've acted like this, I won't stop until I get my revenge on you." ⁸He attacked them viciously and slaughtered many of them. Then he went down and stayed in a cave in the rock of Etam.

⁹The Philistines went up and camped in Judah, spreading out near Lehi. ¹⁰The men of Judah asked, "Why have you come to fight us?"

"We have come to take Samson prisoner," they answered, "to do to him as he did to us."

¹¹Then three thousand men from Judah went down to the cave in the rock of Etam and said to Samson, "Don't you realize that the Philistines are rulers over us? What have you done to us?"

He answered, "I merely did to them what they did to me."

[12]They said to him, "We've come to tie you up and hand you over to the Philistines."

Samson said, "Swear to me that you won't kill me yourselves."

[13]"Agreed," they answered. "We will only tie you up and hand you over to them. We will not kill you." So they bound him with two new ropes and led him up from the rock. [14]As he approached Lehi, the Philistines came toward him shouting. The Spirit of the LORD came upon him in power. The ropes on his arms became like charred flax, and the bindings dropped from his hands. [15]Finding a fresh jawbone of a donkey, he grabbed it and struck down a thousand men.

[16]Then Samson said,

"With a donkey's jawbone
    I have made donkeys of them.[a]
With a donkey's jawbone
    I have killed a thousand men."

[17] When he finished speaking, he threw away the jawbone; and the place was called Ramath Lehi.[b]

[18]Because he was very thirsty, he cried out to the LORD, "You have given your servant this great victory. Must I now die of thirst and fall into the hands of the uncircumcised?" [19]Then God opened up the hollow place in Lehi, and water came out of it. When Samson drank, his strength returned and he revived. So the spring was called En Hakkore,[c] and it is still there in Lehi.

[20]Samson led[d] Israel for twenty years in the days of the Philistines.

[a]16 Or made a heap or two; the Hebrew for donkey sounds like the Hebrew for heap.   [b]17 Ramath Lehi means jawbone hill.
[c]19 En Hakkore means caller's spring.   [d]20 Traditionally judged

15:1a In spite of his outburst toward the Philistines and the apparent abandonment of his wife, Samson still considers himself to be married. Samson waits until the **wheat harvest**, occurring from May until mid-June, **to visit his wife**. He takes **a young goat**, an appropriate present to provide her family with a feast during the harvest.

15:1b-2 Arriving at his father-in-law's house, Samson intends to consummate the marriage, only to discover that his bride's father has given his daughter away to another man. Enough time has passed that the woman's father assumes Samson **hated her** and felt her betrothal to another man is justified. The term used for hatred is an infinitive absolute, making the hatred emphatic. Samson's father-in-law has reasonably assumed that Samson would feel hatred toward his wife after the bitter humiliation he experienced because of her. The man offers his **younger** daughter to Samson as an appealing alternative. He may be concerned about a possibly explosive response from Samson.

15:3 Samson comes to consummate the marriage only after his temper has cooled down. But upon having his desires thwarted, he becomes frustrated and angry once again. Samson justifies his revenge in advance, reasoning that the Philistines themselves are responsible for his marital woes. He states that he has **a right to get even with the Philistines**. Samson claims that he will be blameless (נקה, *nqh*) for the revenge he takes.

15:4-5 Samson expresses his rage by burning **vineyards, olive groves**, and fields full of ripened wheat. He captures **three hundred** jackals, ties a firebrand between their tails, and turns them loose on the ready-to-harvest crops. Samson likely captures jackals rather than **foxes**. The word שׁוּעָל (*šû'āl*) can refer to either animal. Foxes are solitary creatures, and far less common in the region than are jackals. Jackals are the animals more available for Samson's plans. Samson likely ignites the olive orchards by hand, if not the vineyards as well. Frenzied jackals carrying firebrands are not likely to set an olive orchard on fire easily.

A Roman sacrifice during the feast of Ceres is said to incorporate a legend regarding a flaming fox destroying crops. A fox was sacrificed annually at the festival in symbolic retaliation for a fox's once destroying grain fields. Ovid writes,

> She had a son, in childhood frolicsome, who now had seen twice five years and two more. He in a valley at the end of a willow copse caught a vixen fox which had carried off many farmyard fowls. The captive brute he wrapped in straw and hay, and set a light to her; she escaped the hands that would have burned her. Where she fled, she set fire to the crops that clothed the fields, and a breeze fanned the devouring flames. The incident is forgotten, but a memorial of it survives; for to this day a certain law of Carseoli forbids to name a fox; and to

punish the species a fox is burned at the festival of Ceres, thus perishing itself in the way it destroyed the crops.[1]

Ovid's poem and other similar accounts in ancient literature have led some to suggest the Samson narrative is but one of many fox-on-fire-through-the-field legends.[2] But a literary theme common in ancient literature does not by necessity invalidate the historicity of an event. Folklore may easily provide the impetus for original activity — Samson may have obtained the idea of using a flaming animal to light fields on fire from commonly known stories. Rather than considering the narrative of Samson's burning the fields as one in a succession of legends, Samson's actions should be understood as divinely sanctioned malicious vandalism.

Samson's vandalism of the Philistine grain fields is well thought out. In his desire for revenge, Samson destroys the entire range of Philistine diet and trade through fire.[3] Furthermore, capturing such a large number of jackals presents a logistical problem requiring advance planning. The animals would need to be captured and contained, as well as transported to various fields around Philistine territory. It is unlikely that Samson would catch each pair of jackals near each crop he destroys. The Philistines would quickly catch on to the source of the vandalism and move to stop him. More likely is a scenario in which Samson traps and restrains multiple jackals and moves them in pairs to individual fields he intends to destroy.

Samson's plan also requires an extended commitment to the completion of the malicious act. Samson would need both travel and time to round up the large number of animals required. Samson could easily set the fires himself, but prefers the malicious cruelty of exploiting crazed animals instead. Samson is creative, but malevolent. In his anger and desire to retaliate against the Philistines, Samson plans and enjoys the destruction he creates. And it is precisely Samson's spiteful spirit that God so effectively utilizes against Israel's enemy.[4]

The number of three hundred jackals may well be a symbolic

---

[1]Ovid, *Fasti*, 4.701-712.
[2]Soggin, *Judges*, pp. 238-249.
[3]Matthews, *Judges*, p. 152.
[4]Daniel Block notes that the burning of the grain fields may also represent a polemic against Philistine theology. The Philistine deity Dagon was a god of grain (*Judges*, p. 441).

number alluding to the number of troops under Gideon with which God delivers Israel from the Midianites. God uses a small army of three hundred jackals in the same way he uses Gideon's three hundred remaining troops to rout the camp of Midian. The number three hundred is used by the author not because of a concern for accuracy — as if Samson counted out three hundred jackals — but to connect Samson's feat to Gideon.

Robert Alter notes that the subtle literary motif running through the Samson narrative is fire. Jackals and noses burn, bonds melt like burned flax, a woman is threatened and later killed with fire. Fire provides the metaphor for Samson. Fire is all about total indiscriminate destruction, and so is Samson.[5]

Samson's impulsiveness and self-centered androcentric attitude once again causes intense suffering. Just as Midianite oppression devastated Israel's crops, Samson destroys the Philistine sustenance. In the case of the Midianite oppression, Israel could plan their diet and planting through flight and concealment of their harvest. After the seasonal raids by the Midianites, the Israelites would have at least a subsistence-level existence. Samson's deliberate destruction of the Philistine wheat fields, however, strikes a harder blow against the Philistines. Not able to predict the loss of their crops, both dietary and future planting supplies are completely destroyed, guaranteeing difficult times for the Philistines for several seasons. Vandalizing and harassing the Philistines is exactly what God expects Samson to do.

15:6 The Philistines investigate the source of destruction, and all fingers point to **Samson**. Samson is not identified as an Israelite, but as the **son-in-law** of the **Timnite**. The Philistines correctly understand Samson's motive as one of revenge over the giving away of **his wife**. In response to Samson's costly vandalism, the Philistines exact revenge, fulfilling their previous threat to burn the woman **and her father to death**. The Philistines seem uninterested in retaliating against Samson himself, instead punishing the initial source of Samson's frustration. They may be unwilling to confront Samson upon considering the slaughter of the thirty at Ashkelon. Samson's wife and her father make far easier targets.

---

[5]Robert Alter, *The Art of Biblical Narrative* (New York: Basic Books, 1981), pp. 94-95. See Judg 14:15; 15:4-5,6,14.

15:7 Samson's motive seems uncertain at this point. His wife has already been given away to another man, suggesting little need for emotional loyalty on Samson's part beyond possessiveness. Although it is unreasonable to expect the reader to display much sympathy toward the Philistines, it is difficult to avoid seeing Samson's wife as anything but a pawn in a masculine test of wills. Samson's wife suffers at his hands, and his own grief at her loss is ultimately a result of his intertwined impulsivity and ego. The Hebrew does not specify if Samson is avenging himself or his wife and her father, but it clearly indicates that Samson is responding to the murder of his wife and her father. The text records Samson's words as a "since . . . then" construct in which his reaction is linked to the Philistines' initial act. Samson pledges to stop his revenge after this response.

15:8 Samson **viciously** attacks the Philistines, killing an unspecified number. The odd Hebrew idiom is emphatic: "He struck them leg on thigh (with) a great wound." With his calculated revenge complete, Samson heads for **a cave** near **Etam**, some fifteen miles east of Timnah. Samson's hideout is located far enough inside Israelite-controlled territory that Samson deliberately uses the tribe of Judah as a buffer, and the Philistines will need to make a major effort to capture him. The Philistines are prepared to make such an effort after Samson's two murderous rampages. Their desire for vengeance motivates them to send troops to Samson's location within Judah's territory. They make camp near Lehi, close to Etam in Judah.

15:9-10a Judah is perhaps more oppressed by Philistia than the rest of Israel. Judah's territory is adjacent to the majority of Philistine territory. And with Samson's destruction of the year's crops, the Philistines have a motive for both revenge and a need to recoup their losses. Judah is likely the perfect target. For its part, Judah desires to minimize trouble with its more powerful neighbor. Rather than resist, Judah negotiates, asking the Philistines for the reasoning behind their battle formation against Judah.

15:10b The Philistine's response to Judah's query about their motive is one of simple revenge: they desire to extract revenge from **Samson** for his destruction of their livelihood. Rather than locate and confront Samson directly, the Philistines apply pressure on Judah to deliver Samson, perhaps hoping that the men of Judah will eliminate Samson so they will not have to. Samson's two previous outbreaks against the Philistines have revealed that he is an unpredictable and powerful threat. If Judah can be coerced into capturing Samson, so much the better. He is more likely to be compliant toward his own people than toward the Philistines with whom he still harbors the grudge of his wedding humiliation and wife's murder.

15:11-12 Backed into a corner by the Philistines, Judah quickly complies with its enemy's unspoken demand to deliver Samson. A company of **3,000 men** of **Judah** confronts Samson at **the cave** near **Etam**. They ask Samson a rhetorical question, inquiring if he was ignorant about the Philistines' rule over Judah. The question clearly implies that Samson has acted foolishly by upsetting the more powerful Philistines. Like many who exist under oppressive political regimes, the best Judah can do in its daily existence is to minimize conflict with their powerful overlords. Any tension with the Philistines must be quickly rectified in order to prevent the escalation of abuse at their hands.

Samson responds to Judah in much the same way as the Philistines: he matter-of-factly claims his intention has merely been to get even. The Philistines have murdered his wife, so he killed them in retaliation. Samson's response to the whole event seems indifferent, as if vengeance represents a common part of life. He also seems indifferent when the men of Judah relate their intentions to bind him and turn him **over to the Philistines**. His only stipulation for not resisting is that they swear not to kill him.

15:13 The Israelite's reply in the Hebrew is vigorous. They use two emphatic infinitive absolutes and two negative particles to adamantly pledge that while they will certainly bind Samson and deliver him "into the hand" of the Philistines, they certainly will not kill him. Samson, apparently satisfied with their commitment, allows himself to be bound **with two new ropes**. Fresh ropes are the strongest available, and their use on Samson will make observers of his restraints feel secure. The reader, however, knows that God's strong man will not be restrained so easily.

15:14 Upon seeing Samson bound with rope, **the Philistines** begin to cheer. Having subdued this enemy is a cause for celebration. But the text unravels the Philistines' expectations by following their exuberance with the same statement from 14:19: **The Spirit of the LORD came upon him in power.** The strength of the new ropes is compared to "linen that has been with fire" when Samson flexes his muscles. The bonds dropped — literally *melted* (מסס, *mss*) — from his hands. Normal strength in any environment is nonexistent compared to Samson's power.

15:15 The Philistine contingent sent against Samson is large enough that it could overcome Judah's small band of 3,000. The Philistines need not number quite this many, however, since they have superior weaponry. They do have enough of a force to lose **a thousand men** to a single warrior. Samson retrieves a **jawbone** from a donkey carcass. The author's mention of the fresh state of the donkey carcass is yet one more emphasis on Samson's violation of his Nazirite status. Samson has not picked up a dried bone found randomly in a field. He has deliberately reached into a fresh carcass and torn the jawbone from the flesh of the dead animal. Even a dried bone is off limits to the Nazirite. Samson has gone to the extreme to pluck his foot-long weapon from decaying flesh, making him unclean once again in relation to his Nazirite condition.

The battle ends with few details regarding the Philistine camp. The total number of initial troops and survivors are not mentioned. The emphasis is clearly on the accomplishment of Yahweh empowering Samson to kill a thousand troops. The Hebrew word for thousand is אֶלֶף (*'eleph*). In addition to the number "one thousand," *'eleph* can also be used to indicate a large group. As with the number of foxes, the author is not intending to relay an accurate body count, but is instead focusing on one Israelite hero's stand against a large enemy force.

15:16 Surrounded by bodies and covered in blood, Samson utters a poetic testament to his accomplishment. **"With a donkey's jawbone I have made donkeys of them. With a donkey's jawbone I have killed a thousand men"** is a wordplay in Hebrew. The word חֲמוֹר (*ḥămôr*) can mean either "heap" or "donkey." Samson has made piles of donkeys with a donkey's jawbone — he's made fools of the Philistines, besting them physically and piling their bodies in heaps.

15:17 Samson's terse speech is given with the jawbone in his hand as an honored weapon. Proud of having made donkeys of the Philistines, Samson tosses the source of his Nazirite contamination away. The site is named **Ramath Lehi** — "jawbone hill" — in honor of Samson's victory there.

15:18 The Spirit of **the LORD**, once he has come upon Samson, moves to the background while Samson bloodies his hands. Samson's thirst at Lehi returns Yahweh to the front of the narrative: Samson must rely on God for his life.[6] But it seems Samson is still self-centered in his request. He acknowledges God as the source of the victory over the Philistines, but the satiation of his thirst is to prevent his humiliation at the hands of an **uncircumcised** enemy. Samson has not suddenly become a loyal Israelite follower of Yahweh. When considering a wife, Samson demonstrated no preference for a wife from the circumcised Israelites. His own parents implored him to avoid the uncircumcised Philistines, but he refused. Here at Lehi he doubtfully has learned loyalty to his people, but uses both his status as a chosen judge and God's opinion of the Philistines to manipulate God into action.

15:19 God in his generosity provides Samson with water. God provides water for thirsty people in multiple instances (Exod 15:25; 17:1-7; Num 20:7-11; 2 Kgs 2:19-22), in spite of the attitude of the recipients. The water reinvigorates Samson after his protracted battle with the Philistines. The spring produced by God is used by the author as a chronological marker, **still** present **in Lehi** at the time Judges is written.

The name "**En Hakkore**" can mean either "the spring of the one who names" or the "spring of the one who calls." Either interpretation exalts Samson at the expense of Yahweh's generous provision.[7]

15:20 Chapter 15 ends with the summary of Samson's activity on behalf of Israel. Although he served as a judge for **twenty years**, no mention is made at this point of his death. The narrator has chosen to postpone the story of Samson's demise and death for the final section. Verse 15:20 brackets Samson's season of effective ministry, while chapter 16 narrates the downfall of the Israelite hero.

Samson's interaction with the Philistines demonstrates the cold reality of vengeance: Appropriate revenge is in the eye of the beholder. When not restrained by the life centered on the love of Christ, anger over an offense often provides the impetus for justi-

[6]Matthews, *Judges*, p. 154.
[7]Block, *Judges*, p. 447.

fied bitterness and hatred. Hatred, as it grows, gains hands and feet through vengeance and increasingly feels no need for restraint. The cycle of vengeance always escalates, because the receiving party always perceives the response as disproportionate to the offense, and a disproportionate response merits further retaliation. From practical jokes in a college dormitory to inner-city gang violence, retaliation rooted in vengeance is inherently escalatory. Jesus' command in Matthew 5:39 to turn the other cheek is revolutionary because it takes the natural inclination for vengeance and makes it subservient to a deliberate love for the offender. Pursuing vengeance is not what the follower of Christ aspires to; love is.

CHAPTER 16

4. Samson and Delilah (16:1-22)

[1]One day Samson went to Gaza, where he saw a prostitute. He went in to spend the night with her. [2]The people of Gaza were told, "Samson is here!" So they surrounded the place and lay in wait for him all night at the city gate. They made no move during the night, saying, "At dawn we'll kill him."

[3]But Samson lay there only until the middle of the night. Then he got up and took hold of the doors of the city gate, together with the two posts, and tore them loose, bar and all. He lifted them to his shoulders and carried them to the top of the hill that faces Hebron.

[4]Some time later, he fell in love with a woman in the Valley of Sorek whose name was Delilah. [5]The rulers of the Philistines went to her and said, "See if you can lure him into showing you the secret of his great strength and how we can overpower him so we may tie him up and subdue him. Each one of us will give you eleven hundred shekels[a] of silver."

[6]So Delilah said to Samson, "Tell me the secret of your great strength and how you can be tied up and subdued."

[7]Samson answered her, "If anyone ties me with seven fresh thongs[b] that have not been dried, I'll become as weak as any other man."

[8]Then the rulers of the Philistines brought her seven fresh thongs that had not been dried, and she tied him with them. [9]With men hidden in the room, she called to him, "Samson, the Philistines are upon you!" But he snapped the thongs as easily as a piece of string snaps when it comes close to a flame. So the secret of his strength was not discovered.

¹⁰Then Delilah said to Samson, "You have made a fool of me; you lied to me. Come now, tell me how you can be tied."

¹¹He said, "If anyone ties me securely with new ropes that have never been used, I'll become as weak as any other man."

¹²So Delilah took new ropes and tied him with them. Then, with men hidden in the room, she called to him, "Samson, the Philistines are upon you!" But he snapped the ropes off his arms as if they were threads.

¹³Delilah then said to Samson, "Until now, you have been making a fool of me and lying to me. Tell me how you can be tied."

He replied, "If you weave the seven braids of my head into the fabric on the loom and tighten it with the pin, I'll become as weak as any other man." So while he was sleeping, Delilah took the seven braids of his head, wove them into the fabric ¹⁴and^c tightened it with the pin.

Again she called to him, "Samson, the Philistines are upon you!" He awoke from his sleep and pulled up the pin and the loom, with the fabric.

¹⁵Then she said to him, "How can you say, 'I love you,' when you won't confide in me? This is the third time you have made a fool of me and haven't told me the secret of your great strength."
¹⁶With such nagging she prodded him day after day until he was tired to death.

¹⁷So he told her everything. "No razor has ever been used on my head," he said, "because I have been a Nazirite set apart to God since birth. If my head were shaved, my strength would leave me, and I would become as weak as any other man."

¹⁸When Delilah saw that he had told her everything, she sent word to the rulers of the Philistines, "Come back once more; he has told me everything." So the rulers of the Philistines returned with the silver in their hands. ¹⁹Having put him to sleep on her lap, she called a man to shave off the seven braids of his hair, and so began to subdue him.^d And his strength left him.

²⁰Then she called, "Samson, the Philistines are upon you!"

He awoke from his sleep and thought, "I'll go out as before and shake myself free." But he did not know that the LORD had left him.

²¹Then the Philistines seized him, gouged out his eyes and took him down to Gaza. Binding him with bronze shackles, they set him

to grinding in the prison. ²²But the hair on his head began to grow again after it had been shaved.

ᵃ*5 That is, about 28 pounds (about 13 kilograms)* ᵇ*7 Or bowstrings; also in verses 8 and 9* ᶜ*13,14 Some Septuagint manuscripts; Hebrew "I can if you weave the seven braids of my head into the fabric on the loom." ¹⁴So she* ᵈ*19 Hebrew; some Septuagint manuscripts and he began to weaken*

16:1 After an unspecified amount of time following the death of his wife, Samson, independently of both his desire for marriage and his parents' involvement, seeks out **a prostitute** in the Philistine city of **Gaza**. Gaza was the most prominent city within the Philistine confederation. Located some twenty-five miles southwest of Timnah, it would be a full day's journey across easily traveled terrain.

The woman Samson visits is described as a זוֹנָה (*zônāh*). The root is used to indicate sexual unfaithfulness and is used of individuals (Lev 21:9) and communities (Judg 8:33). The word communicates sexual activity in violation of proper relationship. Not only is Samson pictured as expressing out-of-control sexual appetites, he fulfills his desires with a non-Hebrew. He seemingly acts once again without any thought to his special status. Although sexual purity is not an element in the Nazirite status, Hebrew culture avoided fraternization with those existing outside the covenant. When the Benjamites need wives in chapter 21, the thought occurs to no one that women could be obtained from the peoples surrounding Israel. Those outside the Covenant were simply unclean to the Hebrews. Samson knows this fact, but seems to care little.

Three women appear in the larger Samson narrative: his Philistine wife, a prostitute in Gaza, and Delilah. Samson's second interaction with a woman comes when he enjoys this one-night encounter with a prostitute. This text serves a dual purpose in foreshadowing the Delilah narrative. First, the section foreshadows the Delilah narrative by informing the reader that the Philistines are actively conspiring to eliminate Samson. Although they will not be successful in this instance, the reader will not be surprised when they show up again with a scheme concocted to vanquish their enemy.

Samson's encounter with the Gaza prostitute also emphasizes Samson's reckless sexual impulsivity. Samson is sexually driven, and his proclivities place him in danger. Although nothing bad happens to him in this instance, the narrator foreshadows exactly what will happen to him later with Delilah. Samson's objectification of women places him in danger, and he will eventually suffer.

16:2 Samson's reputation among the Philistines likely ensures that traveling in anonymity is impossible. Word quickly spreads of Samson's arrival in Gaza, bringing out a stealthy mob that is willing to wait all night at the city gate. The city gate in the ancient Near East was the setting for community government. Discussions were held and decisions made there. To the ancient mind, the city was only as strong as the walls and the gate. Beyond the power, the meeting of city leaders at the gate communicated stability regarding the city's way of life. When the gates opened in the morning and leaders took their places, everything was as it should be. Samson will soon change that.

16:3 The gates, shut for the evening, will serve to keep Samson trapped in the city, allowing the crowd the leisure of waiting until morning to confront him. Perhaps they planned to leave the gates closed, hoping to back Samson into a corner and minimize his fighting room. That the gates are shut in an attempt to keep Samson confined within the city explains Samson's action. The text makes no mention of any confrontation, but Samson's attempt to exit the city could not avoid a mob lying in wait at the gate. Rather than fight the crowd as a demonstration of his prowess, Samson simply silences them by tearing the gates loose from their foundations and strolling away with them in the dark.

Samson carries the gates some thirty-five miles **to the top of** a **hill** adjacent to **Hebron**. The gate is now within Judah's firmly controlled territory, beyond easy reclamation of its owners. Beyond Samson's strategic placement of the gate, the long-distance relocation may have been Samson's own desire to express his power over the enemies of Israel. Surely anyone who could carry such a weight for such a distance on his back must be supernaturally powered. Yahweh, the power behind Samson, has once again demonstrated his superiority over the Philistine deities. The next morning the crowd, likely still quietly standing around with their mouths open, has experienced the inferiority of their deities and their cities. One lone Israelite has removed the gates, symbol of power and stability in a now uncertain city.

The gates Samson relocated would have been composed of thick layers of wood reinforced by iron, weighing thousands of pounds.

Beyond lifting and carrying such a burden more than thirty miles, Samson would need an even greater force to uproot the gates from their foundations. His actions read like a good but unbelievable story. As with all discussions surrounding miracles, however, presuppositions are crucial. Those who reject either God's presence or his ability to intervene supernaturally in the natural world must consider this story fiction. On the other hand, those who allow for God's deliberate temporary suspension or alteration of natural laws can easily accommodate the historicity behind this text. The reality behind the single miracle of the resurrection forms the foundation for all of Christianity. "Does God act in the natural world?" is a question for which much depends on the answer.

16:4 Delilah's nationality is unknown. The etymology of her name is uncertain. It may easily be a Hebrew theophanic name — a name that includes the name of a particular deity — or it may be a Canaanite name.[1] Delilah's home in the **Sorek** valley also provides little illumination. The valley is close to Samson's hometown of Timnah, but also within Philistine influence. Delilah's collusion with the Philistines suggests a Philistine background, while chapter 17 hints at her identity as a Hebrew.[2]

With the arrival of **Delilah** on the scene, the reader is prepared for the conspiracy against Samson to continue. Indeed, Samson's interaction with both the prostitute of Gaza and Delilah are treated thematically as one literary unit linked by Philistine plots against him. In Gaza, the residents plotted against Samson. In 16:5 the seriousness of Samson's threat is evident to the Philistines, and the five leaders come together to bribe Delilah to betray Samson.

Delilah is nowhere described in the text as the prostitute she is in the popular imagination. The text also nowhere describes a reciprocal love relationship between Samson and Delilah. The two do not share an epic romance. Samson in verse 4 is described as loving Delilah, but Delilah does not return the favor. Greed is the only motive the text allows to be assigned to her. If she is indeed a Philistine, Delilah is likely considered to be patriotic by her people.

16:5 On hearing about Samson's interest in Delilah, the Philistine **rulers** approach Delilah with an offer. After the events at

---

[1]Soggin, *Judges,* p. 253.
[2]See comments on 17:1-2.

Gaza everyone knows that Samson's strength must have a magical source. The Philistines offer Delilah 5,500 shekels in exchange for her discovery and revealing of the **secret of** Samson's **strength**.[3] The desired result is to overpower Samson and deliver retribution.

16:6 Delilah goes quickly to work in verse 6 and immediately asks Samson about the source of his strength. The text follows four cycles of interaction between Delilah and Samson. Delilah asks a question; Samson responds; "Delilah follows Samson's instructions and tests them by crying out 'the Philistines are upon you.'"[4]

In the first cycle, Delilah can easily ask Samson about the secret behind his strength with no fear of discovery of her ulterior motives. Her enticement, **"Tell me the secret of your great strength and how you can be tied up and subdued,"** does not represent a blatantly obvious question. Samson is subject to no individual or group, and how he can be bound and subdued addresses what would be total weakness for the strong hero.

16:7 Samson, fully in charge of his strength and his secret, has no reason to tell the truth to Delilah. It is unlikely that he expects Philistine involvement after Delilah's first question, but the reader knows with certainty what Samson may only suspect: Samson's impulses for women lead him into trouble. The reader immediately knows the trajectory of the narrative as soon Delilah acts on the false information. Samson replies that **seven fresh thongs** will immobilize him. The number seven is likely thought to have magical properties,[5] and Delilah is eager to discover the magical counteragent that will earn her the promised fee.

16:8-9 Delilah contacts the Philistine **rulers**, who in turn provide the fresh catgut twine with which she binds Samson. During the first and second cycles, the text does not mention that Samson is asleep. He is likely awake and playing a lover's game with Delilah. She flirts as she binds him, and he playfully feigns weakness. Delilah alerts Samson to the Philistine troops hidden in the room, and Samson, with his secret safe, easily snaps the cords.

Samson's answer further taints his Nazirite status. The fresh thongs are bowstrings made from animal tendons. "Once again,

[3]There were five Philistine rulers (Judg 3:3; 1 Sam 6:16), each contributing 1,100 shekels.
[4]Matthews, *Judges*, p. 180.
[5]Burney, *Judges*, p. 378.

Samson touches elements belonging to a corpse."[6] Ironically, the cleansing ceremony for defiling one's Nazirite status by contacting the dead involves shaving of the head. (Num 6:9-11), an action Samson will soon experience.

16:10-12 In the second cycle of question and response, Samson finds his motive to lie to Delilah. She presses him to reveal his secret because he has been dishonest with her. The reader cheers for Samson, knowing full well that the hero has met his match in Delilah. Samson knows — or should know — that whatever answer he provides Delilah will be implemented against him. Feeling unthreatened, he lies again. He declares that **new ropes** will render him helpless. The reader sighs with relief, seeing how well new ropes have worked against Samson in 15:13-14. Delilah again warns Samson about the presence of the Philistines, and Samson again is unfazed by Delilah's attempted hindrance.

16:13-14 In the third cycle, Samson wanders perilously closer to the barber. Delilah again complains that Samson has been dishonest with her and repeats her request for his secret a third time. Samson partially reveals the truth, letting Delilah know that his hair is involved. He informs her that if his **hair** is woven **into the fabric** on a weaver's **loom** and secured with a **pin**, he will **become weak**. These instructions seem elaborately bizarre, but Delilah once more slavishly follows them. Her third attempt to secure the Israelite hero fails as Samson wakes from his sleep, removes the pin, and easily resists capture. Delilah's altering Samson's hair "raises the question of how she accomplished the binding in the previous two episodes if not with his conscious complicity. One possible explanation is that it was a game to him; he was humoring her, aware that none of these things would successfully immobilize him." [7]

16:15-17 In the final cycle, Delilah increases the pressure on Samson until he reaches the breaking point. For the first time, she makes his love for her an issue. Delilah defines the parameters whereby Samson's love for her must be demonstrated. If he loves her, he must reveal his secret. The NIV translates Delilah's pressing of Samson as **nagging**. הֵצִיקָה (hēṣîqāh) is the same word used to

---

[6]Soggin, *Judges*, p. 254.
[7]Betsy Merideth, "Desire and Danger: The Drama of Betrayal," in *Anticovenant*, p. 71.

describe the "pressing" of Samson's wife in 14:17. Samson has a demonstrable weakness to women who apply emotional pressure. Samson is described with the idiom וַתִּקְצַר נַפְשׁוֹ לָמוּת (*wattiqṣar naphšô lāmûth*), "and his soul was shortened to death." The hero who kills a thousand troops under a sweltering sun is no match for a nagging woman. Samson breaks down, gives in, and reveals his secret. Rather than Yahweh being the source of his strength, Samson attributes his prowess to his uncut hair, which itself is a product of his Nazirite status. Samson has now revealed his love for Delilah, and in so doing has left himself vulnerable to any action she takes.

Samson, "either so naïve as not to see what was happening, or so arrogant and confident that he had no fear,"[8] is intimate and trusting enough of Delilah that he has no hesitation about playing the same game again. The cycle of Delilah's questioning, Samson's lying response, Delilah's hairstyling attempts, and her increasingly nagging appeal repeats itself three times until the fourth cycle, when Samson tells her the truth. Even though Philistines have three times attempted to subdue him, Samson still tells Delilah his secret. Perhaps he gives in to his heart and trusts that once Delilah knows the truth, she will truly return his love. The reader knows better. "The verbs follow one another in a rapid staccato tempo: She saw, sent, called for, saying, made him sleep, called a man, had him shave, began to torment, said — all these in the space of a few lines. Delilah is as much in control of events as she is of Samson, who sleeps on her knees in a clear position of subordination."[9]

The reader of the narrative cannot help but wonder about Samson's foolishness in finally revealing his secret. The first three cycles are all understandable. He can lie about the source of his strength with impunity. No matter what Delilah attempted, Samson retains his strength. It is difficult to imagine how Samson could be so foolish in light of the three attempts Delilah has made on his life. Proverbs 26:11 could well have been written with Samson in mind: "As a dog returns to its vomit, so a fool repeats his folly." One characteristic of fools is the inability to consider consequences. Fools have little awareness or interest in the future, preferring to cross bridges when they are encountered. Samson, the great hero, is also

---

[8]Schneider, *Judges*, p. 222.
[9]Merideth, "Desire and Danger," p. 72.

the great fool, and his foolishness will soon cost him his eyesight, his dignity, and ultimately, his very life.

16:18a The NIV's translation of verse 18 is somewhat less intensive than the Hebrew. **He had told her everything** is more literally rendered, "he had told her everything on his heart." The Hebrew word for heart, לֵב (*lēb*), communicates not the limited modern idea of a source of emotion and instinct, but the center of the mind and character. For the ancient Hebrews, the heart involved emotions, knowledge, intelligence, wisdom, moral quality, and the source of courage.[10] In sharing his secret with Delilah, Samson reveals his innermost nature and identity to her, making the sting all the worse when she betrays him.

16:18b-19 Having obtained knowledge of Samson's secret, **Delilah** summons the Philistine **rulers**, who return once more with the promised **silver in hand**. She lulls Samson to **sleep** and sends for **a man** who undertakes the task of cutting off the hair of the heavily slumbering hero. The text notes she **began to subdue him**. The cutting of Samson's hair seems to be the affliction Delilah causes. As Samson's locks of hair are removed, his strength dissipates.

16:20 For the fourth time, Delilah cries out that the Philistines have arrived and then disappears from the narrative. Startled awake, Samson assumes he will be easily able to resist a small band of Philistines, either not realizing his hair has been cut, or not believing that his strength has really been connected to his Nazirite condition and the length of his hair. The latter position may be more plausible. Samson no doubt feels the difference in weight as he stands. It is more likely that he assumes that God will support him no matter his actions. This assumption would be a reasonable conclusion for Samson to make. After all, no other violation of his Nazirite status has caused God to depart from him. God provided a spring of water after Samson had made intimate contact with the dead by killing them with a donkey's jawbone. And when Samson killed a lion and later retrieved honey from its carcass, God provided his Spirit to support Samson in his petty revenge. Samson, however, has failed to see the downward descent of his character and obedience. With the shaving of his hair, the last vestiges of his Nazirite status have been removed. Samson has violated every stipulation regarding

---

[10]"לֵב," *BDB*, pp. 524-525.

Nazirite consecration. In the most tragic statement in the narrative, Samson is unaware **that the LORD [has] left him**.

16:21 Without Yahweh's support, Samson is at the complete mercy of his Philistine captors. They **gouge out his eyes**, an action designed to cripple permanently and prevent any independence on the part of the captive ever again. This form of mutilation was a common practice in the ancient Near East, even in Scripture (Num 16:14; 1 Sam 11:2; 2 Kgs 25:7).

Samson's having his eyes removed also serves as a literary irony. Throughout the narrative, Samson's appetites have led him down the path to destruction. Finally, with his head shaved, eyes removed, and weakened body in chains **grinding** grain, Samson has truly become the victim of his own passions. The author has narrated how Samson's eyes continually cause problems. Samson desires women because they look good in his eyes. With his eyes removed, Samson no longer has the ability to follow his lusts. He no longer has the ability to do what is "right in his own eyes."

Samson is bound in **bronze shackles**, likely symbolic when rope will now suffice. He is taken to **Gaza**, where he had removed the city gate, and forced to grind grain, a task commonly assigned to prisoners and slaves.[11] Any work Samson does is clearly secondary to his value as a theological symbol and source of entertainment. The Philistines prefer Samson's permanent enslavement to his death. Part of the worldview in the ancient Near East incorporated a belief in divine retribution. By leaving Samson alive, the Philistines believe they have a testimony to the superiority of Dagon over Yahweh. They also would hold the normal delight over having subdued their enemy. The taunting and humiliation Samson no doubt experiences during this season of his life are an ongoing Philistine celebration of their victory over the Israelite hero.

16:22 With obvious foreshadowing, the author mentions that Samson's **hair** begins to **grow again**. When Samson's hair has grown, he will be purified from the uncleanness created through his violation of his vows. Almost as if his loss of hair and eyes have reconsecrated his Nazirite status, Samson will regain his great strength for one final, mighty act.

---

[11]Karel van der Toorn, "Judges 16:21 in the Light of the Akkadian Sources," *VT* 36 (April 1986): 248-253.

5. The Death of Samson (16:23-31)

[23]Now the rulers of the Philistines assembled to offer a great sacrifice to Dagon their god and to celebrate, saying, "Our god has delivered Samson, our enemy, into our hands."

[24]When the people saw him, they praised their god, saying,

"Our god has delivered our enemy
 into our hands,
the one who laid waste our land
 and multiplied our slain."

[25]While they were in high spirits, they shouted, "Bring out Samson to entertain us." So they called Samson out of the prison, and he performed for them.

When they stood him among the pillars, [26]Samson said to the servant who held his hand, "Put me where I can feel the pillars that support the temple, so that I may lean against them." [27]Now the temple was crowded with men and women; all the rulers of the Philistines were there, and on the roof were about three thousand men and women watching Samson perform. [28]Then Samson prayed to the LORD, "O Sovereign LORD, remember me. O God, please strengthen me just once more, and let me with one blow get revenge on the Philistines for my two eyes." [29]Then Samson reached toward the two central pillars on which the temple stood. Bracing himself against them, his right hand on the one and his left hand on the other, [30]Samson said, "Let me die with the Philistines!" Then he pushed with all his might, and down came the temple on the rulers and all the people in it. Thus he killed many more when he died than while he lived.

[31]Then his brothers and his father's whole family went down to get him. They brought him back and buried him between Zorah and Eshtaol in the tomb of Manoah his father. He had led[a] Israel twenty years.

[a]*31* Traditionally *judged*

16:23-25 Believing that the deity **Dagon has delivered Samson into [their] hands**, the Philistines organize a celebration to honor their god. Samson's oppression of the Philistines has been twofold: his destruction of property and his repeated killing of their people. Dagon was probably a local Semitic deity adopted by the Philistines when the sea-peoples migrated to the area.[12] The deity is known to have had temples at both Gaza and Ashdod,[13] a fact demonstrating another instance of historical accuracy of the text. In the midst of their celebration, the Philistines realize that their worship would be enhanced by the participation of the reason for their festival. Dagon has delivered Samson, and so they **bring Samson** to the event in Dagon's honor.

16:26 Samson is forced to "perform" for the crowd. The root צחק (ṣḥq) means to laugh, toy, or make sport of. The verb is in the third masculine singular, indicating that Samson actively performs for the crowd. Without strength or vision, a slave has little alternative but to endure the indignities thrust upon him as best he can. But Samson's situation seems different. The narrative proceeds as if Samson knows what he intends to do. Samson convinces his young guide to lead him to the central structural **pillars**. Able to **feel** the posts that support the roof, Samson is able to brace himself between them.[14]

16:27-28 Just before the climactic act, the narrator announces the number of Philistines present. Ignorant of their impending death, the 3,000 Philistines continue to look on while Samson performs. Apparently while entertaining the crowd, Samson utters his final prayer. He does not seek repentance, nor does he seek God's glory or deliverance for his people. He wants only vengeance. Samson's final prayer is solely about himself and his desire to pay back the Philistines **for** the loss of his **eyes**. Even after all he has endured, Samson's thinking has not progressed beyond the desire for revenge. He asks God specifically for a final occurrence of supernatural strength to deliver a single devastating blow to the assembly gathered in the temple of Dagon.

16:29-30 In spite of Samson's self-centered prayer, God in his wisdom and for his purposes answers. Samson's last words express his wish to **die with** his Philistine tormentors. Far from a noble desire to end the cycle of vengeance, Samson seeks one last act of retribution against his enemies and sees no benefit in living himself.

---

[12]Burney, *Judges*, p. 385.

[13]Ibid., p. 354.

[14]In spite of skepticism regarding the architectural possibility of such a design, Philistine temples with a dual pillar support structure have been excavated at Tel Miqne (Ekron) and Tel Qasile in Palestine. See Amihai Mazar, "Philistine Temple at Tell Qasile," *BA* 36 (May 1973): 42-48.

Even in expressing his own death wish, he longs to kill as many as he can.

Supernaturally empowered, Samson is able to dislodge the wooden support pillars from their stone bases and cause the collapse of the roof. The roof is likely overloaded because of the occasion, and the excess weight contributes to the building's collapse and casualties. Samson has killed an unknown but significant percentage of the Philistine nobility, crippling the leadership of the Philistine federation. The text does not mention a specific duration of peace brought about by Samson's actions, but does note Samson's final act has been his most significant.

16:31 Samson's story ends where it began in 13:25: **between Zorah and Eshtaol**. Samson's **brothers**, previously unmentioned, travel with family from the broader clan to Gaza and retrieve Samson's body. The death of so many in the Philistine leadership would make retrieval of the corpse attainable, whereas a previous rescue attempt of the symbolic prisoner Samson would have been tenaciously resisted by the Philistines. Samson has **led Israel** for **twenty years**, and as with every judge after Gideon, the text makes no mention of any period of peace he delivered.

Samson's prowess proves no match for the vulnerability caused by his appetites. Samson's attitudes in the text are those of a stereotypically shallow male. While many women are described as beautiful in the Hebrew Bible, their beauty is often incidental to their relationship with their husbands. Genesis 29:17 mentions Rachel's beauty, but Jacob has already met and interacted with Rachel prior to the description of her beauty. In Samson's case, physical beauty is the motive for the relationship. Similarly, his interaction with the prostitute at Gaza is because of sexual desire. The same is implied of his relationship with Delilah. Delilah "perpetrates an age-old and repugnant ruse: using a man's love to bring him down."[15] Samson can conquer men, but he cannot compete when juxtaposed with women.

The text also implies that Samson thinks little of the intellectual capacity of women — that they do not possess the faculty to do him harm. He tells his wife the answer to the riddle, unconcerned that she so desperately wants the answer in the middle of the wedding

---

[15]Lillian Klein, "The Book of Judges: Paradigm and Deviation in Images of Women," in *Feminist Companion to Judges*, p. 66.

celebration. He treats Delilah's queries as a lover's game, exhibiting no apprehension at her repeated requests and not making the connection between Delilah's actions and the arrival of the Philistines. For Samson, women clearly exist as a means of his own sexual satisfaction, objects of his own selfish gratification. The reader understands Samson's selfish mind-set as the cause of his wife's death, his disloyalty to Yahweh, and his ultimate defeat at the hands of Delilah. Samson suffers because he objectifies women.

Samson represents the beloved and classic hero of Israelite literature. He is an instrument of Yahweh, a supernaturally empowered underdog who will win any test of brawn that he encounters. And, like any great hero of classic literature, Samson is saddled with a tragic flaw. His muscles cannot give his heart the strength of wisdom it so desperately needs.

Samson's life serves as a powerful testimony to God's wisdom and graciousness. Samson's impulsive and narcissistic decisions result in consequences and ultimately cost him his dignity and his life. Samson's choices, like so many made before and after him, bear witness to the havoc potential that accompanies sin and selfishness. Wisdom suggests the safer and more stable path of righteousness (Prov 1:7-33). It is also reasonable to imagine that some of Yahweh's best work with Samson occurs while Samson sits, visionless, grinding grain. God often provides the comfort of his presence and teaches wisdom in times of greatest pain and hopelessness. Samson finds himself with significant time on his hands to contemplate his life and his role as God's servant. God uses Samson in spite of himself.

In spite of Samson's burdensome foolishness, God uses him for immense good. Preparing Israel for the monarchy requires the weakening of the Philistines as a viable threat, and Samson's ministry of harassment accomplishes just that. Samson's activity against the Philistines has been sporadic and limited in its scope. By the time of his death, he has achieved a relatively small body count in comparison with some of the other deliverers in Judges. His most significant act is the killing of the Philistine nobility at the end of his life. Samson's ongoing harassment of the Philistines has both softened the underbelly of the Israelite foe and psychologically prepared the Israelites to engage their enemy successfully. A young shepherd years later may very well have Samson's story in mind as he strides toward Goliath, sling in hand.

CHAPTER 17

IV. THE CONCLUSION (17:1–21:25)

Scholarship often treats the narratives in chapters 17–21 as a literary tradition separate from the main section of the book. The section contains a new refrain — "In those days Israel had no king." The section also contains many details that seem contradictory: a trained Levite who has no problem compromising the worship of Yahweh; a Levite who tenderly tries to regain his wife's affections only to later callously shove her out the door into the clutches of a mob; the Benjamite refusal to deliver up the clearly guilty — all seem implausible. Gregory Wong, however, effectively argues that these bizarre details are firmly linked back to sections within the main body of Judges.[1] The epilogue of Judges is anchored to the main section in several ways. The author makes a deliberate connection of the Micah narrative of chapter 17 to the story of Samson and Delilah, both through the amount of silver stolen from Micah's mother and through Micah's identity as a Danite (the same as Samson's). And similar to Samson's violation of his Nazirite status, the Levite methodically violates the components of the priesthood.[2] Similar to Jephthah, Micah is responsible for undermining the religious purity of Israel. Micah steals from his mother, fears a curse, and confesses. Surprisingly, his mother blesses him and leads him into further sin. Rather than demonstrating a true repentance, Micah epitomizes Israel's syncretistic religious tendencies, seen previously in the book.

Goslinga suggests that the lack of mention of judges in 17–21 indicates that this section occurs prior to the activity of the judges and is inserted by the author at the end of the book in order to por-

---

[1]Wong, *Compositional Strategy*, pp. 79-141.
[2]Ibid., pp. 89-96.

tray the overall sense of the time period,[3] but the chronological
markers in this section indicate a retrospective presentation of the
material anchored after the time of the judges. The author of Judges
clearly intends the narratives of 17–21 to be understood as chronologically subsequent to the events previously described in the text.

Bray argues that chapters 17–18 are a smaller unit added to the
book to serve as "a polemic against the ancient shrine of Dan in
Northern Israel."[4] Bray understands the origin of the story to be a
cultic foundation story, explaining the origins of the Danite cult.

A. MICAH'S APOSTASY (17:1-13)

[1]Now a man named Micah from the hill country of Ephraim
[2]said to his mother, "The eleven hundred shekels[a] of silver that
were taken from you and about which I heard you utter a curse—I
have that silver with me; I took it."

Then his mother said, "The LORD bless you, my son!"

[3]When he returned the eleven hundred shekels of silver to his
mother, she said, "I solemnly consecrate my silver to the LORD for
my son to make a carved image and a cast idol. I will give it back
to you."

[4]So he returned the silver to his mother, and she took two hundred shekels[b] of silver and gave them to a silversmith, who made
them into the image and the idol. And they were put in Micah's
house.

[5]Now this man Micah had a shrine, and he made an ephod and
some idols and installed one of his sons as his priest. [6]In those
days Israel had no king; everyone did as he saw fit.

[7]A young Levite from Bethlehem in Judah, who had been living
within the clan of Judah, [8]left that town in search of some other
place to stay. On his way[c] he came to Micah's house in the hill
country of Ephraim.

[9]Micah asked him, "Where are you from?"

"I'm a Levite from Bethlehem in Judah," he said, "and I'm
looking for a place to stay."

---

[3]Goslinga, *Joshua, Judges, Ruth*, p. 210.
[4]Jason S Bray, *Sacred Dan: Religious Tradition and Cultic Practice in Judges 17–18* (New York: T & T Clark, 2006), p. 42.

[10]Then Micah said to him, "Live with me and be my father and priest, and I'll give you ten shekels[d] of silver a year, your clothes and your food." [11]So the Levite agreed to live with him, and the young man was to him like one of his sons. [12]Then Micah installed the Levite, and the young man became his priest and lived in his house. [13]And Micah said, "Now I know that the LORD will be good to me, since this Levite has become my priest."

[a]2 That is, about 28 pounds (about 13 kilograms)   [b]4 That is, about 5 pounds (about 2.3 kilograms)   [c]8 Or *To carry on his profession*
[d]10 That is, about 4 ounces (about 110 grams)

17:1-2 Chapter 17 opens with the confession of the Ephraimite **Micah to his mother** regarding **eleven hundred** pieces **of silver** that had been stolen. Micah himself confesses to being the thief and apparently is afraid of the **curse** his mother has spoken, although he has no compunction about breaking other laws of Yahweh. Micah breaks two commandments regarding his mother: he fails to honor her, and he steals from her. When Micah confesses his theft of the silver, his unnamed mother praises him, apparently for his repentance.

It becomes important to consider the connection between the Micah narrative and the Samson-Delilah narrative. The deliberate placement of the Micah narrative immediately following the story of Samson and Delilah is indicated by the common element in both narratives of the eleven hundred pieces of silver and the similarities between the two women. The Philistine lords each give Delilah eleven hundred pieces of silver, the same amount Micah steals. The question immediately arises as to why the amounts are the same. The easiest answer is that the narrator attempts to establish a connection between the two stories: that Samson is Micah's father and Delilah, his mother.

Not only are they linked by the amount of silver they possess, they are linked by several incidental details. Both women are unattached, free to manipulate those around them. Further, both women are portrayed by the text as interfering with God's religious activity among his people. Delilah betrays a judge God has raised up, and Micah's mother betrays the purity of Israelite religion. The two women are also linked geographically. The hill country of Ephraim is not distant from the Valley of Sorek where Samson meets Delilah and performs many of his activities.

Although the text stops short of equating Delilah and Micah's mother, the association is clear. Some scholars do equate Micah's mother and Delilah. Schneider notes that there are

> circumstantial elements indicating that Micah's mother could have been Delilah. The Micah incident appears directly following Samson's death. The money is exactly same amount as the payment from one of the Philistine lords. The text does not state that all of Micah's mother's money was stolen, only one batch that happened to be in that amount. Micah, the woman's son, has no named father. While many male character's mothers are nameless, this would be the first case in Judges where a main male character did not have a named father, even if his mother was a prostitute. A final link is that in the story Micah has dealings with Dan, Samson's tribe.[5]

Schneider goes on to suggest that Samson is likely Micah's father. Although not explicitly stating the fact, it is cryptically suggested in the author's typical style.

Micah is evidently the head of his household. He has children, and the Levite he hires is described as "young" and "like one of his sons." Micah's mother is wealthy, possessing a large amount of silver that may be stolen. Cultural norms assume a son would care for a widow. Further, a son should inherit his father's estate. In this case, if Micah is the son of a widow, he owns the estate and has no need to steal. Consequently, it is reasonable to assume that Micah has not inherited an estate from his father, due, perhaps, to his lack of a father. Were his mother a prostitute, that would explain both her wealth and the lack of an inheritance for Micah. Jephthah, another prostitute's son, is similarly excluded from an inheritance by his half-brothers.

So rather than encountering a head of household with strong character, the reader meets Micah, a superstitious man afraid of a curse but who yields to his mother's leadership. In both the Samson-Delilah and Micah narratives, eleven hundred pieces of silver is the cost for a woman to betray a man. In Micah's case, his Delilah-like mother returns the silver to Micah in order to promote non-Yahwistic worship through her son; she spiritually pollutes Micah

---

[5]Schneider, *Judges*, p. 232.

and later Israel through her designation of the silver for the creation of an idol. Micah is at the mercy of a cursing, inveigling, manipulative mother.

17:3 Deuteronomy 12:2-20 provides a framework through which Micah's violation occurs. The Law prevented maverick religious expressions, particularly in terms of location. Jerusalem ultimately became Yahweh's designated location for religious expression. Micah violates this law, as well as the Decalogue's commands against graven images.

Idol worship has already occurred in Judges 8:27 with Gideon's creation of the ephod, which the people later worshiped. The text in both Judges 8 and 18 is vague, however, about the focus of the worship. "It would appear that the image was regarded as an embodiment in some sense of the god, a representation of divine presence and potency."[6] After its construction, the idol for the deity was sanctified through rituals. During the life of its use, the idol was routinely served through cleansing, incense, the provision of meals, entertainment, and, of course, sacrifice.[7]

Upon confessing and returning the silver, Micah's mother blesses him and dedicates the **silver to the Lord** for the creation of a graven **image**. The irony of the syncretistic attitude in Israel is clear in this and the remainder of the narrative. Idolatry is dedicated to Yahweh, who forbade idolatry (Exod 20:4; Deut 27:15).

17:4 Although Micah's mother dedicates the eleven hundred shekels for a graven image, only 200 are given to the **silversmith** for the construction of the idol. Some 900 shekels remain unaccounted for. Perhaps in the spirit of Ananias and Sapphira, Micah's mother held back a portion of the payment. She may also have rendered them as payment to the idolsmith,[8] but 900 shekels seems an extravagant fee. The most likely solution is that the remaining silver funded all the aspects of Micah's newly created priesthood.

17:5 Verse 5 describes the elaborate extremes to which Micah goes to create a personal priesthood. He creates a private worship setting that includes **a shrine** (literally, *a house of gods*), priestly raiment, and **idols**. The only thing missing from the environment

---

[6]Bray, *Sacred Dan*, p. 80.
[7]Ibid., pp. 81-83.
[8]Burney, *Judges*, p. 420.

Micah creates is the priest. But he quickly solves that difficulty by (heretically) installing **one of his** own (non-Levite) **sons as priest**. The term used here for **install** is used again in verse 12 when Micah consecrates a Levite he hires. יָד מִלֵּא (*millē' yad*), translating literally as "fill the hand," is a term that indicates ordination — an official appointment for religious service.[9] Micah takes the initiative and creates and applies the parameters for his own religion. The irony of the meaning of his name, "Who is like the LORD?" is telling as Micah assumes for himself prerogatives belonging to Yahweh.

17:6 The phrase, "There was no king in the land" makes its first appearance in 17:6. The term is often used as the filter through which Judges is interpreted, suggesting that righteous leadership is essential to the stability of a society. Gregory Wong argues that rather than referring to the Israelite monarchy and human king, the phrase "No king in Israel" is a comment about the divine King.[10] Numbers 23:21 makes reference to Yahweh as king, and this understanding fits well with the disappointment God expresses to Samuel in 1 Samuel 8:7-8. In his conversation with Samuel, Yahweh speaks as if his natural expectation is to be the King over his people. The flaw with the Israelites is not that they desire a king *per se*, but that they desire the wrong one. God wants no human king for Israel because he himself desires to function in that capacity.

Little has changed for the modern believer. The temptation to look to earthly leaders for spiritual solutions is a constant yet dangerous companion. One need look no further than contemporary political races to see followers of Jesus lining up to back a particular politician because they believe he or she will promote a spiritual agenda. Too often, however, pundits in all areas of the political spectrum cynically see religion as a force to be manipulated for political power. And, in spite of the heavy investment in the political process by the church, unrighteous leadership and the accompanying chaos still flourishes. Jesus repeatedly made it clear that the nature of his kingdom was not cut from the same cloth from which the world is cut. Christians certainly need to be involved in the political process. We should not, however, trust in the political process for spiritual solutions. We must look to our divine King for deliverance.

---

[9]Bray, *Sacred Dan*, pp. 90-94.
[10]Wong, *Compositional Strategy*, pp. 212-223.

Since 17:6 is placed just after Micah's introduction, it summarizes the brief preceding story and brackets the larger narrative of chapters 17–21. Micah, then, becomes the epitome of what is wrong with Israel in the later section of Judges, and, by extension, the entire book: Israel believes it can approach God on its own terms. God's conspicuous absence in the final section, however, betrays the foolishness of that idea.

Everyone did as he saw fit is the NIV's updated translation of the more literal translation, "everyone did what was right in his own eyes." The more literal translation has the advantage of tying instances of seeing and appearance together throughout the book. Samson desires a woman because she appears, as Samson says, "right in my eyes." Oddly, the NIV has retained the phrase for the Israelites' performance of evil (2:11; 3:7,12; 4:1; 6:1; 10:6; 13:1). The author of Judges deliberately juxtaposes standards of righteousness in the eyes of God against the self-centered desires preferable in the eyes of the people. Verses 17:6 and 21:25 form the bookends for the final section, demonstrating that the worst tragedies in the book are caused by the people using their own discretion, doing what is right in their own eyes.

17:7-9 Micah encounters a **Levite** who is living in the land. גֵּר (*gār*) describes an individual who is sojourning temporarily in an area. This traveler might be simply someone passing through, or a resident alien, generally a stranger to the area, often seeking an improvement in circumstances because of famine (Gen 12:10), or seeking wife or fortune (Gen 32:4). Travelers could usually rely on the hospitality of a community to provide for needs in the short term. This particular Levite's journey brought him to Micah's doorstep. The reader has already observed Micah's endeavors toward assembling his own religion. With the introduction of the Levite, the author has yet again skillfully inserted foreshadowing into the narrative as the reader waits to see how a Levite will respond to Micah's religious propensities.

17:10-13 Micah offers the priest an annual salary of **ten** pieces of silver, a change of **clothes**, and living expenses — a comfortable living which the Levite accepts. As he has done with his own son, Micah consecrates the Levite as his **priest**, personally ordaining the Levite for ministry. The Levite's presence in Micah's household is beyond priest; verse eleven notes the father-son relationship

253

between the two men. Micah in every way imagines that he has conveniently embedded access to Yahweh in his household. Micah's spiritual arrogance comes to the forefront in verse thirteen. The author allows Micah's foolishness to be its own commentary. Micah believes that Yahweh will prosper him because he has obtained his own priest. Whether he was neglecting the Law or merely ignorant of it (the latter seeming more likely), Micah has pluralistically crafted his own religion.

Micah's error lies at the core of all idolatry. He believes that God may be accessed through human-designed mechanisms. God as revealed in the Bible differs, however. In both Old Testament and New, it is God who reveals himself, first at Sinai, and then in the person of Jesus of Nazareth. Human efforts to access or control God fail because God cannot be confined by human comprehension. Human religious efforts are an affront to God because they are incapable of encompassing him. The author of Judges makes no editorial comment on Micah because Micah's foolishness is obvious to the reader.

CHAPTER 18

B. THE DANITE MIGRATION (18:1-31)

[1]In those days Israel had no king.

And in those days the tribe of the Danites was seeking a place of their own where they might settle, because they had not yet come into an inheritance among the tribes of Israel. [2]So the Danites sent five warriors from Zorah and Eshtaol to spy out the land and explore it. These men represented all their clans. They told them, "Go, explore the land."

The men entered the hill country of Ephraim and came to the house of Micah, where they spent the night. [3]When they were near Micah's house, they recognized the voice of the young Levite; so they turned in there and asked him, "Who brought you here? What are you doing in this place? Why are you here?"

[4]He told them what Micah had done for him, and said, "He has hired me and I am his priest."

[5]Then they said to him, "Please inquire of God to learn whether our journey will be successful."

[6]The priest answered them, "Go in peace. Your journey has the LORD's approval."

[7]So the five men left and came to Laish, where they saw that the people were living in safety, like the Sidonians, unsuspecting and secure. And since their land lacked nothing, they were prosperous.[a] Also, they lived a long way from the Sidonians and had no relationship with anyone else.[b]

[8]When they returned to Zorah and Eshtaol, their brothers asked them, "How did you find things?"

[9]They answered, "Come on, let's attack them! We have seen that the land is very good. Aren't you going to do something? Don't hesitate to go there and take it over. [10]When you get there,

you will find an unsuspecting people and a spacious land that God
has put into your hands, a land that lacks nothing whatever."

¹¹Then six hundred men from the clan of the Danites, armed for
battle, set out from Zorah and Eshtaol. ¹²On their way they set up
camp near Kiriath Jearim in Judah. This is why the place west of
Kiriath Jearim is called Mahaneh Danᶜ to this day. ¹³From there they
went on to the hill country of Ephraim and came to Micah's house.

¹⁴Then the five men who had spied out the land of Laish said to
their brothers, "Do you know that one of these houses has an
ephod, other household gods, a carved image and a cast idol? Now
you know what to do." ¹⁵So they turned in there and went to the
house of the young Levite at Micah's place and greeted him. ¹⁶The
six hundred Danites, armed for battle, stood at the entrance to the
gate. ¹⁷The five men who had spied out the land went inside and
took the carved image, the ephod, the other household gods and
the cast idol while the priest and the six hundred armed men stood
at the entrance to the gate.

¹⁸When these men went into Micah's house and took the carved
image, the ephod, the other household gods and the cast idol, the
priest said to them, "What are you doing?"

¹⁹They answered him, "Be quiet! Don't say a word. Come with
us, and be our father and priest. Isn't it better that you serve a
tribe and clan in Israel as priest rather than just one man's household?" ²⁰Then the priest was glad. He took the ephod, the other
household gods and the carved image and went along with the people. ²¹Putting their little children, their livestock and their possessions in front of them, they turned away and left.

²²When they had gone some distance from Micah's house, the
men who lived near Micah were called together and overtook the
Danites. ²³As they shouted after them, the Danites turned and said
to Micah, "What's the matter with you that you called out your
men to fight?"

²⁴He replied, "You took the gods I made, and my priest, and
went away. What else do I have? How can you ask, 'What's the matter with you?'"

²⁵The Danites answered, "Don't argue with us, or some hot-tem-
pered men will attack you, and you and your family will lose your
lives." ²⁶So the Danites went their way, and Micah, seeing that they
were too strong for him, turned around and went back home.

²⁷Then they took what Micah had made, and his priest, and went on to Laish, against a peaceful and unsuspecting people. They attacked them with the sword and burned down their city. ²⁸There was no one to rescue them because they lived a long way from Sidon and had no relationship with anyone else. The city was in a valley near Beth Rehob.

The Danites rebuilt the city and settled there. ²⁹They named it Dan after their forefather Dan, who was born to Israel—though the city used to be called Laish. ³⁰There the Danites set up for themselves the idols, and Jonathan son of Gershom, the son of Moses,^d and his sons were priests for the tribe of Dan until the time of the captivity of the land. ³¹They continued to use the idols Micah had made, all the time the house of God was in Shiloh.

^a7 The meaning of the Hebrew for this clause is uncertain.   ^b7 Hebrew; some Septuagint manuscripts *with the Arameans*   ^c12 Mahaneh Dan means *Dan's camp.*   ^d30 An ancient Hebrew scribal tradition, some Septuagint manuscripts and Vulgate; Masoretic Text *Manasseh*

18:1 Chapter 18 begins the descent of Micah's fortunes. The tribe of Dan is still without land at this point in the narrative. Joshua 19:40-46 describes the territory of Dan as being in the plains north of Judah from Joppa to the foothills. The area is valuable farming area, and the small tribe is unable to dislodge the peoples who fight ardently for its possession. Judges 1:34-36 indicates that the Amorites force Dan into their wandering role. The phrase in Judges 18:1 that Dan **had not yet come into an inheritance among the tribes of Israel,** — more literally, "possession had not yet fallen" to Dan — is the author's rather charitable method of pointing out that the tribe had failed in its attempt to conquer its allotted territory. While many assume a negative assessment of Dan is being made in 17–18, the author certainly avoids this obvious opportunity to criticize the tribe, opting for a more diplomatic presentation of their situation. Having failed to capture all of their allotted territory, Dan is relegated to a partial itinerant status, traveling as nomads throughout the region until its excess population can locate or capture an additional place to settle. Judges 18 is an expanded account of the summary of Dan's ultimate settlement as described in Joshua 19:47.

18:2a In good Hebrew tradition, Dan sends out spies to locate territory in which the tribe might settle. These five "men of strength" are described as being **from Zorah and Eshtaol**, a reference to the beginning of Samson's ministry that occurred in the same location (Judg 13:25). The connection with Samson might be intended by the author to portray the presence of men of valor as normative for the tribe: Samson is one of many strong Danites.

18:2b-4 The five spies make their way to **the hill country of Ephraim**. Relying on Jewish hospitality, they lodge at Micah's household. It is here that the Danites recognize the Levite. There apparently existed some kind of a previous relationship between the five Danite spies and the wandering Levite. The nature of their interaction may be nothing more than a previous encounter between sojourners. The nature of the questions the Danites ask the Levite suggest that their familiarity with him is independent of any cultic role. The Levite responds amicably, providing them with details of his employment.

18:5 The priestly role is a new gig for the Levite, one that the Danites are quick to utilize. Common in Hebrew thinking, the Danites **inquire** of the LORD, a typical action when dealing with uncertainty. Inquiry of God often centers on military decisions (Judg 20:18; 1 Sam 30:8; 2 Sam 2:1; 2 Chr 18:7). Inquiry also involves concern over sin (2 Chr 34:21), concern over a pregnancy (Gen 25:22), and even basic unknown facts (1 Sam 10:22). That God replies to simple inquiries demonstrates both his generous concern toward the individual and his management of the larger picture for his purposes. And while the old saying "It is easier to ask for forgiveness than for permission" may have a corner-cutting appeal, the Bible relates the undesirable consequences for failing to seek God's direction prior to decision and action (Josh 9:14; 1 Chr 10:13-14). One characteristic of many of the Bible's great figures is their habit of seeking God when faced with a decision. Moses, David, Jehoshaphat, Josiah, Paul – all are depicted as people who put seeking guidance from the LORD at the forefront of their theology. Contemporary believers often have difficulty thinking in these terms. Our society trains us to make decisions, and provides the information, finances, and technology to empower our choices. It is far easier to trust in military prowess or money in a checking account than to seek God for wisdom. Seeking God's input is too often the last resort, taken after our human resources are ineffective and exhausted.

18:6 The Levite responds to the Danites' query, missing the irony of his own status. The reader knows the Levite can hardly offer the true blessing of the LORD when his status as a priest is entirely illegitimate. Neither he nor the Danites question the efficacy of the priest's blessing, however, and the Danites continue on their journey.

18:7 The spies eventually encounter **Laish** (Leshem in Josh 19:47), a small city in an isolated area near the headwaters of the Jordan River near Mount Hermon next to the modern day Golan Heights. Abundant water makes the location highly valuable to a settlement. The modern day site of Tel Dan has a well-attested archaeological history, occupied as far back as 4500 B.C. At the time of the Danite takeover of the city, Laish is apparently settled by and under the jurisdiction of Sidon. At twenty-five miles to the northwest, Sidon is too great a distance to be of any quick assistance to the smaller city. Laish, a peaceful and isolated city, represents an ideal target for the Danites.

18:8-10 On returning to their home territory, the spies report that the area around Laish is lush and ripe for the taking. As part of the nation of Israel, the Danites have the right, given by God, to conquer the land. The author, however, emphasizes the peaceful nature of the people in Laish that Dan will soon slaughter (Judg 18:7,10,27). The text sympathizes with the people of Laish, while at the same time it notes the divine right granted to Dan (18:10). While the text makes no mention whatsoever of the moral and religious character of the inhabitants of Laish, they are certainly Canaanite and practice Canaanite religion. Merely driving the inhabitants out of Laish would not be an option, since the inhabitants would merely obtain reinforcements from Sidon and return. The difficulties for Christians with divinely sanctioned holy war arise here as well, as innocents in Laish will be killed rather than displaced. Holy war does not present the moral quandary for the author that it does for modern believers. Instead, the issue for the author seems to be that the holy war in which the Danites engage is not holy because their pluralistic and syncretistic worship is not holy. Because the cult that arises from Danite worship is pagan, the attack and slaughter of a Canaanite city represents the murder of innocents. The Danites and the inhabitants are morally equivalent in their religion, which makes the slaughter of Laish by the Danites unjust. When followers of

Yahweh displace or kill a people group because of a divine command, the action is just because God has commanded it. Judges presumes that the Danites are not followers of Yahweh, and therefore have no divine directive to attack Laish.

18:11 Laish is apparently a small enough town that a small task force of 600 soldiers is deemed of sufficient size to capture Laish. The group is more than a small army, however. Judges 18:21 indicates that the 600 have children and possessions with them, hardly effective tools for a military campaign. The 600 are likely the heads of households, making the assembly a fragment of Dan that is planning on permanently migrating to Laish.

18:12-14 The group camps in the foothills at **Kiriath Jearim** and moves along the central ridge through Ephraimite territory. Following the route the spies have taken previously, the group arrives at Micah's household. The five spies describe the cultic contents of Micah's house to the group. Narrated by the author in a way that builds the suspense, the spies tell their kinsmen, **"Now, you know what to do."** Feeling prospered by God at the word of the Levite, the Danites have planned in advance to appropriate Micah's homemade religion for themselves.

18:15-17 The five scouts ask the Levite about his welfare with a humorously ominous group of 600 soldiers standing in the background. The priest, caught off guard, has no option but to allow the looting of Micah's religious household. The Danites are not interested in Micah's wealth, but in the religious objects he possesses. The ancient Greeks were known to have relocated, even through theft, cultic objects for worship.[1] The Danites believe that Micah's cultic objects will be of spiritual benefit to them, and so they have no compunction about absconding with his idols.

18:18-19a The text emphasizes that the Danites exercise coercion by twice mentioning the 600 armed men. When the priest demands to know why the religious objects are being removed, the Danites respond first with a threat, and then with a job offer. They tell the Levite to **"Be quiet! Don't say a word."** This statement is not a command to secrecy, but rather to a humble acceptance of their power and the inevitable. The priest is told literally, "Put your hand over

---

[1]Bray, *Sacred Dan,* pp. 56-57.

your mouth" — a demand to be deliberately silent in the face of authority. Acknowledging God's grandeur, Job willingly performs the action after his encounter with God (Job 40:4).

18:19b-20 The job offered to the Levite is much more calming to his objections than the threat. The Danites offer the Levite the opportunity to serve as priest for their entire group. Because more prestige (and presumably wealth) comes with service to the larger group, the priest joyfully accepts, even to the extent of personally aiding in the removal of the cultic objects from Micah's home. The priest's joy at the Danites' proposal offers another window into the character of this maverick Levite. Even assuming his motives for ministering to a larger group are altruistic, the Levite's choice is fraught with difficulty. For any minister, the spiritual fidelity of a community to God is far more crucial than the size of that community. The assumption that size represents the primary indicator of fidelity is flawed. While a large community size can be one legitimate byproduct of fidelity, demographics, culture, population density, geography, and persecution all factor into the dynamics of any particular congregation. Both the Old and New Testament exhort God's people to pursue fidelity to their maker, trusting him for the results.

Several verses within the narrative suggest that the pluralistic religion practiced by Micah and the Danites is perceived as the worship of Yahweh (17:2; 18:6,10).[2] Nevertheless, the Mosaic Law tolerates no syncretism of religious forms and deities. While Micah and the Danites might be excused similarly to Jephthah for their ignorance of the Law, worship stemming from ignorance is not an adequate substitute for obedience. This reality is even more acute in the New Testament (Acts 3:17; 17:30). God seeks worshipers who are not only enthusiastic followers, but enthusiastically follow based on truth (John 4:23).

18:21 After stealing Micah's idols, the migrating Danites prepare for a violent confrontation with Micah's household. Expecting an attack from behind, they place their families, livestock, and valuables at the front of the procession, allowing for a quick defense if necessary.

18:22 Micah gathers his household and recruits his neighbors in order to confront the Danites. Micah's neighbors may have a spiri-

---

[2]Ibid., p. 139.

tual stake in the return of the cultic objects — Micah may well have made his priest and religious paraphernalia available to his neighbors for their worship. Or he simply may have purchased their assistance. Either way, it is doubtful that Micah intends a military confrontation. More likely, Micah intends to have a large enough group that the Danites will want to avoid such an altercation and return his possessions.

18:23-25 Tempers begin to flare with Micah's arrival. The Danites demand to know the reason behind Micah's pursuit. Micah, for his part, responds with a list of their offenses and the incredulous nature of their feigned innocence. The threat delivered to Micah is thinly veiled: he and his family will be specifically targeted for murder if he continues to protest. The Danites are not interested in violence, but they are prepared to utilize it. Targeting Micah and his family is both a heavy and shrewd threat. They will have no need to fight Micah's hastily assembled group, which has a lower interest in the conflict. If Micah knows that his own life, as well as the lives of his family, will be lost, he would need a certain victory to engage in violence with the Danites.

18:26 The Danites' posturing is successful. Calculating that he has insufficient strength of numbers to defeat the Danites in a skirmish, Micah acquiesces and withdraws, returning home. At this point, Micah drops out of the narrative into the obscurity merited by his foolishness.

18:27 Dan's itinerant status would have brought them difficulty in achieving residency through military means. They have no possessed cities to function as strongholds, and consequently would be at a disadvantage toward people groups that do. Their targets have to be commensurate with their limited ability as nomads to capture them. So when the five Danite scouts encounter the small, quiet town of Laish, they smell the blood of an easily crushed victim. The text again emphasizes that Laish is **peaceful and unsuspecting**, hinting that the city is undeserving of such a fate.

18:28 The Danites cannot risk retaliation by leaving survivors, so in what must be a bref attack, they slaughter all the inhabitants of the city. Laish's distance from their suzerain **Sidon** and its isolation in the immediate region quickly doom the small city. After killing the inhabitants, the Danites burn the city, only later to rebuild and live in it.

18:29-31 In making the city their own, the Danites rename the city **Dan after their** ancestor. Probably because of the remote location of their city, they set up a cultic center as a convenience. They erect Micah's graven image and construct their worship around it. Judges 18:30 finally identifies the priest as **Jonathan son of Gershom, the son of Moses**. "Moses" is the reading found in some versions of the Septuagint and the Vulgate. The Masoretic text reads "Manasseh." English translations are split on the issue, some, like the NIV and NLT, preferring "Moses" while the KJV and NASB opt for "Manasseh." The preference for Moses is likely connected to the name Gershom. Gershom is Moses' son (Exod 2:22) and from the tribe of Levi. The two Hebrew names differ only by the presence of the letter *nun* (נ), and scribal error easily accounts for the omission of the letter and the transformation of Manasseh to Moses. Others suggest the name Manasseh was inserted "to protect the name of Moses."[3]

The comment in verse 30 about Jonathan and his descendants serving the tribe of Dan as priests **until the time of captivity of the land** has several possible meanings and subsequent implications for the date and integrity of the text. First, if Judges is to be considered a unified book, the meaning of the captivity becomes relevant. If it refers to the exile of the Northern Kingdom, then Judges would have been written after 722 B.C. when the Assyrian Empire deported the northern tribes. A second option is that the captivity referred to is indeed the Assyrian exile, but that this particular verse is a later emendation added to elaborate on the Danite cult. While this option is plausible, it undermines the integrity of the text, which is unwarranted in light of Judges' carefully crafted literary structure. The third alternative is simply that the captivity referred to is something other than the exile of the northern tribes. A preferable option, informed by verse 31, is the presence of the Tabernacle at Shiloh. Shiloh has ceased to be Israel's cultic center with the completion of Solomon's temple in Jerusalem, but its disappearance likely occurs much earlier. As early as 1 Samuel 4, the Israelites experience defeat that involves the religious humiliation of the capture of the Ark of the Covenant. In 1 Samuel 4:21-22, Ichabod's mother twice uses the verb form of גלה (*glh*) to express the exile (captivity) of the glory of the LORD. This explanation fits easily, while also adding to the case

---

[3]Schneider, *Judges*, p. 243.

for an early composition date during the early monarchy for the book of Judges.

The narrative of Judges 17–18 explains the background for the polluted and self-styled apostasy occurring at Dan.[4] The text portrays Micah as a spiritual maverick, and that independently determined spiritual practice infects the Danites in the subsequent story of their northward migration, and Dan (Laish) becomes for the Israelites a place of spiritual compromise and disobedience. Ultimately, the cultic practices in Dan are supplemented by one of two golden calves fashioned by Jeroboam to provide an alternative to worship in Jerusalem (1 Kgs 12:28-30). There is no indication that the calf is used in cultic worship prior to the reign of Jeroboam in the north, and the Assyrian invasion ended its worship at Dan.

---

[4]Ibid., p. 241.

CHAPTER 19

C. THE SIN OF GIBEAH (19:1-30)

Judges 19–21 is commonly considered one of the most brutal and offensive passages in the Bible. The rape and murder of an unnamed concubine, her subsequent dismemberment and dispersal throughout the land, the slaughter of a city's innocent inhabitants, and the abduction of 600 women for wives combine for a distressing narrative. Although elements of human depravity appear throughout Scripture, this passage presents depravity at its worst. The human failings — cowardice, brutality, violence, and callous indifference — are extreme.[1]

This dark narrative from the Old Testament begins with the reminder that there is no king in the land. The phrase is repeated in the last verse of chapter 21, effectively bracketing everything that happens in the narrative within Israel's kingless context. The savage inhumanity expressed and experienced in these three chapters is traceable, in the eyes of the author, to the chaos resulting in society that lacks godly leadership.

[1]In those days Israel had no king.
Now a Levite who lived in a remote area in the hill country of Ephraim took a concubine from Bethlehem in Judah. [2]But she was unfaithful to him. She left him and went back to her father's house in Bethlehem, Judah. After she had been there four months, [3]her

---

[1]These extremes are often juxtaposed with various social issues: androcentrism and patriarchy, homosexuality, and hospitality codes, all of which are commonly used as filters for interpreting the narrative. Feminist interpreters have proved particularly scrutinizing of the passage, understanding the unnamed concubine in the narrative as a symbol of both the historical and modern male domination of women.

husband went to her to persuade her to return. He had with him
his servant and two donkeys. She took him into her father's house,
and when her father saw him, he gladly welcomed him. [4]His father-
in-law, the girl's father, prevailed upon him to stay; so he remained
with him three days, eating and drinking, and sleeping there.

[5]On the fourth day they got up early and he prepared to leave,
but the girl's father said to his son-in-law, "Refresh yourself with
something to eat; then you can go." [6]So the two of them sat down
to eat and drink together. Afterward the girl's father said, "Please
stay tonight and enjoy yourself." [7]And when the man got up to go,
his father-in-law persuaded him, so he stayed there that night. [8]On
the morning of the fifth day, when he rose to go, the girl's father
said, "Refresh yourself. Wait till afternoon!" So the two of them
ate together.

[9]Then when the man, with his concubine and his servant, got
up to leave, his father-in-law, the girl's father, said, "Now look, it's
almost evening. Spend the night here; the day is nearly over. Stay
and enjoy yourself. Early tomorrow morning you can get up and be
on your way home." [10]But, unwilling to stay another night, the man
left and went toward Jebus (that is, Jerusalem), with his two saddled donkeys and his concubine.

[11]When they were near Jebus and the day was almost gone, the
servant said to his master, "Come, let's stop at this city of the
Jebusites and spend the night."

[12]His master replied, "No. We won't go into an alien city, whose
people are not Israelites. We will go on to Gibeah." [13]He added,
"Come, let's try to reach Gibeah or Ramah and spend the night in
one of those places." [14]So they went on, and the sun set as they
neared Gibeah in Benjamin. [15]There they stopped to spend the
night. They went and sat in the city square, but no one took them
into his home for the night.

[16]That evening an old man from the hill country of Ephraim,
who was living in Gibeah (the men of the place were Benjamites),
came in from his work in the fields. [17]When he looked and saw the
traveler in the city square, the old man asked, "Where are you
going? Where did you come from?"

[18]He answered, "We are on our way from Bethlehem in Judah
to a remote area in the hill country of Ephraim where I live. I have

been to Bethlehem in Judah and now I am going to the house of the LORD. No one has taken me into his house. ¹⁹We have both straw and fodder for our donkeys and bread and wine for ourselves your servants—me, your maidservant, and the young man with us. We don't need anything."

²⁰"You are welcome at my house," the old man said. "Let me supply whatever you need. Only don't spend the night in the square." ²¹So he took him into his house and fed his donkeys. After they had washed their feet, they had something to eat and drink.

²²While they were enjoying themselves, some of the wicked men of the city surrounded the house. Pounding on the door, they shouted to the old man who owned the house, "Bring out the man who came to your house so we can have sex with him."

²³The owner of the house went outside and said to them, "No, my friends, don't be so vile. Since this man is my guest, don't do this disgraceful thing. ²⁴Look, here is my virgin daughter, and his concubine. I will bring them out to you now, and you can use them and do to them whatever you wish. But to this man, don't do such a disgraceful thing."

²⁵But the men would not listen to him. So the man took his concubine and sent her outside to them, and they raped her and abused her throughout the night, and at dawn they let her go. ²⁶At daybreak the woman went back to the house where her master was staying, fell down at the door and lay there until daylight.

²⁷When her master got up in the morning and opened the door of the house and stepped out to continue on his way, there lay his concubine, fallen in the doorway of the house, with her hands on the threshold. ²⁸He said to her, "Get up; let's go." But there was no answer. Then the man put her on his donkey and set out for home.

²⁹When he reached home, he took a knife and cut up his concubine, limb by limb, into twelve parts and sent them into all the areas of Israel. ³⁰Everyone who saw it said, "Such a thing has never been seen or done, not since the day the Israelites came up out of Egypt. Think about it! Consider it! Tell us what to do!"

19:1 The **Levite** priest referred to in 17:7 is reintroduced in 19:1. Both men are strangers to the area in which they reside. The Levite in chapter 17 is **from Bethlehem in Judah**. Although the author does not mention where the Levite in chapter 19 is from, the latter man travels from the hill country of Ephraim to Bethlehem to obtain a wife. Bethlehem seems a rather random destination unless the man is returning to his hometown where he has familial relationships that could assist him in procuring a bride.

The Levite returns to his hometown of Bethlehem to procure a concubine for himself. Judges 19:1 uses the term פִּילֶגֶשׁ (pîlegeš), indicating that the "concubine was a true wife, though of secondary rank."[2] The terms in 19:3-5 "husband," "father-in-law," and "son-in-law" demonstrate a legal marriage at some level. Some suggest the concubine is not a secondary wife, but a primary wife specifically because of these terms and because a primary wife for the Levite is nowhere mentioned in the text.[3] Mieke Bal suggests the woman in Judges 19 is not a concubine but rather a "patrilocal" wife — a wife who stays with her father and is visited at irregular intervals by a husband who has a nomadic profession — a wandering shepherd.[4] This understanding seems unlikely since the concubine left the Levite, indicating that she normally resides with him. The difference between wife and concubine may well be one of inheritance.[5]

19:2a The NIV translates זָנָה (zānāh) in 19:2 as **she was unfaithful**. Much debate swirls around the understanding of zānāh and its implications for the concubine's actions. Zānāh has been traditionally understood to express the basic idea of fornication.[6]

Some feminist critics interpret zānāh in a way intended to desexualize the term. "Playing the harlot" is considered metaphorical "in a society that so rigorously supervises the sexuality of its women, [that] the daring act of leaving a husband would be judged . . . as a metaphoric act of 'fornication'"[7] Rather than actually committing a sexual act that violated the marriage, the concubine's independence in leaving is equated with a sexual act. Seventeenth-century writer and poet John Milton notes that it would be unlikely for a harlot to

---

[2]Victor Hamilton, "פֶּלֶגֶשׁ (pilegesh), פִּילֶגֶשׁ (pîlegesh)," *TWOT*, 2:724.

[3]Hamlin, *At Risk in the Promised Land*, p. 161.

[4]Mieke Bal, "Dealing with Women: Daughters in the Book of Judges," in *Book and the Text: The Bible and Literary Theory*, ed. by Regina Schwartz (Oxford: Basil Blackwell, 1990), p. 27.

[5]Schneider, *Judges*, p. 249.

[6]"זָנָה," *BDB*, pp. 275-276.

[7]Gale A. Yee, "Ideological Criticism: Judges 17–21 and the Dismembered Body," in *Judges and Method*, p. 162.

bring shame to her father's house by returning there.[8] Many contemporary commentators follow suit, insisting there is no moral-sexual component to the concubine's behavior.

Another way of understanding 19:2 involves looking at the Akkadian root *zenû*, "to be angry," and applying a similar meaning to *zānāh*. This interpretation allows the concubine's departure and the Levite's subsequent "sweet talking" to be indicative of the typical cycle of domestic violence; the concubine angrily leaves an abusive husband, who seeks her out and sorrowfully convinces her he is a different man.[9] Few lexicons adopt this route, however. "Evidence for understanding this one usage to mean 'be angry,' when [sexual immorality] is quite possible, is lacking. Most authorities . . . hold to one root only . . . The basic idea of the word is 'to commit illicit intercourse' (especially with regard to women)."[10] Gerald Hammond summarizes it best, while providing insight as to why the concubine is not punished for her infidelity:

> Commentators . . . propose the emendation of the verb 'played the whore' to 'became angry with him.' . . . [T]heir defence of this emendation is that, in those days, the penalty against the adulteress was death . . . but a heated argument would allow the Levite to seek a reconciliation when the passions of the temper had subsided.' No matter that the rest of the story describes a state of general lawlessness in the land, and that the woman is given the indeterminate state of 'concubine' rather than 'wife', the commentators still emend the text to create a condition where all automatically obey the law.[11]

The Septuagint bolsters the idea of domestic abuse by stating that the concubine "became angry." Matthews argues that the Septuagint reading is preferable since a prostitute would not be able to return

---

[8]Louise Simons, "An Immortality Rather Than a Life: Milton and the Concubine of Judges, 19–21," in *Old Testament Women in Western Literature*, ed. by Raymond Frontain, Jean Frontain, and Jan Wojcik (Conway, AR: UCA Press, 1991), p. 154.

[9]Elaine A. Heath "The Levite's Concubine: Domestic Violence and the People of God," *Priscilla Papers* 13 (Winter 1999): 14.

[10]Leon Wood, "זָנָה (*zānâ*)," *TWOT*, 1:246.

[11]Gerald Hammond, "The Bible and Literary Criticism — Part II," *Critical Quarterly* 25 (Autumn 1983): 9.

to her father.[12] This argument is weak since Judges repeatedly demonstrates the decay of the Law and culture, making what an immoral woman could and could not do far from certain. The argument that the context supports the interpretation of *zānāh* as "angered" or "vexed" is stronger.[13] After his wife leaves, the Levite goes to "persuade her" — literally, "speak to her heart." Wooing her would be unnecessary and highly unlikely unless he is the transgressor. The idea that the Levite is physically abusive is generally inferred from his character. In fact, the Levite's actions will soon reveal that he has no real concern for the woman's well-being, even when there is no threat to him personally. But the text gives no indication that this concubine is a battered wife. *Zānāh* has been understood to have the connotation of either sexual immorality or anger. If the former, the woman is unfaithful to the Levite. If the latter, her anger at her abuse motivates her to return home to her father. But were she a battered woman, her father would be less likely to return his daughter to such a husband.

These first two interpretive schemes both shy away from the concubine as a fornicator. For many, the narrative makes more sense if the concubine is innocent; we are more sympathetic toward her if she is a victim of domestic abuse as opposed to an adulteress. However, this interpretation demeans a woman if she fails to conform to an arbitrary definition of innocence. Why would a sexually promiscuous woman deserve brutal treatment at the hands of a mob any more than an innocent woman? Focusing on the particular character misses the point and blames the victim. No matter the character of the victim, the crime is horrendous and offensive.

A third approach to *zānāh* embraces this line of reasoning and interprets the narrator as blaming the victim. Barry Webb suggests that the narrator believes "there was an element of justice in the concubine's fate," because she, like everyone else in the book, does what is "right in her own eyes."[14] Cheryl Exum extends the argument to assert that the narrative is an "implicit message" to women to keep their sexual place in society.[15] This argument fails in light of the larger narrative of 19–21 and the rest of Judges. If the narrator is intent

---

[12]Matthews, *Judges*, p. 181.

[13]Burney, *Judges*, p. 460.

[14]Barry G. Webb, *The Book of Judges: An Integrated Reading*, in JSOTSupp 46 (Sheffield, Sheffield Academic Press, 1987), p. 188.

[15]Exum, *Fragmented Women*, p. 84.

on blaming the victim for her sexual independence, then Jephthah's daughter, Samson's wife, the town of Jabesh-Gilead, and the daughters of Shiloh would similarly be portrayed as rebellious because of their independence and punished accordingly.

19:2b-4 The Levite follows his wife to her father's house in an attempt to woo her to return with him. The phrase translated **persuade** is literally "speak to her heart," the same description used to describe Shechem's pursuit of Dinah (Gen 34:3) and Joseph's speaking kindly to his brothers (Gen 50:1). The Levite is accompanied by a servant who serves little purpose in the narrative except to provide a foil with whom the Levite can converse. It is the woman who, upon encountering her husband, brings him **into her father's house.** The woman's father is glad to see his son-in-law, not a likely reaction toward a man beating his daughter, but an expected reaction if his daughter has been unfaithful. The Levite is pursuing his wife in spite of her unfaithfulness, which eliminated the father's burden of permanently caring for his now-unmarriageable daughter.

19:5-10 The father offers typical Middle Eastern hospitality to his son-in-law. Travelers could expect to be welcomed into a home at which they stopped, with all their needs being provided for by the host. Both host and guest pass the customary three days together before the young woman's father compels the Levite to stay for another day and following morning. By the afternoon of the fifth day, the host is no longer able to convince the Levite to stay. The Levite, his wife, and his servant set out from Bethlehem and are able to quickly cover the five-mile distance to **Jerusalem**, known as **Jebus** during the time of the Judges.

19:11-13 The servant suggests that with the day ending, the travelers should spend the night in **Jebus**, the nearest city being ten miles farther. The Levite expresses his unwillingness to accept hospitality from a non-Israelite city, instead opting to press on toward **Gibeah**. Irony permeates this foreshadowing in the text. The events that will soon happen in Gibeah invert the expectations of righteousness connected to an Israelite city. With the sad ending of the book of Judges, the degeneration of Israelite society is complete. And with the outcome of his decision, the foolishness of a Levite once again becomes the catalyst for Israelite apostasy.[16]

---

[16]O'Connell, *Rhetoric of the Book of Judges*, p. 264.

19:14-15 By the time the Benjamite city of **Gibeah** is in view, the sun is setting. The three head for the town square, obvious as travelers to inhabitants coming in from the field. Something is immediately amiss as **no one** offers the customary and expected hospitality. The Benjamites of Gibeah display their lack of character early on through this violation of ancient Near Eastern hospitality codes. Leviticus 13:33-34 provides a foundation for treating sojourners well. In spite of the mass ignorance of the Law evidenced in Judges, the reader understands that the Benjamites of Gibeah are breaking societal standards of etiquette.

19:16-19 When someone finally offers the travelers lodging, it is an elderly sojourner **from the hill country of Ephraim** who meets the city's obligation, and not, as verse 16 emphasizes, the Benjamite inhabitants. The man questions the Levite, who is incensed that no one has offered to provide lodging. The Levite states that as guests they will even provide their own supplies, eliminating the expense to a host. The narrator has eliminated financial hardship as a motive for not taking in the guests, emphasizing again that the Benjamites are simply selfishly uncouth toward their fellow Israelites.

19:20-21 The narrator inserts more foreshadowing in the text as the Ephraimite implores the Levite not to **spend the night in the** town **square**. By now, the alert reader knows that the trio is beginning to experience an echo of Genesis 19 and the narrative of the destruction of Sodom and Gomorrah. The story in Judges unfolds in a strikingly similar way: travelers not offered hospitality plan to sleep in the town square; a last-minute, urgent, and fearful offer of hospitality given by a resident alien; men of ill repute surrounding the house and demanding to rape the guests; and the host's offer of two women as substitutes for the male guests. There is little reason to doubt that the narrative of Judges 19 is historical, in spite of the multiple similarities with Genesis 19. The author of Judges has taken the event and framed it in such a way that the reader cannot avoid the connection to the account of Sodom and Gomorrah. The author's intent with the clever literary structure seems clear: Gibeah is every bit as wicked as Sodom. The differences between the two accounts, however, point to a situation far more dire at Gibeah.

19:22 While the Ephraimite and his guests enjoy the evening, a mob of **wicked men** — literally, "sons of Belial" — gathers around the

house where the trio is staying. The term Belial has an uncertain etymology. The word may possibly be connected with Ba'al and is used
often in relationship to evil individuals. E. John Hamlin enigmati-
cally suggests that Belial "is related to the mystery of evil which
enters and dominates the human heart."[17] Evil in character, these
men demand the delivery of the Levite so they might rape him.

Like the narrative of Genesis 19 that it echoes, the nature of the
specific offense in Judges 19 has been the subject of much debate.
Some assume that homosexual conduct is the end of decadence and
worthy of God's judgment. Others, like Victor Matthews, filter the
text through the lens of the hospitality codes of the ancient Near
East, sidestepping the conduct of the mob. Both perspectives seem
too reductionistic. One symptom of decadence within a society is
the combination of sexuality and violence. Further, the moral decay
reflected in that combination is often reflected in a population indifferent to the evil expressing itself in its midst. Beyond any issues of
sexual orientation, violence, or being inhospitable is the underlying
narcissistic obsession with evil. Evil is destructive by nature, seeking
to damage physically, emotionally, psychologically, and spiritually.
The men of Gibeah have willingly and wholeheartedly devoted
themselves to evil. The way that evil is expressed in the text is secondary to their dark hearts that breed their actions.

Part of the desire to rape the Levite involves humiliation. Sod-
omy is an effective tool used to shame a victim. The ancient Near
East understood the glorification of sexual assault, even to the
extent that their deities engaged in it. The inhabitants of Gibeah
may well have been aware of the "myth of Baal and Anath in which
Baal raped her '77 — even 88 times,' causing her to complain that he
had 'raped her with a chisel.'"[18] God's desire to eliminate the memory of a deity that engages in such depravity is easily understood.
Yahweh, unlike the humanized gods of Canaan, is not a sexual
being, and he is immune to humanity's perverted theologies. Even
contemporary society understands the use of rape as a tool of shame
and control.[19] Sadly, equivalent evils in the society in which we live

---

[17]Hamlin, *At Risk in the Promised Land*, p. 163.
[18]Ibid., p. 112.
[19]Gordon James Knowles, "Male Prison Rape: A Search for Causation and
Prevention," *Howard Journal of Criminal Justice* 38 (1999): 267.

no longer hold any surprises for us. Similar nightmarish stories perpetrated on the innocent are becoming commonplace.

19:23-24 Like Lot in Genesis 19, the owner of the home steps outside in an attempt to dissuade the mob from harming his guest. He has a responsibility as a host, which he heartlessly fulfills. In his mind, better the gang rape of two young women than the male guest under his roof. The mob's desire to rape the Levite is communicated by the host to the crowd as wicked. In an attempt to distract the crowd, the host offers the Levite's concubine and his own daughter for the crowd's sexual amusement. He encourages them to **do to them whatever you wish**. In light of the refrain of the larger narrative, the literal translation of the Hebrew is more chilling: "Do to them whatever is good in your own eyes." The atrocity about to occur is the result of the anarchy brought about by a moral relativism that has ended in evil.

When a community accepts that an individual has the capacity to choose his or her own morality, morality becomes relativistic. That a society can accept individual morality should be sobering, if not frightening. An evil heart can justify anything (Jer 17:9). Although an unpopular concept in the contemporary world, a morality that exists outside of the individual and is adhered to by a society is healthier to a community than a morality in which the individual can choose personal standards of right and wrong. Judges 19 is the ultimate example of what can go wrong without a leader to set the moral tone for a community.

The Levite's servant is a נַעַר (na'ar) — a young man. Schneider notes the boy is not considered in the offer. The crowd has little interest in shaming the Levite's subordinates; they want to humiliate the master sexually. This suggests an evil beyond merely the expression of deviant sexual orientation. The mob of Gibeah is willing to use violence to subordinate and violate another human being in the most brutal way possible. Further, from a literary standpoint, the young man who serves the Levite functions in the story only to interject Jerusalem into the narrative. The concubine, who never speaks, is not the character to make the rational request of staying in Jerusalem.

19:25 The mob refuses to listen to the host and rejects his offer of the two women. The Judges story here diverges from the Genesis narrative when there is no miraculous delivery for the men. In

Genesis 19, angels protect Lot and miraculously inhibit the mob's
advance. In Judges, however, there are no angels and no hand of
God to intervene as the young girl is callously shoved out the door.
There is also no deliverance of the righteous from the city, and no
divine wrath and judgment inflicted on Gibeah. God's presence and
activity in Genesis 19 makes their absence all the more keenly felt in
the Judges narrative.

Fearing the worst, the man — whether the Levite or his host, the
text is not specific — forces his concubine outside and delivers her
to the crowd. The text does not go into graphic detail because none
is needed. In malevolent revelry, they "rape and abuse" her throughout the night. The word יָדַע (yd') is the standard Hebrew word used
to communicate sexual intercourse, independent of the willingness
of the participants. The context clearly indicates that this is an act of
gang rape. עלל ('ll) indicates severe treatment. Hamlin suggests that
'll in this case carries a meaning of "making sport of," demeaning
the girl as the evening's entertainment. Meanwhile, four people are
safe inside the host's house.

19:26 The young woman is brutalized until dawn when the
crowd, bored and spent, lets her go. She manages to reach the doorway of the house, where she collapses. The doorway to the house is
what should have provided her with safety, but it instead provides
the Levite with safety while she has been made the sacrifice.

The text has used three other terms besides *pîlegeš* throughout
the narrative to describe the concubine: Prior to the rape, the
woman is referred to six times as נַעֲרָה (na'ărāh), which signifies
youth and "usually refers to a marriageable but unmarried girl."[20]
Presenting his concubine to his host in Gibeah, the Levite refers to
her as אָמָה ('āmāh), the term for "handmaiden." After the rape she
is a "woman" (אִשָּׁה, 'iššāh). Lillian Klein says it best: "It is not a girl
or young woman, na'arah, but a woman, an 'issah who reappears in
the morning; and it is a bitter irony that is implicit in the change of
terms." Also, the Levite is also now no longer referred to as "her
husband" but as "her master."[21]

19:27 While the literary subtlety and cleverness on the part of
the author is astute, it must not be forgotten that the literary devices

[20]Milton Fisher, "נַעֲרָה," *TWOT*, 2:586.
[21]Klein, *Triumph of Irony*, p. 170.

employed are designed to impact the reader with the brutality of the concubine's treatment. As if she has not suffered enough, verse 27 observes how the Levite casually abuses her even more. The Levite stands up, opens the door to the house and prepares to go on his way as if he has forgotten all about his concubine after a good night's rest. The Hebrew text uses the interjection הִנֵּה (hinnēh), usually translated as "behold," to indicate the ghastly scene at the Levite's feet. His wife lies with her hands on the threshold as if trying to crawl her way to the safety on the other side of the door.

19:28 Seemingly oblivious to her plight, the Levite callously commands his wife to stand up so that they can continue their journey, even though the text hints that he was already planning on continuing on his journey without her. "How brutal these words are we cannot be sure, but we are required to guess. We need to guess, too, at the amount of hatred and guilt they contain, and at the possibility of revenge being mixed in with the saving of his skin when he pushed her out of the door into the hands of her murderers."[22] The Levite's treatment of his wife is unfathomable. He perhaps considered it recompense for her earlier unfaithfulness. If so, then the Levite provides a window into how twisted a wounded heart can become as it seeks revenge. Perhaps part of the reason for Paul's exhortation against revenge in Romans 12:19 is God's insightful knowledge that the human desire for justice is too easily corrupted. God alone has the capacity to deal out justice perfectly and vengeance appropriately and proportionately.

When his wife fails to answer, the Levite places the woman on a donkey and heads home. The Septuagint adds the additional ending, "for she was dead," as the reason for the concubine's inability to answer. The Septuagint likely made the emendation to eliminate the possibility that she is still alive(!). Considering what the Levite will soon do with his wife's body, that he himself might have murdered her is difficult to stomach. But the text, as it has been before in Judges, is intentionally vague.[23] Especially in light of the irony in

---

[22]Hammond, "Bible and Literary Criticism," p. 10.

[23]The narrator's comment in 20:4 that the Levite is "the husband of the murdered woman," helps little since this verse also does not identify the killer. The ambiguity on the part of the author may be deliberate to portray both the Levite and the men of Gibeah as responsible for the woman's death.

connection with the Levite's words in 20:5, where the Levite avoids any culpability for his wife's death, the Masoretic text has the preferable reading.[24]

19:29-30 Without specifying whether the concubine is dead, the author narrates as the Levite seizes "the" **knife**, a term found in the Hebrew text only here and in Genesis 22 — the account of Abraham's planned sacrifice of Isaac. It is likely that the use of the definite article relates to a knife used for a ritualistic purpose.

The Levite cuts up his concubine into twelve pieces, and distributes them to the different tribes of Israel. Later in Israel's history, Saul performs the same action on a pair of oxen, distributing the pieces throughout Israel as a rallying cry against the Ammonites. Saul's usage of the divided oxen, however, is intended as a warning. Saul is threatening the oxen and thereby the livelihood of anyone who fails to participate in battle against the Ammonites. The Levite's dismemberment of his wife, on the other hand, is intended to shock the community into action against Gibeah. The plan is effective. The Hebrew community has never experienced such a graphic and depraved action as the mutilation and dismemberment of a human body. As the Israelites receive and discuss the pieces of the dismembered concubine, their shock morphs into outrage and they are galvanized to action.

Judges is a shameful record of the progressive violation of the Covenant by a faithless people. Judges 19, as an echo of Genesis 19, portrays the Israelites as effectively Canaanite. Using Genesis 19 as a lens through which to view Judges 19,

the narrator serves notice that, whereas the travelers had thought they had come home to the safety of their countrymen, they have actually arrived in Sodom. The nation has come full circle. The Canaanisation of Israelite society is complete. When the Israelites look in a mirror, what they see is a nation which, even if ethnically distinct from the natives, is indistinguishable from [the Canaanites] with regard to morality, ethics, and social values. They have sunk to the level of those nations whom they were to destroy and on whom the judgment of God hangs.[25]

---

[24]Schneider, *Judges*, pp. 266-267. See comments on 20:5.
[25]Block, "Echo Narrative," p. 336.

At its most basic level, Judges 19 is simply a story that shocks because of its cold brutality. It is next to impossible to read the story of the Levite and his concubine and not be overwhelmed with the callousness of the Levite, the viciousness of the mob, and the victimization of the young woman. The narrative describes the absolute moral and societal anarchy dominating both communal and personal paradigms. It is a story without heroes, with few innocents, and without the reassuring presence of the divine.

CHAPTER 20

D. THE DESTRUCTION OF GIBEAH AND BENJAMIN (20:1-48)

¹Then all the Israelites from Dan to Beersheba and from the land of Gilead came out as one man and assembled before the LORD in Mizpah. ²The leaders of all the people of the tribes of Israel took their places in the assembly of the people of God, four hundred thousand soldiers armed with swords. ³(The Benjamites heard that the Israelites had gone up to Mizpah.) Then the Israelites said, "Tell us how this awful thing happened."

⁴So the Levite, the husband of the murdered woman, said, "I and my concubine came to Gibeah in Benjamin to spend the night. ⁵During the night the men of Gibeah came after me and surrounded the house, intending to kill me. They raped my concubine, and she died. ⁶I took my concubine, cut her into pieces and sent one piece to each region of Israel's inheritance, because they committed this lewd and disgraceful act in Israel. ⁷Now, all you Israelites, speak up and give your verdict."

⁸All the people rose as one man, saying, "None of us will go home. No, not one of us will return to his house. ⁹But now this is what we'll do to Gibeah: We'll go up against it as the lot directs. ¹⁰We'll take ten men out of every hundred from all the tribes of Israel, and a hundred from a thousand, and a thousand from ten thousand, to get provisions for the army. Then, when the army arrives at Gibeahᵃ in Benjamin, it can give them what they deserve for all this vileness done in Israel." ¹¹So all the men of Israel got together and united as one man against the city.

¹²The tribes of Israel sent men throughout the tribe of Benjamin, saying, "What about this awful crime that was committed among you? ¹³Now surrender those wicked men of Gibeah so that we may put them to death and purge the evil from Israel."

But the Benjamites would not listen to their fellow Israelites. [14]From their towns they came together at Gibeah to fight against the Israelites. [15]At once the Benjamites mobilized twenty-six thousand swordsmen from their towns, in addition to seven hundred chosen men from those living in Gibeah. [16]Among all these soldiers there were seven hundred chosen men who were left-handed, each of whom could sling a stone at a hair and not miss.

[17]Israel, apart from Benjamin, mustered four hundred thousand swordsmen, all of them fighting men.

[18]The Israelites went up to Bethel[b] and inquired of God. They said, "Who of us shall go first to fight against the Benjamites?"

The LORD replied, "Judah shall go first."

[19]The next morning the Israelites got up and pitched camp near Gibeah. [20]The men of Israel went out to fight the Benjamites and took up battle positions against them at Gibeah. [21]The Benjamites came out of Gibeah and cut down twenty-two thousand Israelites on the battlefield that day. [22]But the men of Israel encouraged one another and again took up their positions where they had stationed themselves the first day. [23]The Israelites went up and wept before the LORD until evening, and they inquired of the LORD. They said, "Shall we go up again to battle against the Benjamites, our brothers?"

The LORD answered, "Go up against them."

[24]Then the Israelites drew near to Benjamin the second day. [25]This time, when the Benjamites came out from Gibeah to oppose them, they cut down another eighteen thousand Israelites, all of them armed with swords.

[26]Then the Israelites, all the people, went up to Bethel, and there they sat weeping before the LORD. They fasted that day until evening and presented burnt offerings and fellowship offerings[c] to the LORD. [27]And the Israelites inquired of the LORD. (In those days the ark of the covenant of God was there, [28]with Phinehas son of Eleazar, the son of Aaron, ministering before it.) They asked, "Shall we go up again to battle with Benjamin our brother, or not?"

The LORD responded, "Go, for tomorrow I will give them into your hands."

[29]Then Israel set an ambush around Gibeah. [30]They went up against the Benjamites on the third day and took up positions against Gibeah as they had done before. [31]The Benjamites came

out to meet them and were drawn away from the city. They began to inflict casualties on the Israelites as before, so that about thirty men fell in the open field and on the roads—the one leading to Bethel and the other to Gibeah.

[32]While the Benjamites were saying, "We are defeating them as before," the Israelites were saying, "Let's retreat and draw them away from the city to the roads."

[33]All the men of Israel moved from their places and took up positions at Baal Tamar, and the Israelite ambush charged out of its place on the west[d] of Gibeah.[e] [34]Then ten thousand of Israel's finest men made a frontal attack on Gibeah. The fighting was so heavy that the Benjamites did not realize how near disaster was. [35]The LORD defeated Benjamin before Israel, and on that day the Israelites struck down 25,100 Benjamites, all armed with swords. [36]Then the Benjamites saw that they were beaten.

Now the men of Israel had given way before Benjamin, because they relied on the ambush they had set near Gibeah. [37]The men who had been in ambush made a sudden dash into Gibeah, spread out and put the whole city to the sword. [38]The men of Israel had arranged with the ambush that they should send up a great cloud of smoke from the city, [39]and then the men of Israel would turn in the battle.

The Benjamites had begun to inflict casualties on the men of Israel (about thirty), and they said, "We are defeating them as in the first battle." [40]But when the column of smoke began to rise from the city, the Benjamites turned and saw the smoke of the whole city going up into the sky. [41]Then the men of Israel turned on them, and the men of Benjamin were terrified, because they realized that disaster had come upon them. [42]So they fled before the Israelites in the direction of the desert, but they could not escape the battle. And the men of Israel who came out of the towns cut them down there. [43]They surrounded the Benjamites, chased them and easily[f] overran them in the vicinity of Gibeah on the east. [44]Eighteen thousand Benjamites fell, all of them valiant fighters. [45]As they turned and fled toward the desert to the rock of Rimmon, the Israelites cut down five thousand men along the roads. They kept pressing after the Benjamites as far as Gidom and struck down two thousand more.

⁴⁶**On that day twenty-five thousand Benjamite swordsmen fell, all of them valiant fighters. ⁴⁷But six hundred men turned and fled into the desert to the rock of Rimmon, where they stayed four months. ⁴⁸The men of Israel went back to Benjamin and put all the towns to the sword, including the animals and everything else they found. All the towns they came across they set on fire.**

ᵃ*10* **One Hebrew manuscript; most Hebrew manuscripts** *Geba,* **a variant of Gibeah** ᵇ*18* **Or** *to the house of God*; **also in verse 26** ᶜ*26* **Traditionally** *peace offerings* ᵈ*33* **Some Septuagint manuscripts and Vulgate; the meaning of the Hebrew for this word is uncertain.** ᵉ*33* **Hebrew** *Geba,* **a variant of Gibeah** ᶠ*43* **The meaning of the Hebrew for this word is uncertain.**

20:1 Outraged at the extremity of the wickedness, Israel rallies together troops at **Mizpah**. Mizpah apparently served as a military rallying point prior to and early during the monarchy (Judg 10:17; 1 Sam 7:5-6; 10:17). Because the tribes must confront the tribe of Benjamin, Mizpah is an ideal location, only a few miles from Gibeah on the edge of Benjamin's territory.

The author provides two significant spiritual details regarding Israel's assembly. First, they assembled **as one man**, indicating that for the first time in Judges, there is powerful consensus among the people. Ephraim will not be sitting out the battle, only later to complain about being omitted.

The second detail mentions that the people assembled **before the LORD**. In spite of the plethora of spiritual compromises throughout the book, the people's response is made in commitment to Yahweh. Even the pluralistically compromised tribe of Dan will be present for the confrontation. The dismemberment of the Levite's concubine is so repulsive to the Israelites that they quickly unify in their resolve to punish those responsible. Perhaps shocked into their awareness of Yahweh, they assemble in his name. As flawed as their fidelity to God is, the people still attempt, commendably, to place him at the forefront of their actions.

20:2 Throughout Judges, tribal participation has often been difficult to manage — there's a sense that community and loyalty among tribes is heavily fractured. In Judges 20, any division among the tribes no longer exists. The 400,000 battle-ready soldiers is by far the largest force assembled by the Israelites for a military purpose in Judges. The next largest force has been Gideon's army of 32,000.

Ironically, such a large number will not be focused externally for deliverance. The 400,000 will be directed at an internal purge of evil within the community. The Israelites are at their most unified when they confront one of their own tribes over the events at Gibeah.

20:3 That the Israelites were outraged at Gibeah's treatment of the concubine rather than the Levite's dismembering her is suggested by the fact that Benjamin is mentioned in 20:3 as aware of the army being assembled against them. The assembly has not gathered to confront the Levite; the atrocity that led to the concubine's dismemberment is apparently already known. For the sake of the reader, the assembled Israelites ask the Levite for details.

20:4 The Levite recounts the story to the Israelites, immediately fingering the town of **Gibeah** and its possession by **Benjamin**. The designation of Gibeah as part of Benjamin places the responsibility for dealing with the abominable act that occurred there squarely on Benjamin's shoulders.

20:5 The Levite carefully frames his account to present himself as a victim. The reader already knows the Levite's responsibility for his wife's death when he shoved her out the door to the crowd. Similarly, the text observed the Levite's unfeeling callousness as he prepared to step over his wife's prostrate form. But when he relates his version of the events, he carefully omits his pitilessly shoving her out the door and uncaring attitude toward her the following morning. He also claims that the mob intended **to kill** him, when that motive was further down the list than their desire to debase him.

20:6-7 The Levite clearly claims that his wife was murdered by the mob after their prolonged assault. The Levite's comments to the assembly only illuminate his disreputable character. The deliberate ambiguity of the Masoretic text in 19:28 places his reliability in doubt and leaves open the question of who murdered his concubine. He relates that he has indeed dismembered his wife and distributed her pieces throughout the region, but that he has done so in response to the evil perpetrated on her by Gibeah. His challenge to the assembly is to render a **verdict**, literally, to give advice or counsel. The Levite intends to provoke action against Gibeah, and he serves as the catalyst for what follows.

20:8 Verses 8-11 again emphasize the solidarity of the Israelites as they prepare to deal with Gibeah. Approaching the situation with a common mind **as one man**, the entire assembly commits to staying to see through Gibeah's punishment, even though the size of the army will relegate most to the sidelines.

20:9 To determine who will fight against Gibeah, the Israelites decide to cast lots to select ten percent of the initial force. Lots are used throughout the Bible as a method to decide between two or more equal alternatives. Lots were used to determine property division (Josh 14:2), individuals for spiritual or other service (Neh 11:1; Acts 1:21-26), or revelation of hidden sin (Jonah 1:7). The underlying premise is that God directs the outcome of the lots for his purposes, making the decision his.

20:10-13a The lots are used to select an army of 40,000, a force deemed adequate to destroy a small village like Gibeah. Unfortunately for the Israelites, their task will not be so simple. The text has already hinted in verse three that the Benjamites will get involved in the confrontation. Because the inhabitants of Gibeah are Benjamites, the tribe maintains control over what will happen to the immoral town. The other tribes make their initial appeal to Benjamin, demanding an explanation for Gibeah's actions. The ultimatum is not far behind. The assembly demands Benjamin surrender the men of the city for execution. Their reason is **to purge the evil from Israel**. Oddly, much evil that has already occurred in Judges has been overlooked by the people. No one has demanded punishment for Jephthah after he has sacrificed his own daughter, and no one has become upset over the blasphemous worship connected with Gideon or Dan. Because Israel has become desensitized to Yahweh and his Law, the people have acquired a very high threshold of tolerance for sin and false worship. Sadly, it takes the gang rape, murder, and dismemberment of a helpless woman to shock the community to its senses. Now that the nation's moral indignation has finally been aroused, Israel will not hesitate to act. The tribes' desire to punish Gibeah may be rooted in the way the tribes dealt with the sin of Achan.[1] God's blessing would not be available to a people that tolerated wickedness in its midst.

20:13b The **Benjamites** refuse to surrender the men of Gibeah. The reason behind their decision is uncertain. The rest of the tribe may have been morally equivalent to Gibeah, hence seeing nothing wrong with the town's action. This seems unlikely considering the

---

[1]Matthews, *Judges*, p. 194.

common repulsion shared by every other tribe, making it difficult to believe that a single tribe would have been corrupt. A more likely explanation understands Benjamin as choosing clan loyalty over punishing evil. Benjamin may well recognize Gibeah's actions as despicably vile, but because Gibeah is family, the larger tribe is willing to overlook — or at least deliver a less severe retribution for — Gibeah's sin.

20:14-17 The city where the atrocity occurs becomes the rallying point for the soldiers of Benjamin. The tribe mobilizes 26,000 troops to bolster Gibeah's small contingent of 700. About three percent of the Benjamite army are like Ehud — military elite trained to fight with the left hand.[2] Beyond the sword-fighting advantage held by lefthanders, these Benjamite soldiers possess a long-range tactical advantage. The text notes that these 700 **could sling** a baseball-sized rock with deadly accuracy, effectively striking at military opponents long before the two lines meet. Although the 40,000 troops against Gibeah have been designated, verse 17 returns to the total number of 400,000, foreshadowing that the smaller group will not be sufficient against Benjamin's army.

20:18 As the Israelites prepare for war, the assembly moves a short distance northeast to the cultic center at **Bethel**. The town has already played a formative role in the Hebrew mind-set ever since Jacob gave the name Bethel (*House of God*) to the city of Luz. The city will be home to prophets and the other golden calf placed by Jeroboam, figuring prominently as an alternative cultic center. The people have come to Bethel for the purpose of seeking God's guidance. Throughout Judges, God has spoken primarily to individuals and has interacted with the larger community through the detached actions of placing the people in the hands of oppressors or sending a judge to deliver them. At Bethel, he will interact with the people three times as they confront Benjamin.

Desiring God's blessing and guidance for the battle, the Israelites inquire as to which tribe should attack Benjamin **first**. God responds by commanding the largest tribe, **Judah**, to be the first to attack. Because Judges opens with Judah going first into battle (1:2), the writer may be intending another symbolic connection of the Benjamites to the Canaanites. The second and third attacks against

---

[2]See comments on 3:15.

Benjamin do not mention what tribe is moving against Benjamin; rather, the whole of the Israelite army is moving against the renegade tribe. Benjamin is acting like the Canaanites, and so will be destroyed in the same manner.

It may seem easy to attribute the cause of this civil war to the Levite's stubbornness in rejecting the counsel of his servant that they lodge in Jerusalem. Or the cause could be considered the actual rape and murder of his wife, and the evil of the inhabitants of Gibeah. Schneider calls the basis for civil war "false," because the "rape of one woman" serves as an illegitimate impetus for war.[3] The response against Benjamin, however, is not because of the initial rape, but because of Benjamin's refusal to allow the guilty to be punished, which is interpreted by Israel as tacit approval. The roots of the war lie in the societal degeneration caused by years of spiritual and moral decay. Chaos is the natural by-product of a moral vacuum. By defeating the Benjamites, the rest of Israel hopes to restore societal morality.

20:19-22 The day following the query at Bethel, the Israelite army makes the brief five-mile journey and sets up their military camp at **Gibeah**. Schneider notes that the previous focus in Judges has been on the leader rather than the battle, but for the remainder of the narrative, the details of the individual battles will be catalogued.[4] The Israelite army and Benjamites take up battle formations in front of Gibeah. Not waiting for the enemy to control the timing of the attack, the **Benjamites** attack first. The strategy is successful, and 22,000 Israelite soldiers are slain in the battle. Licking its wounds, the Israelite army retreats to its initial position, its soldiers encouraging each other in the face of the rout.

20:23 In verse 23 the Israelites "go up," returning to Bethel to inquire further of the LORD. The narrative adds additional details not present in the first query in verse 18. First, the assembly weeps, expressing grief over their fallen kinsmen. Beyond this grief is a theological grief, in which the Israelites must reconcile their obedience to God with the defeat he allows at the hands of the Benjamites. The Israelite army has assumed far too easily that obedience will always be met with success. They are learning — with two more lessons to go — that obedience can be extremely costly.

[3]Schneider, *Judges,* pp. 271-285.
[4]Ibid., p. 277.

The second additional detail is the duration of weeping. The assembly weeps **until evening**, an indicator that the day has been set aside for the occasion. The army will not have time to devise and implement a plan on the same day. Instead, they are seeking God, more wholeheartedly than before the first battle.

The third addition is the altered nature of the Israelites' question. Rather than assuming the battle needs to be fought and then asking God how to fight the battle, the congregation steps back from their assumption and asks God if they should be fighting Benjamin at all. In spite of their determination to expunge the evil from the midst of Israel, their defeat at the hand of Benjamin has shaken them to the core.

The fourth additional detail is the designation of Benjamin as **our brothers**. In seeking God's counsel, the people put their relationship to their fellow tribe clearly in God's view. It may be fair to suggest that God is testing the people's resolve to obtain purity. Will the Israelites be willing to suffer loss and attack family in order to regain purity? For the second time, offering the promise of success, God commands the Israelites to attack Benjamin.

20:24-27a The number equivalent to the ten percent levy of the original 400,000 troops has now been killed. A total of 40,000 Israelite troops have fallen in two battles against Benjamin. The union's best plan has failed, and so they return to Bethel. More details are again added, suggesting that the Israelites are learning as they go what it means to seek the LORD. After years saturated with sinful disobedience and pluralism, Israel is rediscovering the God of Abraham, Isaac, and Jacob. Before any question is asked, they worship. This time, they sit while weeping. They go without food and offer burnt offerings to Yahweh, something they have neglected to do during their first two visits to Bethel. This is the first instance of corporate worship in Judges since the burnt offerings at Bokim in 2:5. In the former instance, the worship is related to sorrow over God's rebuke for the people's disobedience. Now at Bethel, the people have been driven into deeper worship of Yahweh as they desperately seek a solution to the war.

20:27b-28a The text notes the presumed advantage of the presence of the Ark of the Covenant, the only mention of the sacred object in Judges. The text adds the odd detail that the ark is in Bethel **in those days**, which suggests that the ark is normally at Bethel, and that the people did not fetch it from Shiloh for the occasion as is done later in 1 Samuel 4. The ark's presence at Bethel may possibly be attributed to the ministry of Deborah in the area (Judg 4:5). At this time, the ark is maintained by Phinehas, the grandson of Moses' brother Aaron (Num 25:6-13). It has been under Phinehas's leadership that another civil war has been avoided with Reuben and Gad over a misinterpreted altar (Josh 22:10-34).

Phinehas's presence in the narrative places the events within a generation of the wilderness wanderings. The early date for these events seems somewhat surprising, considering that the men of Gibeah have descended to such depravity in such a short period of time. It should again be noted that while Judges is historical, the author has not necessarily arranged events in chronological order, but in a way that furthers his purpose of promoting leadership as necessary for maintaining fidelity to Yahweh.

20:28b Initially, the Israelites plan to attack Benjamin and seek Yahweh's input only in terms of how to conduct the battle. After being defeated, they ask if they should be fighting against Benjamin at all. On this third occasion they ask, **"Shall we go up again to battle with Benjamin our brother, or not?"** "Or not" is the translation of חדל (ḥdl), Hebrew for "to refrain." Israel is asking the question with the realization that God may desire them to cease fighting. God answers with the command to go, but this time promises that the Israelites will be successful in battle.

20:29-32 Utilizing the military strategy used at the second battle for Ai, the Israelite army capitalizes on their previous two defeats. They assume the same battle positions as they have on the two previous occasions. Offering a gambit that costs the lives of thirty men, the Israelites draw Benjamin away from Gibeah. Being conditioned by their success in the two previous battles, the Benjamite army falls for the ruse, leaving Gibeah undefended.

20:33-36a With Gibeah lacking military protection, 10,000 Israelite troops attack so ferociously that Benjamin has no time to assess the hopelessness of its military situation (20:34). Verses 35-36a summarize the outcome of the battle, even though the text provides additional details concerning Benjamin's defeat. Like the Israelite victories over its various enemies throughout Judges, the victory over Benjamin is considered Yahweh's victory. Twenty-five thousand, one hundred Benjamites have died because of their rebellious refusal to follow the LORD.

20:36b-44 Verse 20:36b provides a more detailed description of the third battle and Benjamin's defeat. After the Benjamite army has been drawn away from the city, Israelite troops wait under cover to ambush Gibeah. The entire population of the city is slaughtered, and a smoldering fire created to signal the retreating Israelite troops. The Benjamites see the smoke signal ascending from Gibeah just as the Israelite army reverses direction and attacks. The Benjamite troops head for the wilderness, but are cut off. The Benjamites are surrounded and 18,000 are slain.

20:45 The Benjamites flee to the northwest toward the cliffs of **Rimmon**. Some 5,000 Benjamites are killed during the pursuit, and 2,000 more are killed at the presently unknown site of **Gidom**, where they make their last stand. The total number of Benjamite casualties from verse 35 has been broken down into three separate groups. With their military defeated, the remaining towns of Benjamin are easy prey for the Israelite army. Destroying the Benjamite population more effectively than they have the Canaanites, the Israelites methodically work their way through the territory of Benjamin, killing women, children, and livestock. The Israelites have loosely followed Deuteronomy 13:12-18 as their basis for destroying the Benjamite cities.[5] Apostasy in Israel is to be dealt with in the harshest terms possible. Although Gibeah alone demonstrated aberrant behavior, Benjamin, by defending Gibeah's deviancy, placed itself under the same sanction Gibeah would receive.

20:46-48 As with the case of Achan's family, this severe treatment of noncombatants seems to be a disproportionate reaction to the initial offense. Women and children have not been the instigators at or defenders of Gibeah. The Israelites, however, are treating the families not as individuals, but as extensions of the men who have been slain. This patriarchal approach considers even cattle to be tainted by the Benjamite immorality. As inhabitants are killed, cities are burned. The tribe of Benjamin has been decimated, leaving only 600 survivors hiding in the rugged territory surrounding **Rimmon** for **four months**.

---

[5]O'Connell, *Rhetoric of the Book of Judges*, pp. 229-240.

CHAPTER 21

E. PROVISION FOR THE LOST TRIBE (21:1-25)

¹The men of Israel had taken an oath at Mizpah: "Not one of us will give his daughter in marriage to a Benjamite."

²The people went to Bethel,ᵃ where they sat before God until evening, raising their voices and weeping bitterly. ³"O LORD, the God of Israel," they cried, "why has this happened to Israel? Why should one tribe be missing from Israel today?"

⁴Early the next day the people built an altar and presented burnt offerings and fellowship offerings.ᵇ

⁵Then the Israelites asked, "Who from all the tribes of Israel has failed to assemble before the LORD?" For they had taken a solemn oath that anyone who failed to assemble before the LORD at Mizpah should certainly be put to death.

⁶Now the Israelites grieved for their brothers, the Benjamites. "Today one tribe is cut off from Israel," they said. ⁷"How can we provide wives for those who are left, since we have taken an oath by the LORD not to give them any of our daughters in marriage?" ⁸Then they asked, "Which one of the tribes of Israel failed to assemble before the LORD at Mizpah?" They discovered that no one from Jabesh Gilead had come to the camp for the assembly. ⁹For when they counted the people, they found that none of the people of Jabesh Gilead were there.

¹⁰So the assembly sent twelve thousand fighting men with instructions to go to Jabesh Gilead and put to the sword those living there, including the women and children. ¹¹"This is what you are to do," they said. "Kill every male and every woman who is not a virgin." ¹²They found among the people living in Jabesh Gilead four hundred young women who had never slept with a man, and they took them to the camp at Shiloh in Canaan.

¹³Then the whole assembly sent an offer of peace to the Benjamites at the rock of Rimmon. ¹⁴So the Benjamites returned at that time and were given the women of Jabesh Gilead who had been spared. But there were not enough for all of them.

¹⁵The people grieved for Benjamin, because the LORD had made a gap in the tribes of Israel. ¹⁶And the elders of the assembly said, "With the women of Benjamin destroyed, how shall we provide wives for the men who are left? ¹⁷The Benjamite survivors must have heirs," they said, "so that a tribe of Israel will not be wiped out. ¹⁸We can't give them our daughters as wives, since we Israelites have taken this oath: 'Cursed be anyone who gives a wife to a Benjamite.' ¹⁹But look, there is the annual festival of the LORD in Shiloh, to the north of Bethel, and east of the road that goes from Bethel to Shechem, and to the south of Lebonah."

²⁰So they instructed the Benjamites, saying, "Go and hide in the vineyards ²¹and watch. When the girls of Shiloh come out to join in the dancing, then rush from the vineyards and each of you seize a wife from the girls of Shiloh and go to the land of Benjamin. ²²When their fathers or brothers complain to us, we will say to them, 'Do us a kindness by helping them, because we did not get wives for them during the war, and you are innocent, since you did not give your daughters to them.'"

²³So that is what the Benjamites did. While the girls were dancing, each man caught one and carried her off to be his wife. Then they returned to their inheritance and rebuilt the towns and settled in them.

²⁴At that time the Israelites left that place and went home to their tribes and clans, each to his own inheritance.

²⁵In those days Israel had no king; everyone did as he saw fit.

ᵃ2 Or *to the house of God*   ᵇ4 Traditionally *peace offerings*

21:1 Chapter 21 opens with a flashback to a vow that the entire nation made, apparently as part of the larger deliberations regarding Benjamin's protection of the renegade city of Gibeah. Verse 1 sets the stage for Benjamin's problem. With only 600 surviving warriors, the tribe is in danger of extinction. The tribe's women and children have all been killed. To prevent Benjamin's ultimate disappearance, wives for the survivors need to be found. But the people have already made a vow, obviously as foolish as the one made by

Jephthah in chapter 11. The vow is a commitment by the people not to **give** [their] **daughter**[s] **in marriage to a Benjamite**. The people are clearly designating Benjamin as a pagan group, existing outside of the privileges of the Covenant. Beyond being a statement of spiritual rebuke, the move is also likely intended as a way to prevent spiritual contamination. Intermarriage with polytheistic religions results in trouble for Israel whenever it occurs (Deut 7:1-4; 1 Kgs 11:4; 16:31; Ezra 9–10). It is both blessing and curse that few relationships have the capacity to affect us as does marriage. The Israelites realized this fact on some level, but their spiritual resentment echoes as somewhat shallow given the people's corruption described throughout the book.

21:2-3 Realizing the mistake of their vow, **the people** return to the spiritual center at **Bethel** to weep and worship. Oddly, the question, "**Why**?" is asked of God. The answer is obvious to the reader. Gibeah deserved destruction and Benjamin tried to prevent it. Therefore Benjamin's fate is linked to the fate of Gibeah. Benjamin is destroyed because its people refuse to allow evil to be punished. Of all the narratives in the book of Judges, it has been with regard to Benjamin's apostasy that the people have demonstrated the most loyalty to Yahweh. Israel has endured 40,000 of its own casualties, and is now facing the extinction of one of their kindred tribes. They have finally learned that obedience is costly.

The people follow a three-step progression in their actions at Bethel. First, they weep. This is simply an expression of deep sorrow over the loss of a brother tribe. At a deeper level, their grief may include — properly so — an element of self-examination. This first step is easily bypassed. Many find it too easy to worship a God of overwhelming love, neglecting their own role in the relationship. Every relationship is a two-way street, and it's important for us to be aware how we're driving toward the relationship on our side of the road.

Second, the people question. At a deeper level, the loss of Benjamin as a tribe calls to mind God's covenant to be with his people. Many of God's attributes are taken for granted. The Israelites are little different than believers today. Basic assumptions about God are part of who we are, but rarely enter conscious thought: God is all-powerful. God is all-loving. God is all-knowing. But in the face of real tragedy, these characteristics can easily sound like trite clichés.

Grief forces us beyond head knowledge toward an experience of God himself. The Israelites are wondering if God has abandoned his people because he has allowed Benjamin to be destroyed. Questioning God is healthy; it drives us toward the third step taken by the Israelites: worship.

21:4 After expressing their grief and questioning, the Israelites worship. The proper destination of grief is worship. The Israelites express their worship through **burnt offerings** and peace offerings. Burnt offerings are intended as an offering for corporate sin, and in this case the Israelites express repentance at the corporate level. This is the second corporate worship scene occurring at Bethel. Previous instances of crying out for deliverance to God have not involved repentance nor worship, but have been merely plaintive cries from a desperate people. Here, however, the people worship through sacrifice. But the reader wonders if their repentance hasn't come too late. God has grown completely silent and does not speak or act for the remainder of the book.

Not receiving an answer from God, the Israelites make yet again another impulsive decision that results in some of the vilest conduct in the book. Without spiritual directive, the people, perhaps impatient and unwilling to wait, devise a solution to the problem of Benjamin's demise. The author refers to a second part of the deliberations at Mizpah: a promise of execution to any Israelite who refuses to participate in the council at Mizpah against Benjamin. For the second time in Judges, a foolish and impulsive vow dooms the life of the innocent.[1]

21:5-9 The curse of **death** against any town refusing to participate at **Mizpah** is perhaps bravado. Clearly, no one knows the identity of **Jabesh-Gilead** until the matter has been investigated. Without the need to supply Benjamin with wives, it is doubtful that such an investigation would have ever taken place. Using one vow to fulfill another, Jabesh-Gilead becomes the scapegoat to rescue Benjamin from Israel's impulsiveness.

21:10-14 The Israelites send an overwhelming force of 12,000 to slaughter the Gadite town of **Jabesh-Gilead**, ostensibly for their nonparticipation against the Benjamites. The location of Jabesh-Gilead

---

[1]Wong, *Compositional Strategy*, pp. 132-135.

is uncertain, but many place it on the eastern side of the Jordan River, within the territory of Gad. Gad has more reason than Benjamin to defend its own kindred, but after observing what has happened to Benjamin for its refusal to comply with the rest of Israel, Gad is hardly likely to raise any objections. The men of the city will be sacrificed to repopulate Benjamin. Entire families are destroyed, but 400 virgin girls are preserved as wives for the Benjamite remnant. To restore Benjamin to its status as a tribe, the other tribes host a reconciliation ceremony at Shiloh. As part of the reconciliation, the remaining Benjamites are presented with the 400 survivors of Jabesh-Gilead as wives.

The town of Jabesh-Gilead is later to function as bookends for the reign of the Benjamite Saul. Saul, echoing the division of the concubine's body in Judges 19, divides and distributes an ox throughout Israel in a rallying summons for the Israelites. Saul powerfully delivers the city from the Ammonites, and earns their loyalty (1 Sam 11:5-11). Later, after Saul's death and beheading by the Philistines, it is men from Jabesh-Gilead who rescued and buried his body (1 Sam 31:8-15). One would assume that the city would have no great love for any Benjamite, but it is crucial to remember that the inhabitants of the city have been slaughtered with the exception of 400 girls. The city Saul delivers in 1 Samuel 11 is a repopulated Jabesh-Gilead.

Nor should the reader miss that Saul's home city is the city where the concubine is assaulted and murdered. Burney suggests that both narratives in Judges — Gibeah and Jabesh-Gilead — are designed to promote a "deep antipathy to the memory of Saul and his adherents."[2] Avoiding the connection between Judges 19–21 and Saul is difficult. Consequently, many consider the final section in Judges to be a rhetorical device attempting to undermine Saul and support the Davidic monarchy. The overall tenor of the narrative, however, faults the entire nation, not just Gibeah and Jabesh-Gilead. Further, the people of Jabesh-Gilead in the Judges narrative are innocent victims. If anything, the Judges account hints that the city needs the deliverance of a hero like Saul.

21:15 Still 200 wives short, the Israelites continue to mourn Benjamin's situation in verse 15, laying the responsibility for the tribe's decimation at the LORD's feet. Again, the Israelites under-

---

[2]Burney, *Judges*, p. 490.

stood God as culpable not because of his direct involvement, but because of his *lack* of involvement; because God is all-powerful, he is often blamed for what he allows or fails to prevent.

21:16-17 Desiring to **provide wives for** the remaining survivors of **Benjamin** in order to maximize the tribe's chances for survival, the elders of Israel concoct a scheme whereby the remaining 200 Benjamite men who lack wives travel to Shiloh to abduct virgin female worshipers during an annual celebration. The Israelite army is already camping at Shiloh, and has presented the 400 girls from Jabesh-Gilead to the Benjamites there. The worship setting probably sparks a reminder of the annual festival undertaken by young girls there, giving birth to the dark idea as the situation is discussed.

21:18-19 Although the Israelites will not give their daughters to the Benjamites, nothing prevents the elders from directing the 200 men to abduct and rape the young women, making them wives according to the Law. This is most probably a perversion of Deuteronomy 22:28-29. The Mosaic Law made the provision of marriage for a female rape victim. In a patriarchal society, a rape victim is treated as damaged goods and considered unmarriageable. God insightfully prevented women from societal ostracism by forcing the attacker to marry his victim and pay a fine to the girl's father. It is a command that certainly seems strange and even cruel by modern standards, but within the sociological context of the ancient world God is intending to provide for the victim and minimize her consequences. This text is likely the basis for the reasoning justifying the elders' encouragement of Benjamin's abduction of the daughters of Shiloh. The law is misapplied at a community level in order to justify rape as a guarantor of marriage. A fifty-shekel payment to the girl's father legitimizes the union, and everyone is able to comfortably sidestep the vow made at Mizpah.

21:20-22 Hiding in the **vineyards** in the hills around **Shiloh**, the 200 remaining Benjamites wait for the young female worshipers to make their appearance. In action reminiscent of the Roman history tale, *The Rape of the Sabine Women*, the soldiers kidnap the young women and force them into what is at least a coerced marriage. Objections from any of the girls' **fathers** are deflected by the diplomacy of Israel's leaders. The fathers themselves will be **innocent** of violating the vow against Benjamin because they have not consented to the marriages.

21:23 The 600 Benjamites and their wives return to the previously destroyed cities throughout their territory and rebuild and repopulate. Even Gibeah will be repopulated and will be the home of the young Saul when he is made king over Israel.

The passage is bracketed by the refrain, "There was no king in Israel," in 19:1 and 21:25. Verse 25 adds the final chilling punctuation: "Everyone did what was right in his own eyes." The author's placement of the story between the two refrains suggests the paradigm for interpreting the narrative. It is the refrain that is often referred to in considering the book of Judges to be primarily a polemic for the monarchy.[3] But the undertone of the narrative is the chaos and anarchy that result in a societal context of moral relativism.

21:24-25 The civil war over, the **Israelites** return in 21:24 to their **inheritance** as if nothing is wrong. Sixty-five thousand Israelites have been killed in the war, along with numerous noncombatants in Benjamite cities, and young women have been abducted and forced into marriages, with the blessing and counsel of Israel's elders. The peaceful and happy ending of verse 24 is belied by the events that have just preceded it. Home, family, and inheritance are enjoyed with a backdrop saturated with their own blood. Verse 25 strips away the spiritual haze and leaves the reader with the twofold refrain as a caveat: Because Israel lacks a king, morality has become individualistically pragmatic.

Judges concludes with the narrative of 19–21. The brutal rape and murder of a concubine, her dismemberment, the slaughter of Gibeah, the Benjamites, and Jabesh-Gilead, as well as the abduction of the daughters of Jabesh-Gilead and daughters of Shiloh, are clearly rooted in the anarchy of a kingless Israel. Underneath the surface of the narrative, however, lies the author's castigation of the cowardly, the sexually perverted, the callous, the brutal, and the self-centered. The narrator critiques both the passivity and the deliberate evil that causes the innocent to suffer. The message of Judges is clear: Israel needs a godly leader who will eliminate the anarchy permeating society. Judges is followed in the canon with the story of God's provision of just such a leader. David will unite Israel and become the model of righteous leadership.

---

[3]Block, *Judges*, pp. 57-59.

CONCLUSION

GOD'S TRAJECTORY TOWARD THE CROSS

Judges is ultimately part of the story of Jesus. The Old Testament is interpreted by followers of Christ to be the record of God's interaction with humanity for salvation. Through his sovereignty, God ensured that Jesus of Nazareth would die on a cross at a deliberate point in history (Rom 5:6). In order to do so, God created the religious and cultural circumstances through which those events would occur. A large part of his plan involved creating an identity for a nation that was cohesive enough to provide that framework. Through the Exodus, Conquest, Judges, Monarchy, and Exile, God shaped the mind-set of the nation to ensure the right religious elements were present when he walked the streets of Israel as Jesus of Nazareth. The judges played a key role in preserving that national identity until it could be further shaped by the monarchy.

JUDGES AND EXAMPLES OF FAITH

When considering the lives of Gideon, Barak, Samson, and Jephthah, Hebrews 11:32 seems confusing. The author of Hebrews certainly seems to have chosen questionable examples in these four Judges. How are disobedience, cowardice, and testing God examples of faithfulness? How can idolaters, the sexually immoral and murderers be examples to modern Christians? Gideon continually tests God, seeking validation for the command he has been given. Near the end of his life, he is responsible for idolatry in Israel. Barak is simply disobedient. Jephthah violates the Law and the heart of God by attempting to manipulate him with a vow of human sacrifice. He later fulfills that abominable vow. Samson is a self-centered, revenge-seeking womanizer whose passions cause suffering to everyone around him. How are these men servants of God, let alone models of faith that should be emulated? Some things to remember:

1. Strong faith sometimes coexists with immoral behavior.

This statement is disconcerting to believers, who ardently pursue moral character and behavior in order to please God. Both the Old and New Testaments are clear that a lifestyle that embraces and pursues immorality alienates people from God. But the ministry of Jesus encounters spectacular faith springing from those who find themselves ensnared by evil. Prostitutes, greedy tax collectors, and sinners in general are somehow at the front of the line to enter the Kingdom of God because they are keenly aware of the empty depths of their own depravity and hunger for deliverance. God can work with that kind of person. Within Christian circles, morality has often become a substitute for faith. But it was the most moral in Jesus' time who most stridently resisted his offer to redeem them. Relying on our own morality provides a feeling of greater security than relying on the grace of God that justifies and sanctifies our ever-wandering hearts.

2. Faith may waver and change over time. God does not.

Second Timothy 2:13 states, "If we are faithless, he will remain faithful, for he cannot disown himself." Ultimately, the character deficiencies in Judges are not about trying to reconcile Samson's or Jephthah's wicked acts with their faith. No matter how imperfect their character and faith, the object of their faith — God himself — is perfect. The same is true for us. Faith is not as much about our ability to believe as it is about the object of our painfully imperfect and inadequate faith — God himself. Even great believers often blunder. But our blundering and meandering hearts don't diminish us — they exalt our heavenly Father because of his grace and compassion.

3. Faith is a process as much as a possession.

Faith is often mistakenly assumed to be a mere possession: one has a strong faith, weak faith, or no faith. But Scripture repeatedly makes it clear that faith is developed (Phil 2:12-13; Heb 12:2; 2 Pet 1:5-8). Through revealing himself to a man or woman with imperfect faith, God often strengthens faith and trust. Just as he did with Gideon, God — sometimes gently, sometimes roughly, always graciously — incrementally builds faith. Like physical prowess and stamina, strong faith is developed over time.

THE RELEVANCE OF JUDGES FOR TODAY

While entertaining, Judges is not merely a collection of good stories about ancient peoples. The modern era would do well to learn from the wisdom God has revealed in the book. The anarchic society and horror stories of the ancient world are no longer events isolated in the past. Similar events are commonplace in our day. The church must learn from Judges in order to provide clarity to a suffering world.

THE PROBLEM OF COMMUNAL SIN

Much of the difficulty Israel experienced in the book of Judges is tied to the problem of their communal sin. Many dangerous consequences sprout and flourish when a society learns to accommodate immorality at the corporate level.

Desensitization

Sin functions within a group the way it does in an individual. The evil are quickly bored with depravity and seek to recapture the temporary thrill sin offers. The righteous, on the other hand, endure evil around them. Over time, both groups, because of overexposure to wickedness, can become deadened to the hideousness of evil. Our entertainment culture is saturated with sexuality, crimes against children, narcissism, violence, foolishness — all wrapped in the attractive package of a prime time television show, popular novel, or catchy pop song. When the wicked pursue evil and the righteous ignore it, society inevitably decays.

Progression

One of the consequences of desensitization is the natural progression to more extreme expressions of evil. As the righteous become desensitized to sin, their voice becomes deadened and they provide diminishing resistance to evil. Meanwhile, the wicked explore evil, with devastating results. Today's tantalization becomes tomorrow's naiveté.

Lack of Communal Moral Standards

As a community decays, its group standards for ethical conduct are replaced by the relative and subjective preferences of the individual. Modern American society is experiencing this very phenomenon. There are academics who seriously argue for the validity of genocide, euthanasia, and pedophilia. Without a belief in an absolute moral standard, a society will reflect an unhealthy pluralism of moral views.

Religious Confusion

One of the hallmarks of Judges is the tainted religious life through which the characters approach God. Gideon believes he can bribe God. Samson gives no thought to his own nature when he makes demands of God. Jephthah sacrifices his daughter because of his ignorance of the Law. Micah and the Danites believe they can approach God through the hiring of a personal priest. Societal decay sees not only a decline in communal ethical standards, but also in the understanding of truth. Truth, rather than being an objective standard to which a community agrees, becomes an individual preference. And because beliefs undergird actions, people do what is true — or right — in their own eyes.

WHAT CAN A BELIEVER DO IN AN UNCERTAIN WORLD?

Remember That Chaos Is an Opportunity for the Gospel

Wherever unrest exists, the gospel of Jesus can bring peace. One of the byproducts of anarchy is fear, and our media culture has selling fear down to a fine art. Fear of the future, fear of violence, fear of the economy, fear over what to eat, drink, or wear. The gospel of Jesus reminds us that the fear that saturates a life apart from God is removed in the life of the believer (Matt 6:25-34).

Wherever immorality exists, the gospel of Jesus can bring meaning and healing. A by-product of sexual immorality is boredom. Because the world has lost the idea of mystery and sacredness, sexuality has become the mere search for pleasure. And yet that search has cost

many very dearly in terms of damaged relationships, ruined reputa-
tions, illness, and addictive enslavement. The sexual immorality inun-
dating our culture exists because society has forgotten that sexuality is
God's gift. It's the gospel that offers a theology of the sacred, restor-
ing the delightful mystery of sexuality to its natural wholeness.

Wherever confusion exists, the gospel of Jesus can bring clarity.
A by-product of religious pluralism is confusion. But Jesus in John
14:6 makes a reasonable claim — that he himself is the embodiment
of truth. God intervened in human history in the person of Jesus to
supply us with the solution to our own sin. As offensive as that idea
is to a religiously pluralistic culture, its simple message provides a
welcome relief to confusion.

Avoid Desensitization

Popular culture trivializes brutality. The news outlets, the
Internet, television, movies, and even music depict with disturbing
ease images of torture, rape, drug abuse, and violence. As those
images percolate through our consciousness, becoming apathetic to
the reality is a serious danger. It is past time for Christian leaders to
challenge the church to pursue a holiness that reflects God's nature.

Meet the Needs of Victims

Abuse, particularly abuse that is sexual or violent in nature,
leaves permanent scars on the victims. The wounded experience
physical, emotional, social, and economic hurdles in addition to the
initial trauma. An important part of the ministry of the church is
bringing healing to those who are broken. Part of that ministry
requires speaking out for justice. As pluralism makes the definition
of both sin and justice murky, the church must clearly define both
terms and boldly proclaim the solution in the cross of Christ.

Pray for Godly Leaders

Judges is a book that cries out for men and women reflecting the
heart of God to be upstanding leaders in their sphere of influence.

Church, school, job, community — all are desperate for leaders who will powerfully communicate that the world has the potential to be a better place than it is. Life can be full of security, power, and wonder for a people whose heart is fully committed to God.

THE BOOK OF
RUTH

PREFACE AND ACKNOWLEDGEMENTS

Life in a marginal zone can be unsettling. Patterns of rainfall, disease, and political power veer to the right and to the left. Winds that carry feasting for a season can bring famine in the next. Successful herders and farmers of the biblical *Heartland* lived life close to the earth and were keenly aware of these dynamics. Their survival hinged upon the ability to communicate, flex, and move as a group.

Even so, mounting challenges have a way of reaching a tipping point; they can overwhelm the human ability to respond, individually as well as collectively. In such extreme circumstances, not only does the intellect and emotion grow numb, in an act of mutilation we gnaw off that which is most precious and necessary for our recovery: personal relationships. It is a bitter act of self-destruction indeed, for what else is left when power, pretensions, and possessions are stripped away? In this state, how does one carry on? And with whom? And for whom? Such questions are hardly unique to the windswept highlands of Moab. For all who ponder such questions, the book of Ruth provides some answers.

For me, the opportunity to spend a season of study with the text of Ruth is the result of the kindness of many people. The administration of the Cincinnati Christian University offered the time needed to initiate this work with a semester sabbatical away from my teaching duties. In addition to this one-time kindness, they have, so far, supported six seasons of archaeological investment at the site of Tell Jalul in the country of Jordan. That commitment has given me — and a host of students — the chance to regularly walk the paths of Ruth's homeland.

Within the CCU family, thanks also goes out to my colleagues, Sara Fudge and Jody Otte. Both read this manuscript and offered improvements. David Toundas, my graduate assistant, helped with many details. Rob Fleenor has been an enormous help to me as a student, librarian, and friend. He knows that our work is bound together in ways beyond the cover to this book.

Finally, given the subject matter of this commentary, it is appropriate to honor the contribution of resourceful women who understand the need for cooperation, flexibility, and mobility while living life in a marginal zone. I consider myself blessed to have such a grandmother, a mother, a wife, and a daughter. To Doris Spencer, Karen Ziese, Vicki Ziese, and Moriah Ziese, I dedicate this work.

"Your people will be my people and your God my God."

Mark Ziese
November 17, 2008

RUTH
INTRODUCTION

Every so often in the course of life, ordinary people discover God at work. This possibility gives courage in the face of uncertainty, strength in moments of exhaustion, and comfort in times of trouble. In the book of Ruth, the work of God is discovered — truly — but not in lightning flashes or in rumbly thunder as upon Sinai. Neither does it beckon from a cool garden path as did a voice in Eden. Here, the discovery is much more unobtrusive and restrained, perhaps even unnoticed by all except the narrator (and careful reader!). Yet despite a quietness, it is no less effective than the larger "displays" favored by those who prefer a God who swoops down and dashes in, in might and fury. Such vindications are, without a doubt, terrible and wonderful to behold, but quite removed from the experiences of most folk.

The charm — even mystique — of the book of Ruth rests in the ability of the narrative to suggest the work of God in the midst of ordinary life. Who could guess that the earthy smell of an open grave, the golden hues of the harvest sun, the whisper of voices in the dark, or the legal maneuvering of a public hearing are actually the ingredients for a monarchy, much less a Messiah! By means of this superbly crafted narrative, the reader finds himself or herself drawn into a world that is, in some ways, quite different than his/her own, and yet, in other ways, is very much the same. Like Naomi, we grow bitter. Like Orpah, we go home. Like Ruth, we try to be loyal. Like Boaz, we seek to do the right thing. Understanding how these characters relate to each other, to the story-line, and ultimately to us, is essential to understanding the book and the God who works in it. So grows the task.

Through careful attention to language and syntax — what is said as well as what is not said — the goals of the book may be approached. But before this can begin in earnest, the contours of some larger contexts must be traced. This is attempted in five moves here: text and language, presentation and structure, time and space, literature and law, and finally, message and faith.

TEXT AND LANGUAGE

The Hebrew text of the book of Ruth is relatively free of problems. Some 1,300 words are organized into 85 verses and grouped into four chapters. Within this well-defined set, those responsible for preserving and pointing (vocalizing) the text identified ten occasions where they believed alterations were necessary.[1] These are of little consequence, however, consisting mostly of spelling corrections. Only one (4:5) is significant enough to impact the text's understanding. Not surprisingly, it has generated much discussion and will be addressed below.[2] Other linguistic debates center around examples of what appear to be gender disagreements,[3] the presence of the "paragogic *nun*,"[4] and the presence of possible Aramaisms.[5] Such debates are recognized, but cannot be pursued here. Suffice it

---

[1]1:8; 2:1; 3:3 (two instances); 3:4; 3:14 (two instances); 4:4; 4:5; and 4:6.

[2]To tap into this discussion see the work of D.R.G. Beattie, either his "Kethibh and Qere in Ruth IV 5," *VT* 21 (1971): 490-494, or his "Ruth III: A Response," *JSOT* 5 (1978): 39-48.

[3]Robert L. Hubbard outlines these disagreements into three categories. In the first category there is an apparent disagreement between a 2 mas. pl. verb and a fem. pl. subject (1:8). In the second category there is an apparent disagreement between suffixial pronouns (2 or 3 mas. pl.) and their antecedents (f) (1:5,8,9,11,13,19; 4:11). In the third category, a 3 mas. pl. pronoun is used with a fem. antecedent (1:22). Hubbard also offers a brief bibliography of proposals for dealing with these grammatical issues. See his *The Book of Ruth*, NICOT (Grand Rapids: Eerdmans, 1989), p. 4.

[4]2:8,21; 3:4,18 all contain verbal forms with a final, unexplained, "paragogic *nun*" (נ). GKC (para. 47m) points out that these are found especially in the "older books" and may possibly be the result of euphony or the remnants of a still older form.

[5]Four examples of possible Aramaisms have been noted. וַיִּשְׂאוּ (*wayyiś'û*, "to take [wives]") in 1:4, תְּשַׂבֵּרְנָה (*tᵉśabbērnāh*, "would you wait") of 1:13, לְקַיֵּם (*lᵉqayyēm*, "to confirm") of 4:7, and שָׁלַף (*šālaph*, "took off") of 4:7. As Edward F. Campbell, Jr. writes, "there is nothing compelling about any of these, either as Aramaisms or as necessarily late vocabulary" (*Ruth*, AB [Garden City: Doubleday, 1975], p. 24). Robert Polzin notes how difficult it is to use lexicographic items to draw conclusions regarding the development of biblical Hebrew. More telling, in his opinion, is grammar and syn-

to say, the language of Ruth is classical Hebrew in form and is reminiscent of the patriarchal stories in style.

Apart from that which has been preserved by the Masoretes (the Masoretic Text or MT), other texts of Ruth are known and noted for their comparative value. Fragments from the caves along the Dead Sea have been recovered, studied, and published.[6] The Greek tradition of the Old Testament (the Septuagint or LXX) has been carefully combed in search of clues some believe to be helpful for determining the development of the Hebrew text.[7] The more "free-flowing" Syriac version is currently being studied and published.[8] Early elaborations on Ruth are available in Josephus (*Jewish Antiquities* V, ix), the Aramaic Targum to Ruth,[9] and the aggadic midrash known as *Ruth Rabbah*.[10] All these weigh in during the opening centuries of the first millennium AD and are helpful witnesses.

PRESENTATION AND STRUCTURE

The book of Ruth is a short story celebrated for its artistry and drama. It can be read in a single sitting, and, at a glance, appears

---

tax. See his *Late Biblical Hebrew: Toward an Historical Typology of Biblical Hebrew Prose* (Missoula, MT: Scholars, 1976), pp. 2, 123, 159. Evaluated according to Polzin's criteria, the text of Ruth clearly has more in common with classical biblical Hebrew than with Late Biblical Hebrew.

[6]Fortunately, a critical edition to the Megilloth is now available in the *Biblia Hebraica Quinta* series (Vol. 18, Deutsche Bibelgesellschaft, 2004). This valuable resource utilizes material from the Dead Sea Scrolls as well as other recent textual discoveries in its apparatus.

[7]For a survey of the study of the Greek text of Ruth and an outline of how this has prompted theories concerning the development of the Hebrew text, see Campbell, *Ruth*, pp. 36-40.

[8]An English translation has been available for many years as a result of the work of George M. Lamsa (*The Holy Bible from Ancient Eastern Manuscripts* [Philadelphia: A.J. Holman, 1957]). A critical edition is forthcoming from the Peshitta Institute at the University of Leiden.

[9]Etan Levine, *The Aramaic Version of Ruth*, AnBib 58 (Rome: Pontifical Biblical Institute, 1973).

[10]Access to the text in English is available in the work of H. Freedman and Maurice Simons, eds., *The Midrash*, vol. VIII, *Ruth and Ecclesiastes*, 2nd ed. (London: Soncino, 1951), and in the work of Jacob Neusner, trans. *Ruth Rabbah: An Analytical Translation*, Brown Judaic Studies 183 (Atlanta: Scholars, 1989).

quaint and simple. However, a quick read is not always the best one; the subtleties of presentation can be easily overlooked. This is especially true here, where expectations of (or a distant familiarity with) what the story says may run ahead of what is actually written. A slow read reveals a small cast of round, flat, and functionary characters. Naomi is perhaps the most fully revealed (or round) of these. She is, in many ways, at the book's center. Ruth is a foreigner and yet *the* namesake for reasons beyond the sympathy that she so naturally attracts. She is less revealed as a character (flatter) than Naomi; her words are few and weighty. Boaz appears pious, clever, and vigorous, in contrast to other male characters of the book. These are functionary, impious, part of an anonymous chorus, or dead! Together, this small cast of Naomi, Ruth, and Boaz speaks and acts in ways that may not be as straightforward as expected. Word choice, surprise, ambiguity, gapping, repetitions, inter- and intratextual play are among the sharpened tools in the narrator's kit. Taken together, these direct the plot and purpose of the book. In connection with this, it should be remembered that the recognition of this narrative artistry need not imply raw invention; put differently, well-told stories cannot be relegated to the category of fiction simply because they are well told! Successful historians have always been those who truly understand the craft of language and engage it toward specific goals.

The book of Ruth is organized chronologically, clearly marked with a beginning and an end. Scenes, or "acts," are composed of dialogue, usually limited to two characters at a time, or a character and a "chorus."[11] Each dialogue is framed by the cues and comments of an anonymous and omniscient narrator. When the text is considered carefully, it is surprising to note how little action is actually encountered; the characters move into position at the beginning of

---

[11]Terms such as *novelle, novella,* or "little novel" have been used as form-critical terms to describe the genre of Ruth (e.g., Campbell, *Ruth,* pp. 3-4; Richard L. Pratt, Jr., *He Gave Us Stories* [Phillipsburg, NJ: P&R, 1993], p. 300). Such terms are reminders that Ruth is a brief presentation, composed of episodes, has a purpose, and, in the minds of many, is fictional in character. On this last point, a snippet from Meir Sternberg is appropriate: "Were the narrative written or read as fiction, then God would turn from the lord of history into a creature of the imagination, with the most disastrous results" (*The Poetics of Biblical Narrative* [Bloomington, IN: Indiana University, 1985], p. 32).

each scene and stay put (with the possible exception of 1:8-18 where Naomi urges Ruth and Orpah to return home seemingly as they travel down the road). The actions of the characters are mostly functionary, moving them from one scene to the next. The real "guts" of the story are carried in conversation.

Some measure of symmetry is achieved when these scenes are considered end to end against the larger construction.[12] Elements of chapters one and four correspond at points: family histories are given (1:1-5 and 4:18-22); Naomi and the women of Bethlehem converse (1:19-21 and 4:14-17). Similarly, chapters two and three follow similar trajectories: Ruth and Naomi exchange plans (2:2 and 3:1-5); Ruth's identity is sought by Boaz (2:5-7 and 3:9); Boaz gives Ruth food and protection (2:8-16 and 3:10-15); and Ruth reports to Naomi (2:18-23 and 3:16-18). This balanced structure (a chiasm of sorts) is identified by most commentators, although few are bold enough to make the leap from structure to purpose.[13]

One other note should be offered. Critical scholars are prone to dismiss the genealogy of 4:18-22 as a later addition, coda, or appendix. This conclusion bespeaks an assumption that, at some point, the narrative existed independently, apart from the genealogy (or perhaps is offered as an explanation of it?). Against this critical view stands a host of recent literary approaches that view the genealogy as essential to the narrative. This is a view maintained here, not only on the grounds of literary analysis, but also given the unanimous consensus of text traditions that deliver the book to us as a seamless whole (always including 4:18-22).

---

[12]Stephen Bertman, "Symmetrical Design in the Book of Ruth," *JBL* 84 (1965): 165-168.

[13]Tod Linafelt is an exception to this. He points out how this structure assists the argument that Ruth "bridges the gap" between the text of Judges and the story of David found in Samuel. Additionally, he notes how the structure of Ruth finds a parallel in 2 Sam 5:13–8:18. See his contribution in *Ruth and Esther* (Collegeville, MN: Liturgical, 1999), pp. xx-xxv. Some of Linafelt's other points will be taken up below.

Daniel I. Block suggests an outline of the book that zigzags between complications and solutions. However in his exposition, he uses a more dramatic model that divides the work into four "Acts" and an "Epilogue." See his *Judges, Ruth*, NAC (Nashville: Broadman and Holman, 1999), pp. 616-621.

TIME AND SPACE

The book of Ruth is firmly rooted in time and space. Within the text, time is sensed irregularly and at different speeds. The cadence increases and decreases with the story's focal adjustment. Years and years are "gapped" in the grinding struggle between life and death described in the first five verses of the book. The events of the remainder of chapter one and all of chapter two transpire in only a matter of weeks. Chapter three brings focus to arresting events that transpire in a single night. The bulk of chapter four is concerned with the morning after (the night of chapter three), while in a quick dash to the finish, the closing verses of chapter four describe the passing of the months, years, and even centuries that are required to describe the conception, birth, and the enduring legacy of a child. In the end, the reader feels like an observer standing beside a long straight stretch of highway. A car is noted in the distance, moving almost imperceptibly at first. But sound and speed are increasingly experienced, until, in a roar, the car passes in a blaze of fury, and then it's gone, slowly disappearing over the horizon. This is how Ruth moves.

In the larger sweep of time, almost external to the book itself, two notations are discovered. Each is pivotal for different reasons. The first is the mention that these events occurred "in the days when the judges ruled" (1:1). This statement places the narrative within a context that is obviously clear to the reader, both ancient and modern.[14] The days of the judges may be characterized by many things, few of which are positive: infidelity, genocide, anarchy. For the modern reader of the English text, the eye ambles up the page and locks on a single phrase that says it all: "In those days Israel had no king; everyone did as he saw fit" (Judg 21:25). The book of Ruth is a welcome respite against this dark background, or, in the words of others, "a moment of serenity in the stormy world."[15] In the place of infidelity, Ruth offers loyalty. In the place of genocide, Ruth offers

---

[14]2 Kgs 23:22 also alludes to the period of the judges in a way that assumes recognition by an ancient audience.

[15]Danna Nolan Fewell and David Miller Gunn, *Compromising Redemption: Relating Characters in the Book of Ruth* (Louisville, KY: Westminster John Knox, 1990), p. 11.

ḥesed-kindness. In the place of anarchy, Ruth offers a picture of conscientious law keeping. This temporal note of 1:1, therefore, offers a setting that speaks as much to *mood* as years. Still, the years are there, vaguely. Given the conventions of modern scholarship, the described events are located in the closing centuries of the second millennium B.C. In other configurations, this might be called the end of the Late Bronze Age, the beginning of the Iron Age, or, for biblicists, the stretch between the conquest of Canaan and the establishment of the monarchy.

The second temporal note of importance comes as a result of the genealogy found in the closing verses. Assuming a genetic unity to the work, the mention of the lineage of the great king David makes it clear that the account would not have been written before his day. But how much time passes after David before the writing occurs? Such questions have occupied scholars for generations. Early interpreters felt constrained to offer early dates: could the book have been written even while David was alive?[16] Later critical scholars think not, and on the basis of language, themes, and the explanatory note of 4:7 ("Now in earlier times"), push the date of authorship well out of the lifetime of Israel's monarchy altogether.[17] Campbell has prudently grappled with these issues, outlining the arguments with their presuppositions, and suggests that the book emerged early in the period between 950–700 BC.[18] It is a comfortable conclusion.

Not only is time given definition in the book of Ruth, the same is true of space. Bethlehem is at the center. Its fields, threshing floor, and gateway offer stages for successive scenes. With respect to

---

[16]The Jewish tradition recorded in the Babylonian Talmud (*Baba Bathra* 14b) presents the opinion that Ruth is an early book in Israel's history, written by the prophet Samuel. Such an early date is difficult to accept, given the testimony to the character of David. For the tradition, see I. Epstein, ed., *The Babylonian Talmud. Seder Nezikin, Baba Bathra* (London: Soncino, 1935).

[17]Frederic W. Bush (*Ruth, Esther*, WBC [Dallas: Word, 1996], pp. 18-30) is a recent champion of a postexilic date for Ruth. The hinge of his argument swings on the conclusion that a number of instances of Late Biblical Hebrew appear in the text. Of course, others such as Hubbard, work from the same data and suggest a preexilic date for the composition of Ruth. As this disparity demonstrates, these lines of thinking are troubled, convoluted, loaded with assumptions, and as the conclusions themselves show, are prone to manipulation.

[18]Campbell, *Ruth*, pp. 23-28.

its fields, the highlands of Judah and its agricultural potential have been variously described.[19] Terraced hillsides and pockets of fertile fields mark rolling terrain. Likewise, the dynamics of cereal farming are recognized, particularly as a means of subsistence in the Judean highlands. Unfortunately, little is known of Bethlehem's history as a result of archaeological investigation; modern construction has prevented exploration. For this reason, no specifics with respect to structures or installations may be offered. There are simply no discoveries to report.

Curiously, as Linafelt has already suggested, this Bethlehem center may also add gravity to a view that slips Ruth into the gap between the book of Judges and the book(s) of Samuel. As argued, the author is fully aware of both accounts and practices literary reflection and anticipation.[20] Hence, the tragic story of the unfaithful concubine that closes down the book of Judges unwinds from Bethlehem. As a vignette of life "in the days when the judges ruled," it threads into Ruth's beginning. On the back side, it continues to the anointing of David, also in Bethlehem (1 Samuel 16). At risk of overreading, could it be said that the arrival of monarchy and the end of the period of judges is signaled, in part, by the use of this important place name? Some might call it clever fiction; other presumptions demand different conclusions.

Apart from the immediate environs of Bethlehem, the region of Moab is mentioned. No specifics are offered in the text though; Elimelech's family sojourns in the "fields of Moab." It is possible that these "fields" are located in the Jordan Valley, northeast of the Dead Sea.[21] However, by the period known as the Iron Age II, the likely time of the book's composition, the kingdom of Moab is developed and well known.[22] From a geographical perspective, this "essential Moab" is

---

[19]For excellent examples, see David C. Hopkins, *The Highlands of Canaan* (Sheffield: Almond, 1985), or Denis Baly, "The Hill Country of Judah," in *The Geography of the Bible* (New York: Harper and Row, 1974), pp. 177-190.

[20]In the classroom I encourage students to do this kind of intertextual exercise by reading "with their lights on and their mirrors adjusted."

[21]John Gray (*Joshua, Judges, and Ruth*, NCB [London: Nelson, 1967], p. 408) takes this position.

[22]No indication of state formation in Moab is suggested by the text. Undoubtedly, "Moab" in the time of the judges and "Moab" in the period of the monarchy were different. Moab, like Israel, experienced dramatic social development between the second and first millennium B.C.

concentrated on the western edge of an elevated plateau (soaring up to 4,500 feet) in what is now the Hashemite Kingdom of Jordan. It is strung between people groups known as Ammonites and Edomites, and between the Madaba plains on the north and the Wadi el-Hesa (biblical Zered) on the south.[23] A final observation notes that this "essential Moab" rests on the far side of the Dead Sea, only 35 miles due east of Bethlehem. Interestingly, because the village of Bethlehem and the region of Moab are both situated in elevated areas, they are within eyeshot of each other on a clear day. This raises the possibility that the scarps of Ruth's Moab may have been visible from Naomi's front door.

LITERATURE AND LAW

The NIV follows the well-worn tradition of the English Bible and the tradition of the LXX in positioning the book of Ruth between Judges and Samuel. Reasons for this placement have already been raised and discussed.

The MT, alternatively, places Ruth in the third part of the Hebrew canon known as "the Writings" (*Kethubim*). Within this section, it is grouped with other books (collectively known as the *Megilloth*, or the five "scrolls") designated for public reading on special days of feasting and fasting.[24] Within this tradition, Ruth is slated for the second day of Pentecost (*Shabu'ot*, or "Weeks"). Connections between the harvest celebration of Pentecost and the harvest context of Ruth are clear. Christian interpreters recognizing this link may anticipate the

---

[23]For more on Moab, see G.L. Mattingly, s.v. "Moab," in *Eerdmans Dictionary of the Bible*, ed. by David Noel Freedman, Allen C. Myers, and Astrid B. Beck (Grand Rapids: Eerdmans, 2000); Denis Baly, "The Tableland of Moab, the Land of the Shepherd," in *The Geography of the Bible*, pp. 229-233; or Burton MacDonald, "Moabite Territory and Sites" in *"East of the Jordan": Territories and Sites of the Hebrew Scriptures* (Boston: ASOR, 2000), pp. 171-183.

[24]Robert Gordis suggests that the book of Ruth, like its companions in this section of the Hebrew Bible, is concerned with questions of חָכְמָה (*hokmāh*) or "wisdom." It is a narrative that shows how *hokmāh* "operates and succeeds in human affairs." See his "Love, Marriage, and Business in the Book of Ruth" in *A Light unto My Path: Old Testament Studies in Honor of Jacob M. Myers*, Howard N. Bream, Ralph D. Heim, and Carey A. Moore, eds. (Philadelphia: Temple, 1974), p. 243.

mission of the New Testament and explore how Ruth, a Moabite, prefigures the announced movement of God in the "last days."[25] Here, as in Acts, the "Kingdom" is extended to one "who calls on the name of the Lord" (Acts 2:21). Similarly, the position of Jesus as the ultimate "descendent of David" is also a point of contact between Ruth and Peter's Pentecost sermon of Acts 2.

Legal, familial, and social customs are among the most interesting, yet tangled, aspects of the book's interpretation. This is due to the fact that specific dynamics such as the practices of inheritance, adoption, property vesting, kinship marriage, and *gō'ēl*-redemption consist of elements drawn from the larger Near Eastern setting generally and from *torah* specifically. As will be noted, the narrative not only assumes — but requires — these precedents in order for tensions to be created and relieved. That being said, two responses are raised. One is a caveat, the other is an observation.

First, the caveat. It must be recognized that the story of Ruth is precisely this: a story, and a dramatic one at that! As such, selectivity is expected of the storyteller, and some degree of "social memory" is expected of the audience.[26] If Ruth were intended to be an article of jurisprudence, it would undoubtedly have a very different flavor. Many other details, such as the questions asked by the elders in the gateway, for example, would be provided. For now, it is sufficient to note that the story "works," as generations of readers and a steady stream of commentaries attest. Moreover, the story is consistent with what is known about law and custom from this time and place.[27] The evidence for this continues to be drawn out slowly, but drawn out nonetheless.[28] Still, care must be taken not to squeeze the text needlessly for details that are beyond the point of the narrative or

---

[25]Alternatively, the feast of Pentecost is also connected to the issue of the Law at Sinai. This connection may be significant, elevating the character of Ruth for her willingness to honor *torah*.

[26]I thank my colleague Tom Thatcher for pointing out the value of this approach. See his work on this in his *Why John Wrote a Gospel: Jesus-Memory-History* (Louisville, KY: Westminster John Knox, 2005).

[27]As Hubbard states, the story is coherent (it meets the test of intelligibility), it is complete (it meets the test of self-sufficiency), and it is believable (it meets the test of credibility). See his *Ruth*, pp. 49-50.

[28]See the recent bibliography on the "Legal and Social World Studies" by Victor H. Matthews in his *Judges and Ruth* (Cambridge: Cambridge University, 2004), pp. 215-216.

the purpose of the narrator. If given, such "fine print" would, in all likelihood, derail the story line and detract from the simple elegance of its telling.

Beyond this caveat is an observation. The legal code offered in Leviticus, Numbers, and Deuteronomy is not substantially different from legal codes known elsewhere. Such codes are often written in general and generic ways. They are not intended to cover every case imaginable. Interpretation is required to match the intent of the code with the particulars of the situation. This basic principle of law appears to be the case here. As an example, kinship marriage, as codified in Deuteronomy 25, requires that the brother of the dead marry the widow of the dead for the purpose of raising an heir for the dead. But what if the dead has no brother? And what if the widow is not an Israelite? Must this code still be honored? By whom? How elastic is the law? If such questions challenged those who sought to apply legal principles in their own time (and may have required a meeting of the elders to sort it out), how much more challenging is it for us to *interpret the interpretations* of those living in a distant time and place? It is, therefore, no wonder that the book of Ruth has become a textual playground for expositors of all stripes. Naturally, predispositions plug the gaps every time.

MESSAGE AND FAITH

Corresponding to this wide field of predispositions, a number of responses to the book of Ruth have been offered. Given the complexities of the text, this is not just expected, but appropriate.[29] Some of these responses grow from inquiry that is more intrinsic in nature, summarizing the text's message through the lens of presented characterizations, scenes, and structures. Other responses grow

---

[29]As Pratt suggests, "Old Testament authors wrote univalent, coherent texts for their audiences. Each passage has one original meaning. But univalence is not the same as simplicity (original emphasis). Writers, documents, and audiences interacted in numerous ways to produce the original meaning. Paradigmatic, syntagmatic, and pragmatic angles reveal just how complex these interactions were. Consequently, as we investigate Old Testament stories, the best we can do is to make many different summaries of the one original meaning" (*He Gave Us Stories*, p. 125).

out of inquiry that is more extrinsic in nature, summarizing the text's message through the lens of what is perceived to be the needs of the audience, either ancient or modern. Both types of summaries are helpful, although one must carefully sort the underpinnings of each. Decisions to accept or reject "controls" — such as the truth-claim of the text, the interpretive community in which the message is forged, and the larger scriptural context — seriously affect the outcome. Still, all inquiries here revolve around the same poles, albeit releasing at different points to form different trajectories. Important poles to consider include Ruth's "foreignness," societal justice, Davidic ancestry, and the *ḥesed*-kindness of Yahweh.

Many see the book of Ruth as protest or proselyte literature. As literature of protest, it is argued that the text contains a message directed toward those seeking to narrowly define the "people of God."[30] As such, the text deliberately undermines (or subverts) a so-called "purity position" seeking to expel "good" aliens (like Ruth) from the Jewish community. A variation of this view considers the message of the book to be an encouragement directed toward the gentile wives of Jewish husbands. In this, Ruth is the poster child: a model proselyte for all foreigners to imitate. Naturally, for this message to be fully embraced, the front-loaded assumption that the book is a product of the postexilic period must be accepted. This is a questionable suggestion at best. This view of the book as a polemic against "nationalistic" tendencies (such as those described in Ezra 9–10) begins with the assumption of manipulation and ends with a conclusion of conflicted Scripture.

Others find a message in the book of Ruth directed toward identifying and correcting the injustices of society. Such perspectives exploit the contrast between the powerless and the powerful, but more specifically (and indicatively of predisposition), tend to highlight the struggle of women to achieve a meaningful place in a male-dominated, patriarchal society. Moreover, it is claimed that the text collapses from within, demonstrating that the powerful may be manipulated and the pious may be corrupted.[31] While these views

---

[30]An example of this approach is found in the work of Marjo C.A. Korpel, *The Structure of the Book of Ruth* (Assen: Van Gorcum, 2001).

[31]As an example, consider the work of Fewell and Gunn, *Compromising Redemption*.

highlight important themes and are even prophetic in a sense,[32] they cannot be embraced for many reasons: primary is a cracked methodological foundation. Such presentations crush the elegance of the ancient text under the weight of concerns that are terribly modern. Roles, attitudes, categories of thought, and at times, even language are transferred from the present and imposed upon the past. This kind of work may create grist for popular messages today, but is ultimately a cheap substitute for solid exegesis, much less, the responsible inquiry into the history and literature of the ancient world. As above, this approach begins with the assumption of manipulation and ends with a conclusion of conflicted Scripture.

Perhaps the most visible and explored purpose of the book of Ruth concerns the Davidic connection. The position of the genealogy at the conclusion of the book suggests the importance of this point (4:17 and 4:18-22); it is the bull's-eye at the end of the arrow's flight. Here, David's amazing ancestry is realized: he has roots that are, at once, poor and rich, Moabite and Israelite, landless and landed, and ultimately engineered by both Yahweh and man. In terms that are strictly political, such a realization would seemingly endear him (and his heirs) to a wider audience and dispel any reservations some might have about his Moabite connections (i.e., remember that Ruth is a model of faithfulness). In larger, biblical terms, this realization continues the theme of God's amazing program to bring a Messiah to earth.[33] As elsewhere, threats to derail this holy program are regularly encountered and overcome. Accepting this view

---

[32]As presented elsewhere in Scripture, people with a passion for God's reign must be open to the dispossessed and marginalized (Zech 7:10; Matt 5:14-16), must be quick to feed the hungry (Matt 5:7; Act 6:1), care for children and the elderly (Ps 139:13-14; Isaiah 61), and cannot become complacent with injustice (Amos 5:7ff; Micah 6:8). Without a doubt, such themes are essential to Kingdom-life and may be explored in the book of Ruth. However, it is difficult to see such calls to social action as "the purpose" for the text.

[33]Kirsten Nielsen observes how Yahweh is central to the book because of the position "he assumes in the dialogues. The sheer number of times he is mentioned (1:8-9,13,17,20-21; 2:12,19-20; 3:13; 4:11-12,14) creates an awareness of his never-failing presence, whether it be disaster striking, or dearth turning to wealth. This book can thus be read as homage to the God who performs his will despite all obstacles" (*Ruth: A Commentary*, OTL [Louisville, KY: Westminster John Knox, 1997], p. 30).

satisfies not only the need posed by the book's contents but the
need to read it within its canonical-historical context. Taking this
Davidic target seriously satisfies the implicit truth-claim of the book
itself and endows it with enduring, positive, qualities.[34]

In keeping with this last thought, a final purpose of the text must
be mentioned. Naomi's blessing of 1:8 has often been viewed as thematic for the book as a whole: "May Yahweh show *ḥesed*-kindness to
you, as you have shown to your dead and to me." In the end, Ruth
is shown to be a personal example of faithfulness. She exceeds all
the expectations of her society and perhaps even the letter of *torah*.
Her industry and selfless choices trigger healing and are honored by
those in the gateway and by God, the ultimate source of all *ḥesed*-
kindness. Thus, the message of the book of Ruth may be considered
from at least two vantage points. Viewed in strictly human terms, it
underlines the importance of persistent relationships in moments of
crisis.[35] Viewed from a faith perspective, it communicates confidence
in the ongoing work of God to fill the empty, to protect the vulnerable, and to bring joy into a broken world. In a small way, Ruth's
story anticipates that which is only fully realized on this side of the
cross. As Paul put it:

> We wait for the blessed hope—the glorious appearing of our
> great God and Savior, Jesus Christ, who gave himself for us to
> redeem us from all wickedness and to purify for himself a people
> that are his very own, eager to do what is good (Titus 2:13-14).

---

[34]Contra Linafelt, who begins with the assumption that David was an abus-
er of power and represents "the failure of the institution of monarchy in
Israel" (*Ruth*, p. xxiv). This presumption is consistent with other recent negative evaluations of David that idealize the decentralized, tribal nature of the
period of the judges over and against the monarchy. Armed with these
reversed values, Linafelt can then conclude that the story of Ruth "may not
have the unequivocally happy ending that commentators so often claim for
it" (*Ruth*, p. xxv). This kind of extreme thinking can only be followed when
a methodology of reading is accepted that holds the text is internally inconsistent, is "shot through" with propaganda, and is either deliberately or inci-
dentally detached from its canonical-historical context.

[35]In this, Jesus' parable of the "persistent widow" (Luke 18:1-8) is recalled.
This parallel and some cross-textual applications are considered in Victor H.
Matthews and Don C. Benjamin, *Social World of Ancient Israel 1250–587
B.C.E.* (Hendrickson, 1995), pp. 138-141.

RUTH
OUTLINE

I. **THE FLIGHT, TRAGEDY, AND RETURN OF NAOMI —** 1:1-22
   A. The Flight and Tragedy — 1:1-5
   B. The Road of Return — 1:6-18
   C. Arrival in Bethlehem — 1:19-22

II. **QUESTIONS AND ANSWERS IN THE HARVEST FIELD** — 2:1-23
   A. Ruth Goes to the Field — 2:1-3
   B. Ruth Meets Boaz — 2:4-16
   C. Ruth Returns to Naomi — 2:17-23

III. **SEEKING, SHAKING, AND PROMISE-MAKING IN THE NIGHT —** 3:1-18
   A. Naomi's Risky Plan — 3:1-6
   B. Ruth Modifies and Executes the Plan — 3:7-15
   C. Ruth Reports Back — 3:16-18

IV. **RESOLUTIONS ACHIEVED —** 4:1-22
   A. Boaz Negotiates — 4:1-12
   B. Ruth Bears a Legacy — 4:13-22

RUTH

BIBLIOGRAPHY

Alter, Robert. *The Art of Biblical Narrative*. New York: Basic, 1981.

Atkinson, David. *The Message of Ruth*. The Bible Speaks Today. Downers Grove, IL: InterVarsity, 1983.

Baly, Denis. *The Geography of the Bible*. Rev. ed. New York: Harper and Row, 1974.

Beattie, D.R.G. "Kethibh and Qere in Ruth IV 5." *Vetus Testamentum* 21 (1971): 490-494.

_____. "Ruth III: A Response." *Journal for the Study of the Old Testament* 5 (1978): 39-48.

Bertman, Stephen. "Symmetrical Design in the Book of Ruth." *Journal of Biblical Literature* 84 (1965): 165-168.

Biblia Hebraica Quinta. Deutsche Bibelgesellschaft. Vol. 18. 2004.

Block, Daniel I. *Judges, Ruth*. New American Commentary. Nashville: Broadman & Holman, 1999.

Borowski, Oded. *Agriculture in Iron Age Israel*. Boston: American Schools of Oriental Research, 2002.

_____. *Daily Life in Biblical Times*. Atlanta: Society of Biblical Literature, 2003.

Botterweck, G. Johannes, Helmer Ringgren, and Heinz-Josef Fabry, eds. *Theological Dictionary of the Old Testament*. 15 vols. Grand Rapids: Eerdmans, 1974–2006.

Brichto, Herbert Chanan. "Kin, Cult, Land, and Afterlife—A Biblical Complex." *Hebrew Union College Annual* 44 (1973): 1-54.

Britt, Brian. "Unexpected Attachments: A Literary Approach to the Term *Chesed* in the Hebrew Bible," *Journal for the Study of the Old Testament* 27 (2003): 289-307.

Brown, F., S.R. Driver, and C.A. Briggs, *The New Brown–Driver–*

Briggs–Gesenius Hebrew and English Lexicon of the Old Testament. Oxford: Clarendon, 1952.

Bush, Frederic W. *Ruth, Esther.* Word Biblical Commentary. Dallas: Word, 1996.

Campbell, Edward F., Jr. *Ruth.* Anchor Bible. Garden City, NY: Doubleday, 1975.

Carasik, Michael. "Ruth 2, 7: Why the Overseer Was Embarrassed." *Zeitschrift für die Alttestamentliche Wissenschaft* 107 (1995): 492-494.

Clark, Gordon. *The Word Hesed in the Hebrew Bible.* Journal for the Study of the Old Testament Supplement Series 157. Sheffield: Journal for the Study of the Old Testament, 1993.

Coote, Robert B. "Tribalism: Social Organization in the Biblical Israels." In *Ancient Israel: The Old Testament in Its Social Context,* pp 35-49. Ed. by Philip F. Esler. Minneapolis: Fortress, 2006.

Davis, Barry C. *God behind the Seen. Expositions of the Books of Ruth and Esther.* Expositor's Guide to the Historical Books. Grand Rapids: Baker, 1995.

Dearman, Andrew, ed. *Studies in the Mesha Inscription and Moab.* Atlanta: Scholars, 1989.

deVaux, Roland. *Ancient Israel.* New York: McGraw-Hill, 1965.

Epstein, I., ed. *The Babylonian Talmud: Seder Nezikin, Baba Bathra.* London: Soncino, 1935.

Fewell, Danna Nolan, and David Miller Gunn. *Compromising Redemption: Relating Characters in the Book of Ruth.* Louisville, KY: Westminster John Knox, 1990.

Freedman, David Noel, Allen C. Myers, and Astrid B. Beck, eds. *Eerdmans Dictionary of the Bible.* Grand Rapids: Eerdmans, 2000.

Freedman, H., and Maurice Simons, eds., *The Midrash,* Vol. VIII, *Ruth and Ecclesiastes.* 2nd ed. London: Soncino, 1951.

Gelb, I.J. "The Ancient Mesopotamian Ration System." *Journal of Near Eastern Studies* 24 (1965): 230-243.

Gesenius, W., E. Kautzsch, A.E. Cowley. *Gesenius' Hebrew Grammar.* 2nd English ed. Clarendon: Oxford, 1910.

Gordis, Robert. "Love, Marriage, and Business in the Book of Ruth: A Chapter in Hebrew Customary Law." In *A Light unto My Path: Old Testament Studies in Honor of Jacob M. Myers*, pp. 241-262. Ed. by Howard N. Bream, Ralph D. Heim, and Carey A. Moore. Philadelphia: Temple University, 1974.

Gow, Murray D. *The Book of Ruth: Its Structure, Theme and Purpose.* Leicester: Apollos, 1992.

_____. "Ruth Quoque—A Coquette? (Ruth 4:5)." *Tyndale Bulletin* 41 (1990): 302-311.

Gray, John. *Joshua, Judges, and Ruth.* New Century Bible. London: Nelson, 1967.

Harm, Harry J. "The Function of Double Entendre in Ruth 3." *Journal of Translation and Textlinguistics* 7 (1995): 19-27.

Harris, R. Laird, Gleason L. Archer, and Bruce K. Waltke. *Theological Wordbook of the Old Testament.* 2 vols. Chicago: Moody, 1980.

Herzog, Zeev. "Settlement and Fortification Planning in the Iron Age." In *The Architecture of Ancient Israel from the Prehistoric to the Persian Periods*, pp. 231-274. Ed. by Aharon Kempinski and Ronny Reich. Jerusalem: Israel Exploration Society, 1992.

Hillel, Daniel. *The Natural History of the Bible: An Environmental Exploration of the Hebrew Scriptures.* New York: Columbia University, 2006.

Hopkins, David C. *The Highlands of Canaan.* Sheffield: Almond, 1985.

Hubbard, Robert L. *The Book of Ruth.* New International Commentary on the Old Testament. Grand Rapids: Eerdmans, 1989.

Hunter, Alistair. "How Many Gods Had Ruth?" *Scottish Journal of Theology* 34 (1981): 421-436.

Kempinski, Aharon, and Ronny Reich, eds. *The Architecture of Ancient Israel from the Prehistoric to the Persian Periods.* Jerusalem: Israel Exploration Society, 1992.

Killebrew, Ann E. *Biblical Peoples and Ethnicity: An Archaeological Study of Egyptians, Canaanites, Philistines, and Early Israel 1300–1000 B.C.E.* Atlanta: Society of Biblical Literature, 2005.

King, Philip J., and Lawrence E. Stager. *Life in Biblical Israel.* Louisville, KY: Westminster John Knox, 2001.

Kitchen, K.A. *On the Reliability of the Old Testament*. Grand Rapids: Eerdmans, 2003.

Koehler, Ludwig, and Walter Baumgartner, eds. *The Hebrew and Aramaic Lexicon of the Old Testament*. Leiden: Brill, 1994–2000.

Korpel, Marjo C.A. *The Structure of the Book of Ruth*. Assen: Van Gorcum, 2001.

LaBianca, Øysten. *Hesban 1. Sedentarization and Nomadization*. Berrien Springs, MI: Andrews University, 1990.

LaCocque, André. *Ruth: A Continental Commentary*. Trans. by K.C. Hanson. Minneapolis: Fortress, 2004.

Lamsa, George M. *The Holy Bible from Ancient Eastern Manuscripts*. Philadelphia: A.J. Holman, 1957.

Levine, Etan. *The Aramaic Version of Ruth*. Analecta biblica 58. Rome: Pontifical Biblical Institute, 1973.

Linafelt, Tod, and Timothy K. Beal. *Ruth and Esther. Berit Olam*. Collegeville, MN: Liturgical, 1999.

Luter, A. Boyd, and Barry C. Davis. *God behind the Seen. Expositions of the Books of Ruth and Esther. Expositor's Guide to the Historical Books*. Grand Rapids: Baker, 1995.

MacDonald, Burton. *"East of the Jordan": Territories and Sites of the Hebrew Scriptures*. Boston: American Schools of Oriental Research, 2000.

Matthews, Victor H. *Judges and Ruth*. Cambridge: Cambridge University, 2004.

Matthews, Victor H., and Don C. Benjamin. *Social World of Ancient Israel 1250–587 BCE*. Peabody, MA: Hendrickson, 1995.

Mattingly, Gerald L. "Moab." In *Eerdmans Dictionary of the Bible*. Ed. by David Noel Freedman, Allen C. Myers, and Astrid B. Beck. Grand Rapids: Eerdmans, 2000.

_____ . "Moabite Religion and the Mesha' Inscription." In *Studies in the Mesha Inscription and Moab*. Ed. by Andrew Dearman. Atlanta: Scholars, 1989.

Miller, Max. "Ancient Moab: Still Largely Unknown." *The Biblical Archaeologist* 60 (Dec. 1997): 194-204.

Moore, Michael. *"Haggo'el*: The Cultural Gyroscope of Ancient Hebrew Society." *Restoration Quarterly* 23 (1980): 27-35.

Morris, Leon. *Judges and Ruth*. Tyndale Old Testament Commentaries. Grand Rapids: Eerdmans, 1968.

Myers, Eric M., ed. *The Oxford Encyclopedia of Archaeology in the Near East*. New York: Oxford University, 1997.

Neufeld, Edward. "Hygiene Conditions in Ancient Israel [Iron Age]." *The Biblical Archaeologist* 34 (1971): 42-66.

Neusner, Jacob, trans. *Ruth Rabbah: An Analytical Translation*. Brown Judaic Studies 183. Atlanta: Scholars, 1989.

Nielsen, Kirsten. *Ruth: A Commentary*. Old Testament Library. Louisville, KY: Westminster John Knox, 1997.

Polzin, Robert. *Late Biblical Hebrew: Toward an Historical Typology of Biblical Hebrew Prose*. Missoula, MT: Scholars, 1976.

Pratt, Richard L., Jr. *He Gave Us Stories: The Bible Student's Guide to Interpreting Old Testament Narratives*. Phillipsburg, NJ: P&R, 1993.

Rebera, Basil A. "Yahweh or Boaz? Ruth 2:20 Reconsidered." *Bible Translator* 36 (1985): 317-327.

Roop, Eugene F. *Ruth, Jonah, Esther*. Believers Church Bible Commentary. Scottdale, PA: Herald, 2002.

Sakenfeld, Katharine Doob. *The Meaning of* Hesed *in the Hebrew Bible: A New Inquiry*. Missoula, MT: Scholars, 1978.

——————. *Ruth*. Interpretation. Louisville, KY: John Knox, 1999.

Sasson, Jack. *Ruth: A New Translation. With a Philological Commentary and a Folkloristic-Formalist Interpretation*. Baltimore: Johns Hopkins University, 1979.

Saxegaard, Kristin Moen. "'More Than Seven Sons': Ruth as Example of the Good Son." *Scandinavian Journal of the Old Testament* 15 (2001): 257-275.

Shepherd, David. "Violence in the Fields? Translating, Reading, and Revising in Ruth 2." *The Catholic Bible Quarterly* 63 (July 2001): 444-463.

Sternberg, Meir. *The Poetics of Biblical Narrative*. Bloomington, IN: Indiana University, 1985.

Thatcher, Tom. *Why John Wrote a Gospel: Jesus–Memory–History*. Louisville, KY: Westminster John Knox, 2005.

Tischler, Nancy M. "Ruth." In *A Complete Literary Guide to the Bible.* Ed. by Leland Ryken and Tremper Longman, III. Grand Rapids: Zondervan, 1993.

Trible, Phyllis. "Two Women in a Man's World: A Reading of the Book of Ruth." *Soundings: An Interdisciplinary Journal* 59 (Fall 1976): 251-279.

Waltke, Bruce K., and M. O'Connor. *An Introduction to Biblical Hebrew Syntax.* Winona Lake, IN: Eisenbrauns, 1990.

Wright, Christopher J.H. *God's People in God's Land: Family, Land, and Property in the Old Testament.* Grand Rapids: Eerdmans, 1990.

RUTH 1

I. THE FLIGHT, TRAGEDY, AND RETURN OF NAOMI
(1:1-22)

The opening chapter describes the origins of an unlikely union between Naomi of Israel and Ruth of Moab. Their story is one of journeys. For Naomi, it is a journey of descent: from full to empty, from sweet to bitter, and from Bethlehem to Moab and back again. For Ruth, the trek is equally unsettling. She chooses to leave the familiar behind to embrace the unknown. The chapter may be followed in three moves. The first (1:1-5) describes the flight of Naomi from Bethlehem and the subsequent tragedies that unite her with two younger widows. The second (1:6-18) is largely dialogue between those widows as they attempt to make sense of the present and sort options for the future on the road of return. The third (1:19-22) describes what happens when Naomi and Ruth arrive in Bethlehem.

A. THE FLIGHT AND TRAGEDY (1:1-5)

¹In the days when the judges ruled,ᵃ there was a famine in the land, and a man from Bethlehem in Judah, together with his wife and two sons, went to live for a while in the country of Moab. ²The man's name was Elimelech, his wife's name Naomi, and the names of his two sons were Mahlon and Kilion. They were Ephrathites from Bethlehem, Judah. And they went to Moab and lived there.

³Now Elimelech, Naomi's husband, died, and she was left with her two sons. ⁴They married Moabite women, one named Orpah and the other Ruth. After they had lived there about ten years, ⁵both Mahlon and Kilion also died, and Naomi was left without her two sons and her husband.

ᵃ1 Traditionally *judged*

1:1-2 Deftly, in a single paragraph, the author sketches the outline of primary characters, their setting, and the series of escalating crises from which the story is launched. The drama is drawn against the dark and distant background of premonarchial Israel, **in the days when the judges ruled**.[1] Individuals are introduced. **Naomi** ("Sweetie"[2]) is the wife of **Elimelech** ("My god is king") and the mother of two sons, **Mahlon** and **Kilion**. This small family hails from a village in Judah, although they are specifically identified as **Ephrathites**. This problematic term may refer either to a specific clan within the tribe of Judah, or the tribe of Ephraim.[3] Regardless, they are ultimately Israelite in origin and, as the text presents, worshipers of Yahweh. Such identities are key to the unfolding narrative, as a **famine** prompts their flight out of the land of promise, and from their home in **Bethlehem** (loosely, "The Breadbasket"), ironically, to seek bread outside of Israel.[4] **The fields of Moab** are located in southern Transjordan, on the far side of the Dead Sea, where a narrow and grassy plateau is cut sharply by deep canyons.[5] While the flight of Elimelech's family from Israel to Moab raises questions of

---

[1]The book begins with the verbal form וַיְהִי (*wayᵉhî*) followed by a circumstantial clause. This syntax is rare in late Biblical Hebrew and may suggest an earlier date for the book. See Polzin, *Late Biblical Hebrew*, p. 56, or Bruce K. Waltke and M. O'Connor, *An Introduction to Biblical Hebrew Syntax* (Winona Lake, IN: Eisenbrauns, 1990), para. 33.2.4.

[2]BDB (s.v. נעמ) suggests that the name Naomi grows from a verbal root meaning "to be pleasant, delightful," or "lovely." Cf. with Ruth 1:20.

[3]The use of the term Ephrathites in 1:2 is debated. It is likely both a place name and a personal name. Elsewhere Ephrathite is clearly applied to members of the tribe of Ephraim (e.g. Judg 12:5 and 1 Sam 1:1). However, it is also used in parallel with the village of Bethlehem (e.g., Ruth 4:11 and Micah 5:2). Gray suggests that it refers to a district within Judah, possibly named after a specific clan that settled there. See his *Joshua, Judges and Ruth*, p. 385.

[4]The vicissitudes of rainfall within the biblical *Heartland* create a fluctuating edge between "zones of possibility," where life is sustainable, and "zones of impossibility," where life is not sustainable. It is possible for the inhabitants of the Judean hills to suffer an acute famine that does not extend into the more elevated highlands of Moab. Consider the recent presentation of rainfall in the *Heartland* hills by Daniel Hillel, *The Natural History of the Bible: An Environmental Exploration of the Hebrew Scriptures* (New York: Columbia University, 2006), pp. 140-162.

[5]For a description of Moab and a brief survey of interpretive issues, see Max Miller, "Ancient Moab: Still Largely Unknown," *BA* 60 (Dec. 1997): 194-204.

faith and failure (What is God doing here? Why doesn't Elimelech "stick it out"?), the text provides no easy answers. It does tap into themes familiar to Bible readers, famine and migration, starve-or-run dynamics, and makes it clear that this family has opted to run before it is too late. Their lifeway choice is also a familiar one to the reader of the biblical text, that of the mobile pastoralist moving among strangers, likely herding sheep and goats.[6]

1:3-5 In this time and place, far from home, Elimelech dies. His sons take Moabite wives. The terse description of these events offers no elaboration, no explanation. Certainly, suspicions creep forward though, as Israelite-Moabite relations are fraught with problems in periods before (e.g., Numbers 22–25) and after (e.g., 1 Kgs 11:1-8; Neh 13:1-3) the time of the judges. Readers are apt to remember such animosities and use them to color the narrative.[7] In this case, the names of the Moabite wives are curious and unattested elsewhere. **Orpah** may mean "Neck" or "Nape," a term referring to the back of the head and alluding to her future action.[8] **Ruth** is appro-

---

[6]The infinitive לָגוּר (lāgûr) may be translated "to sojourn" or "to camp around." The NIV translates it "to live for a while." Such temporal and mobile lifeways are a common survival tactic in the marginal zones of the Bible lands. Those who live as "sojourners" are subject to the hospitality of permanent residents. For more on the biblical use, see *TDOT*, s.v. גּוּר (gûr). For a discussion of pastoralist lifestyles in the region of ancient Moab, see Øysten LaBianca, *Hesban 1. Sedentarization and Nomadization* (Berrien Springs, MI: Andrews University, 1990).

[7]Traditions are mixed regarding the fate of Elimelech and his sons. Early Jewish interpretations suggest that Elimelech's death is a result of his choice to flee specifically to Moabite territory. The death of Elimelech's sons is due to their choice in taking Moabite wives, an action deemed illegal by early Jewish exegetes. *Ruth Rabbah* concludes that Elimelech was a rich man who would rather flee than share his wealth. For these acts of raw selfishness, he and his sons were punished. It is difficult to find such explanations rising from the text. Instead, they come from a coupling of curiosity with extra-biblical concerns.

[8]The name Orpah is connected with the root ערף ('rp) for which BDB offers two distinct meanings. The first option refers to the place on the back of the head and finds an Arabic parallel describing the mane of a horse. This gives rise to the traditional interpretation and connects to 1:14-15 where Orpah does an about-face (lit., she "turns around," from שׁוּב, šûb) for home and in so doing, shows the back of her head. This prompts Matthews and Benjamin to suggest "Deserter" as a meaning for her name (*Social World of Ancient Israel*, p. 137). The second option is connected to the act of dip-

priately named "Companion."⁹ In a further twist of ironic and dramatic elements, the two sons of Elimelech fail to sire children
through these Moabite daughters and eventually die as well, **after
they had lived there about ten years**. Irony arises from the meaning
of the sons' names and their premature deaths: *Mahlon* may mean
"Wimpy," and *Kilion*, "Perishing."¹⁰ Drama arises from the resulting
situation: due to these losses, Naomi is reduced to the most vulnerable of characters. She is a widow living without progeny in a foreign
land. Hence, in this crisp, staccato-like cadence of narrative delivery,
she is tragically and systematically deprived of her home, blood-fam-
ily, security, a decade of life, and quite possibly, the blessing of
Yahweh. Her future could not be bleaker.

B. THE ROAD OF RETURN (1:6-18)

⁶**When she heard in Moab that the LORD had come to the aid of
his people by providing food for them, Naomi and her daughters-
in-law prepared to return home from there. ⁷With her two daughters-in-law she left the place where she had been living and set out
on the road that would take them back to the land of Judah.**

---

ping or dropping. Sasson prefers this connection and playfully suggests
Orpah means, "a handful of water," something challenging to hold (see Jack
M. Sasson, *Ruth, A New Translation with a Philological Commentary and a
Formalist-Folklorist Interpretation* (Baltimore: Johns Hopkins, 1979), p. 20.

⁹This meaning of the name Ruth is regarded as tentative at best. BDB suggests it is built from the root of רעה (r'h), providing the idea of "friend," or
"companion." Others have questioned this traditional connection, arguing
that the *'ayin* (ע) could not easily be dropped. Hubbard (*Ruth*, pp. 94-95, n.
15) provides a summary of views, offering other West Semitic parallels.

¹⁰Just as the names of Elimelech's sons suggest that their place (or non-
place!) in the story is temporary at best, so too, the matter-of-fact manner of
reporting their deaths. (We struggle to even learn who is married to whom.)
The men in Naomi's life are rushed on and off the page so quickly that the
reader only later discovers that this is not a typical story about men, but an
atypical story of women. Tischler is certainly edgy and perhaps even right in
her comment, "Ruth is a woman's story in many ways. It is about women,
for women — and perhaps even, in its earliest form, by women." See Nancy
M. Tischler, "Ruth," in *A Complete Literary Guide to the Bible*, ed. by Leland
Ryken and Tremper Longman III (Grand Rapids: Zondervan, 1993), p. 153.

For more on the problematic etymology of the names *Mahlon* and *Kilion*,
consult Hubbard, *Ruth*, pp. 89-90.

[8]Then Naomi said to her two daughters-in-law, "Go back, each of you, to your mother's home. May the LORD show kindness to you, as you have shown to your dead and to me. [9]May the LORD grant that each of you will find rest in the home of another husband."

Then she kissed them and they wept aloud [10]and said to her, "We will go back with you to your people."

[11]But Naomi said, "Return home, my daughters. Why would you come with me? Am I going to have any more sons, who could become your husbands? [12]Return home, my daughters; I am too old to have another husband. Even if I thought there was still hope for me—even if I had a husband tonight and then gave birth to sons— [13]would you wait until they grew up? Would you remain unmarried for them? No, my daughters. It is more bitter for me than for you, because the LORD's hand has gone out against me!"

[14]At this they wept again. Then Orpah kissed her mother-in-law good-by, but Ruth clung to her.

[15]"Look," said Naomi, "your sister-in-law is going back to her people and her gods. Go back with her."

[16]But Ruth replied, "Don't urge me to leave you or to turn back from you. Where you go I will go, and where you stay I will stay. Your people will be my people and your God my God. [17]Where you die I will die, and there I will be buried. May the LORD deal with me, be it ever so severely, if anything but death separates you and me." [18]When Naomi realized that Ruth was determined to go with her, she stopped urging her.

1:6-7 Eventually, word arrives in Moab that the famine in Israel has lifted. This may be the result of departing invaders, the end of pestilence, or the return of rain, but according to the text, it is triggered by a divine visitation. Interestingly, this is the first mention of Yahweh's direct intervention in human affairs by the narrator. Could it hint at providential care in the midst of disaster? If so, it inserts a quiet reassurance that despite all appearances; the situation is *not* spinning out of control.[11] Food is now available in Judah and

---

[11]There are two instances in the book of Ruth where God's actions are explicitly described by the narrator. The first is here, in the case of the famine relief. The second is in the conception of Ruth's child (4:13).

Naomi is determined to return there. In tow are her Moabite daughters-in-law.

The conversation that develops en route emphasizes their collective plight, cultural differences, and future options. It is littered with the language of travel: "come," "go," "stop," "return." Such patterns may suggest the physical context of anguished debate along a dirt path. However, the language may also be read more figuratively as allusions to the halting and erratic course that, more often than not, marks life's way.

1:8-13 In a patriarchal society where support systems are engaged at the level of clan or family, there are few real choices to be made. Naomi chooses to return to the place of her extended family and encourages her daughters-in-law to do the same. **"Go back, each of you."** The rare use of **"mother's home"** here, as opposed to "father's home," has raised some debate.[12] Perhaps the easiest solution is to view Naomi's encouragement as an appeal to the mother-daughter bond. She says, in essence, "Go home. I am not your birth-mother. Stop following me."

The only gift she can leave them is a blessing: **"may the LORD show kindness to you, as you have shown to your dead and to me."** Acts or attitudes of *hesed*-kindness have been demonstrated, recognized, and appreciated. Such acts may include the faithfulness shown in staying with Naomi through the difficult days of death. Now Naomi prays that Yahweh return that same *hesed*-kindness to

---

Sakenfeld finds these instances to be structural, as they create "a narrative bracket" where "the two problems (famine and barrenness) raised by the story's prologue are addressed by divine intervention at the very beginning and very end of the main narrative." See Katharine Doob Sakenfeld, *Ruth*, Interpretation (Louisville, KY: John Knox, 1999), p. 22.

[12]Hubbard connects this use of the "mother's home" to the bedroom where marriages are arranged and feminine love is shared (cf. Gen 24:28; S of S 3:4; 8:2) (*Ruth*, pp. 102-103). Other proposals include the suggestion that Ruth and Orpah had lost their fathers to death or, more simply, that this phrase is a tender way of referencing home (i.e., remember the smell of chocolate-chip cookies fresh from the oven?).

Curiously, one rabbinic tradition suggests that Ruth and Orpah were sisters and the daughters of Eglon, the fat "Calf"-king of Moab (Judg 3:12-17)! This is surely an interpretive grope, but one that would explain why they had no "father's house" to return to. Ehud had already dispatched him. For this tradition, see the comments on Ruth 1:4 in *Ruth Rabbah*.

them.[13] It is possible that such a blessing may also be read as a release from self- or culturally imposed loyalties (cf. 2 Sam 15:20). Orpah and Ruth are free to find their own place within the care of God. Naomi further prays that through Yahweh they will experience **"rest in the home of another husband."** Only in this way will security, provision, and children be achieved. In Naomi's opinion, such an opportunity is best found among their Moabite kin. (Would it be a miracle in Israel?) This interethnic, interfamily, and possibly interreligious, experiment must come to an end for the well being of all. Still, Naomi's blessing and kiss of separation prompts their tears and protest, **"we will go back with you to your people."**

Naomi urges a different course with compelling logic. She has no hope to offer. **"Am I going to have any more sons, who could become your husbands?"** By means of this comment, the subject of kinship-marriage is raised, an important concept in discussions of the book of Ruth.[14] As described in *torah* (Deut 25:5-10), this prac-

---

[13]חֶסֶד (*ḥesed*) is a term often translated as "kindness" or "loyalty," but may be extended beyond a simple gracious act. Context suggests that *ḥesed* is assistance specifically given to those in need. For a brief discussion see Eugene F. Roop, *Ruth, Jonah, Esther*, BCBC, (Scottdale, PA: Herald, 2002), pp. 268-269. For a more extended study, see Katherine Doob Sakenfeld, *The Meaning of* Khesed *in the Hebrew Bible: A New Inquiry* (Missoula, MT: Scholars, 1978), or Gordon Clark, *The Word Hesed in the Hebrew Bible*, JSOTSup 157 (Sheffield: JSOT, 1993). A more recent presentation is Brian Britt's "Unexpected Attachments: A Literary Approach to the Term *Chesed* in the Hebrew Bible," *JSOT* 27 (2003): 289-307.

[14]This ancient "social-security net" is sometimes referred to in the literature as kinship-marriage or levirate-marriage (from the Latin, *levir*, "husband's brother"). How this principle found its way into practice in Israel, or even in areas outside of Israel for that matter, is not well known. Beyond this mention in the book of Ruth, the other primary text for the subject in a narrative context (as opposed to legal) is Genesis 38, the account of Judah and Tamar. For extrabiblical connections see the bibliography in Hubbard, *Ruth*, p. 49, n. 3.

As will become clear, beyond this mention in 2:11-13, the dynamic of kinship-marriage as presented in Ruth does not easily mesh with the legal descriptions of Deuteronomy 25. This incongruity may be explained, first, as a reflection of the evolution of the practice (and critical views regarding the evolution of the Hebrew Bible). Second, it may be explained as an imperfect legal application in a troubled time (remember, this is the "period of the judges"!). Third, explanation may be found in the unique literary needs of the author: legal quibbles are glossed in order to make the story

tice requires the brother of a dead man to take his childless widow as wife. By this action, the dead man's legacy, lineage, and, most importantly for this context, his widow, are given protection in a forgetful and dangerous world. Naomi's point at the moment, however, is that she is beyond childbearing years. She is *not about* to produce sons to marry her daughters-in-law. And even if by some miracle she could have **"a husband tonight, would you wait until they grew up?"** The answer is clearly "no." There will be no kinsman-marriage here. There will be no miraculous rescue here. Time is against all of them. Separation is their best choice for survival.

Naomi not only assesses the grim situation, she offers an interpretation of events. **"It is more bitter for me than for you, because the LORD's hand has gone out against me."** As is often the case when submerged in tragedy, it is difficult to see beyond the circle of self. Naomi shoulders the blame for recent events and believes that her suffering is without equal. She asserts that it is Yahweh who is behind it all, and states that she is the one who is experiencing the most bitterness (מַר, *mar*), possibly as wife *and* mother of the dead.[15] One can only wonder if, like Job, her words are directed heavenward.[16] To follow Naomi is to risk the very wrath of God. Again, tears erupt among the tragic trio.

1:14-18 Finally, a separation does occur. Orpah is convinced. She accepts the advice of her mother-in-law, kisses her, and departs,

---

"work." Or finally, as will be suggested here, it is possible that the marriage of Ruth (either to the unnamed kinsman or to Boaz) is so unique in circumstances, due to her foreignness and the death of appropriate male candidates, that the principles of levirate-marriage do not apply in this case at all.

[15]Alternatively, the comparative *min* used in this construction may be rendered as a "comparison of capability," viz., "I am *much too bitter* for you," or loosely, "I am *toxic!*" See Waltke and O'Connor, *Biblical Hebrew Syntax*, para. 14.4f. While this may, in the end, say the same thing, it does introduce a sharper edge to the relationship between Naomi and her daughters-in-law.

[16]Like Job, Naomi suffers without knowing why. She views herself as the recipient of some kind of divine "backhand." Compare her statement, "the LORD's hand has gone out against me" (1:13) with Job's, "for the hand of God has struck me" (Job 19:21). Here, as elsewhere in the Old Testament, the issue of theodicy is raised, but not resolved. As passages such as Hab 2:2-4 and Ps 73:21-23 point out, a faith position recognizes that answers will eventually be revealed. In the meantime, focus must be given to the presence and goodness of God.

ostensibly for **her people and her gods**. Ruth, however, chooses differently. Her choice causes the narrative to lurch forward unexpectedly. She trails, clings, or even sticks to Naomi, like skin to a body.[17]
Neither logic nor peer pressure can drive Ruth away. Instead, her
voice is heard for the first time: poignant, tender, soaring. Two elements are crucial. The first is a description of her intentions in
"clinging" to Naomi, **"Where you go I will go, and where you stay I
will stay. Your people will be my people and your God my god.
Where you die I will die, and there I will be buried."** Each clause
ratchets up the dialogue to a level of greater intensity: going, lodging, identifying, worshiping, dying. This statement of intension portrays a journey of sorts, a dangerous journey through barriers and
over boundaries. It is no short run, but persistent to the grave. It further underlines the _ḥesed_-kindness mentioned by Naomi.

Why, exactly, Ruth is loyal to Naomi is part of the mystery (and
charm) of the book (see, however, 4:15). Equally curious is Ruth's
willingness to embrace the people and god of her mother-in-law.
Certainly she must realize the difficulty of her proposal.[18] She cannot be ignorant of the risk of rejection and the difficulty of shaking
pejorative labels. Does her experience of Naomi's people go beyond
the little family of Elimelech? Does her experience of Naomi's god
extend beyond Naomi's blunt interpretation of their collective loss?
Given Naomi's declaration that it is Yahweh's hand that forced this
bitter situation, how or why would such a deity ever be attractive to
Ruth? Along these lines, the text is silent. A down-to-earth explanation suggests that the ten-year relationship between Ruth and Naomi
has knitted their spirits together in friendship. A more lofty explanation suggests that a seed of faith has taken root inside of Ruth.
Both may very well be true.

A second crucial element of Ruth's speech is an oath, cast in familiar language: **"May the LORD deal with me, be it ever so severely, if**

---

[17]The Hebrew דָּבַק (_dābaq_) is applied to human relationships in many
ways. It may suggest a friendly or hostile relationship. It may describe a sexual union (e.g., Gen 2:24) or simply a friendly affection (Prov 18:24). For
skin on a body, see Job 19:20.

[18]Consider the opening comments of Ann E. Killebrew in her _Biblical
Peoples and Ethnicity: An Archaeological Study of Egyptians, Canaanites, Philistines, and Early Israel 1300–1000 B.C.E._ (Atlanta: SBL, 2005).

anything but death separates you and me." This oath-formula
becomes exceptional only when it is remembered that it is coming
from the mouth of a woman with Moabite roots.[19] Her oath is in the
name of Yahweh! One would expect to find the name of a local deity
such as *Chemosh* or *Nabu* in her mouth, e.g. "May Chemosh do to
me . . . ."[20] Naomi's encouragement to Ruth to return to her people
and her gods is offered in vain. Could this be because Ruth has nothing left to return to? Details of her previous life are unknown. Has
Ruth's transformation from a Moabite to a Judahite context moved
beyond recall? Finally, and most significantly, does the language of
this oath-formula indicate that Yahweh is now Ruth's god?[21] Additional support for this position comes from Naomi's words in 1:8-9
where she invokes Yahweh's blessing on Orpah and Ruth, not in
Israel, but in Moab. Ruth's faith orientation may be enigmatic, but
Naomi's blessing is not. Her words recognize that the sovereignty —
and blessing — of God is not limited by human boundaries.

In the end, there is no turning back for Ruth. She is daring
enough to challenge Naomi.[22] The word used to describe her determination is not a finite verb but a participle that carries a durative
connotation.[23] The task ahead will require that she muster "all her
physical and mental resources."[24] When Naomi recognizes Ruth's
resolution, possibly at the level of personal relationship as well as

---

[19]Compare the oath-formula used here with that used in 1 Sam 14:44;
1 Kgs 2:23; 19:2, and elsewhere.

[20]Gerald L. Mattingly surveys what is known of Moabite religion in his
"Moabite Religion and the Mesha' Inscription," in *Studies in the Mesha
Inscription and Moab*, ed. by Andrew Dearman (Atlanta: Scholars, 1989), pp.
211-238. See also Alastair Hunter, "How Many Gods Had Ruth?" *SJT* 34
(1981): 427-436.

[21]Ruth is the epitome of a proselyte in Jewish tradition. According to the
commentary on 1:16 in the *Targum to Ruth*, Naomi explains what the Law
demands of the convert. Later (3:11), she is described as one "strong
enough to bear the yoke of the Lord's law" (Nielsen, *Ruth. A Commentary*,
p. 49).

[22]Ruth's daring is raised again in her request to glean (2:2) and in the
threshing floor scene where she challenges Naomi's instructions by changing the plan (3:9).

[23]מִתְאַמֶּצֶת (*mith'ammeṣeth*) is a Hithpael participle built from the root, אמץ
(*'mṣ*), "to be strong." Taken reflexively, "she is strengthening herself."

[24]Hubbard, *Ruth*, p. 121.

faith commitment, she stopped urging her, or more literally, she simply falls silent.[25]

C. ARRIVAL IN BETHLEHEM (1:19-22)

[19]So the two women went on until they came to Bethlehem. When they arrived in Bethlehem, the whole town was stirred because of them, and the women exclaimed, "Can this be Naomi?" [20]"Don't call me Naomi,[a]" she told them. "Call me Mara,[b] because the Almighty[c] has made my life very bitter. [21]I went away full, but the LORD has brought me back empty. Why call me Naomi? The LORD has afflicted[d] me; the Almighty has brought misfortune upon me." [22]So Naomi returned from Moab accompanied by Ruth the Moabitess, her daughter-in-law, arriving in Bethlehem as the barley harvest was beginning.

[a]20 Naomi means pleasant; also in verse 21. [b]20 Mara means bitter. [c]20 Hebrew Shaddai; also in verse 21 [d]21 Or has testified against

1:19-21 No details of the journey from Moab to Judah are given; the narrator quickly telescopes to the moment of arrival. When Naomi and Ruth enter Bethlehem, **the whole town is stirred**. The return of Naomi creates a tumult of excitement or confusion, shock or joy.[26] Having not seen her for more than a decade, this sudden appear-

---

[25]The Hebrew וַתֶּחְדַּל לְדַבֵּר (wattehdal l°dabbēr) suggests that Naomi "ceased speaking." Some interpret her silence as the result of anger, notably Fewell and Gunn, who interpret the relationship between Naomi and Ruth in icy terms. Using cues such as this ambiguous phrase, they propose that Naomi's interest in sending Ruth home is less than altruistic. According to their reading, "Naomi is attempting to shake free of Moab and the calamity she associates with that place and its people. Resentment, irritation, frustration, unease may well lie behind her silence. Ruth the Moabite may even menace her future." For Fewell and Gunn, antagonism lies beneath the surface of the widows' relationship and regularly threatens it; only their mutual plight keeps them together (see their Compromising Redemption, p. 74).

A less cynical interpretation is suggested by the NIV text. Given Ruth's passionate speech, Naomi is taken aback. She grows quiet and "stops urging" Ruth to return home. Naomi's silence may even be interpreted as contemplative; she, like the reader, is stunned by Ruth's loyalty.

[26]The root הוּם (hûm) is also used in 1 Sam 4:5 to mark the exciting arrival

ance without husband or sons — and with a Moabite daughter-in-law — causes many tongues to wag. **"Can this be Naomi?"**[27]

The question prompts an outburst that expands upon the interpretation of events offered by Naomi in 1:13. Previously, she stated that her bitterness was greater than that of Orpah and Ruth. Now, she answers the question of the village women, saying in essence, "No, I am not Naomi ('The sweet one'), I am **Mara**, ('The bitter one'[28])." Note the wordplay. She also claims that her newfound emptiness is a direct result of God's work: Yahweh **has afflicted me; the Almighty has brought misfortune upon me.** One can rightly challenge Naomi's interpretation of events, but her self-description will stand. The situation, whether chalked up to ill-luck, providence, punishment, or merely the consequence of living in a fallen world, has changed Naomi forever. What starts in Bethlehem, ends in Bethlehem. Even so, Naomi is not the same as at the start. She may return to her hometown, she may again walk familiar streets or even sleep in her old home, but her previous life will not be recovered. Time and circumstances prevent such complete returns. Expositors of this text would do well to explore similar attempts in modern life.

1:22 The narrator's statement brings closure to the flight, tragedy, and return of Naomi. It also serves as a narrative bridge for what comes next, as it just so happened[29] that **the barley harvest was**

---

of the Ark-box in the Israelite camp and in 1 Kgs 1:45 to describe the ruckus in Jerusalem when Solomon was announced as king.

[27]The verbal form תֹּאמַרְנָה (tō'marnāh) is clearly a feminine plural, suggesting that this question of identity comes from the women of Bethlehem. This voice is raised again in 4:17 at the close of the book, where it is specifically attributed to "the women living there." Assuming that this chorus at the beginning of the book is the same as the chorus at the end of the book, their presence becomes structurally significant and is worth exploring further. See the comments below related to 4:17.

[28]The term מָרָא (mārā') is likely built from the root מרר (mrr, "to be bitter"). The pungent incense known as myrrh (mōr) is from the same word family, as are the bitter herbs (marōr) of the Passover meal.

[29]Invisible in the NIV is the Hebrew clause of v. 22, וְהֵמָּה בָּאוּ (wᵉhēmmāh bā'û). What is the antecedent of the 3mp pronoun hēmmah? If it is the women, why the masculine gender? Moreover, if it refers to the women, why is it necessary at all, given the presence of bā'û, ("they came," from בּוֹא, bô')? Some commentators suggest it is a gender confusion on the part of the author. Alternatively, Campbell suggests that the hēmmāh is not a pronoun at all, but rather, an emphasizing particle with Ugaritic parallels. If correct

beginning. According to the agricultural calendar of the region, the barley harvest takes place from mid-March to late April.[30] This detail not only propels the story forward, it prompts one last look over the shoulder. The long famine that initiated the flight of Naomi and her men has now given way to harvest. Similarly, Naomi's life is about to change yet again, as a result of events in a harvest field and the actions of Ruth, still identified as **the Moabitess.**

---

in this, his following conclusion becomes reasonable: the odd grammar of this emphasizes "the entire circumstance" and injects "a note of sly and good-humored wonder: 'Well, what do you know, they arrived in Bethlehem for barley-harvest — just the right time.'" For the full discussion see Campbell, *Ruth*, p. 78.

[30]The agricultural calendar was full of labor-intensive activity. A tenth-century-B.C. tablet known as the Gezer Calendar outlines this work.

Line 1: two months of [olive] harvest;
Lines 1-2: two months of sowing;
Line 2: two months of late sowing;
Line 3: a month of hoeing weeds;
Line 4: a month of harvesting barley;
Line 5: a month of harvesting and [measur]ing;
Line 6: two months of cutting grapes
Line 7: a month of [collecting] summer fruit.

While some of the terms used in this "calendar" are disputed, it clearly shows a twelve-month schedule of activity beginning in the fall. For more, see *OEANE*, s.v. "Gezer Calendar," or Oded Borowski, *Daily Life in Biblical Times* (Atlanta: SBL, 2003), pp. 26-28.

RUTH 2

II. QUESTIONS AND ANSWERS
IN THE HARVEST FIELD (2:1-23)

Food returns to the land of Israel, but it must be harvested. For the returning Naomi and her daughter-in-law, Ruth, securing a meal from this harvest is an immediate need.[1] But how will this be accomplished? A "chance encounter" between Ruth and Boaz proves sufficient and is suggestive of more to come. Narratively, the plot is advanced by a series of questions and answers. Ruth asks to glean in the fields (2:1-3). Boaz inquires as to Ruth's story (2:4-16). Naomi wonders who Ruth's gracious benefactor could be (2:17-23).[2] Through it all, the theme of hidden providence continues to rise and fall.

A. RUTH GOES TO THE FIELD (2:1-3)

¹Now Naomi had a relative on her husband's side, from the clan of Elimelech, a man of standing, whose name was Boaz.
²And Ruth the Moabitess said to Naomi, "Let me go to the fields and pick up the leftover grain behind anyone in whose eyes I find favor."

---

[1]To suggest that food is not a pressing issue for Ruth and Naomi (e.g. Sasson, *Ruth*, p. 42), seemingly overlooks the thrust of the first chapter — the obvious dynamics of famine, migration, and return — that set this story in motion.

[2]Roop offers a chiastic structure of Ruth 2. He pairs the opening (2:1) and concluding (2:23) statements, dialogue between Ruth and Naomi (2:2 with 2:18-22), scene in the field (2:3 with 2:17), and the dialogue between Boaz and the workers (2:4-7 with 2:15-16). This leaves the dialogue between Boaz and Ruth as the apogee (2:8-14). See his *Ruth, Jonah, Esther*, p. 45.

Naomi said to her, "Go ahead, my daughter." ³So she went out
and began to glean in the fields behind the harvesters. As it turned
out, she found herself working in a field belonging to Boaz, who
was from the clan of Elimelech.

2:1 New information is revealed in the notice that **Naomi had a
relative**. One might assume that Elimelech had connections in Bethlehem; this is now made explicit.³ The notice is of great interest, as
this connection is **from the clan⁴ of Elimelech** and is **a man of standing**, or more traditionally, a "mighty man."⁵ Such a description may
refer to his strength, size, prowess, possessions, or virtue. The translation choice of the NIV emphasizes his role in the community; as
such, he is set in sharp contrast with the lowly Naomi.⁶ The name

---

³Still, the precise relationship between Naomi and Boaz is difficult to
determine. Clearly, Boaz is of the family of Elimelech, but how is he connected to Naomi? The grammar here is vexed with a *ketib/qere* problem.
Following the *ketib*, Boaz is מְיֻדָּע (*mᵊyuddā'*), or "friend" (from the root ידע,
yd', "to know") or acquaintance of Naomi via her husband. Following the
qere, Boaz is a מוֹדַע (*môda'*), a "relative" (a nominal form likewise from the
root *yd'*) to Naomi via her husband. The NIV follows the latter, likely bol-
stered by his description in 3:2. Elsewhere within the book, Boaz is termed
a גֹּאֵל (*go'ēl*), "redeemer" (2:20; 3:9,12). Hence, questions arise concerning
the semantic overlap of these terms, *mᵊyuddā'*, *môda'*, and *go'ēl*. However
translated, the point of the clause in question is that Boaz is familiar to
Naomi and is therefore in a position to be of help.

⁴"Clan" here is derived from מִשְׁפָּחָה (*mišpaḥāh*), a term used to describe
extended family connections. Anthropological studies point out that early
Israel was a "segmented society." As such, it was composed of various seg-
ments: households, clans, and tribes. For more, consult Robert B. Coote,
"Tribalism: Social Organization in the Biblical Israels," in *Ancient Israel. The
Old Testament in Its Social Context*, ed. by Philip F. Esler (Minneapolis:
Fortress, 2006): 35-49.

Hubbard (*Ruth*, p. 134) suggests that the term from 1:2, Ephrathites, may
designate the particular clan described here.

⁵A גִּבּוֹר חַיִל (*gibbôr ḥayil*) is one who has outperformed others in some area
of excellence. This area of excellence is frequently connected to military
activity but is not limited to such. A tighter definition must be determined
by context (s.v. גָּבַר [*gābar*] in *TWOT*). What specific activities in Boaz's past
might attract the label of *gibbôr ḥayil* are not offered. What is clear here is
that he is a man of some substance, possessing land and servants. He also
demonstrates wisdom and virtue in his dealings with others.

⁶Phyllis Trible captures these surges in her early and influential essay,
"Two Women in a Man's World: A Reading of the Book of Ruth," *Soundings:*

Boaz, tentatively rendered as either "Shrewd" or "Strong," offers additional commentary on his person.[7] In this, though, it is the narrator who is shrewd: this piece of information is casually dropped at the end of this notice. Anticipation is stirred.

2:2-3 Meanwhile, Ruth dares to take the initiative and gently requests permission from Naomi: "Please, let me **go to the fields and pick up the leftover grain.**" Subsistence farming in the vicinity of Bethlehem utilized small open valleys or terraced hillsides that took advantage of the fertile soil. Barley, in particular, was a more hearty cereal than wheat, and could be sown in areas or periods of limited rainfall.[8] Hand harvesting was done by pulling the stalks from the ground or by cutting them close to the ground with a sickle. Each handful of stalk with its grain head would be piled, tied into bundles or sheaves, and transported to a threshing area where the grain would be separated from the chaff and stalks. Grain could be eaten directly by humans or animals, allowed to ferment for drink, or ground to flour for baking. Even the remaining chaff and stalks were valuable. They served as fodder or bedding for animals or used as a binder in clay destined for bricks, ceramic pots, or mud plaster. In the labor-intensive process of hand-harvesting cereals, it would not be uncommon for stalks to be missed, dropped, or trampled. The act of collecting this lost produce is known as gleaning.[9] Ruth here proposes to enter the fields where the harvest was taking place in order to glean. Such activity is described in Israel's *torah* as a right of the poor who had no fields of their own to harvest (Lev 19:9-10;

An Interdisciplinary Journal 59 (Fall 1976), p. 259. She writes, "This kinsman . . . opposes Naomi's emptiness, poverty, and powerlessness."

[7]Linafelt not only outlines the possibilities, he raises the mention of the name Boaz in the context of Israel's temple architecture (1 Kgs 7:21). Here the name Boaz is applied to one of two columns in the hall entrance. He also fails to resist the pun, noting how Boaz in the book of Ruth is a "pillar in the community" (*Ruth*, p. 25). For a more linguistically sensitive presentation, see Sasson, *Ruth*, pp. 40-42.

[8]Compare and contrast the description of these two cereals in the description of Oded Borowski, *Agriculture in Iron Age Israel* (Boston: ASOR, 2002), pp. 88-92.

[9]For more on food-production practices in Israel see Philip J. King and Lawrence E. Stager, *Life in Biblical Israel* (Louisville, KY: Westminster John Knox, 2001), pp. 85-122. Also helpful is Borowski's presentation on "Field Work and Grain Production," in *Agriculture in Iron Age Israel*, pp. 45-83.

23:22; Deut 24:19-21).[10] As this request is generated by Ruth (specifically called **a Moabitess** again), it raises a question concerning how widespread this practice could have been (did the poor have similar rights in Moab?) or Ruth's familiarity with Mosaic teaching. At the very least, it underlines the daring of Ruth who ventures as a foreigner into the matrix of strange fields, manners, and customs of the people she has proposed to adopt (1:16).

Since the practice of gleaning relied, in part, on the kindness (or sloppiness!) of the harvesters, Ruth states that she will go and work **"behind anyone in whose eyes I find favor."** Following the NIV, she is, in essence, willing to take "a random shot" at finding food by following the harvesters, whoever they are, wherever she can.[11] As a

---

[10]This activity may be likened to picking up aluminum cans along the side of the road, a subsistence tactic practiced by the poor in areas of the U.S. today. This parallel is noted by Hubbard, *Ruth*, p. 138.

[11]Our reading differs from that of Sasson, Matthews, and others in several ways. First, they have argued that the reason why Ruth proposes to enter the field to glean is not necessarily motivated by hunger. This is why the idea does not originate with Naomi nor does Naomi accompany Ruth to the field. Second, translators (here, Sasson particularly) creatively render the question in the middle of v. 3 as, "Shall I go to the fields and glean among the ears of grain, in the hope of pleasing *him*?" (Emphasis mine). Matthews similarly suggests that Ruth's proposal is not as much a deliberate hunt for food, as for a man. See Sasson, *Ruth*, p. 42-43, and Matthews, *Judges and Ruth*, p. 225.

Sasson's reading at this point strains the text and context unnecessarily. His three points may be countered as follows: (1) even though the law gives Ruth permission to glean wherever she wishes, it is not necessarily true that all fields will be equally productive. Some harvesters will be more careful than others; some harvesters will be more generous to gleaners than others. What Ruth voices here is a hope to find a place where she can gather as much grain as possible. (2) Naomi's failure to go to the field is easily explained by her age, the difficulty of the work, or by her loss of hope. The fact that she may have land (did she already sell it?) is immaterial at this point (4:3). She has been removed from it for more than a decade and could hardly have tilled or planted it in time for the present harvest. Her question at Ruth's return (v. 19) suggests that she was not a part of any manhunt, raising a further question, if she wasn't involved, how would Ruth, a foreigner, have identified Boaz, much less his field(s)? The context itself suggests that the Ruth-Boaz encounter was "accidental" (see comments on v. 3 below). (3) Finally, the subordinate clause Sasson uses as a hinge-pin to his argument, אֲשֶׁר אַחַר (*'aḥar 'ăšer*), must be read alongside of other passages within the book, noticeably the *very next verse* that says she gleaned in the field *after* or

gleaner, she is not bound by property limits (probably set by boundary stones) and is free to work an area once it has been harvested.
Her statement specifically raises the subject of finding the "favor" of
a superior and voices her hope to fall into a situation where hospitality will be shown.[12] Curiously, this effort to "find favor" is partially anticipated by the prayer in 1:9 where Naomi prays that through
Yahweh, her daughters-in-law will "find rest." Could the text be edg-
ing toward a theology of "finding" that is as much a divine grant as
it is a human endeavor?

So much is suggested by the phrase **as it turned out**. This loaded
vocabulary (more literally, "her chance encountered"[13]) intentionally
understates the results of Ruth's quest.[14] First Samuel 6:9 provides a
curious allusion to the role of "chance" in the OT and a parallel to
this passage.[15] In 1 Samuel 6, the Ark-box of Yahweh is returned to
Israel by the Philistines via an unmanned cart drawn by cattle. The
Philistine diviners suggest that the direction the Ark-box travels will
reveal if their fate has been determined by a divine hand or by
"chance." As it turns out, there is no "chance" involved. Similarly,
here, like the Ark-box to the harvesters, Ruth **found herself working
in a field belonging to Boaz**. The thread left dangling in 2:1 is picked

---

behind the harvesters (v. 3). The difference between a singular and plural
usage of *'aḥar* is scarcely sufficient to overturn a more conventional reading.

[12]Depending on how one interprets 2:7 (see below), it may also anticipate
the request of Ruth for permission to glean. Read in this way, her statement
is loosely translated, "Let me go . . . behind anyone who will give me permission." If this is indeed the case, it relieves the difficulty of how Ruth
could be aware of the provision for gleaners in *torah* (see above).

[13]וַיִּקֶר מִקְרֶהָ (*wayyiqer miqrehā*). Verb and noun are built from the root,
קרה (*qrh*), "to encounter, meet, or befall." BDB (s.v. קרה) suggests that this
activity is "without pre-arrangement" and usually involves Yahweh.
Likewise, the LXX renders the passage with the verb, περιπίπτω (*peripiptō*)
used of a situation where a man falls among robbers or a ship strikes a reef.
The narrator steers as widely as possible to avoid the conclusion that the
meeting of Ruth and Boaz is humanly engineered.

[14]This turning of divine providence as key to the book of Ruth is readily
apparent in most commentaries. Still, some attempts have been offered to
dispute it, e.g., Linafelt, *Ruth and Esther*, p. 28. A recent, more popularly
written work favoring the providence of God in Ruth is the work of A. Boyd
Luter and Barry C. Davis, *God behind the Seen: Expositions of the Books of Ruth
and Esther*. Expositor's Guide to the Historical Books (Grand Rapids: Baker,
1995), pp. 43-53.

[15]Suggested by Campbell, *Ruth*, p. 112.

up again. Connecting Boaz to the **clan of Elimelech** is hardly redundant; it reinforces the conclusion that this "finding" is no accident.

B. RUTH MEETS BOAZ (2:4-16)

[4]**Just then Boaz arrived from Bethlehem and greeted the harvesters, "The LORD be with you!"**

"The LORD bless you!" they called back.

[5]**Boaz asked the foreman of his harvesters, "Whose young woman is that?"**

[6]**The foreman replied, "She is the Moabitess who came back from Moab with Naomi. [7]She said, 'Please let me glean and gather among the sheaves behind the harvesters.' She went into the field and has worked steadily from morning till now, except for a short rest in the shelter."**

[8]**So Boaz said to Ruth, "My daughter, listen to me. Don't go and glean in another field and don't go away from here. Stay here with my servant girls. [9]Watch the field where the men are harvesting, and follow along after the girls. I have told the men not to touch you. And whenever you are thirsty, go and get a drink from the water jars the men have filled."**

[10]**At this, she bowed down with her face to the ground. She exclaimed, "Why have I found such favor in your eyes that you notice me—a foreigner?"**

[11]**Boaz replied, "I've been told all about what you have done for your mother-in-law since the death of your husband—how you left your father and mother and your homeland and came to live with a people you did not know before. [12]May the LORD repay you for what you have done. May you be richly rewarded by the LORD, the God of Israel, under whose wings you have come to take refuge."**

[13]**"May I continue to find favor in your eyes, my lord," she said. "You have given me comfort and have spoken kindly to your servant—though I do not have the standing of one of your servant girls."**

[14]**At mealtime Boaz said to her, "Come over here. Have some bread and dip it in the wine vinegar."**

When she sat down with the harvesters, he offered her some roasted grain. She ate all she wanted and had some left over. [15]As

she got up to glean, Boaz gave orders to his men, "Even if she gathers among the sheaves, don't embarrass her. ¹⁶Rather, pull out some stalks for her from the bundles and leave them for her to pick up, and don't rebuke her."

Events described in this section take place in the harvest field. The exchange of dialogue alternates between Boaz and the harvesters (2:4-7), Boaz and Ruth (2:8-14), and again, Boaz and the harvesters (2:15-16).

2:4-7 With respect to the dialogue between Boaz and the harvesters: 2:4 builds upon what has already been presented in 2:3. Not only is it a "coincidence" that Ruth ended up in the field of Boaz, the drama is heightened by the sudden (and even surprising) arrival of Boaz. **Just then** masks the Hebrew הִנֵּה (*hinnēh*), "look" or "behold," that emphasizes the "here-and-now-ness" of this character already introduced.[16] The reader can exclaim, "I just knew you would come!" Unfortunately, Ruth is not yet in on the secret shared between narrator and reader.

Boaz arrives in the field and greets the harvesters, "May Yahweh **be with you!**" Whether anything can be made of his words from a historical perspective is questionable. It is likely that such a greeting was common and followed social conventions of the day within Judah. The same is likely true of the harvesters' response, "May Yahweh **bless you.**" However, narratively, this exchange is a cue to the presence and blessing of God in what follows. It also alerts the reader to the fact that there is a group of harvesters working for Boaz under the direction of a foreman (v. 5). This group involves young men and young women (v. 9).[17]

Following this greeting, Boaz inquires concerning the presence of Ruth. He asks the young man who functions as the harvest foreman, **"Whose young woman is that?"** The question is a bit more complicated than a simple question of identity ("Who is this?"). As

---

[16]See *TWOT*, s.v. הִנֵּה (*hinnēh*).

[17]The harvest team is composed of נְעָרִים (*nᵉʿārîm*, "lads") and נַעֲרֹת (*naʿărôth*, "lasses") (v. 9). Such terms refer specifically to young people, mature enough to be married, but often single. People of this class may be personal servants, attendants, or hired laborers. See *HALOT*, s.v. נַעַר or נַעֲרָה. The repeated use of these terms suggests a thematic role for "youth" within the book as a whole and within this section particularly.

such, the possessive suggests there is a story here.[18] "What is going on here?" This is what Boaz wants to know.[19]

The young man answers, **"She is the Moabitess who came back from Moab with Naomi."** No name is offered. More immediately significant is Ruth's social standing (she is a foreigner) and Ruth's relationship to Naomi (she has stuck with her). Story told. **"She said, 'Please let me glean . . . and has worked steadily.'"** By this, the young man explains Ruth's activity in the field.[20] She has been persistent, if not industrious, clearly one who has gone "above and beyond" the expected.

---

[18]Campbell, *Ruth*, p. 94. Others have suggested that this indirect style is a reflection of the cultural situation. See Gray, *Joshua, Judges, and Ruth*, p. 391, or Hubbard, *Ruth*, p. 146.

[19]Again Fewell and Gunn expand this notion dramatically, and pack it with sexual overtones (*Compromising Redemption*, pp. 36-38, 42). Whether Boaz is physically attracted to this stranger in his field is impossible to say; his thoughts are opaque as presented. Similarly, the reader cannot know at this point whether his motive is driven by benevolence or kindness. What is clear is that Ruth's presence is a surprise.

[20]The grammar of 2:7 is notoriously difficult and has prompted many different interpretations. Three observations may be offered. First, Ruth requests permission (via the cohortative as 2:2) to work in a particular place or in a particular way. While it is assumed that permission to glean was not necessary per Mosaic Law, it certainly is consistent with Ruth's "above and beyond" attitude and would likely be in her best interests as a foreigner. Connected to this is her request to "gather among the sheaves." Does she request to sort through the already-cut sheaves, work only in the gaps between them, or something else (gather and pile now, carry away later)? The text is not clear. Second, the passage is problematic with respect to her "standing" (תַּעֲמוֹד, *ta'ămôd*) "from morning till now" (or till "evening," following LXX). The NIV loosely translates this verb as working on her feet, or "working steadily" throughout this time. However, a more literal reading suggests she has been "standing" since morning, ostensibly to receive an answer to her request to glean. It should be noted that these two interpretations move in very opposite directions. In the first scenario, Ruth asks permission to glean and then commences to do so almost tirelessly. In the second scenario, Ruth asks permission to glean and then stands patiently awaiting an answer. In light of comments raised above (cf. 2:2) and the "permission granted" statement from Boaz below (2:9), this latter reading is preferred here (against the NIV). The third and final problem of the verse, the mention of the "house," hinges on how one reads Ruth's actions (working or waiting). If she has been working steadily all day (per NIV) the report may be a statement of amazement: she took only one short break, perhaps for the shade or bathroom (?). If she has been standing and waiting for an

2:8-14 With respect to the dialogue between Ruth and Boaz: Boaz speaks three times, Ruth twice responds, humbly. In the first statement of Boaz, permission to glean is granted. **"Don't go and glean in another field."**[21] Ruth is told to stay within the reach of the field-parcel and people of Boaz. Despite her role as a "free grazer," she is given permission to work among his **servant girls** by following after them. Connected to this is the notice of Boaz to the young men **not to touch** her. While some interpreters are quick to read the potential for illicit sexual contact into these words (i.e. "molest"),[22] it is not necessary.[23] This order to the young men is conjoined to the clause giving permission to Ruth to stay in the field. Their touch, in this case, is more likely to come in the form of driving her away as an unwanted irritant or obstruction.[24] Almost as an underline to this

---

answer all day, the passage may be read, per Hubbard, as the nervous joking of the foreman who whispers sideways to Boaz, "she has practically taken up residence here!" (*Ruth*, p. 151).

For still one more reading option, see Michael Carasik, "Why the Overseer Was Embarrassed," *ZAW* 107 (1995), pp. 493-494.

[21]The commands of Boaz in 2:8 are cast as a negative, "Do you not hear, my daughter?" Such circumlocution gives emphasis to his words and amounts to a way of assertion, viz, "certainly you hear, my daughter." See GKC, paragraph 150*e*. Compare with Josh 10:13 or with Naomi's words later in the book (3:1,2). Some see the similar speech patterns of Boaz and Naomi as stylistic indications that they are from the same generation (Campbell, *Ruth*, p. 116).

The phrase "my daughter" should obviously not be understood literally. BDB refers to such use as "kindly address" (s.v. בַּת) or a term of endearment. It may even suggest a difference of status or age between Boaz and Ruth. Naomi, similarly, refers to Ruth as "my daughter" (1:11; 2:2). Used in the context of chapter two, it may continue the thematic use of youth in general and specifically the description of Ruth as a "lass" (*na'ărāh*).

[22]David Shepherd considers the history of English translations with respect to this particular passage in his "Violence in the Fields? Translating, Reading, and Revising in Ruth 2," *CBQ* 63 (July 2001), pp. 444-463.

[23]Again, Fewell and Gunn leap to a particular reading of this comment consistent with their presentation, i.e., "molest," "sexual assault" (*Compromising Redemption*, p. 76). However, the root נגע (*ng'*) may also refer to the grabbing, striking, or stoning that might occur if Ruth were forcibly driven out of the field. The latter is a more likely possibility, given the public nature of the field (full of harvesters) and larger, sociocultural norms. This is not a secret place.

[24]It is difficult to overlook Gray's use of words, "though the poor might glean, evidently they might be churlishly handled" (*Joshua, Judges, and Ruth*, p. 308).

interpretation, Ruth is given access to the drinking water supplied by the young men. In short, she is shown hospitality. Ruth has claimed the people of Naomi as her own; in return, Naomi's people, via Boaz, welcome her.

Ruth's response to this offer is marked by gratitude. She bows, face to the ground, and exclaims, **"Why have I found such favor in your eyes . . ."** Her question raises again the idea of "finding favor" (cf. 2:2) and establishes it firmly as a theme. Ruth has found exactly what she asked for. **". . . that you notice me—a foreigner?"** The two terms translated as the verbal idea "to notice" and as the noun, "foreigner" may be built from the same root, "to recognize."[25] But even if they are not, the poetic assonance of the well-turned phrase cannot be missed.[26] Ruth is, by self-description, an alien, one who is "strange." Boaz has done more than gawk or simply acknowledge that difference. Why is this?

Boaz answers: **"I've been told all about what you have done."** Ruth's actions have not been kept secret. Some details of her journey from homeland to Bethlehem and from her natural parents to the surrogate Naomi have been shared. How or when Boaz acquired this knowledge is not important. What is significant is that his language echoes actions and even exact vocabulary used in the telling of the story from the first chapter, "death," "abandoning," "your father," "your mother," etc.[27] In a distant way, they may even echo patriarchal moves.[28] Boaz is fully informed. He turns this information into a blessing. **"May you be richly rewarded by the LORD, the God of Israel, under whose wings you have come to take refuge."** The blessing of Boaz stresses compensation and reward for right

---

[25]BDB suggests that the verbal form "to recognize" and the noun "foreigner" come from two different roots, both however based on the three consonants, נכר (*nkr*). Other lexicons, such as *TWOT* and *HALOT*, treat them together.

[26]לְהַכִּירֵנִי וְאָנֹכִי נָכְרִיָּה (*l°hakkîrēnî w°'ānōkî nokrîyāh*), lit., "to notice me since I (am) a foreigner." Hubbard attempts to convert the pun into English, "You have noticed the unnoticed" or "recognized the unrecognized" (*Ruth*, p. 163).

[27]The phrase used by Boaz, "to abandon (or leave) your father and mother" appears only here and in Gen 2:24, a passage celebrating marriage. This connection has not been lost on those studying the text of Ruth. Narratively, it describes the past and anticipates future events.

[28]Hubbard, *Ruth*, p. 164.

actions. These right actions undoubtedly include Ruth's choices to stick to Naomi and adopt her God (1:16-17). With poetic flair, Boaz likens the refuge of Yahweh to that of the security found beneath a bird's wings. This is a common motif within the Old Testament (e.g., Ps 17:8; 36:7[8]; 91:4) and one that finds its way into the teaching of Jesus as well (Matt 23:37-39; Luke 13:34-35).[29] The image is captured here by Ruth and will be eventually returned to Boaz (cf. 3:9). At present, other conclusions may be drawn. Just as Naomi's people have welcomed Ruth, the blessing of Boaz invokes Yahweh's welcome, and correspondingly, Ruth's admittance into the people of God. The border between Moab and Israel is seemingly more porous than expected.

Ruth's second response to Boaz is similar to the first. She expresses an acknowledgment that she has found grace and comfort, and that it is unmerited, for she does **not have the standing** of one of Boaz's **servant girls**.

Some time later, Boaz invites Ruth to draw even closer. She will not only share in the harvest gathering, but in the harvester's meal as well. **"Come over here. Have some bread and dip it in the wine vinegar."** She joins the group, eats her fill, and still has leftovers. In this case it is לֶחֶם (*leḥem*), or "bread," that is eaten in the harvest fields of Beth-*lehem*, a dramatic turnaround from the days of famine. As presented, the *lehem* is dipped in vinegar or a tart wine and is consumed. Such a meal would provide the necessary energy to complete the day's labor. The fact that she is invited into a position close enough to reach into the dip, suggests she is brought into their circle.[30] In addition to the meal, Ruth is offered **roasted grain**. She eats her fill and still has leftovers; she prepares to return to glean.

2:15-16 At this point the dialogue shifts back to Boaz and the harvesters. As Ruth prepares to leave the meal, the order is given to

---

[29]The root itself, כנף (*knp*), suggests the idea of finding or offering a protecting embrace or a hiding place. *HALOT*, s.v. כָּנָף. For use as a metaphor in the context of marriage, see Ezek 16:8.

[30]When describing the place where Ruth sat, the preposition translated in the phrase "with the harvesters" is מִצַּד (*miṣṣad*). Perhaps a closer translation is "beside the harvesters" or even "at the hip of the harvesters." Elsewhere it is used to describe the place where an infant is carried, i.e., on the hip (Isa 60:4; 66:12). This position is contra that of Campbell who suggests Ruth took a more modest or subordinate position (*Ruth*, p. 102).

allow her to glean between the sheaves (echoing her request communicated via the foreman in 2:7). The harvesters are told not only to avoid embarrassing or rebuking her, but to pull some stalks from the bundles specifically for her to pick up. Just as Ruth is characterized as one who goes "above and beyond," so too, Boaz. Pulling stalks from the cut sheaves and leaving them behind exceeds the legal obligations for field owners with respect to gleaners. It is unclear if Ruth heard any or all of these words.

C. RUTH RETURNS TO NAOMI (2:17-23)

[17]So Ruth gleaned in the field until evening. Then she threshed the barley she had gathered, and it amounted to about an ephah.[a] [18]She carried it back to town, and her mother-in-law saw how much she had gathered. Ruth also brought out and gave her what she had left over after she had eaten enough.

[19]Her mother-in-law asked her, "Where did you glean today? Where did you work? Blessed be the man who took notice of you!"

Then Ruth told her mother-in-law about the one at whose place she had been working. "The name of the man I worked with today is Boaz," she said.

[20]"The LORD bless him!" Naomi said to her daughter-in-law. "He has not stopped showing his kindness to the living and the dead." She added, "That man is our close relative; he is one of our kinsman-redeemers."

[21]Then Ruth the Moabitess said, "He even said to me, 'Stay with my workers until they finish harvesting all my grain.'"

[22]Naomi said to Ruth her daughter-in-law, "It will be good for you, my daughter, to go with his girls, because in someone else's field you might be harmed."

[23]So Ruth stayed close to the servant girls of Boaz to glean until the barley and wheat harvests were finished. And she lived with her mother-in-law.

[a]17 That is, probably about ⅗ bushel (about 22 liters)

2:17 The work of gleaning kept Ruth busy. Toward the end of the day, **she threshed the barley she had gathered**. Threshing usually took place in a flat, clean, breezy area. The sheaves were beaten, trampled, or crushed by a sledge on the ground in order to break open the hard shell or husk that surrounded the kernel in the cereal head. The broken stalks would then be thrown into the air, possibly with a large wooden pitchfork, in a process called winnowing. Lighter materials such as the stems and chaff were blown downwind while the heavier material, including the cereal kernels, fell back down at the feet of the winnower. In this way that which was edible was separated from that which was not.[31] Following the threshing and winnowing, Ruth possessed **about an ephah** of barley. An ephah is a standard unit of dry measure in biblical times, approximately twenty to forty dry quarts in size.[32] According to ancient Mesopotamian records, this portion is equal to the wage earned by a female worker over a four-week period.[33] This is what Ruth produced in just one day! Only with difficulty could such an amount even be carried.

2:18-20 Ruth lugs her load back into Bethlehem and shows it, along with the leftovers from the field meal, to Naomi. **"Where did you glean today? . . . Blessed be the man who took notice of you."** This is no ambush plot for a husband. Naomi is puzzled, if not astonished, by what Ruth has brought home. It is, by far, a greater portion than what one might expect from a day's gleaning. Where could it have come from?

Ruth's answer is convoluted and climatic. The verbal idea of "working" and the prepositional phrase "with him" are awkwardly repeated. In the end though, the name of her benefactor tumbles out: **Boaz**. The revelation now connects Naomi to Boaz, a link anticipated since 2:1 by the reader, but not realized until now. The previously laconic Naomi is spurred into offering yet another blessing. **"The LORD bless him! . . . He has not stopped showing his kindness."** The author continues to repeat and weave words artfully. Just as Ruth refused to "abandon" Naomi (1:16), so too the ḥesed-kindness so integral to the story has not been abandoned.[34] The **living and the dead** presumably apply to Naomi and the family of Elimelech.

---

[31]For more on the work of threshing and winnowing, see Borowski, *Agriculture in Iron Age Israel*, pp. 62-69.

[32]*TWOT*, s.v. אֵיפָה (ʾêpâ).

[33]See I.J. Gelb, "The Ancient Mesopotamian Ration System," *JNES* 24 (1965): 236.

[34]Is it the ḥesed-kindness of Yahweh that is referred to here or is it the ḥesed-kindness of Boaz? Both have been argued. Maybe both are intended!

Moreover, Naomi adds, **"That man is our close relative; he is one of our kinsman-redeemers."** One wonders if this statement is simply part of Naomi's exclamation or if it is offered as explanation to Ruth. Two descriptors are applied to Boaz, one builds upon another. First, Boaz is literally "near to us" (cf. 2:2). Second, he is a *gō'ēl*-redeemer. The reference to nearness is general; the reference to *gō'ēl*-redeemer is specific and technical. According to biblical use, the *gō'ēl*-redeemer offers assistance to family members threatened by difficult circumstances or legal obligation. Such assistance takes four forms.[35] First, if a field or person is sold in a desperate move, a *gō'ēl*-redeemer could "buy back" that land or person, and provide restoration (Lev 25:25ff,48ff). Second, if property or animals are dedicated to Yahweh, but wished to be "bought back," a *gō'ēl*-redeemer could redeem them (Lev 27:11ff). Third, if a family member is wrongfully killed, the *gō'ēl*-redeemer may become the "avenger of blood" who takes the life of the life-taker (Num 35:6-15; Deut 19:6,12). Fourth, in exceptional cases, the *gō'ēl*-redeemer is God himself who redeems his people in troubled times through judgment (Isa 43:1-3). Which, if any, of these assisting roles of the *gō'ēl*-redeemer Naomi envisions is difficult to discern. Three issues grow clearer as a result of such a survey. First, the assistance of the *gō'ēl*-redeemer is meant to preserve the life and possessions of family members. Second, exchange for life and possessions was viewed as possible and satisfactory. Third, the practice of kinsman marriage is not *specifically* linked anywhere to the work of the *gō'ēl*-redeemer. This point will be touched upon again. For the moment it is enough to note that Naomi identifies Boaz as a potential *gō'ēl*-redeemer. He could become, in Moore's words, a "cultural gyroscope" who brings balance into an off-kilter situation.[36] Boaz can act. The question is, will he?

2:21-23 After all this, Ruth (still called **the Moabitess**) responds with one additional piece of information. **"He even said . . . 'Stay with my workers until they finish.'"** The *ḥesed*-kindness shown on

---

For a survey of the argument, see Basil A. Rebera, "Yahweh or Boaz? Ruth 2:20 Reconsidered," *BT* 36 (1985): 317-327.

[35]*TWOT*, s.v. גאל (gā'al).

[36]Michael Moore, "*Haggo'el*: The Cultural Gyroscope of Ancient Hebrew Society," *RQ* 23 (1980): 27-35.

this particular day will not be a unique event, Boaz has invited her back! Ruth reports being told to "cling" to the young men (even as she did to Naomi [cf. 1:14]).[37]

Naomi encourages Ruth to heed his instruction, else **you might be harmed**. The verbal form appearing here is different from the one that appeared in the command of Boaz (2:9). In 2:9 the report suggests Boaz instructed his young men not to "touch" Ruth. Here Naomi counsels Ruth to stay close to the young women of Boaz lest someone literally "happens upon" her.[38] While the NIV's rendering is possible, and even probable (given the explanation at 2:9 above), the verbal idea used here by itself simply poses the possibility of a chance meeting for good or ill. Other translation options include "lest someone woo you" raising the possibility of other potential suitors in the field or even "lest someone catch you" either in a possessing sense or in the sense that her presence discovered elsewhere might be reported to Boaz as ingratitude.

Ruth avoids these problems, however, and clings **to the servant girls of Boaz**. The concluding statement of the narrator communicates at least three important points. First, it communicates that Ruth follows the counsel of Boaz and Naomi. By doing so, she avoids trouble and is in a position to come into contact with Boaz

---

[37]Ruth's report here has raised a few eyebrows. Boaz specifically told her to "stick with my young women" (*na'ărōth*). Here, however, she tells Naomi that she was told to "stick with the young men" (*nᵊ'ārîm*). Why the difference? Some view this as a deliberate prodding of Naomi. Others suggest that Ruth did not clearly understand the words of Boaz, perhaps owing to her foreignness. Neither suggestion is likely. The masculine plural ending is the default form for a general reference (cf. the contemporary use of "you guys" to refer to male and/or female parties), hence the NIV's "my workers." Here, as elsewhere, interpreters such as Fewell, Gunn, and Linafelt insert their own agenda into the text. Gender, with respect to grammar is a feature of syntax, not sex. Consider Waltke and O'Connor, *Biblical Hebrew Syntax*, para. 6.4.1.

More useful is Hubbard's observation that Ruth's report of the words of Boaz to Naomi contains a shift of emphasis from place to people. Boaz emphasized that Ruth was to work in this *place*. Ruth reports that she is to work with Boaz's *people*. See Hubbard, *Ruth*, p. 190. Hubbard raises the possibility that the clause "which are mine" may refer back to Ruth. This is a questionable move, but interesting, especially since in this verse Ruth is again called "the Moabitess."

[38]Translation alternatives are discussed by Shepherd in his "Violence in the Fields?" pp. 444-463.

again, possibly even on a daily basis. Second, as she works to the conclusion of **the barley and wheat harvests**. Her experience is length-
ened. As wheat matures more slowly than barley, it is harvested later
in the season, well into the month of May.[39] Hence, this "season of
plenty" is extended for several weeks through the barley *and* the
wheat harvests. Finally, the notice of the chapter also communicates
a specific end point to the harvesting season, raising the question,
would these established relationships continue? In this light, the last
statement becomes significant, Ruth lives **with her mother-in-law**.
Ruth is true to her intention to go where Naomi goes and stay where
Naomi stays. However, the reader is left wondering if this will continue? How long can the gathered food last? Will Boaz act in the role
of *gō'ēl*-redeemer and help the widows? Finally, will Ruth truly "find
rest in the home of another husband" (1:9) and be "richly rewarded" (2:12)? In the short run, some of the problems facing Ruth and
Naomi have been resolved: food is in storage, new relationships
have been cultivated, and Naomi's disposition concerning God has
certainly improved. Still, one has the feeling that these improvements are tenuous at best. In the long run, has anything really
changed?

---

[39]Borowski, *Daily Life in Biblical Times*, p. 28.

RUTH 3

III. SEEKING, SHAKING, AND PROMISE-MAKING IN THE NIGHT (3:1-18)

Through a "chance encounter," Ruth entered the orbit of Boaz, a family friend. Boaz was kind to Ruth, granting her admission into his harvest circle. Now, Naomi proposes a risky plan to draw the intentions of Boaz out into the open. Ruth carries out that plan in the dark of night, where her acts are shrouded in mystery, marked by innovation, and concluded in promise. Like chapter 2, the movements of chapter 3 develop through the speeches of key characters located in home and in the field. Dialogue is exchanged between Ruth and Naomi (3:1-6), Ruth and Boaz (3:7-15), and Ruth and Naomi (3:16-18).

A. NAOMI'S RISKY PLAN (3:1-6)

¹One day Naomi her mother-in-law said to her, "My daughter, should I not try to find a home[a] for you, where you will be well provided for? ²Is not Boaz, with whose servant girls you have been, a kinsman of ours? Tonight he will be winnowing barley on the threshing floor. ³Wash and perfume yourself, and put on your best clothes. Then go down to the threshing floor, but don't let him know you are there until he has finished eating and drinking. ⁴When he lies down, note the place where he is lying. Then go and uncover his feet and lie down. He will tell you what to do."

⁵"I will do whatever you say," Ruth answered. ⁶So she went down to the threshing floor and did everything her mother-in-law told her to do.

[a]*1* Hebrew *find rest* (see Ruth 1:9)

3:1-2 The chapter begins at home with Ruth and Naomi. **One day** implies that an undetermined amount of time elapses between Ruth's introduction to Boaz and the narrative present.[1] It is clear that the harvest season is not yet complete; a span of weeks or a few months have passed at best.[2] Unlike chapter 2 where Ruth announces a plan to her mother-in-law, here it is Naomi who takes the initiative with a rhetorical question, **"My daughter, should I not try to find a home for you?"**[3] Obscured by the NIV translation of the word "home" is the root idea of "rest."[4] What Naomi resolves to find is literally a "place" or "condition of rest" for Ruth. "Rest" is a key word in this chapter (appearing later in 3:18), but also appearing in the blessing of Naomi, "may the LORD grant . . . *rest* in the home of another husband" (1:9). In such a relationship, Ruth **will be well provided for**, a striking contrast from the present situation. Why Naomi makes such a resolution at this time is curious, although her words do bespeak some level of care, responsibility, and perhaps even gratitude for Ruth (cf. "*my* daughter," or more particularly, "a kinsman of *ours*" [3:2], emphases mine).

The revelation of Naomi's risky plan begins with the recognition that Boaz is **a kinsman**, a relative (cf. 2:1), a fact that ought to make him more kindly disposed to the widow's plight.[5] Whether Boaz will

---

[1]Recognize that this clause is added by the NIV editors. It represents a conclusion drawn from the content of the chapter and is not a translation from the original text.

[2]It is not uncommon today in the country of Jordan to find threshing and winnowing activities continuing throughout the summer months. Curiously, the text of 3:2 suggests that Boaz is winnowing only barley. No mention is made of wheat. Could that be because the wheat is still being gathered in the field? Given the harvest schedule of these crops, a time earlier in the summer is preferred to a time later in the summer.

[3]Naomi's statement in 3:1 and 3:2 begins with the negative interrogative הֲלֹא (hălō'), a syntactical feature that links her with Boaz (2:8,9). See footnote connected to 2:8 above.

[4]The term מָנוֹחַ (mānôaḥ) has נוּחַ (nûaḥ, "to rest" or "be quieted"), as a root, BDB, s.v. נוּחַ. The NASB offers a closer reading: "shall I not seek security for you?"

[5]At the start of this chapter as at the start of the previous chapter, Boaz is described. In 2:1 Boaz is מְיֻדָּע (mᵉyuddāʿ), or "friend" or מוֹדָע (môdaʿ), a "relative," depending upon one's choice of the *ketib* or *qere* reading. Here, no such problem exists. Boaz is clearly מוֹדַעְתָּנוּ (môdaʿtānû), "our relative," supporting the *qere* reading of 2:1.

act upon his own recognition of this relationship, however, is the question, and hence, that which gives birth to the risky plan. Such a plan must be subtle enough to stay within the boundaries of cultural norms,[6] yet forceful enough to press his hand to action.[7] The revelatory הִנֵּה (*hinnēh*), "behold," or "look," connects the announcement of Boaz's identification to the immediate situation and signals that such a plan is now possible. "Look — **tonight he will be winnowing barley on the threshing floor.**" As previously described, the threshing floor is a place where the work of separating grain from chaff occurs.[8] From elsewhere, it is known that threshing floors were often communal, shared by the members of a village. As such, threshing floors could be used for other public purposes, such as mourning (Gen 50:10-11), meeting (1 Kgs 22:10), or the redistribution of resources (Num 18:30; Deut 26:12-13). Sometimes they were located by the city gate (cf. 1 Kgs 22:10) or in another centrally located place as a laborsaving measure.[9] In light of the time required for the processing of grain and the value of the produce, workers might

---

[6]Unfortunately, what is known of such norms in minimal at best. Gray (*Joshua, Judges, and Ruth*) is comfortable leaning on 19th-century Arab customs as demonstrated by his many references. How much alteration of this social fabric is due to the arrival of Islam, however, is an issue that must be raised in critique.

[7]To what goal is Boaz's hand pressed? As this risky plan unfolds, it becomes clear that Ruth is placed before Boaz as a potential wife. However, it is argued here that this relationship is not governed by the dynamics of kinsman marriage recorded in *torah* — at least as far as Naomi is concerned. From Naomi there is no legal appeal, no welfare request, and quite possibly (if Ruth is truly a "free agent"), no direct benefit for herself. The pressure generated by Naomi's risky plan is a simple appeal to Boaz's basic instincts: Ruth will speak through her presence, "Look, I am needy, attractive, and available. Take me." The ambiguities that shade the threshing floor narrative seem to confirm this approach. However, according to our reading, Ruth will dare to "tweak" Naomi's plan at the last moment.

[8]An Arabic cognate to the Hebrew גֹּרֶן (*gōren*), "threshing floor," suggests that the place was "worn smooth" or "rubbed clear" (BDB, s.v. גרן; Gray, *Joshua, Judges, and Ruth*, p. 309). A stone or packed-earth surface is needed to allow for the careful sweeping, collecting, measuring, and even drying of grain.

A description of threshing and winnowing is found in Isa 41:14-16. Here, the subject is Israel and the acts are figurative. Still, some details of process are communicated.

[9]Here, it appears that the threshing floor is removed some distance from the village. In 3:3 Ruth is told to "go down" to the threshing floor. Later,

sleep on the premises.[10] Texts and tradition also allude to the fact that harvest work was marked by celebration, the final act in a prolonged effort to obtain and stockpile cereal for another year.[11] Hence, the threshing floor was a public place of working, sleeping, celebrating, eating, and drinking. As Boaz is there at night, likely to avoid the heat of the summer day, Naomi identifies it as a place where Ruth might be able to approach him directly, yet discreetly.[12]

3:3-6 Her plan proceeds to the obvious. **"Wash and perfume yourself."** Such tactics would make Ruth as appealing as possible, and may, narratively, allude to the preparations for marriage.[13] Bathing with water would cleanse the body of filth and sweat. "Being anointed," presumably with some kind of scented oil, would soften her skin and mask odors of body and clothing.[14] The rendering of the NIV, **put on your best clothes** speaks to modern ears but is improbable in light of what is known of the ancient world. One possibility is that Ruth is told to exchange her "widow's garments" for "regular" clothes.[15] An

---

Boaz "went up to the town gate" (4:1). How much distance is between the threshing floor and the village? For the sake of efficiency, threshing floors were located at crucial junctions between fields and even villages (see Hopkins, *Highlands of Canaan*, p. 226). Unless Campbell's unlikely correction of 3:2 is accepted ("the threshing floor near the gate," [*Ruth*, p. 117-119]), the text suggests only that Ruth made the journey there and back in less than one night and on the return trip carried six measures of barley (3:15). Nothing more of location is known, and unfortunately, archaeology has yet to be helpful in the case of Bethlehem.

[10]Gray, *Joshua, Judges, and Ruth*, p. 309.

[11]Passages such as Isa 9:2[3] suggest the joy of the harvest.

[12]This raises the question: would Ruth be able to approach Boaz elsewhere? Was it difficult for a woman to approach a man in this time and place? How would local custom regard the approach of a foreigner like Ruth? Much of the tension in this chapter swirls around issues of public male-female relations. Many explanations of this chapter are based upon assumptions regarding this cultural milieu, thousands of years removed, and are therefore suspect.

[13]Some see these preparations as similar to those taken by a bride (cf. Ezek 16:8-12; Esth 2:12). As such, Naomi's words are interpreted as that of a mother preparing her daughter for her wedding night. See Sasson, *Ruth*, pp. 66-67, among others.

[14]For more on anointing see BDB, s.v. סוּךְ, סִיךְ. For more on personal hygiene, see the classic article by Edward Neufeld ("Hygiene Conditions in Ancient Israel [Iron Age]," *BA* 34 [1971]: 42-66).

[15]Widow's clothing is mentioned in Gen 38:14 and possibly in 2 Sam 14:2. In the former passage, Tamar exchanges such garments for a clothing style (?)

even simpler reading may yet be offered. Because clothing was expensive and rarely changed by common folk, Ruth is told to "set" or "fix" her garment, she arranges or adjusts the drapes and folds that frame her face, round her shoulders, or fall about her waist.[16] The visual of a mother carefully preening her daughter comes to mind. Whatever, the case, these preparations are viewed as an essential part of the plan.

As an aside: while many have wondered about Ruth's physical appearance, no specific biblical descriptions of her features are recorded. More significant to the narrative are disclosures of social status (she is a widow, she is Moabite), details that anticipate future events (she is a נַעֲרָה [na'ărāh, "youth"], i.e., still in her child-bearing years), or descriptions of overt actions (she is obedient, unflinching, creative). These characterizations elicit a sympathetic response from the reader, particularly when set beside Naomi (whose complexities arouse a host of mixed reactions).[17]

The words that follow (3:4) are mysteriously incomplete and have been at the center of critical discussions for literally thousands of years. When Ruth is clean and ready, she is told to go secretly to the threshing floor area. **"Don't let him know you are there until he has finished eating and drinking."** Even the identity of Boaz is hid-

---

that suggested she was a prostitute. This parallel is all the more striking because of the blessing in Ruth 4:12.

[16]For "set," "arrange" consult BDB, s.v. שׂוּם, שִׂים. For "garment," realize the *ketib/qere* issue here revolves around a singular or plural construct form of שִׂמְלָה (*śimlāh*), a term referring to an "outer cloak" or "mantle." This term is used of a sleeping wrap (cf. Exod 22:26-27). However, note Gen 45:22 and the suggestion that this may refer to "festive" wear. The *ketib* reading suggests this is a single item of clothing. It is unlikely that this is the same garment as the מִטְפַּחַת (*miṭpāḥath*), or "shawl" of 3:15. Sasson suggests the latter may have been "used by Ruth to veil herself in order to avoid recognition" (*Ruth*, p. 68).

For a brief discussion of women's clothing, see King and Stager, *Life in Biblical Israel*, p. 272.

[17]Characterization within Hebrew narrative is typically revealed through speech (either direct or indirect) and action; only rarely are appearances or inner thoughts revealed. This is certainly the case with Ruth. At no time is the reader privy to her thoughts. Consider Robert Alter's depiction of David within this vein (*The Art of Biblical Narrative* [New York: Basic, 1981], pp. 114-130), or Pratt's more formal presentation of characterization (*He Gave Us Stories*, pp. 129-150).

den, in the dark he is simply "the man" (3:8). Naomi's plan is to let
the evening run its course, let Boaz eat his fill, drink until he is satisfied, and let him drift off to sleep. **"When he lies down, note the
place."** Although it is not explicitly mentioned, it is unlikely that
Boaz would be alone at the threshing floor participating in these
activities of working, eating, and drinking. He has hired hands harvesting for him. Why would he tackle the job of threshing and winnowing alone?[18] His aloneness would be particularly acute if the
threshing was accomplished by a heavy wooden sledge pulled by
traction animals (such as an ox or mule).[19] The conclusion that Boaz
is not alone also explains why Ruth is told to identify Boaz and mark
his spot: she must separate him from the others. **"Then go . . .** No
indication of timing is given, **. . . and uncover his feet."**[20] Village

---

[18]Some have suggested that Boaz was not there to work, but to participate
in some kind of cultic activity. Such a conclusion is based upon presuppositions about the evolution of Israelite religion. As it begs the question, it does
not merit attention here.

In farming regions it is not unusual for field owners to take full part in
agricultural activities, leading by example. To argue that Boaz is "too important" to be at the threshing floor is a conclusion that is simply out of step
with rural traditions.

[19]Threshing sledges used in the preindustrial period in Palestine were large
implements, between three and four feet long and two and three feet wide.
They were equipped with basalt or metal chips or "studs" that "chewed" the
stalks. Scripturally, see Deut 25:4, Isa 41:15, or Amos 1:3 for examples. For
illustration, see Borowski, *Agriculture in Iron Age Israel*, p. 63-65.

[20]Three terms merit further comment here. The first, translated as
"uncover" is built from the root גָּלָה (*gālāh*). Objects of this verb may be
secrets, edicts, or even eyes! However, *gālāh* is also used in conjunction with
intimate parts of the body (e.g., Exod 20:26, "reveal your nakedness," or Lev
18:6-19 where the repeated phrase to "uncover the nakedness" is congruent
with sexual relations). Given these examples, the sexual overtones of this
word choice cannot be simply dismissed.

The common understanding of the second word, מַרְגְּלֹת (*marg^elôth*), is
the "place of the feet." As Sasson points out, this word is derived from the
term רֶגֶל (*regel*, "foot') and a מ (*ma-*) preformative. "As is clear from other
vocables . . . this preformative indicates the place (localites), rather than the
means (instrumentalis), which affects the *regel*" (*Ruth*, p. 69). She is to
uncover the place of the *regelîm* not specifically the *regelîm*, (note how
Nielsen uses this point to absurdly suggest that what Ruth is to uncover is
her own body! [*Ruth*, p. 68-69]). Outside of Ruth, the only other occurrence
of this form is in Dan 10:6 where it appears in a parallel construction with
arms. "Legs" in this case, is an easy and natural choice.   *Continued* ➤

men typically wore three pieces of clothing: a kilt or loincloth that functioned as an undergarment; a long tunic (like a nightshirt), made of wool and reaching the ankles; and finally, over the tunic, a cloak that would also function as a blanket in the night.[21] Boaz will likely be wrapped in his outer garment. Naomi's plan calls for Ruth to pull up that outer garment to expose his feet, ankles, possibly his lower legs. Such an action will in all probability awaken him, and prompt a reaction. When this happens, the plan calls for Ruth to **lie down. "He will tell you what to do."**

The plan is bold and remarkably open-ended. How will Boaz respond to Ruth's forwardness? What will he say? What will he do? Why does Naomi propose it at all? Why does she not confront Boaz more openly and directly? Many questions remain unanswered. Whatever Naomi is thinking, it is not communicated. Ruth's thoughts are equally opaque; she agrees without objection to follow through with the plan, **"I will do whatever you say."** Perhaps Ruth's fears are allayed by Naomi's opening line (3:1), assuring her that however audacious the plan sounds, it has her own interests at heart. Perhaps the situation is desperate enough to offset any risks inherent in the plan. In the end, however, Ruth's easy agreement is sus-

---

However, the discussion migrates to other forms and occurrences of the base term *regel*. A handful of passages faintly suggest that as a dual, *regelîm*, may refer euphemistically to the upper legs or even genitalia (cf. of male, Exod 4:25, Judg 3:24; Isa 7:20; 1 Sam 24:4; of female [?], Deut 28:57). This conclusion is, at best, inconclusive in each and every case. Nowhere is *regel* the object of some verbal form of *galah*, nor does the LXX insert any connection between *regel* and the genitalia. To argue that Naomi bids Ruth to expose the private parts of Boaz is possible, but strains the bonds of linguistic analysis.

Having said this, the tension of the text is not fully relieved. Naomi's next command to Ruth is to "lie down." This term, שָׁכַב (*šākab*), is regularly used in the context of sexual intercourse. As Sasson points out, though, this meaning is usually achieved by the use of *šākab* with a preposition "with," missing in this context (*Ruth*, p. 70).

In the case of each of these three selected terms, the text may be read innocently or provocatively. It edges forward in the dark, leaving the reader wondering what exactly is Naomi asking Ruth to do? Such ambiguity is undoubtedly purposeful. Consider Harry J. Harm, "The Function of Double Entendre in Ruth 3," in *Journal of Translation and Textlinguistics* 7 (1995): 19-27.

[21]Matthews and Benjamin, *Social World of Ancient Israel*, p. 41. King and Stager, *Life in Biblical Israel*, pp. 266-271.

pect; she may be just daring (or intuitive?) enough to challenge the script as handed to her.

B. RUTH MODIFIES AND EXECUTES THE PLAN (3:7-15)

[7]**When Boaz had finished eating and drinking and was in good spirits, he went over to lie down at the far end of the grain pile. Ruth approached quietly, uncovered his feet and lay down.** [8]**In the middle of the night something startled the man, and he turned and discovered a woman lying at his feet.**

[9]**"Who are you?" he asked.**

"I am your servant Ruth," she said. "Spread the corner of your garment over me, since you are a kinsman-redeemer."

[10]**"The LORD bless you, my daughter," he replied. "This kindness is greater than that which you showed earlier: You have not run after the younger men, whether rich or poor.** [11]**And now, my daughter, don't be afraid. I will do for you all you ask. All my fellow townsmen know that you are a woman of noble character.** [12]**Although it is true that I am near of kin, there is a kinsman-redeemer nearer than I.** [13]**Stay here for the night, and in the morning if he wants to redeem, good; let him redeem. But if he is not willing, as surely as the LORD lives I will do it. Lie here until morning."**

[14]**So she lay at his feet until morning, but got up before anyone could be recognized; and he said, "Don't let it be known that a woman came to the threshing floor."**

[15]**He also said, "Bring me the shawl you are wearing and hold it out." When she did so, he poured into it six measures of barley and put it on her. Then he**[a] **went back to town.**

[a]**15 Most Hebrew manuscripts; Vulgate and Syriac** *she*

3:7-9 Events transpire exactly as Naomi predicts. Boaz eats, drinks, and lies down. It has been a pleasant evening, he is **in good spirits**, literally "his heart is good."[22] He goes **over to lie down at the**

---

[22]This phrase, coupled with the word for drinking, suggests inebriation but does not require it. The narrative may be assisted by this notice, though, as it renders Boaz more susceptible to Ruth's stealthy approach and may

far end of the grain pile. The place Boaz chooses to rest is located in the loose pile of cereal, but specifically on the "edge."[23] This may be significant as it suggests that the place where Boaz chooses to sleep is away from the center of activity. It may be a more private place. Others might still be eating, drinking, laughing, talking. Boaz is, in essence, just "around the corner" from them. There he drifts off to sleep. In this condition, he is most vulnerable.

At this point, Ruth does as Naomi instructs. The text says she approached Boaz **softly**, or in secrecy (due to the presence of others?), then **uncovered his feet and lay down**. How much time passes is unknown but the result is predictable. **In the middle of the night, something startled the man**. Boaz is shaken. Two words are used to describe his actions. First, he "shudders."[24] This may be a response to the cold or a sudden surprise. Second, he "twists," "clutches himself," or "gropes" for his cover.[25] This rare verb (it appears only three times in the OT) is of interest. Sasson derives meaning from it courtesy of an Arabic cognate that describes the winding path of a desert caravan.[26] Boaz twists and turns — this way then that — like one who is attacked. Without a doubt, it is a climactic moment in the story. It should come as no surprise that this master storyteller slows the pace of the narrative before releasing it again. Boaz jerks and jumps into the night air, white-eyed, out of control, and much to the delight of the listener! Precisely what causes this to happen to the "mighty man" is not offered. Is it the cool air on his exposed skin? The movement of Ruth? Her touch? A bad dream? A noise? Whatever the cause, Boaz discovers what the reader already knows. "Look!" exclaims the narrator: **a woman lying at his feet**, an image of humility and supplication. This is certainly

---

explain his delayed reaction at his own exposure. On the other hand, Boaz appears quite sober in his conversation with Ruth later that night. Taken at face value, the text suggests Boaz eats, drinks, is happy, and sleeps — a natural progression after a long day of labor!

[23]The "edge" or the קָצֶה (qāṣeh), suggests the extremity or the outskirts of the grain pile.

[24]The Hebrew חָרַד (ḥārad) captures the idea of "trembling" or "quaking." See BDB, s.v. חָרַד.

[25]See HALOT, s.v. לפת. Block suggests Judg 16:29 is parallel. Here, Samson blindly "gropes about" for the temple columns. See his Judges, Ruth, p. 690, n. 35.

[26]Sasson, Ruth, p. 78-79.

unexpected! In his daze he exclaims, **"Who are you?"** Boaz has no idea who this figure is or why she is there. She answers, **"I am your servant Ruth."** Despite the NIV's consistent reading, the term for "servant" appearing here is different from the term used in 2:13. In her first meeting with Boaz, Ruth describes herself among the lowest ranks in society, a handmaid functioning in "deep servitude."[27] Here, her language shifts to a self-depreciating term that demonstrates that same brand of humility, yet one that cracks open the door to a future relationship.[28]

At this crucial moment, Ruth deviates from the script given to her by Naomi. The close reader cannot miss this. Naomi's final instructions to Ruth were to lie down and let Boaz take over, "he will tell you what to do" (3:4). However, Ruth seizes the initiative by a bold plan, apparently of her own design (as in 2:2). Instead of waiting for instruction from Boaz, she voices a request, a petition that is at once delicate, electrifying, and perhaps even culturally inappropriate: **"Spread the corner of your garment over me."** The statement contains several levels of meaning, each interconnected, nuanced, and teasing for different reasons. At one level, Ruth's statement alludes back to her action and anticipates an action from Boaz. Has she not pulled the garment corner off of the feet of Boaz? Now she asks him to cover her with it.[29] At another level, the words reach across the

---

[27]שִׁפְחָה (*šiphḥāh*), a term of "deep servitude" is used to describe Hagar in Gen 16:1. It is used of the handmaid who tends to the needs of the woman of the house. It is also used in self-depreciating introductions, such as 1 Sam 1:18. See *HALOT*, s.v. שִׁפְחָה.

[28]אָמָה (*'āmāh*) is likewise a humble term, but one that is frequently used to describe a second wife or concubine. Ruth's choice to use this term at this time is hardly coincidental, and may reveal her vision of a future with Boaz.

To contrast the use of *šiphḥāh* with *'āmāh*, see 1 Sam 25:41 where it reads, Abigail "arose and bowed with her face to the ground and said, 'Behold, your maidservant (*'āmāh*) is a maid (*šiphḥāh*) to wash the feet of my lord's servants.'"

[29]Again Fewell and Gunn manage to degrade the narrative, subverting, undermining, and, in some cases, even ignoring the very text they seek to "explain." In their reading, Ruth challenges the piety of Boaz, "You can afford to wait for YHWH to recompense, reward and offer refuge. I can't. How about putting your action where your fine words of faith are . . ."And later, "Not only does she (Ruth) pull her religiosity to the level of human interaction, she pulls it to the most basic level of human interaction — sexual intercourse" (Fewell and Gunn, *Compromising Redemption*, p. 103). Fewell

pages of the Old Testament to passages that are clearly matrimonial such as Deuteronomy 22:30 (23:1, MT) or Ezekiel 16:8.[30] From this perspective, Ruth's request is clear: make me your *'āmāh*.[31] Finally, her statement turns the words of Boaz back onto himself. In the blessing of 2:12, Boaz asked that Ruth be rewarded by Yahweh "under whose wings you have come to take refuge." The word translated in 2:12 as "wings" and the word translated here as "garment" are one and the same.[32] In short, through a cunning reference that is at once direct and indirect, physical and symbolic, Ruth challenges Boaz to *become the blessing that he requested of Yahweh!*

Ruth further exclaims, "Surely, you are a *gō'ēl*-redeemer!"[33] But is he? It is obvious that Ruth is off the script, away from the page, working far ahead of Naomi's instructions. Does she truly realize what she asks? Perhaps. Perhaps not. A freer translation might read Ruth's exclamation as a question: "You *are* a *gō'ēl*-redeemer, aren't

---

and Gunn's interpretation may be challenged on any number of points, not least of which include their definition of "the most basic level of human interaction." Could that "most basic level" be simply conversation — or must it be sex?

[30]Many see Ezek 16:8 as particularly useful for interpreting Ruth's request as a marriage proposal. Note the parallel vocabulary: "Later I passed by, and when I looked at you and saw that you were old enough for love, I spread the corner of my garment over you and covered your nakedness. I gave you my solemn oath and entered into a covenant with you, declares the Sovereign LORD, and you became mine."

[31]This may be a bit bold, but a proposal is needed. Exactly what kind of relationship with Boaz did Ruth envision? Would she become his wife? Concubine? Servant? Mistress? Girlfriend? Ruth's choice of the term *'āmāh* is key to answering this question.

Did Boaz already have a wife? The rabbis of old believe he did (*Baba Bathra*, 91a). However, she died coincidentally (and conveniently) at the moment of Ruth's arrival from Moab!

[32]The term כָּנָף (*kānaph*) is used to describe the four "corners" of Israelite garments, which, according to Deut 22:12, were marked by a tassel.

[33]Sasson points out the possibility of rendering the particle כִּי (*kî*) here in the sense of a wish exclamation, e.g., "surely" or "verily." (See his *Ruth*, p. 82; and grammatical explanations in GKC, para. 148d, and Waltke and O'Connor, *Biblical Hebrew Syntax*, para. 40.2.2). This reading is quite different from the NIV "since you are a kinsman-redeemer." The practical effect of this is the separation of the issue of Ruth's marriage from the issue of Naomi's redemption. The former was the plan of Naomi; the latter launches the question from Ruth.

you?" Obviously, Naomi sent Ruth on a mission to snag a man. It is not clear if Ruth requests this or something more.

It is easy to imagine a prolonged silence at this point in the narrative. Boaz has been suddenly awakened from a deep sleep by an unexpected woman voicing a profound request. Perhaps the silence of the night was punctuated only by the sounds of snoring coming from other nearby sleepers.

3:10-13 True to form, when he speaks, Boaz responds with a blessing, **"The LORD bless you, my daughter. . . . This kindness is greater than that which you showed earlier."** What is the earlier kindness and what is the later kindness? The answer must be pulled from the context of the phrases that precede and follow. As the preceding statement has already been dealt with, namely, Ruth's request for "cover," it is the latter statement of Boaz that requires comment. **"You have not run after the younger men,[34] whether rich or poor."** Instead of pursuing the "choice men" of any ilk, Ruth has demonstrated *ḥesed*-kindness by making astonishing choices. She could have returned to Moab to seek a man there, but instead chose to stick with Naomi. Similarly, now that she is in Bethlehem of Judah, she could have pursued the *nᵊ'ārîm* (or "young men") — as she herself corresponded to them as a *na'ărāh* ("young woman") — but instead she has pursued Boaz.[35] From his perspective, such an unexpected choice demonstrates that Ruth is a person of rare character. Her loyalty to Naomi and possibly to the seed of Elimelech, has superseded her own quest for personal gain or happiness.

After collecting himself and praising Ruth for her *ḥesed*-kindness, Boaz responds with a plan of his own. This plan confirms that which is known, but adds a twist. He emphasizes that he will move on Ruth's proposal. **"Don't be afraid. I will do . . . all you ask."** Boaz is

---

[34]The term בָּחוּר (*bāḥûr*) refers to a choice, vigorous, young man. The "young men and virgins" functions as a hendiadys for all those in the prime of life (e.g. Deut 32:25).

[35]The text offers no details on the age of Boaz, beyond the obvious: he is mature. Jewish tradition makes him quite old, in his eighties, and suggests that he died on his wedding night! (André LaCocque, *Ruth: A Continental Commentary*, trans. by K.C. Hanson [Minneapolis: Fortress, 2004], pp. 98, 120). Sasson believes that this is done to defuse the possibility of sexual contact on the threshing-room floor and to emphasize his purely functionary role (*Ruth*, p. 86).

willing to follow through with the marriage proposed by Ruth.[36] The reason? **"All of my fellow townsmen know that you are a woman of noble character."** Two points must be offered here. First, those who are in-the-know are literally, those in "the gate-house of all my people." This is an awkward and rare syntactical arrangement[37] that may refer generally to all who pass through the gate (i.e., everyone in town), or it may more specifically refer to those who meet in the gate-house (i.e., the town council). The latter interpretation is particularly appealing, given the location of the legal meeting in chapter four. No introductions will be necessary when the subject of Ruth arises. Her character precedes her physical presence. A second point drawn from this verse is focused on the content of their knowledge. Those who are in the gate know that Ruth is a "mighty woman."[38] The NIV's rendering, "woman of noble character," is a good interpretation given the larger context, but it still misses the nuance. In order to capture it, it must be remembered how other men are described in the book as "young," or "choice"; but only Boaz is "mighty" (2:1). Clearly, the alert reader cannot escape the conclusion that the pairing of this "mighty man" with this "mighty woman" makes perfect sense. It may even explain why Ruth has not pursued others. No one else was her match! No one else was her equal!

Earlier it was proposed that Boaz confirms the marriage plan but adds a twist of his own making. This twist comes by way of a new character. Boaz continues: **"Although it is true that I am near of kin, there is a kinsman-redeemer nearer than I."** His words drop to the ground heavily (and may explain his own hesitancy to act). Until this revelation, it has been clear to the reader that Boaz is one of several close relatives, but to date, no other candidates have surfaced. Now that Ruth has drawn Boaz out (and now that the reader knows that they are the perfect match), there appears to be a technical (or

---

[36]Note the reversal from 3:4, "He (Boaz) will tell you (Ruth) what to do," to 3:11, "I (Boaz) will do all you (Ruth) ask."

[37]Variations of כָּל־שַׁעַר עַמִּי (kol šā'ar 'ammî) appear in Micah 1:9 and Obad 13.

[38]The phrase אֵשֶׁת חַיִל ('ēšeth ḥayil), "mighty woman," of 3:11 corresponds to גִּבּוֹר חַיִל (gibbôr ḥayil), "mighty man," of 2:1. The question of the passage however is this: what makes Ruth an 'ēšeth ḥayil? May whatever quality this is, be the same quality in the case of Boaz? Elsewhere, Scripture defines the 'eset hayil, "mighty woman," by means of an acrostic poem (Prov 31:10-31).

legal) glitch. Looming questions are these: does this glitch affect the marriage plans of Boaz and Ruth, does it affect the ability of Boaz to serve as *gō'ēl*-redeemer for Naomi, or does it affect both? Details revealed in the next chapter will help relieve this ambiguity; such questions should be suspended for the moment.

"Stay here for the night, and in the morning if he wants to redeem, good; let him redeem. But if he is not willing . . . I will do it." While in one sense, the picture has fogged due to the presence of another, it has cleared insofar as revealing the intentions of Boaz. Ruth is assured that the period of waiting is over. Change is on the horizon, possibly as near as the sunrise. Boaz instructs Ruth to "spend the night," using a verb free of sexual connotation.[39] In the morning the "nearer kinsman" will have his opportunity to exercise his role as *gō'ēl*-redeemer. If he chooses not to exercise it, Boaz will. *Either way*, Ruth is still covered. This idea must be carried forward into the next chapter.

Again Boaz urges her to **"lie here until morning."** Unlike the previous choice of verb, this one is used, at times, with sexual connotations.[40] Such a liaison, however, is hardly a foregone conclusion from the perspective of grammar or story, much less theology or ethics. Her character, involving a strong sense of loyalty and *ḥesed*-kindness, has driven the narrative thus far. To compromise that character now could jeopardize Ruth's future. From the perspective of Boaz, his words and actions have suggested that he is a man of integrity. He functions as the agent of Yahweh's blessing.[41] Finally, if it is accepted that the threshing floor is a public place — where Boaz and Ruth are surrounded by sleeping workers — the notion of a steamy tryst here is difficult to accept. A straightforward reading seems best: **she lay at his feet until morning.**

3:14 In the end, the meeting is kept confidential. **She . . . got up before anyone could be recognized.** In the wee hours of the morn-

---

[39]Sasson, *Ruth*, p. 90. See BDB, s.v. לִין, לוּן.

[40]Consult BDB, s.v. שָׁכַב.

[41]Campbell's words need another hearing. "It is not prudery which compels the conclusion that there was no sexual intercourse at the threshing floor; it is the utter irrelevance of such a speculation. What the scene must end with is something far more fitting, the clear evidence of Boaz's determination to care for these two widows as custom and generosity dictate" (*Ruth*, p. 138).

ing, Ruth leaves her place at the feet of Boaz. He instructs her to leave the same way she came: in secret.[42] An additional statement explains why he thinks this best. **"Don't let it be known that a woman came to the threshing floor."** Why is her presence at the threshing floor a problem? One possibility may be because this midnight meeting could jeopardize their new alliance. As suggested by the Mishnah, a sexual encounter, either real or imagined could become an issue in future negotiations concerning Ruth.[43] Another possibility steps back into the larger cultural backdrop, i.e., "Go secretly because women (in a general sense) should not be at the threshing floor." Insight here is gained from Hosea 9:1 stating that prostitutes may be found on the threshing floor. Interpreted in this light, Boaz may be saying in essence, "Go secretly because good girls like you should not be seen in a place like this." Unfortunately, so little is known of cultural customs that it is impossible to say how real these possibilities are.

3:15 Before Ruth leaves, Boaz gives her a gift: **"Bring me the shawl you are wearing and hold it out."** One is tempted to connect this passage with the word for garment used by Naomi in her instructions to Ruth to "put on your best clothes" (3:3). However, as stated above, this "shawl" is likely distinct from Ruth's outer garment.[44] Boaz **poured into it six measures of barley.**[45] This gift is yet another example of Boaz's role as provider. Ruth is given food in parting, then he (or she) **went back to town.**

---

[42]Gray points out that "a woman stirring in the early morning would attract less suspicion, since work, until lately, began before light in Arab villages. The first task of the day being grinding, Ruth, with her load of barley, would be a natural figure" (*Joshua, Judges, and Ruth*, p. 310).

[43]According to Morris, the Mishnah states that a Jewish man who has sexual relations with a Gentile cannot enter into a Levirate marriage with her. See Leon Morris, *Judges and Ruth*, TOTC (Grand Rapids: Eerdmans, 1968), p. 293.

[44]Campbell suggests the two references refer to the same garment (*Ruth*, p. 127). This might be possible if he envisions her filling the folds and carrying the grain on her person. Context however, seems to suggest she takes the garment in question off, holds it tightly while he fills it, then braces herself while he lifts it back on her again (3:15). This would be an awkward move indeed if this is the only garment she is wearing!

[45]The text reads literally, "he measured six barleys." No unit of measure is offered. This prompted early interpreters to suggest that Boaz gave Ruth only six single grains! See LaCocque, *Ruth*, p. 103.

C. RUTH REPORTS BACK (3:16-18)

¹⁶**When Ruth came to her mother-in-law, Naomi asked, "How did it go, my daughter?"**

Then she told her everything Boaz had done for her ¹⁷and added, "He gave me these six measures of barley, saying, 'Don't go back to your mother-in-law empty-handed.'"

¹⁸**Then Naomi said, "Wait, my daughter, until you find out what happens. For the man will not rest until the matter is settled today."**

3:16-17 The final section of the chapter witnesses the return of Ruth to her home and the dialogue that takes place between Ruth and Naomi. The first question Ruth faces is a loaded one. The NIV's **"How did it go?"** masks the fact that this is the exact same question asked by the startled Boaz in the night, "Who are you?" Here though, it can hardly be a question of identity; Naomi adds the familiar **"my daughter."** She knows exactly *who* this is. A preferred translation here renders the interrogative מִי (*mî*) not as a question of condition (per NIV) but as a question of possession, i.e., *"whose are you?"*[46] Naomi may ask the same question as Boaz, but certainly drives it in a different direction! Her question inquires as to Ruth's status. Is she still the possession of Naomi ("my daughter") or the possession of another ("his wife")? In short, she asks if her risky plan has been successful.

As an answer to the question, Ruth gives a full report of the night's activities right down to the gift of the grain. New information in Ruth's report are Boaz's words **"Don't go back to your mother-in-law empty handed."** The question arises as to whether these words were spoken by Boaz or not. Clearly, they are not reported earlier. Some commentators believe that the report was simply left out. Others believe this line was an addition contrived by Ruth to promote Boaz to Naomi as benefactor or to assuage Naomi's fears in losing her daughter-in-law. As Ruth will not speak again in the text, it would be tragic to believe that the last reported words of Ruth, a character elevated for her loyalty, are false and manipulative.

Narratively, it is much more profitable to refocus on the vocabulary of the phrase for a closer read. The term used is רֵיקָם (*rêqām*),

---

[46]Sasson reads this the same way, *Ruth*, pp. 100-101.

"empty," or "empty-handed." Ruth is not to return to Naomi "empty" (3:17). This statement should be placed alongside of Naomi's statement of 1:21 where she bitterly laments that Yahweh brought her back "empty." This sets up a powerful contrast. Through the actions of Boaz and the initiative of Ruth, Yahweh is about to fill her again.

3:18 Naomi has the last word in the chapter, stating implicitly that Boaz is a man of character, and explicitly, because he is a man of character, he **"will not rest until the matter is settled today."** Again the notion of "rest" appears. In this case, Boaz will not be "at rest" until resolution has been achieved. Fortunately, he will not have long to wait.

RUTH 4

IV. RESOLUTIONS ACHIEVED (4:1-22)

While the future of Ruth and Naomi seems assured as a result of promises offered on the threshing floor, legal issues remain unresolved. In this final chapter to the book, events shift from dark to light and from private to public as Boaz steps forward to negotiate with the unnamed kinsman of 3:12. Personal rights and social obligations are discussed in legal terms that thrust the reader into the gathering crowd to witness this "courtroom" finish. The end reveals that this small story, opening with the smell of death, is really about the triumph of life, and that the feelings of hopelessness associated with the annihilation of a family name, will grow into the celebration of a dynasty. This final chapter breaks into two pieces: the first piece (4:1-12) describes negotiations in the gateway, while the second piece (4:13-22) outlines the legacy of a newborn child.

A. BOAZ NEGOTIATES (4:1-12)

¹Meanwhile Boaz went up to the town gate and sat there. When the kinsman-redeemer he had mentioned came along, Boaz said, "Come over here, my friend, and sit down." So he went over and sat down.

²Boaz took ten of the elders of the town and said, "Sit here," and they did so. ³Then he said to the kinsman-redeemer, "Naomi, who has come back from Moab, is selling the piece of land that belonged to our brother Elimelech. ⁴I thought I should bring the matter to your attention and suggest that you buy it in the presence of these seated here and in the presence of the elders of my people. If you will redeem it, do so. But if youᵃ will not, tell me, so

I will know. For no one has the right to do it except you, and I am next in line."

"I will redeem it," he said.

[5]Then Boaz said, "On the day you buy the land from Naomi and from Ruth the Moabitess, you acquire[b] the dead man's widow, in order to maintain the name of the dead with his property."

[6]At this, the kinsman-redeemer said, "Then I cannot redeem it because I might endanger my own estate. You redeem it yourself. I cannot do it."

[7](Now in earlier times in Israel, for the redemption and transfer of property to become final, one party took off his sandal and gave it to the other. This was the method of legalizing transactions in Israel.)

[8]So the kinsman-redeemer said to Boaz, "Buy it yourself." And he removed his sandal.

[9]Then Boaz announced to the elders and all the people, "Today you are witnesses that I have bought from Naomi all the property of Elimelech, Kilion and Mahlon. [10]I have also acquired Ruth the Moabitess, Mahlon's widow, as my wife, in order to maintain the name of the dead with his property, so that his name will not disappear from among his family or from the town records. Today you are witnesses!"

[11]Then the elders and all those at the gate said, "We are witnesses. May the LORD make the woman who is coming into your home like Rachel and Leah, who together built up the house of Israel. May you have standing in Ephrathah and be famous in Bethlehem. [12]Through the offspring the LORD gives you by this young woman, may your family be like that of Perez, whom Tamar bore to Judah."

[a]4 Many Hebrew manuscripts, Septuagint, Syriac and Vulgate; most Hebrew manuscripts *he*   [b]5 Hebrew; Vulgate and Syriac, *Naomi, you acquire Ruth the Moabitess*

4:1-2 At the conclusion of chapter 3, Naomi made it clear that Boaz would not rest until a resolution to the situation was found.[1] This appears to be the case at the beginning of chapter 4. Now, it is

---

[1]Similarly, Boaz himself vowed that the matter would be resolved directly (3:13).

not Elimelech (1:1), Ruth (2:2), or Naomi (3:1) who takes the initiative that opens a new stage; it is Boaz. He goes **up to the town gate** and positions himself for an interception.

The city gate is a likely place of meeting. Archaeology reveals how this civic feature was much more elaborate than a simple opening in the city wall.[2] In large, fortified cities, towers were built over a series of chambers and entry doors. These might be flanked by stairs, secondary walls, guardhouses, and even small, well-defined plazas. The overall effect of this complex, however, was to restrict the flow of traffic and simplify the defensive task. But just as fearsome attackers could be funneled through these narrows, so too, ordinary folk. On busy days vendors, shoppers, judges, beggars, and prophets crowded outside, inside and within the gated area. Consequently, the city gate in the biblical period served social as well as military functions. Plastered benches found within gate chambers suggest places of gossip (Ps 69:12), judgment (Deut 21:19), and mercantile pitch (Neh 13:15-22). Such finds also underline texts such as Proverbs 31:23, Joshua 20:4, and possibly Genesis 19:1, where the city gate appears in a more technical sense as a place of civic administration. If Boaz is a civic administrator is not known, but certainly as a prominent landowner and "mighty man," his voice is valued. Hence, Boaz takes a seat inside the bustling gate complex where he could monitor all who enter and leave Bethlehem.[3]

The careful use of הִנֵּה (hinnēh), "behold" or "look," gives immediacy to the action and hints again at providential operation, as the gō'ēl-redeemer previously mentioned by Boaz (3:12-13) just happens to pass by. Boaz speaks to him, inviting him to come over and sit. The NIV kindly renders Boaz's bid as **"my friend"** although the Hebrew text is less congenial, reading his direct address more curtly as "certain one," a "so-and-so," or, as we might be inclined to put

---

[2]For more on city gates, see Zeev Herzog, "Settlement and Fortification Planning in the Iron Age," in *The Architecture of Ancient Israel from the Prehistoric to the Persian Periods*, ed. by Aharon Kempinski and Ronny Reich (Jerusalem: Israel Exploration Society, 1992), pp. 231-274.

[3]Unfortunately, the remains of Bethlehem in the period of the Old Testament rest quietly beneath the modern village. Some 10th–8th-century-B.C. remains have been unearthed in the vicinity of the Church of the Nativity, but few conclusions have been drawn. Only future excavations may reveal the presence and complexity of the defensive systems in this place.

it today, "Mr. Whatever."[4] As Boaz would have undoubtedly known
the man's true name (he clearly grasps the man's familial connections and place of nearness to Naomi), it is possible that this is a
deliberate gloss by the narrator. As such, it devalues the character in
the eyes of the reader. This kinsman, who has no name of his own
(Whatever!), is hardly in a position to rescue the name of another.[5]
In addition to "Mr. Whatever," Boaz also beckons ten **elders of the
town** to join them. These men play no active role in the negotiations; rather they serve as witnesses to the conversation and guarantee its fair outcome.[6]

4:3-4 With all parties in place, Boaz deftly proceeds to **bring the
matter** to the attention of the anonymous kinsman. What is apparently at stake is a piece of land that previously belonged to Elimelech, but is now being sold by Naomi. This launch comes as a complete surprise. Thus far in the narrative, no mention has been made
of this family land; as such, it raises immediate questions. What is
the significance of this land? Was it sold by Elimelech in the days
before he took his wife and boys and fled to Moab? How does the
"buying" (back?) of this land relate to the responsibility of the gō'ēl-
redeemer in Leviticus 25:25-28? When and how was the sale of this
land discovered? This opening statement of Boaz grows ever more

---

[4]The phrase פְּלֹנִי אַלְמֹנִי (peˀlōnî ˀalmōnî) appears rarely (elsewhere in 1 Sam
21:3 and in 2 Kgs 6:8 of "such and such a place"). The LXX translates this
address as κρύφιε (kryphie, "O hidden one"). Campbell offers a complete discussion of this "nonsense name" in his Ruth (pp. 141-143).

[5]The verb used of the kinsman's action in 4:1 is also a hint. The verbal עֹבֵר
(ˀōbēr) here is well served by the NIV's "came along," having at the core a
meaning of "crossing over." But it can also be translated as, "to cross over
the line," or even "to transgress." This nuance is not overlooked: at first
meeting this man wanders in namelessly and dangerously. It will not get any
better for him.

[6]Moore points out that elders appear in five legal contexts within the
book of Deuteronomy: blood redemption (19:12), expiation of murder
(21:1-9), rebellious sons (21:18-21), defamation of virgins (22:13-21), and
levirate marriages (25:5-10). He further observes that the string that ties
these contexts together is family. "Judges, not elders, habitually deal with
cases involving criminal law" (See his Ruth, p. 361). The context of Ruth 4
is the arbitration of a family matter not an issue of criminal law.

In addition to their legal role as witnesses, the elders' appearance here
may also add pressure to the kinsman from the perspective of social account-
ability.

perplexing given the fact that *personal* concerns, not *property* concerns have driven the plot thus far; all gather at the gate expecting to hear something of Ruth's marriage request, not a discussion of real estate.[7] Still, it must be remembered that Boaz himself is not introduced until 2:1 and the unnamed kinsman, a key player to be sure, is not brought up until late in the story (3:12). Surprise is a sharp tool in this narrator's kit!

Boaz urges the kinsman to exercise his option to buy (back) the land. Hubbard captures the precision of this formula by his translation, "Now for my part, I hereby say, let me inform you as follows: Buy it (the land)."[8] Three issues must be noted. First, this is legal language concerned with the activity of buying and selling. Efforts to recast the dynamic into something else (i.e., mortgage relief, obligation rights, etc.) are interesting but outrun our knowledge of ancient practices.[9] A second issue concerns the relationship between the purchase of the land and care for Naomi specifically. It may be inferred that this land purchase encouraged by Boaz involves some care-giving responsibility toward Naomi, but this is not made explicit. Perhaps she would be cared for through the profits gained by working the land, the purchase price itself, or both. Connected to

---

[7]Some commentators have suggested that the announcement of land is a fabrication on the part of Boaz to divert the attention of his listeners from his true goal (see Linafelt, *Ruth*, p. 67). This reading is possible only if the clear descriptions of Boaz by the narrator are subverted and are assumed to hide some other "true agenda." This raises the question, if modern interpreters are suspicious of the claim of Boaz from this distance (where nothing is really at stake), would not those who gathered at the gate be even more so? In the case of the kinsman, particularly, the truthfulness of Boaz's claim will seriously impact his estate. Are we to believe that Boaz "pulled the wool" over all their eyes, while only we moderns know better?

[8]Hubbard, *Ruth*, p. 236.

[9]Some of these ideas are prompted by the LXX that glosses מָכְרָה (*mākrāh*) altogether and inserts ἣ δέδοται Νωεμὶν (*hē dedotai Nōemin*), [the land] "that was given to Naomi." Sasson devotes several pages to a discussion of the verb *mākrāh* and a host of proposals for understanding it within the context of the book (*Ruth*, pp. 108-115).

H.C. Brichto's argument that the land was sold in the past, perhaps even by Elimelech, is helpful. The land could have been sold after all other resources were exhausted, prior to their flight to Moab. Naomi's wish is that the land be "bought back," in line with Leviticus 25 principles of land tenure. See his "Kin, Cult, Land, and Afterlife—A Biblical Complex," *HUCA* 44 (1973), pp. 1-54.

this is the point that no mention is made of Ruth yet, although the language of redemption (gō'ēl) is identical to that used on the threshing floor (3:9,13). Boaz obviously has Ruth in mind. The gnawing question is this: does the kinsman? Third and finally, the introduction of land here challenges the reader to look closely at two dynamics of *torah*. The first concerns kinsman marriage.[10] The second concerns the redemption of land by a *gō'ēl*-redeemer.[11] While some interpreters link these two dynamics in reading the book of Ruth, it is proposed here that these dynamics are different in both nature and goal and should therefore be kept separate in order to best understand Ruth's story.[12]

In a move that creates even more leverage, Boaz offers an "out." If "Mr. Whatever" does not exercise his first option to buy, Boaz will exercise his second. There will be no more dillydallying. What is striking here is the verb used to describe this entire string of information. Literally, Boaz "uncovers" this hidden knowledge, even as his own feet were "uncovered" previously (3:4,7).[13] One cannot help but smile at the narrator's wry connection between these two acts. Just as Boaz did not "see Ruth coming," neither does this anonymous kinsman. Ruth continues to be a revelation in the purest sense.

---

[10]Key texts for kinsman marriage include Deut 25:5-10 and Genesis 38. The Deuteronomy 25 passage makes it clear that kinsman marriage involves brothers who are living together. If one of these dies without an heir, the widow of the dead man is taken by another brother who is obligated to sire a child through her to perpetuate the name of his brother. How this principle found its way into practice, however, is difficult to know. Certainly Genesis 38, a narrative drawn from a setting prior to the giving of *torah* is of some help. But how much?

[11]Key texts for land redemption include Leviticus 25. A helpful secondary source on the subject is Christopher J.H. Wright's *God's People in God's Land: Family, Land, and Property in the Old Testament* (Grand Rapids: Eerdmans, 1990).

[12]Untangling these dynamics is tough, as the narrative itself blends some of the features. The *gō'ēl*-redeemer introduced at the threshing floor (3:12) is seemingly revealed in the context of kinship marriage. However, here in Boaz's opening discussion of land redemption, the same man is the key player. Likewise the language of redemption, גָּאַל (gā'al), is used of both people and land, kinship marriage and land redemption.

[13]In 4:4 the phrase אֶגְלֶה אָזְנֶךָ ('egleh 'oznᵉkā) reads more literally, "I will uncover your ear." This expression may be suggestive of the motion of lifting a head covering or parting the hair to gain clear access to the ear of another.

"Mr. Whatever" meets the challenge and replies in a way that suggests both emphasis and perhaps even enthusiasm, **"I will redeem it."**[14] Acquiring this land appears to be a good investment.[15] The transaction could give the new owner and his heirs a parcel of land for use and profit, and may even impart additional status to this anonymous one as a gracious benefactor within the community. Since Naomi has no sons and is apparently past her child-bearing years herself, there are no other obvious claimants on the horizon. Even in a year of jubilee when all property is theoretically returned to original families, it cannot be lost. With this reply, the narrative tension rises in an uncomfortable crescendo; the trajectory of events is moving in a way that does not seem to favor Boaz.

4:5 However, with this assent in place, Boaz drops one last piece of additional information, his gateway *coup d'etat*. **"On the day you buy the land from Naomi and from Ruth the Moabitess, you acquire the dead man's widow, in order to maintain the name of the dead with his property."** Suddenly, "Mr. Whatever" is informed that there is more at stake here than land alone. Understanding the exact nature of Boaz's revelation and why it prompts such a startling backpedal on the part of the kinsman is a demanding task. Word choice, word order, and the larger context of 4:5 collide in an interpretive crux that significantly impacts how the larger story is to be understood. To approach some resolution, a pause to ask and answer three questions must be made.

First, from whom is the land acquired? Clearly Naomi is owner in some fashion (past or present), but how does Ruth fit in? The NIV renders the "seller" of the land using a conjunction: the land is bought "from Naomi *and* from Ruth the Moabitess." However, the syntax is quite awkward, a disjunctive (or separating) accent on the name of Naomi suggests otherwise, and even logically, it seems odd

---

[14]The use of a personal pronoun preceding the finite verb creates an explicit antithesis between the kinsman-redeemer and Boaz, viz. "I, even I, will redeem!" For more on this structure see Waltke and O'Connor, *Biblical Hebrew Syntax*, para. 16.3.2d.

[15]So why has the anonymous kinsman not moved on it already? It seems possible—but unlikely—that he did not know about the situation. Could it be that he was waiting for the aging Naomi to die. At her death, as the closest relative, he would eventually inherit the land without having to pay a redemption price!

to credit the land parcel *to* Ruth, here specifically termed a foreigner. Ultimately, the issue here is grammatical and revolves around the question of a simple conjunction. Does the conjunction link phrases or clauses?[16] The reading of the NIV suggests conjoined phrases is the answer, i.e., the "seller" is both Naomi *and* Ruth. However, if the conjunction links independent clauses, a very different reading is produced, viz., the land is bought "from Naomi (full stop); (new idea here) *and as for* Ruth the Moabitess. . . . "[17]

Growing from this first issue is the second. Who is the "wife of the dead" that will be acquired? Does this phrase refer back to Naomi or back to Ruth? Both are obviously widows. Again, how one reads the conjunction is key. On one hand, it is attractive to attach the phrase to Naomi. She is, after all, the primary "seller" and the wife of Elimelech who originally owned the land. However, if it refers to Naomi, how will she fulfill the purpose of the redemption, i.e., preserve "the name of the dead with his property"? Preserving the "name of the dead" presumably requires the birthing of a child, an act that appears unlikely for Naomi (1:11). On the other hand, Ruth is young enough to bear children, and syntactically, the phrase immediately follows the description of her as from Moab. It may be proposed, therefore, that the translation be reconsidered: (new idea here) "and as for Ruth the Moabitess, wife of the dead. . . ."

---

[16]The disjunctive accent on Naomi suggests a break at this point that would relegate the following description of Ruth to another clause. Key to the awkwardness of this passage is the particle וּמֵאֵת (*ûmē'ēth*). Syntactically, how does this function? Many emendations have been proposed to resolve this awkwardness. See Waltke and O'Connor (*Biblical Hebrew Syntax*, p. 648, n. 2) for a brief discussion of the grammatical form.

[17]This translation has been termed problematic for lack of a direct object. This is alleviated, however, if the second clause is rendered using a *casus pendens*, a possibility that takes the *ēth* as an accusative particle (as rendered here). There is precedent for such use (cf. 1 Kgs 15:13), although the *mem* (מ) remains a problem.

Solutions to this *mem* problem include deleting the *mem* altogether (a dittographical error prompted by the preceding Nao*m*i) or by emending it in some fashion (either by inserting a *gimel* (ג) in the place of the preceding *waw* (ו) or by adding a *gimel* to produce some form of גַּם־אֵת רוּת (*gam-'ēth rûth*).

For a tightly written survey of options, see Murray D. Gow, "*Ruth Quoque*—A Coquette? (Ruth 4:5)," *TB* 41 (1990), pp. 302-311. To place these thoughts in the larger context of his view, see Gow's *The Book of Ruth: Its Structure, Theme, and Purpose* (Leicester: Apollos, 1992).

Third, what is the verb of this second clause? Unfortunately, a *ketib/qere* issue is encountered and suggests that this verse has been problematic since ancient times. The rabbinic recommendation (*qere*) is adopted by the NIV, hence, "on the day you [i.e., the gō'ēl-redeemer] buy . . . *you will acquire* Ruth." Put this way, the redemption of Ruth is firmly attached to the redemption of the land and the redemption of Naomi. Grammatically and traditionally (at least according to the Masoretes) this reading has been accepted. However, apart from this one troubled passage no biblical connection between kinsman marriage and land redemption is attested, and even here, it does not make the best sense of the evidence. Atkinson makes a noble attempt to explain this passage as an encouragement from Boaz to the kinsman to "go above and beyond" *torah* (as both Ruth and Boaz have done previously). This is hardly satisfactory though for a simple reason: why should the kinsman go beyond *torah*?[18] How would meeting the letter of *torah* possibly be viewed as unsatisfactory?

Setting the rabbinic tradition aside (*qere*), another reading is possible, that of the unencumbered text itself (*ketib*). If this reading is adopted, the following translation is the result, "and as for Ruth the Moabitess, wife of the dead, *I* (Boaz) *will acquire* (her) for the purpose of raising up the name of the dead and his property." Note the contrast of actions. What Boaz announces is nothing less than a preemptive strike: "on the day *you* acquire the land . . . *I* will acquire Ruth." If the kinsman intends to honor the tradition of gō'ēl-redeemer and purchase Naomi's land, he must do so with the full knowledge that Boaz is planning to marry Ruth, a "free agent,"[19] not

---

[18]David Atkinson, *The Message of Ruth: Wings of Refuge*, Bible Speaks Today Old Testament. Downers Grove, IL: InterVarsity, 1983), pp. 113-115.

[19]Having lost her husband and without children, Ruth and Orpah were free to choose future options. Orpah chose to return to her Moabite family. Ruth chose to link her future to that of Naomi. The freedom of Ruth to seek a man of her own choosing is emphasized in Boaz's words of 3:10, "you have not run after the younger men, whether rich or poor."

Sasson argues that Ruth chose to submit herself in an obliging way to the will of Naomi. This explains why she gleaned for herself and for Naomi, why she stayed with Naomi even after attaching herself to the "girls" of Boaz, and why she did not object to Naomi's proposal to meet Boaz in the night. More controversial is Sasson's suggestion that the "purchase" of 4:5 is compensation given to Naomi for the release of Ruth from this obligation. See his *Ruth*, pp. 124-125.

attached to the redemption of the land nor to the redemption of Naomi.[20] Furthermore, Boaz intends to honor the "name of the dead" by producing a child from that union and dedicating it to Ruth's dead husband. Such a bold declaration stuns those assembled in the gateway and especially the close relative. However, it does not stun the close reader who has watched Ruth enter the circle of harvesters in 2:8-16, has heard Naomi describe Ruth as one of Boaz's "household" in 3:2, and has secretly witnessed Ruth ask Boaz for "cover" in 3:9. Hence, if this reading is adopted, a most helpful conclusion is reached, one that comes close to satisfying the grammatical demands of a tricky passage and one that explains the reaction of the kinsman. Boaz's words are a threat due to an "heir potential." The logic of this threat is as follows. When Boaz takes Ruth to wife, Ruth *may* bear a child. If she bears a child, *it is possible* that this offspring dedicated to Ruth's dead husband *could* eventually make a viable claim upon the land in question. If such a claim is successfully validated, Elimelech's possessions will revert to Ruth's child. If this were to happen, "Mr. Whatever's" investment would be entirely lost, either to him personally or to his heirs. Note that this scenario is laced with hypothetical strings and fraught with improbabilities. As a starter, it assumes that Ruth can conceive a child, something that did not happen in ten years of marriage to her first husband.

4:6 However, when faced with even a remote possibility, the kinsman balks. The reason offered is an ironic overstatement, connected to ability rather than will. **"I cannot redeem it,"** says "Mr. Whatever," **"because I might endanger my own estate."** The term translated here as "endanger" suggests an utter waste.[21] The kinsman is unable (or better put, unwilling) to purchase the land of Elimelech.[22] This is *not* because he will acquire Ruth as wife; indeed, as our reading goes,

---

[20]This is a controversial reading as many commentators link the redemption of the land (*gō'ēl*-redeemer) to the redemption of Ruth (kinsman marriage). This link is here challenged and shares perspectives previously voiced by Gordis ("Love, Marriage, and Business," p. 247, 252) and Sasson (*Ruth*, pp. 125-129).

[21]The term שׁחת (*šḥt*) is used of the action of massacring people, battering a city wall, or making a corrupting choice. See *HALOT*, s.v. שׁחת.

[22]Hubbard cites other reasons traditionally cited including problems with his present wife, lack of faith, and fear of contamination of his seed due to foreign influence (*Ruth*, p. 246, n. 52).

it is precisely because *he will not acquire* Ruth as wife, *and therefore cannot fully control the future of his own investment.* Suddenly, he backpedals: **"You redeem it yourself."** In the end, "Mr. Whatever" is exposed for the whatever that he is! His own self-interests are revealed to be a higher priority than his personal responsibility to care for a widow in distress or even his social responsibility to keep a family name in Israel from total annihilation. His generosity is exhausted where the possibility of sacrifice begins. The reader is not surprised, though, for at least two reasons. First, this nameless one was viewed with suspicion from the moment he crossed over the threshold.[23] Second, his example is all too familiar to every reader. Who has not witnessed the shrinking of a generous spirit in the face of personal sacrifice? "Mr. Whatever" is an example of the selfishness that lurks in the gateway of every human heart.

4:7-8 In earlier times makes it clear that the narrator is writing to a generation that is removed at some distance from the described events. To bring the readers "up to speed" culturally, a parenthetical statement is offered describing the ceremony of the sandal, **for the redemption and transfer of property.** As explained here, this ancient practice finalized arrangements both civic and commercial in nature. **One party took off his sandal and gave it to the other.** Some similarities between this ceremony as described in Ruth, and the ceremony described in Deuteronomy 25:5-10 are noted. However, enough differences exist between these two passages to dismiss their direct connection. It is also worth noting that in the literature of the Old Testament and the ancient Near East other links may also be found.[24]

4:9-10 At the conclusion of this ceremony, **Boaz announced . . . "Today,[25] you are witnesses."** The words of Boaz are both judicial and jubilant. He states for the record what he is acquiring at this

---

[23]Others attempt to read the kinsman in a less critical way, e.g., Hubbard, *Ruth*, p. 246-247.

[24]See Roland deVaux, *Ancient Israel* (New York: McGraw-Hill, 1965), p. 169.

[25]Hubbard and others connect this use of "today" with the statement of Naomi in 3:18, "the man will not rest until the matter is settled today." Naomi was exactly right about Boaz (*Ruth*, p. 257).

[26]The claim of Boaz here is quite large, perhaps even larger than expected. His purchase includes "all the property of Elimelech, Kilion and

moment in time: the family property of the clan of Elimelech,[26] and Ruth, as wife.[27] The latter is expected, the former is not. The latter is a result of a private agreement on the threshing floor, the former is a result of a public hearing in the gateway. Given our reading above, it is necessary to understand these acquisitions as two distinct actions, linked here by due process and practical outcome. The purpose in both will be **"to maintain the name of the dead with his property, so that his name will not disappear."**[28] Boaz's words underline yet again the importance of name preservation (and create contrast with the abdicating *gō'ēl*-redeemer who remains nameless). Moreover, his words underline a generosity as previously witnessed, his piety in making and keeping promises, his ability to outwit a selfish and possibly evil opponent, and finally, his honor in upholding social traditions. In short, he is truly a "mighty man."

4:11-12 In answer to this call for notarization, **the elders and all those at the gate** respond. The first part of this response acknowledges their role **"We are witnesses."** As revealed, this exchange is witnessed by more than the assembled elders. One can rightly imagine a space crowded by spectators, young and old, keen to see and

---

Mahlon." If this includes more property than the field parcel of 4:3 is not known. One explanation for this inclusive language may be the legal context in which it is offered: Boaz seeks to eliminate any future claims.

[27]Ruth is here identified as a Moabite and as the wife of Mahlon. These details fix her identify for the sake of the legal proceeding, but perhaps even more importantly, they tie the conclusion of the book to its introduction by reminding the reader of Ruth's misfortune and by underscoring the fulfillment of the blessing of Naomi offered in 1:9 ("May you . . . find rest in the home of another husband").

[28]A further outcome will be the permanent uniting of Ruth and Naomi in the same household. By virtue of marriage, Boaz acquires responsibility for Ruth. By virtue of land acquisition, he acquires responsibility for Naomi. Both remain together under his care, a move that carries forward the echo of 1:16-17, only "death" can separate them.

This interpretation also bolsters a view that finds these two widows caring for each other and making moves that benefit the other. In an act of affection, Naomi dispatches Ruth to the threshing floor to get a husband that will provide "rest" for her daughter-in-law. However, as it turns out, Ruth works "beyond the script" and presses Boaz to accept the role of *gō'ēl*-redeemer. As a result of Ruth's act of affection (requested knowingly or unknowingly), the land of Naomi is redeemed and the "name of the dead with his property" is preserved.

hear the negotiations. What has happened is now a matter of public record; the transaction initiated by Ruth in the dark of the night is brought into the open and given public approval. The second part of the response at the gate is directed toward blessing. Invoking the name of Yahweh, the blessing moves the three directions, each back-loaded and front-loaded with meaning.

First, the gateway blessing is directed toward Ruth. **"May the LORD make the woman who is coming into your home like Rachael and Leah, who together built up the house of Israel."** Although she does not appear in this scene, the journey of Ruth from Moabite to Israelite is now complete.[29] Her own statement of intention quietly resurfaces, "your people will be my people and your God, my God" (1:16). Amazingly — despite her "outsider" roots as a Moabite — she is not only acknowledged as a member of Boaz's household, but placed in elite company. She is likened to Rachel and Leah, famous women who "built Israel" in the past. Just as Rachel and Leah initi-ated a legacy through childbirth, the reader anticipates the same for Ruth. In this vein one cannot miss the significant vocabulary of "building up" and "house," terms that prefigure Yahweh's promises to David in 2 Samuel 7.

Second, the gateway blessing is directed toward Boaz, **"May you have standing in Ephrathah and be famous in Bethlehem."** Ephra-thah and Bethlehem were connected in 1:1-2 to the family of Elime-lech, and obviously here, to the family of Boaz. While the significance of this place in Israel's past is not altogether clear, it will play an enormous role as a birthplace for others in Israel's future. Boaz will sire a famous family.

Third and finally, the blessing is directed toward a child yet to be

---

[29]Still resisting the larger thrust of this verse (and our own work with the text of Joshua), the Targum makes it clear that Israel here refers specifical-ly to "our father" Jacob, rather than the nation. See Levine (*The Aramaic Version of Ruth*, pp. 105-106). For more on what it means to "be" or "become Israel," see our thoughts on the subject in the commentary on *Joshua* (Joplin, MO: College Press, 2008).

[30]Literally, "from the seed given by Yahweh." Some connect this phrase to previous images of Boaz giving grain and barley. Certainly, in the immedi-ate context, the suggestion is made that Yahweh is the ultimate benefactor. Yet, taken even more broadly, "seed" is a collective noun often used in nar-ratives recounting the redemptive movements of God (cf. Gen 3:15; 12:7; 2 Sam 7:12-13; Ps 18:50, etc.). Given the genealogical context that follows,

born. **"Through the offspring**[30] **the LORD gives you by this young woman, may your family be like that of Perez, whom Tamar bore to Judah."** Two points of note may be made. First, the biblical concept of Yahweh as the one who opens and closes the womb is raised again (e.g. Gen 30:2; Ps 22:9[10]; 127:3). These words may be viewed as a prayer for the miraculous, given Ruth's present barrenness and Boaz's presumed age. They anticipate 4:13 and may even offer a theological explanation for why Ruth did not bear any children through her first husband. Second, the words of blessing bring to mind Genesis 38, a story involving Tamar, a widow who gained a legacy through initiative and persistence. How much of Tamar's story is meant to be carried into this context can only be guessed at.[31] What is certain is that the birth of Perez is an important genealogical link that unites the assembled crowd at the gate to their heritage. This link also serves as a bridge into the conclusion.

B. RUTH BEARS A LEGACY (4:13-22)

[13]**So Boaz took Ruth and she became his wife. Then he went to her, and the LORD enabled her to conceive, and she gave birth to a son.** [14]**The women said to Naomi: "Praise be to the LORD, who this day has not left you without a kinsman-redeemer. May he become famous throughout Israel!** [15]**He will renew your life and sustain you in your old age. For your daughter-in-law, who loves you and who is better to you than seven sons, has given him birth."**

[16]**Then Naomi took the child, laid him in her lap and cared for him.** [17]**The women living there said, "Naomi has a son." And they named him Obed. He was the father of Jesse, the father of David.**

[18]**This, then, is the family line of Perez:**

Perez was the father of Hezron,
[19]**Hezron the father of Ram,**

---

it is not overreaching to suggest the place of Ruth and Boaz in that larger testimony. For more on "seed," see *TWOT*, s.v. זֶרַע (*zeraʿ*) or *TDOT*, s.v. זָרַע *zāraʿ*; זֶרַע *zeraʿ*.

[31]Fewell and Gunn develop this link extensively, and use it as a lens through which Ruth's story is interpreted. See their *Compromising Redemption*, pp. 23-25, 46-48, 57-58, 63-64.

Ram the father of Amminadab,
[20]**Amminadab the father of Nahshon,**
Nahshon the father of Salmon,[a]
[21]**Salmon the father of Boaz,**
Boaz the father of Obed,
[22]**Obed the father of Jesse,**
and Jesse the father of David.

[a]*20* A few Hebrew manuscripts, some Septuagint manuscripts and Vulgate (see also verse 21 and Septuagint of 1 Chron. 2:11); most Hebrew manuscripts *Salma*

4:13 That which was announced in 4:10 is enacted, as the story rushes to a conclusion. **So Boaz took Ruth and she became his wife.** Naomi's blessing of 1:8-9 is fulfilled as Ruth receives *ḥesed*-kindness and goes to "the home of another husband." Beyond this, Boaz **went to her, and the LORD enabled her to conceive, and she gave birth to a son.** The one whose existence was only a threat in the gateway, and a remote one at that, becomes a reality. In terms reminiscent of a host of other Old Testament narratives, the previously barren wife conceives and produces a son. Biblically such things are chalked up to miracle. Interestingly, this is the second overt action of God described in the narrative. As such it provides a working frame: He relieves the problem of famine by giving his people food (1:6); he relieves the problem of family by giving Ruth a child (4:13). The latter passage may also indirectly confirm the innocence of the threshing-floor meeting between Ruth and Boaz. Only now are they physically united and only now is a child conceived.

---

[32]Trible's proposal ("Two Women," pp. 277-278) that the chorus of Bethlehem women functions in opposition to the chorus of male elders is too strong. Certainly, as one compares the blessing of 4:11-12 and the blessing of 4:14-15 there are different interests expressed, e.g., the gateway blessing is concerned for the "name of the dead," while the blessing of the women includes a naming of the living. Against this reading, two things must be remembered. First, the two blessings are voiced in two different contexts. One concludes a legal decision, the other is offered in the midst of a nativity scene. Different issues arise in different settings. Second, it is hardly a foregone conclusion that "*all* the people" of v. 9 and "the elders and *all those at the gate*" of v. 11 are strictly male. Removing this unnecessary gender-loading allows each chorus to function in a way that is both complete and complementary.

4:14-15 The birth prompts the chorus of women to speak to Naomi.[32] It must be remembered that at one time, a female chorus questioned her identity. When she returned from Moab, bitter and sad, they asked "Can this be Naomi?" (1:19). Now they speak again, gathering together closing words like loose threads that function on no less than two levels. At one level, their words are a blessing or prayer, opening in formulaic phrase, "blessed be Yahweh." At another level, however, their words expand into a series of final assessments, circling again around the question of identity: Who is Yahweh? Who is Ruth? Who is the *gō'ēl*-redeemer?

The blessing begins, **"Praise be to the LORD, who this day has not left you without a kinsman-redeemer."** Through these words, Yahweh is identified and praised. He "has not ceased" or "put an end to" a *gō'ēl*-redeemer for you. Note that the activity of this *gō'ēl*-redeemer, as recognized, is rightly applied to Naomi. One expects this special one to be identified as Boaz; however, a closer read reveals an unexpected twist.[33] **"May he become famous throughout Israel! He will renew your life and sustain you in your old age. For your daughter-in-law, who loves you and who is better to you than seven sons, has given him birth."** Three directions are fruitful for exploration. First, a description of the *gō'ēl*-redeemer is noted.[34] His name will become famous in Israel; he will "return" life to Naomi,[35] and he will support (or even "nourish") Naomi when her hair turns grey. Second, the relationship between Ruth and Naomi is underlined. While Ruth offers a child (but has no voice) in this closing chapter, it is significant that her love for Naomi provides the final

---

[33]Nonetheless, some have tried to argue for Boaz as this *gō'ēl*-redeemer. Note Sasson's arguments against Bewer (*Ruth*, p. 163-164).

[34]Besides Boaz, it is tempting to read Yahweh as the subject of these statements. Grammatically, it is possible as Campbell has shown (*Ruth*, p. 163-164). However, the final line describing his "birth" makes this a difficult reading, as Campbell concedes.

[35]The notion of "return" has been thematic throughout the book, albeit more often than not with a negative edge. Recall in 1:12 Naomi encouraged her two daughters-in-law to "return" home, and later in the chapter Naomi laments that Yahweh caused her to "return" from Moab empty (1:21). Still, Ruth refused to "return" (1:16), and, of course, here it is the newborn who will cause Naomi's life to "return." Hence, the greatest "return" is saved for the last; she who once spewed bitterness, has no need to even open her mouth.

word on her character. Here, the chorus uncharacteristically (for Hebrew narrative) pulls back the curtain and reveals inner feelings, suggesting in part, why this daughter-in-law has been so loyal to Naomi. Who is Ruth? She is the one who truly loves Naomi.[36] In fact, this attachment is so strong, that from the perspective of the chorus, such a daughter-in-law is preferable to a whole battery of sons, a remarkable statement given Naomi's personal loss and the male-oriented world in which she lives.[37] Third and finally, the identity of the gō'ēl-redeemer is revealed. Although it is the same word used by Naomi to describe Boaz (2:20), and by Boaz and the narrator to describe the anonymous kinsman (3:12; 4:1,3,6,8), neither of these is the focus. Who is the gō'ēl-redeemer? In a twist, the women proclaim that he is *the son* born to Ruth! It is the newborn child who will become famous, be a restorer of life, and will maintain Naomi in her old age.

The introduction of this child provides the final piece of the gō'ēl-redeemer puzzle for the book. Boaz has heroically functioned in this role in order to achieve legal satisfaction. But as the chorus points out, there is more at stake here than *torah*. Their words suggest that Naomi, the returning one, has returned, but the genealogical list makes it clear that there are greater issues than Naomi's place in the world or even her personal comfort. Perhaps it is better to hold this idea at arm's

---

[36]The term אהב (*'āhab*) is used of the affection shared between a parent and a child (Gen 22:2; 25:28), a husband and a wife (Gen 24:67; Judg 16:4), a slave and a master (Exod 21:5), or friends (1 Sam 16:21; 18:1,3). This is a very broad term that describes both pure and impure feelings.

Certainly to achieve the reading of Fewell and Gunn, Ruth's "love" cannot be taken at face value and rests somewhere between pure and impure. "We suggest a loyal friendship that is not without mixed motives. Sacrificial love? Perhaps—but not a love that recklessly loses sight of the self" (*Compromising Redemption*, p. 98).

[37]Kristin Moen Saxegaard presents an interpretation of the book of Ruth through the expression, "more than seven sons." Several points are of interest. First, she points out that Ruth functions as both daughter and son to Naomi, challenging conventional gender roles. Second, she compares the phrase found here, "more to you than x sons," to a similar expression in 1 Sam 1:8. Third, she briefly offers the observation that Ruth has become the "eighth son" to Naomi, and as such can be compared, as a type, to David, also an eighth son (cf. 1 Sam 16:10-11). Both Ruth and David go beyond the perfect. See her "'More Than Seven Sons': Ruth as Example of the Good Son," *Scandinavian Journal of the Old Testament*, 15 (2001): 257-275.

length for a moment, consider Naomi's embrace first, and then return to it in the context of the closing genealogical discussion.

4:16-17 Whereas before Naomi responded to the women in complaint (1:20-21) — trading her identity as "sweet" for "bitter" — her response now is one of actions, not words. She takes the child and tenderly cares for him. The women see this action and proclaim, **"Naomi has a son."** Rather than view this statement as a sentimental exercise, or, even worse, a factual error (isn't Ruth the child's mother?), the twist prompts the reader to think narratively. The words of the women may be a play on imagery. The child is quietly pressed to Naomi's bosom; she "cares for him," possibly even "nurses him."[38] While it is physically unlikely that she suckled the child, the raw symbolism of her action cannot be missed. As Boaz promised, a son born to his union with Ruth would be dedicated to preserve the name of the dead (4:5), and, in time, fit into a larger construct (4:21-22). To this is the cleverly added point that the newborn also functions in the place of Mahlon and therefore becomes, in a round about way, the son of Naomi.[39] A further thought on this phrase emphasizes a contrast. When Naomi returned to Bethlehem and spoke to the women, her self-assessment was that of empty. Now, as a result of described events, she has become "full." The disasters in Moab, while not explained, have been reversed. Food and family are now secure.

Just as the identity of Naomi is key to the closing of the book, so too is the identity of the child. In the final surprise of this book of surprises, the reader learns of the child's name and lineage. **They named him Obed**. The name attached to the child means "Worker" or "Servant," or in a more pious context, one who performs acts of service, "Worshiper." This is a unique biblical example where the

---

[38]While the verb may suggest a suckling child (Num 11:12), it certainly does not require it (cf. 2 Sam 4:4, Esth 2:7).

[39]Naomi's act here has been variously debated. Some have even seen it as a legal action formalizing adoption. Compare with statements elsewhere of a child "placed on the knees" (e.g., Gen 30:3; 50:23). It is safe to say that this text offers no further information about who specifically would rear the child, nor are details of childcare in ancient Israel very illuminating.

Along another line, while it is clear here that this newborn will, in a sense, serve in Mahlon's place, the pedigree of the child will clearly be that of Boaz. Mahlon will not be mentioned again.

women of the village offer a name, rather than the parents. Hubbard observes this in the context of reversals, "In 1:19-21, they (the chorus of women) listened while Naomi lamented; here she listens while they rejoice."[40]

4:18-22 It is his lineage, though, that is most striking, as offered in a concluding genealogy. **"This, then, is the family line of Perez"** echoes with vocabulary from the book of Genesis and suggests a measure of continuity with that book.[41] It also provides a kind of bridge over the tumultuous period recorded by Joshua and Judges. By means of these names, the reader may step carefully from the Patriarchs into the Davidic Monarchy with the confidence that this path is not outside of the will or blessing of Yahweh. Ten generations link **Perez** to **David**, the great king of Israel (cf. 1 Chr 2:5-15).[42] Wrangling over the question of exact succession is hardly useful, as "father" may simply mean "ancestor."[43] More crucial is the demonstration of directness, and even possibly, a consciously crafted structure that is parallel to the genealogies of Genesis 4 and 5. Just as ten generations separate Adam from Noah, ten generations are offered here. It is fascinating to observe that just as Enoch (the man who "walked with God") occupies the seventh position in the Genesis 5 account, here, Boaz fills this key slot. Could such placement be coincidence? No. The great action plan of God, initiated in the beginning, continues in Ruth.

In the end, the genealogy demonstrates the fulfillment of the gateway pronouncement, "may your family be like that of Perez" (4:12), and, most significantly, the realization that this child of Ruth

---

[40]Hubbard, *Ruth*, p. 276.

[41]The phrase אֵלֶּה תּוֹלְדוֹת (*'ēleh tôlᵉdôth*) ("these are the generations" or better, "this is the legacy") is a well known structuring formula used in the book of Genesis. See Gen 2:4; 10:1; etc.

[42]Reading the text with this end in mind causes a second glance to be given to Elimelech (of Ruth 1:2), a name meaning, "My God is king." While other voices emphasize David's role as king, Hubbard wisely points out, "that David was born at all amply attested the presence of . . . providence. . . . David's ascent to power provided weighty corroborating evidence, God is, indeed, King!" (Hubbard, *Ruth*, p. 285).

[43]Kitchen, Hubbard, and others observe how this list must have gaps if it is to be correlated with what is currently known of chronological fix points in and out of the Bible. See K.A. Kitchen, *On the Reliability of the Old Testament* (Grand Rapids: Eerdmans, 2003), p. 357, or Hubbard, *Ruth*, p. 284.

and Boaz is a link in the chain the stretches from the Patriarchs, through David, and ultimately, to the Messiah (Matt 1:1-17; cf. Luke 3:23-38). From this broad biblical perspective, the complete picture of the *gō'ēl*-redeemer is finally realized. How can a *son* "become famous throughout Israel," "renew your life, and sustain you in your old age" (4:14)? A temporary and local fulfillment, to be sure, is seen in the image of what must have been regarded as a miracle baby, resting in the arms of widowed Naomi. However, an eternal and worldwide fulfillment is recognized in the image of another miracle baby, likewise born in Bethlehem, some thousand years later. Through his teachings and actions, this *son* will offer the final and fullest meaning to the expression *gō'ēl*-redeemer.